*Readings in Discipline-Based Art
Education: A Literature of
Educational Reform*

Readings in
Discipline-Based Art Education
A Literature of Educational Reform

EDITED BY

Ralph A. Smith

University of Illinois

at Urbana-Champaign

National Art Education Association
Reston, Virginia

About NAEA . . .
Founded in 1947, the National Art Education Association is the largest professional art education association in the world. Membership includes elementary and secondary teachers, art administrators, museum educators, arts council staff, and university professors from throughout the United States and sixty-six foreign countries. NAEA's mission is to advance art education through professional development, service, advancement of knowledge, and leadership.

© 2000 National Art Education Association, 1916 Association Drive, Reston, VA 20191-1590. Archival Series.

ISBN 1-890160-12-1

To Leilani Lattin Duke

*for unparalleled leadership
in art education*

———————

Acknowledgments

Appreciation is extended to the writers and publishers for granting permission to reprint the following:

"Mind Building and Arts Education" by Leilani Lattin Duke is from *Design for Arts in Education* 91, no. 3 (1990): 42-45. Reprinted with permission of the author and the Helen Dwight Reid Educational Foundation. Published by Heldref Publications, 1319 Eighteenth St., N.W., Washington, D.C. 70036-1802. Copyright © 1990.

"Art as General Education" by Harry S. Broudy is from the *Alaska Journal of Art* 1 (1989): 4-9. Reprinted by permission of the Alaska Art Education Association.

"Disciplined-based Art Education: Becoming Students of Art" by Gilbert A. Clark, Michael D. Day, and W. Dwaine Greer is excerpted (pp. 130-36, 180-83) from *The Journal of Aesthetic Education* 21, no. 2 (1987): 129-93. © 1987 by the J. Paul Getty Trust. Reprinted by permission of the authors and the J. Paul Getty Trust..

"What Is Disciplined-based Art Education?" by Elliot W. Eisner is excerpted (pp. 13-21) from *The Role of Discipline-Based Art Education in America's Schools* (Los Angeles: Getty Center for Education in the Arts, n.d.). © by the J. Paul Getty Trust. Reprinted by permission of the author and the J. Paul Getty Trust.

"DBAE: A Humanities Interpretation" by Ralph A. Smith is a condensation of remarks in *Art Education: A Critical Necessity* by Albert William Levi and Ralph A. Smith (Urbana: University of Illinois Press, 1991), pp. 174-79. © 1991 by the J. P. Getty Trust. Reprinted by permission of the author and the J. Paul Getty Trust.

"The General Characteristics of DBAE" by Stephen Mark Dobbs is excerpted (pp. 5-12) from *Learning in and through Art: A Guide to Discipline-Based Art Education* (Los Angles: Getty Education Institute for the Arts, 1998). © 1998 by the J. Paul Getty Trust. Reprinted by permission of the author and the J. Paul Getty Trust.

"The Creation of Art" by Albert William Levi is excerpted (pp. 39-45, 49-52) from *Art Education: A Critical Necessity* by Albert William Levi and Ralph A. Smith (Urbana: University of Illinois Press, 1991). © 1991 by the J. Paul Getty Trust. Reprinted by permission of the Levi estate and the J. Paul Getty Trust.

"DBAE: Opening a Bridge between Art History and Art Education" by David Ebitz is from the *Alaska Journal of Art* 1 (1989): 10-15. Reprinted by permission of the author and the Alaska Art Education Association.

"Types of Art Criticism" by Theodore F. Wolff is excerpted (pp. 14-22, 30-32) from *Art Criticism and Art Education* by Theodore F. Wolff and George Geahigan (Urbana: University of Illinois Press, 1993). © 1993 by the J. Paul Getty Trust. Reprinted with permission of the author and the J. Paul Getty Trust.

"Philosophical Aesthetics: A Way of Knowing and Its Limits" by Marcia Mueldar Eaton is excerpted (pp. 19-24) from *The Journal of Aesthetic Education* 28, no. 2 (1994): 19-31. © 1994 by the Board of Trustees of the University of Illinois. Reprinted by permission of the author and the University of Illinois Press.

"The Artworld and the Disciplines of DBAE" by Anita Silvers is from *The Preservice Challenge: Discipline-Based Art Education and Recent Reports on Higher Education* (Los Angeles: Getty Center for Education in the Arts, 1988), pp. 94-101. © 1988 by the J. Paul Getty Trust. Reprinted by permission of the author and the J. Paul Getty Trust.

"Experiential Learning and DBAE" by Richard Lachapelle is excerpted (pp. 137-142) from *Visual Arts Research* 23, no. 2 (1997): 135-44, a special issue on the evolution of DBAE edited by Ronald MacGregor, Christine Thompson, and Nancy Gardner. © 1997 by the Board of Trustees of the University of Illinois. Reprinted by permission of the author and the University of Illinois Press.

"In Praise of Practice: A Defense of Art Making in Education" by Stuart Richmond is excerpted (pp. 13-20) from *The Journal of Aesthetic Education* 32, no. 2 (Summer 1998): 11-20. © 1998 by the Board of Trustees of the University of Illinois. Reprinted by permission of the author and the University of Illinois Press.

"Art Making in the Classroom" is excerpted (pp. 95-103) from *Art Making and Education* by Maurice Brown and Diana Korzenik (Urbana: University of Illinois Press, 1993. © 1993 by the J. Paul Getty Trust. Reprinted by permission of the author and the J. Paul Getty Trust.

"Building the Mind through Art" by David N. Perkins is excerpted (pp. 82-90) from *The Intelligent Eye: Learning to Think by Looking at Art* (Santa Monica, Calif.: Getty Center for Education in the Arts, 1994). © 1994 by the J. Paul Getty Trust. Reprinted by permission of the author and the J. Paul Getty Trust.

"Teaching Art History as Inquiry" by Mary Erickson is excerpted (pp. 124-32) from *Art History and Education* by Stephen Addiss and Mary Erickson (Urbana: University of Illinois Press, 1993). © 1993 by the J Paul Getty Trust. Reprinted by permission of the author and the J. Paul Getty Trust.

"Art Criticism and Art Education" by George Geahigan is excerpted (pp. 141-47) from *Art Criticism and Education* by Theodore F. Wolff and George Geahigan (Urbana: University of Illinois Press, 1997). © 1997 by the J. Paul Getty Trust. Reprinted by permission of the author and the J Paul Getty Trust.

"Learning Outcomes in Aesthetics" by Marilyn Galvin Stewart is excerpted (pp. 80-86) from "Aesthetics and the Art Curriculum," *The Journal of Aesthetic Education* 28 , no. 3 (1994): 77-88. © 1994 by the Board of Trustees of the University of Illinois. Reprinted by permission of the author and the University of Illinois Press.

"Aesthetic Scanning" by Harry S. Broudy is excerpted (pp. 49-53) from *The Role of Imagery in Learning* (Los Angeles: Getty Center for Education in the Arts, 1987). © 1987 by the J. Paul Getty Trust. Reprinted by permission of the J. Paul Getty Trust.

"The Characteristics, Benefits, and Problems Associated with Implementing DBAE" by Michael D. Day is from the *NASSP Bulletin* 73, no. 517 (1989): 43-52. Reprinted by permission of the author and the *NASSP Bulletin*.

"Improving Visual Arts Education" by W. Dwaine Greer is excerpted (pp. 101-9) from *Improving Visual Arts Education: Final Report of the Los Angeles Getty Institute for Educators on the Visual Arts, 1982-1989* (Santa Monica, Calif.: Getty Center for Education in the Arts, 1993). © 1993 by the J. Paul Getty Trust. Reprinted by permission of the author and the J. Paul Getty Trust.

"DBAE and Educational Change" by Brent Wilson and Blanche Rubin is excerpted (pp. 90-96) from *Visual Arts Research* 23, no. 2 (1997): 89-97, a special issue devoted to the evolution of DBAE edited by Ronald MacGregor, Christine Thompson, and Nancy Gardner. © 1997 by the Board of Trustees of the University of Illinois. Reprinted by permission of the authors and the University of Illinois Press.

"Designing and Implementing a Curriculum for Multicultural Art Education" by F. Graeme Chalmers is excerpted (pp. 63-70) from *Celebrating Pluralism: Art, Education, and Cultural Diversity* (Los Angeles: Getty Education Institute for the Arts, 1996). © 1996 by the J. Paul Getty Trust. Reprinted by permission of the author and the J. Paul Getty Trust.

"The Arts and Cross-Disciplinary Study" by Bruce O. Boston is excerpted (pp. 18-28) from *Connections: The Arts and the Integration of the High School Curriculum* (Los Angeles and New York: College Board and Getty Center for Education in the Arts, 1996). Reprinted with permission from *Connections*. Copyright © 1996 by College Entrance Examination Board and Getty Center for Education in the Arts. All rights reserved.

"Symbolic Literacies: The Developmental Portrait Research Has Provided" by Jessica Davis and Howard Gardner is excerpted (pp. 111-20) from "The Cognitive Revolution: Consequences for the Understanding and Education of the Child as Artist" in *The Arts, Education, and Aesthetic Knowing*, edited by Bennett Reimer and Ralph A. Smith, Ninety-first Yearbook of the National Society for the Study of Education, Part II (Chicago: University of Chicago Press, 1992), pp. 92-123. Reprinted by permission of the authors and the National Society for the Study of Education.

"Five Phases of Artistic Development" by David J. Hargreaves and Maurice J. Galton is excerpted (pp. 128-35) from "Aesthetic Learning: Psychological Theory and Educational Practice" in *The Arts, Education and Aesthetic Knowing*, edited by Bennett Reimer and Ralph A. Smith, Ninety-first Yearbook of the National Society for the Study of Education, Part II (Chicago: University of Chicago Press, 1992), pp. 124-50. Reprinted by permission of the authors and the National Society for the Study of Education.

"Stages of Aesthetic Development" by Michael J. Parsons is excerpted (pp. 21-26) from *How We Understand Art: A Cognitive Developmental Account of Aesthetic Experience* (New York: Cambridge University Press, 1987). Reprinted with the permission of the author and Cambridge University Press.

"Museums in Age of Pluralism" by Abigail Housen is excerpted (pp. 29-34) from *Art Education Here* (Boston: Art Education Department, Massachusetts College of Art, 1987). Reprinted by permission of the author and the Massachusetts College of Art.

"Aesthetic Literacy" by Jean Rush is excerpted (pp. 3-6) from "The Arts and Education Reform: Where Is the Model for Teaching 'The Arts,'?" in *Arts Education Policy Review* 98, no. 3 (1997): 2-9. Reprinted with permission of the Helen Dwight Reid Educational Foundation. Published by Heldref Publications, 1319 Eighteenth Street, N.W. Washington, D.C. 20036-1802. Copyright © 1997.

"Phases of Aesthetic Learning (K-12)" by Ralph A. Smith is excerpted (pp. 60-67) from "Toward Percipience: A Humanities Curriculum for Arts Education" in *The Arts, Education, and Aesthetic Knowing*, edited by Bennett Reimer and Ralph A. Smith, Ninety-first Yearbook of the National Society for the Study of Education, Part II (Chicago: University of Chicago Press, 1992), pp. 51-69. Reprinted by permission of the author and the National Society for the Study of Education.

"The Interrelationship between Preservice and Inservice Education for Art Teachers and Specialists" by Frances Schoonmaker is from *The Preservice Challenge: Discipline-Based Art Education and Recent Reports on*

Higher Education (Los Angeles: Getty Center for Education in the Arts, 1988), pp. 201-12. © 1988 by the J. Paul Getty Trust. Reprinted by permission of the author and the J. Paul Getty Trust.

"Preparing Teachers for Excellence" by Michael D. Day is excerpted (pp. 11-12, 14-21, 22-23) from "Preparing Teachers of Art for 2000 and Beyond" in *Preparing Teachers of Art* edited by Michael D. Day (Reston, Va.: National Art Education Association, 1997). © 1997 by the J. Paul Getty Trust. Reprinted by permission of the author and the J. Paul Getty Trust.

"DBAE and Staff Development" by Katherine A. Schwartz is excerpted (pp. 64-68, 70) from *Visual Arts Research* 23, no. 2 (1997): 89-97, a special issue devoted to the evolution of DBAE, edited by Ronald MacGregor, Christine Thompson, and Nancy Gardner. © 1997 by the Board of Trustees of the University of Illinois. Reprinted by permission of the author and the University of Illinois Press.

"Aesthetics in Teacher Preparation" by E. Louis Lankford is excerpted (pp. 12, 15-16) from "Of Chickens, Eggs, and Expertise: Observations Complimentary and Contrary to *The Quiet Evolution*" in *Arts Education Policy Review* 100, no. 3 (January/February, 1999): 12-16. Reprinted with permission of the Helen Dwight Reid Educational Foundation. Published by Heldref Publications, 1319 Eighteenth Street, N.W. Washington, D.C. 20036-1802. Copyright © 1999.

"Artist-Teacher: A Problematic Model for Art Education" by Michael D. Day is from *The Journal of Aesthetic Education* 20, no. 4 (1986): 38-42. © 1986 by the Board of Trustees of the University of Illinois. Reprinted by permission of the author and the University of Illinois Press.

"Elitism" by Ralph A. Smith is excerpted (pp. 100-5) from *Excellence II: The Continuing Quest in Art Education* (Reston, Va.: National Art Education, 1995). Reprinted by permission of the author and the National Art Education Association.

"Informing the Promise of DBAE: Remember the Women, Children, and Other Folk" by Georgia Collins and Renee Sandell is excerpted (pp. 57-62) from the *Journal of Multicultural and Cross-cultural Research in Art Education* 6, no. 1 (1988): 55-63. Reprinted by permission of the authors and the *Journal of Multicultural and Cross-cultural Research in Art Education*.

"Art Education and Postmodernism" by H. Gene Blocker is excerpted (pp. 62-65) from *Aesthetics and Education* by Michael J. Parsons and H. Gene Blocker (Urbana: University of Illinois Press, 1993). © 1993 by the J Paul Getty Trust. Reprinted by permission of the authors and the J. Paul Getty Trust.

"Museums and their Functions" by Harold Osborne is excerpted (pp. 45-51) from *The Journal of Aesthetic Education* 19, no. 2 (1985): 41-51. © 1985 by the Board of Trustees at the University of Illinois. Reprinted by permission of the University of Illinois Press.

"The Art Museum as an Agency of Culture" by Albert William Levi is excerpted (pp. 31-40) from *The Journal of Aesthetic Education* 19, no. 2 (1985): 23-40. © 1985 by the Board of Trustees of the University of Illinois. Reprinted by permission of the Levi estate and the University of Illinois Press.

"Notes on Art Museum Experiences" by Mihaly Csikszentmihalyi is from *Insights: Museums, Visitors, Attitudes, Expectations: A Focus Group Experiment* (Los Angeles: Getty Center for Education in the Arts and the J. Paul Getty Museum, 1991), pp. 123-31. © 1991 by the J. Paul Getty Trust. Reprinted by permission of the author and the J. Paul Getty Trust.

"Issues in Evaluating Museum Education Programs" by Elizabeth Vallance is excerpted (pp. 233-36) from *Evaluating and Assessing the Visual Arts in Education: International Perspectives* edited by Doug Boughton, Elliot W. Eisner, and Johan Ligtvoet (New York: Teachers College Press, 1996), pp. 222-36. Reprinted with permission of the publisher. © 1996 by Teachers College, Columbia University. All rights reserved.

Photo Credits

Full copyright information is provided below. Shorter captions are used in the text.

1. Boccioni, Umberto. *Unique Forms of Continuity in Space* (1913). Bronze (cast 1931), 43 7/8 x 34 7/8 x 15 3/4" (111.2 x 88.5 x 40 cm). The Museum of Modern Art, New York. Acquired through the Lillie P. Bliss Request. Photograph © 1999 The Museum of Modern Art, New York.

2. Arp, Jean (Hans). *Human Concretion* (Replica of plaster, cast stone, 1949). Cast authorized and approved by artist. Cast stone, 19 1/2 x 18 3/4 x 25 1/2" (49.5 x 47.6 x 64.7 cm). The Museum of Modern Art, New York. Purchase. Photograph © 1999 The Museum of Modern Art, New York.

3. Matisse, Henri (1869-1954), *Still Life on a Green Buffet*, Musée Nationale d'Art Moderne, Centre Georges Pompidou, Paris, France. © 2000 Succession H. Matisse, Paris/Artists Rights Society (ARS), New York/Giraudon/Art Resource, NY.

4. Matisse, Henri (1869-1954). *L.D.*, 1937. Pen and India Ink. 14 1/4 x 11 in. © 2000 Succession H. Matisse, Paris/Artists Rights Society (ARS), New York.
5. Veronese, Paolo (1528-1588). *Feast in the House of Levi*. Accademia, Venice, Italy. Alinari/Art Resource, NY.
6. Eyck, Jan van (c. 1390-1441). *The Arnolfini Wedding Portrait* (Giovanni Arnolfini and his wife). National Gallery, London, Great Britain. Alinari/Art Resource, NY.

Contents

PART THREE: CURRICULUM

Introduction   119

A. TEACHING AND LEARNING

B. IMPLEMENTING AND EVALUATING DBAE

PART SIX: ISSUES

Introduction 347

PART SEVEN: MUSEUMS AND MUSEUM EDUCATION

Introduction 377

Introduction: The Changing Image
of Art Education

Over the past half century and notably since the sixties theorists of art education have been recasting the aims of teaching art in the schools. This tendency may be characterized as efforts to increase the intellectual content of aesthetic learning by engendering in young people a well-developed sense of art requisite for the intelligent engagement with works of art and other things from an aesthetic point of view. Writers have argued that building such a sense of art involves acquisition of a rudimentary capacity to create works of art, a general knowledge of art history, a grasp of some basic principles of aesthetic judgment, and an ability to reflect thoughtfully about the values and uses of art. Such assumptions were adopted by policymakers of the Getty Center for Education in the Arts (later renamed the Getty Education Institute for the Arts) upon its arrival on the educational scene in the early eighties.[1] This introduction discusses the theoretical origins of the Getty educational venture and comments briefly on the evolution of its outlook.

In the mid-eighties I was invited by the Getty Center to identify the theoretical antecedents of discipline-based art education. Other writers were asked to detect antecedents in curriculum documents, state education requirements, and teacher education programs, while still others were asked to prepare a systematic rationale for DBAE, describe the nature of the disciplines associated with the approach, and indicate the relevance of developmental psychology to aesthetic learning. These studies, which constitute a good introduction to DBAE, were printed in a special issue of *The Journal of Aesthetic Education* (1987) that was subsequently published as a book. The Getty Center gave the journal issue generous distribution, and at the time of this writing a second printing of the book is still available.[2]

My account of the origins of DBAE differs from others in placing the emergence of the Getty educational venture in a larger context than is usually done, one that takes into account what I call the two faces of the cognitive revolution in thinking about the character of mind and human development, in short, inquiries into knowing and the known. But while it is possible to speak of two faces of cognition, it is apparent that cognitive studies have been predominantly psychological and centered on the child as creative artist.[3] Yet several theorists who chose to endorse DBAE, including myself, came to it from a background more solidly rooted in the humanities and philosophy of education. For example, early efforts to implement and evaluate DBAE drew significantly on the philosophical writings about general and aesthetic education by Harry S. Broudy.[4] And my own interests have been strongly influenced by work in art history, aesthetics, and art criticism. In truth, the emphasis on aesthetic education in the sixties and seventies had a major impact on the Getty venture, and because its influence on Getty policymaking has not been adequately recognized the following refers to writings, in addition to those of Broudy, that may be said to have anticipated DBAE.

Going back somewhat, Broudy's mid-century essay "Some Duties of an Educational Aesthetics"[5] discussed the types of relevant problems any theory of aesthetic education must address, such problems as the nature of aesthetic experience, the peripheral status of aesthetic education, and the justification question. He also believed it was important that philosophers of education explain the low level of taste in the society and specify criteria of artistic value, all problems that need continual attention. Just as Broudy had, other writers during the fifties found aesthetics a useful resource in thinking about the problems of art education. Thomas Munro, whose career is associated with the American Society for Aesthetics, *The Journal of Aesthetics and Art Criticism*, and the educational activities of the Cleveland Museum of Art, and who understood by aesthetics both philosophical and psychological studies, believed in establishing close relationships between aesthetics and school learning. The latter, he said, provides data for aesthetics to interpret and translate for purposes of teaching.[7] The writing team of David W. Ecker and E. F. Kaelin likewise discussed ways in which principles of modern aesthetics can help clarify the purposes of an art education program,[8] while Edmund B. Feldman went so far as to assert that all research in art education should take its lead from aesthetics in order to detect the philosophical assumptions that inform teaching and learning.[9]

Such thinking about the aesthetic in effect set the agenda for the sixties, which found Manuel Barkan saying that the future of reform in art education would consist of making "the aesthetic life" a reality for theorists, teachers, and students alike, an objective that prescribed an important role for the discipline of aesthetics.[10] Sensing what was in the air, Elliot Eisner wrote that the emerging interest in the aesthetic constituted a new era in art education. He regarded aesthetic education as humane education in and through the arts, the realization of which necessitated plumbing not just the behavioral sciences but also art history and philosophy for ideas.[11] I likewise acknowledged the changing image of art education and during the mid-sixties founded *The Journal of Aesthetic Education* and published an anthology that contained essays on educational theory and the disciplines of aesthetics, art history, art criticism, and artistic creation which, as it turned out, were the disciplines that were to become associated with DBAE.[12] The same can be said about some of the essays in *Readings in Art Education*, edited by Eisner and Ecker and published at about the same time.[13] In fact, the decade of the sixties was something of a watershed in American cultural life and education. It was not only that New York City became the center of the international art world; the two national endowments for the arts and humanities were established, and there was support for a rash of seminars, symposia, and conferences, one of which produced what was to become a major influence on aesthetic education and an antecedent of DBAE, *A Seminar in Art Education for Research and Curriculum Development*.[14]

Interest in aesthetic education carried over into the seventies which may well be regarded as the decade of aesthetic education. Indicative is Brent Wilson's statement in a handbook about educational evaluation that "the central purpose of art instruction is to assist students in achieving reasonably full aesthetic experiences with works of art and other visual phenomena which are capable of eliciting such a response."[15] Continuing their collaboration, Ecker and Kaelin in a chapter in an NSSE yearbook identified a peculiarly aesthetic domain of educational research in which the principal concern is with aesthetic experiences of works of art. As if in anticipation of DBAE, the authors also describe discourse that attempts to capture the quality not just of direct experiences of works of art but also that of theoretical accounts of the nature of art and art criticism, and of reflective thought about the place of art in philosophical systems.[16] I also edited two anthologies in the seventies bearing on aesthetic education; one examined the relations of a number of aesthetic concepts to education generally, including arts education, while the other subsumed writings under the rubrics of historic ideas of aesthetic education, aims, curriculum design and validation, and teaching and learning.[17]

The shift in thinking also produced a number of textbooks that either stressed the idea of aesthetic education or were compatible with it. Edmund Feldman's *Becoming Human Through Art: Aesthetic Experience in the School* is noteworthy for its subtitle alone. Feldman remarked that "aesthetic education" was the best term for describing his text, which is to say "it can be regarded as either an art education text with a strong aesthetic bias, or an aesthetic education text with a strong art education bias."[18] Typically, Feldman drew attention to the overemphasis in the field of art education on artistic expression which several writers in the field believed adversely affected students' capacities for intelligent viewing and interpretation of works of art. Eisner's major contribution during the seventies to what he had earlier termed a new era in art education was *Educating Artistic Vision*. It set forth a conception of curriculum consisting of three domains—the productive, the critical, and the historical—which were exemplified in a curriculum project designed for the early years of schooling.[19] The similarity of Eisner's domains to those of DBAE is apparent. The significance of Feldman's and Eisner's texts was recognized in the decision of the NAEA to reprint them in its archival series marking the Association's fiftieth anniversary. Coming near the end of the decade, Laura Chapman's *Approaches to Art Education* is also worth mentioning for its exemplification of the tendency to supplement creative activities with historical and critical studies. Writing with a good working knowledge of school life, Chapman asserted that art programs should be eclectic and provide instruction in both Western and non-Western artistic traditions. As if in anticipation of writings that would later influence DBAE, she also stressed the need to take account of the cross-cultural insights of anthropology.[20] Yet what stands out more than anything else in the seventies so far as aesthetic education is concerned is the aesthetic education program of the Central Midwestern Regional Educational Laboratory (CEMREL). An appreciation of the scope and accomplishment of CEMREL's program, which was the most ambitious project to reform art education prior to the Getty venture, as well of the problems it faced, can be gained by examining *Through the Arts to the Aesthetic*, written by Stanley S. Madeja and Sheila Onuska. Consistent with the temper of the time, CEMREL emphasized a comprehensive approach to the study of art and is yet another important antecedent of DBAE.[21]

It is to the credit of Getty policymakers that in large they adopted the premises of the aesthetic theorists of art education—a rare instance, it might be said, of cumulative development in educational thinking. Yet the aesthetic education origins of DBAE are not the whole story. As Getty policy evolved some of the aesthetic theorists altered their views, and a new generation of writers with a different agenda and with careers to build stressed themes of social reform. Although it oversimplifies matters, I'll refer to this trend as social reconstructionism.[22] Committed to social change and the advocating of cultural diversity, they have been successful in giving DBAE a stronger social dimension than it might otherwise have had.

Among those who have made a serious and responsible contribution to defining a social aspect of art education are June McFee, Rogena Degge, and F. Graeme Chalmers. A decade before the advent of the Getty Center, McFee's *Preparation for Art* set forth a broad anthropological concept of art education that, in contrast to the normative idea of culture, defined it as patterns of living in social groups that shared values, beliefs, and opinions. McFee further held that the major purposes of art education were to provide a basis for understanding the functions of art and how they vary from culture to culture.[23] Her influence is further apparent in a volume co-authored with Rogena Degge,[24] and in a series of articles by F. Graeme Chalmers, who was later invited by the Getty Center to write a monograph about cultural pluralism. Chalmers has called for studies of art education that would not only complement its historical, philosophical, and psychological foundations and integrate the arts into social studies, but also for the teaching of art history in a way that accommodates popular, folk, and environmental art as well as recognized artistic traditions.[25] The writings of Vincent Lanier are further noteworthy in this context. A proponent of aesthetic education whose writings are distinctive for not providing a role for creative activities, Lanier also stresses the social dimension of art education and the expansion of the art curriculum beyond studying the cultural heritage. However, contrary to the literature produced by social reconstructionists, the notions of aesthetic value and aesthetic experience figure prominently in Lanier's thinking, as his major statement on aesthetic education indicates.[26]

Efforts to effect reform are always accompanied by debate and controversy, not to mention acrimonious criticism and hostile behavior. The idea of DBAE has generated its fair share of both. But I believe DBAE, or art education generally, has reached the point where its various problems and dimensions need to be systematically integrated into a comprehensive philosophy. For example, Monroe C. Beardsley's little-known essay titled "Art and Its Cultural Context" indicates the need for a coherent account of the relations of art and other segments of culture that does not deny art's special character. This would involve articulating the nature of artistic and aesthetic values and indicating what they contribute to the quality of both personal and social life, all the while protecting such values from political and economic forces that would either distort, repress, or trivialize them.[27] Contributors to this volume may be understood as providing working materials to accomplish this formidable task, but there is still much to be done.

A special note. As this introduction was being written, word came of the resignation of Leilani Lattin Duke, director of the Getty Trust's educational activities for seventeen years (1981-1998). In guiding the Trust's educational program, Duke exhibited unparalleled leadership and earned the respect and admiration of many both within and without the field. She spelled out her role as a member of a private organization in an article written a few years after the establishment of the Getty Center for Education in the Arts.[28] Choosing the word "synergism" to characterize the style of appropriate involvement, Duke discussed the importance of cooperation with relevant players in striving to attain a common goal as well as the special function of private organizations and their responsibilities. The private sector, she wrote, can take philosophic and economic risks and identify needs that it is in a special position to address. Such a vision of functions, responsibilities, and limits has informed Getty policy for art education and made it a major force for reform and change.

The writings selected for this volume were drawn largely from a comprehensive annotated bibliography of the literature of DBAE prepared by the editor with support from the Getty Education Institute and now available on ArtsEdNet. A more selected bibliography prepared by the editor appears in Stephen Mark Dobbs, *Learning in and through Art: A Guide to Discipline-Based Art Education* (Los Angles: Getty Education Institute for the Arts, 1998), pp. 121-42. In the suggested readings following each section, books precede articles and other references, and the period covered is from 1982 to 1998. The bibliography and this collection are limited principally to the literature of DBAE and sources that obviously bear on it. For a comprehensive bibliography of art education generally and of the disciplines associated with teaching art other sources would have to be consulted. In short, the collection is intended to constitute a basic document of the Getty intervention into art education. The collection moreover, consists of an interpretation of the literature and does not necessarily reflect the views of the Getty Institute for Education in the Arts.

In addition to Leilani Lattin Duke whose efforts helped generate the literature from which a selection of readings was made for this volume, my thanks go to Thomas Hatfield, Executive Director of the National Art Education Association, for his support and assistance, and to NAEA Board members who thought the volume was worth including in the archival series of the Association's publishing program.

Notes

1. Getty Center for Education in the Arts, *Beyond Creating: The Place for Art in America's Schools* (Los Angeles: Getty Center for Education in the Arts, 1985). Foreword by Harold M. Williams, Preface by Leilani Lattin Duke.

2. Ralph A. Smith, ed., *Discipline-Based Art Education: Origins, Meaning, Development* (Urbana: University of Illinois Press, 1989).

3. See, e.g., Jessica Davis and Howard Gardner, "The Cognitive Revolution: Consequences for the Understanding and Education of the Child as Artist," in *The Arts, Education, and Aesthetic Knowing*, ed. Bennett Reimer and Ralph A. Smith, Ninety-first Yearbook of the National Society for the Study of Education, Part II (Chicago: University of Chicago Press, 1992), pp. 92-103.

4. See, e.g., Harry S. Broudy, *Enlightened Cherishing: An Essay on Aesthetic Education* (Urbana: University of Illinois Press, 1994). First published in 1972 and reprinted with Getty assistance. For discussions of Broudy's influence on DBAE, see W. Dwaine Greer, "Harry Broudy and Discipline-Based Art Education (DBAE)," and Margaret Klemplay DiBlasio, "The Road from Nice to Necessary: Broudy's Rationale for Art Education" in a special issue of *The Journal of Aesthetic Education* (Winter 1992) devoted to Broudy's career. Cf. Jack H. Hobbs and Jean C. Rush, *Teaching Children Art* (Saddle River, N. J.: Prentice-Hall, 1997), who dedicate their volume to Broudy.

5. Harry S. Broudy, "Some Duties of an Educational Aesthetics," *Educational Theory* 1, no. 3 (November 1951): 190-98.

7. See Thomas Munro, *Art Education: Its Philosophy and Psychology* (New York: Liberal Arts Press, 1956).

8. David W. Ecker and E. F. Kaelin, "Aesthetics in Public School Art Teaching," *College Art Journal* 18, no. 4 (1958): 382-91.

9. Edmund B. Feldman, "Research as the Verification of Aesthetics," *Studies in Art Education* 1, no. 1 (1959): 19-25.

10. Manuel Barkan, "Transition in Art Education: Changing Conceptions of Curriculum and Theory," *Art Education* 15, no. 7 (1962): 27.

11. Elliot W. Eisner, "Toward a New Era in Art Education," *Studies in Art Education* 6, no. 2 (1965): 54-62.

12. Ralph A. Smith, "Images of Art Education," *Studies in Art Education* 7, no. 1 (1965): 56-61; *Aesthetics and Criticism in Art Education: Problems in Defining, Explaining, and Evaluating Art* (Chicago: Rand McNally, 1966). The *Journal of Aesthetic Education* was initiated with two trial issues in 1966 (Vol. I) and became a subscription quarterly published by the University of Illinois Press in 1968.

13. Elliot W. Eisner and David W. Ecker, eds., *Readings in Art Education* (Waltham, Mass.: Blaisdell, 1966).

14. *A Seminar in Art Education for Research and Curriculum Development*, Cooperative Research Project V-002 (University Park, Pa.: The Pennsylvania State University, 1966). Edward L. Mattil Project Director. Final Report, Kenneth R. Beittel and Edward L. Mattil.

15. Brent Wilson, "Evolution of Learning in Art Education," in *Handbook on*

Formative and Summative Evaluation of Student Learning, ed. Benjamin S. Bloom, J. T. Hastings, and G. F. Madaus (New York: McGraw-Hill, 1971), p. 510.

16. David W. Ecker and E. F. Kaelin, "The Limits of Aesthetic Inquiry: A Guide to Educational Research," in *Philosophical Redirection of Educational Research,* ed. G. Thomas, Seventy-first Yearbook of the National Society for the Study of Education, Part I (Chicago: University of Chicago Press, 1972), p. 261.

17. Ralph A. Smith, ed., *Aesthetic Concepts and Education* (Urbana: University of Illinois Press, 1970); *Aesthetics and Problems of Education* (Urbana: University of Illinois Press, 1971).

18. Edmund B. Feldman: *Becoming Human Through Art: Aesthetic Experience in the School* (Englewood Cliffs, N. J.: Prentice-Hall, 1970), v.

19. Elliot W. Eisner, *Educating Artistic Vision* (New York: Macmillan, 1972).

20. Laura Chapman, *Approaches to Art Education* (New York: Harcourt Brace Jovanovich, 1978).

21. Stanley S. Madeja and Sheila Onuska, *Through the Arts to the Aesthetic: The CEMREL Aesthetic Education Curriculum* (St. Louis: CEMREL, Inc., 1977).

22. Arthur Efland, in *A History of Art Education: Intellectual and Social Currents in Teaching the Visual Arts* (New York: Teachers College Press, 1990), characterizes the reconstructionist stream as one that believes in the power of schooling to transform society.

23. June McFee, *Preparation for Art,* 2nd ed. (Belmont, Calif.: Wadsworth, 1971).

24. June McFee and Rogena M. Degge, *Art, Cultures and Environment: A Catalyst* (Belmont, Calif.: Wadsworth, 1977).

25. Representative is F. Graeme Chalmers, "A Cultural Foundation for Education in the Arts," *Art Education* 27, no. 1 (1974): 21-25.

26. See Vincent Lanier, "Aesthetic Literacy as the Product of Art Education," in *The Product of a Process,* Proceedings of the 24th INSEA World Congress (Amsterdam, the Netherlands: De Trommel, 1982), pp. 115-21.

27. Monroe C. Beardsley, "Art and Its Cultural Context" in *The Aesthetic Point of View: Selected Essays,* ed. Michael J. Wreen and Donald M. Callen (Ithaca, N.Y.: Cornell University Press, 1982), pp. 352-70. In this essay Beardsley acknowledges that artworks can be considered from a view wider than that of a more circumscribed aesthetic criticism, for example, that of cultural criticism. Yet "Cultural criticism does not eliminate or replace aesthetic criticism, but embraces and builds upon it; its own enterprise must acknowledge, make room for, and preserve the distinctively aesthetic point of view" (p. 370).

28. Leilani Lattin Duke, "The Role of Private Institutions in Art Education," *The Journal of Aesthetic Education* 20, no. 4 (1986): 48-49.

PART ONE

Interpretations

Introduction

Leilani Lattin Duke served as the director of the Getty's educational activities for seventeen years and exerted unparalleled leadership in advancing arguments for a more substantive conception of art education. Her discussion of DBAE is thus important not just for its being a director's review of the Getty Center's activities but also for its highlighting of the cognitive revolution in human understanding. The effect of this revolution in aesthetic education has been a greater emphasis on substantive subject matter and the psychological dynamics of knowing, in short the two faces of cognition. Duke points out that cognitive studies are not narrowly cognitive but encompass affective aspects of understanding as well. The overall contribution of DBAE can be characterized in different ways, but it may well be that its harvesting of the cognitive revolution, to borrow a phrase from Margaret DiBlasio, will be a lasting one.

In "Art as General Education" Harry S. Broudy, a distinguished philosopher of education whose writings on general and aesthetic education have influenced a generation of educational theorists, argues that a case for art education must show that art is not just a distinctive subject of study but that it also pervades all aspects of life. In doing so, he discusses the range, potency, value, and function of images in shaping human thought and action, in particular the ways in which images constitute an important part of a person's allusionary stock. The primary responsibility of the schools in regard to teaching sensitivity to images is to convey the high points of a civilization's value imagery. A principal consultant to the Getty Center in its early years, Broudy refers to its efforts to design a defensible curriculum and pedagogical methodology that would put art education on a par with other subjects. The essay is essentially a condensation of arguments in his *The Role of Imagery in Learning* and *The Uses of Learning*, in which Broudy emphasizes the importance of the associative and interpretive uses of learning for enabling persons in later life to perceive the quality and import of works of art.

The contribution by Gilbert Clark, Michael Day, and W. Dwaine Greer consists of excerpts from their comprehensive monograph-length essay that describes what they call a paradigm shift in art education, one that stipulates the general goal of DBAE to be the development of abilities to understand and appreciate art within a program of general aesthetic education, with some attention to specialist training. Such abilities encompass a range of creative, historical, and critical skills found in the basic disciplines of DBAE (aesthetics, art criticism, art history, and art production). Works selected for study are drawn from Western and non-Western cultures and include, in addition to works of fine art, applied and folk art. Special attention is given to the importance of written sequential curricula and systematic district-wide implementation and assessment, while other topics are the aesthetic domain of human experience, perception, imagic store, metaphor, administrative support, and institutional resources. The excerpts reprinted explain the meaning and purposes of DBAE and compare and contrast DBAE and traditional thinking.

In an argument essentially from cognitive philosophy and psychology and the theory of multiple intelligences, Elliot W. Eisner likewise understands DBAE and visual arts generally as basic to general education, especially in connection with his view of art as a distinctive form of literacy that makes a significant contribution to the development of mind and sensitivity. Discussions of the biological and environmental bases of learning precede explanations of the special values of the arts and the functions they suggest for teaching. The excerpt reprinted here concentrates on the assumptions informing DBAE, the nature of meaning and human development, the disciplines associated with DBAE, and the kind of objectives appropriate for teaching art.

My interpretation of DBAE from a humanities point of view is a condensation of the argument presented in *Art Education: A Critical Necessity*, co-authored with Albert William Levi, which is the initial volume in a series of five titled Disciplines in Art Education: Contexts of Understanding. In this volume a philosopher of culture and the humanities and a theorist of aesthetic education provide an interpretation that draws parallels between the functions of the four disciplines of DBAE and such basic human needs as personal expression and communication, a sense of historical identity and continuity, and reflective criticism. Chapters that discuss the personal and social values of art precede descriptions of the four disciplines of DBAE, while concluding chapters center on the teaching of art as a humanity. Smith recommends a curriculum scenario that features five phases of aesthetic learning (see Part Four on Artistic and Aesthetic Development).

The discussion of the distinguishing characteristics of DBAE by Stephen Mark Dobbs is taken from the section on definition in *Learning in and through Art*, which is a revision of a handbook published by the Getty several years earlier, also authored by Dobbs. The revision differs from its predecessor in that it details not only what remains constant in DBAE but also ways in which earlier formulations have been modified.

In addition to the topic of definition, Dobbs organizes discussion under such rubrics as the disciplines of art, features (which encompass program requirements, professional roles, and performance assessment), and the future of DBAE.

LEILANI LATTIN DUKE

Mind Building and Arts Education

A complex challenge faces those of us who want the public, and more specifically parents and educators, to recognize the value of arts education. Many positive signs would seem to indicate a greater appreciation for the arts. Attendance increases are evident for a wide variety of visual, performing, and literary arts events. Artists often command celebrity attention and recognition, and new cultural facilities continue to spring up in the U.S. landscape. Some surveys even show that parents rank arts education as a subject that ought to be in the core curriculum.

And yet, despite these encouraging signs, I have been impressed with the sheer numbers of parents, teachers, school administrators, and elected public officials I continue to meet who tenaciously hold to some beliefs about arts education that result in their relegation to the margins of the curriculum. For example, they believe that the arts do little, if anything, to develop reasoning skills and the intellect. After all, so this argument goes, while the arts develop affective, emotional, and sensory capacities, these are of less importance to children's educational development than is developing their intellectual and reasoning capabilities. Our society tends to regard the arts as intellectually undemanding when compared to such subjects as chemistry and trigonometry, which are perceived as rigorous and tough because they require skills of abstraction, conceptualization, and computation. The arts, on the other hand, are perceived to appeal to our emotions, feelings, and sensibilities and to require little exercise of discrimination, interpretation, and judgment.

This artificial and spurious dichotomy between the affective and cognitive domains makes those of us who devote our professional and personal lives to the arts and to children's education in the arts want to beat our chests and pull out our hair. But the dichotomy is real. And the prognosis for its survival is quite good if one listens to what parents voice as their expectations for schooling: language proficiency, computational skills, and critical thinking capacities. Over the past eight years I have become convinced that unless arts education programs become better understood by parents, teachers, and school administrators as "mind-builders," they are destined to remain a marginal subject in the curriculum, relegated to the sidelines of schooling.

Schools have traditionally been preoccupied with the cultivation of a specific range of skills, namely, those focused on words and numbers. Even though we, as human beings, create and communicate through a much wider array of symbols and languages, such as visual, audile, and kinesthetic forms, the curriculum has emphasized linguistic and mathematical modes of thinking. Meanwhile, the capacity of the arts to build minds generally has gone unappreciated.

Arts educators have often argued for the cognitive importance of the arts in schooling but generally seem to have made little progress in justifying a place for the arts in the core curriculum with such arguments. Over the last twenty-five years, leading theorists and educators, including Rudolf Arnheim, Harry Broudy, Elliot Eisner, and Howard Gardner, have advocated the centrality of the senses and the development of mind and intellect. But the cognitive approach has been far less successful in attracting the attention even of art educators themselves than have the rationales that provide art with an educational role through its personal, social, and therapeutic consequences. The paradigm that primarily values creative self-expression, for example, sees art as an opportunity for experiences that are sharply at variance with the modes of learning practiced through such subjects as language, mathematics, history, and social studies. These subjects place a premium on written and oral response, whereas art usually has emphasized the making of visual objects employing techniques and materials utilized by artists.

During the 1970s, when "basic skills" swept over the educational landscape, many arts educators began speaking of "visual literacy" and "reading through the arts." These efforts to benefit art education by aligning it to schooling's primary mission to develop intellectual capacities existed more in rhetoric than reality. But there were noteworthy exceptions. Curriculum experiments, such as those at the Central Midwestern Regional Educational Laboratory (CEMREL) and Stanford University's Kettering Project did encourage increased reflection, reading, and discussion about art. Additionally, a number of theorists and arts educators contributed to the 1977 conference on "The Arts, Cognition, and Basic Skills" held at Aspen, Colorado, to explore the relationships between perception, human development, cognition, and arts education. And in the twelve years since the Aspen conference, the writings of Rudolph Arnheim, Harry Broudy, Elliot Eisner, and Howard Gardner provide well-reasoned and compelling arguments that support the role of the arts in mind building.

But it was difficult for parents and school policymakers to place much confidence in an art education that claimed it was contributing to developing a child's reasoning and problem-solving capabilities when the preponderance of classroom instruction in art continued to emphasize art-making activities and creative, self-expressive experiences through the manipulation of art materials.

Affect and Cognition

In 1982, as the cognitive approach to arts education was gaining greater currency, the Getty Center for Education in the Arts was created. After a year-long study of arts education in U.S. schools, the center began its work to improve the quality and status of arts education, deciding to concentrate its initial programs on the visual arts. During its extensive review of arts education, the center's staff was impressed by the emergence of a new, more comprehensive approach to arts education advocated by the College Board, the National Art Education Association, and an increasing number of arts curriculum guides published by state departments of education. The center's programs were informed by these developments and by several conclusions derived from its year-long review of arts education: Education in the arts contributes to every child's emotional and intellectual development and deserves to be part of the core curriculum, and education in the arts develops affective *and* cognitive capacities and its teaching should reflect both.

The approach to teaching art education adopted by the center has become known as discipline-based art education (DBAE) because it draws its content from four constituent disciplines that lead to the creation, understanding, and appreciation of art: studio art, art history, art criticism, and aesthetics.

The reason for the convergence of DBAE with the affective and cognitive rationales for art education has to do with the multiplicity of learning modes it utilizes. In the center's first national publication, *Beyond Creating: The Place for Art in America's Schools,*[1] it is suggested that the art lesson addresses a range of experiences it is possible to have with art, including but not limited to those involved with making art. By learning to respond and articulate through an art vocabulary the properties in visual phenomena (including works of art) to which one can respond, students can develop critical judgment that makes them independent observers capable of making informed choices and reasoned judgments about art. This is the task of art criticism. By learning about the role that artists play in different cultures and the contributions of visual art to societies of many kinds throughout the world, the student comes to appreciate art in a historical and cultural context and can develop a consciousness that extends beyond his or her own inheritance and background. That is the task of art history. By learning to think about the nature of art and the kinds of purposes that art objects serve, the student can develop a conceptual ability to understand and appreciate the relationships between ideas and objects. That is the task of aesthetics.

Interactive Modes

In other words, DBAE involves considerable learning activity that complements, supplements, and integrates the studio component—the shaping of form to have aesthetic character—with other kinds of activities and experiences. These other modes of learning require discursive attention to art—the speaking and writing and reading about imagery. Such modes are pursued to bring about a wider encounter with art than is likely when the exclusive focus of art is upon the technical and making side. These are viewed as interactive, the understanding and appreciating with the creating. They are not isolated or independent, but are integrated and interdependent. Indeed, to become more artistically creative, a child requires the kind of intellectual support nurtured by a curriculum that acknowledges the role of mind.

DBAE lends itself to *mind building* and to the effort of many arts educators to bring to the attention of school boards, administrators, and other educational policymakers the role of the arts in supporting general education goals of intellectual development. The current idiom of this primary mission of the schools is often called "critical thinking" or "higher order thinking skills." It really seems to be another version of the back-to-basics movement of a decade ago. But in contrast to previous eras in which arts educators talked about the arts building minds but usually failed to realize such aspirations, arts education today is showing stronger signs of developing the cognitive approach. Through DBAE and other versions of a multifaceted, comprehensive arts education, students' minds are stretched by activities and exercises that promote the use of language, problem solving, and reflection about works of art. This has proceeded along with a basic respect for the centrality of the art object and the making that brings it into existence. But, in a DBAE program, the children's art products now reveal the acquisition of concepts because their art production has a purposive character reflecting the goals of art and of general education.

Research

Even as we make the claim that DBAE can help build minds through the cognitive skills that are a consequence of the modes through which children can experience art, we recognize that the field of art education has far to go to understand empirically the kinds of results that are increasingly realized in DBAE instruction. Relatively little hard data are available on the transfer implied by the claims for mental development. Educational theory, such as that of Piaget, provides some support. Gestalt and developmental psychology, such as in the work of Arnheim and Gardner, provides further evidence. The testimony and anecdotes of teachers and principals, and of superintendents and school board members, about increases in reading scores, increased verbal fluency, and enhanced divergent thinking are impressive but need scientific study and elaboration. With the continuing researches of Project Zero at Harvard University, the efforts of the National Endowment for the Arts-supported National Arts Education Research Centers at New York University and the University of Illinois, and the growing interest in teacher education institutions for a research agenda that directs doctoral and professional investigations toward this general area, the prospects for additional support for the cognitive view increases as time passes.

Arts education is only one of a number of subjects in the school curriculum that can build minds and support the general mission of U.S. education to nurture intellectual functioning. Arts educators can fulfill their part of this task through the creative and comprehensive use of arts experiences for students. Thus, arts education remains one of the most underutilized assets and resources of learning in our schools.

The potential for the arts to build minds through a comprehensive multifaceted approach is beginning to be realized because more national organizations—such as the Association for Supervision and Curriculum Development, the Council for Basic Education, the Council for Chief State School Officers, and the National PTA—advocate this approach. More state education departments are also embracing a multifaceted or DBAE approach in their curriculum guides, and an increasing number of leading art education practitioners are shaping its classroom implementation. The future for arts education programs to be recognized as mind-builders never looked brighter.

Note

1. Getty Center for Education in the Arts, *Beyond Creating: The Place for Art in America's Schools* (Los Angeles: Getty Center for Education in the Arts, 1985).

HARRY S. BROUDY

Art as General Education

The public for the fine arts is composed of artists, professional and amateur, galleries, museums, auction houses, art scholars, critics, plus a selection of citizens who are interested in some or all of these activities. All in all, this public is relatively small and esoteric. This bothers those who believe that public schools should produce "cultural" as well as linguistic, scientific, mathematical, and social literacy. Yet literature aside, the fine arts are still regarded as specialties that regular classroom teachers cannot, and often do not want to handle, and from which only talented pupils can benefit.

In recent years an increasing number of states have mandated arts education programs, but the movement still has far to go before art instruction is taken for granted on a par with the standard required subjects in the curriculum. To convince a School Board—even a well meaning one—that all pupils should be subjected to regular instruction in art requires more than praising the arts. The argument has to make two major points: (1) that art experience is distinctive, and therefore cannot be subsumed under other subjects, yet (2) that it affects *all* aspects of experience. The School Board must be convinced that the aesthetic experience (of which art is a special form) pervades every phase of life—cognition, judgment, feeling, and action.

Consider, for example, how much we depend on appearances for guides to judgment on a person's occupation, economic status, race, nationality, and personality traits. When modes of dress, hair styles, carriage, speech do not send clear messages on these matters, we are uneasy and confused. When professors and students look and dress alike; when joggers and muggers present similar images, we become wary of both. We retreat into situations where the signs/appearances are clear—in our own social cocoons.

Banks and government buildings are supposed to *look* dignified and even majestic. Perhaps this accounts for the misplaced confidence people had in the scores of savings and loans that belied their appearance.

We do not know how images acquire their potency. Psychologists, anthropologists, aestheticians have their answers, which, sooner or later, reduce to the fact that images convey information by externalizing feelings that are occurring in the glands and nervous system. They provide a unique combination of knowledgeful feeling and feelingful knowledge that constitutes a basic underground connection between language and imagery.[1]

The arts, of course, are founded in this power of imagery, mysterious though it may be. Pine trees are not *really* lonely, yet to be on the trail of the lonesome pine makes aesthetic sense. Compare the report "These trees have been standing for hundreds of years" with "This is the forest primaeval/The murmuring pines and hemlocks."

Although Gertrude Stein proclaimed that "a rose is a rose is a rose," the unabridged dictionary lists columns of rose words. "Roses that bloom in Picardy," the "sacred soldiery of Christ" that Beatrice revealed to Dante was in the form of a white rose—what would the arts do without roses? And what can those with meager stores of rose images do with art?

Subcultures in a society develop diverse imagery banks. Slang is one example of esoteric imagery; in-house jargon (e.g., computers) is another. Washington's rhetoric is highly esoteric. Sometimes the babbles become ambiguous, as when a vehicle servicing computers bears a sign reading "Terminal Repairs."

ART, EDUCATION, AND LEARNING

Art contrives images to portray feeling by using what Susanne K. Langer called "presentational" rather than "discursive symbols." Art, therefore, contributes a unique component to the curriculum. However, not all art forms require a place and time in the curriculum, especially in that of a public school. Popular art needs no formal school instruction. Neither does the school have to take on functions of museums, orchestras, arts councils, and generous corporate endowments. Finally, if only certain classes in society and prospective professions need such instruction, a public school is under no obligation to provide it for everyone.

Only when lack of art instruction leaves an intolerable cultural gap in the resources of the mind does it become a public necessity. For what a culture deems important, it enshrines in art. The origin of the tribe, its tragedies and victories are presented in legends, drama, music, architecture, and dance. They become the images *with* which we construe cultures: the *Iliad*, the Parthenon, the Statue of Liberty, the *Marseillaise*, the raising of the flag at Iwo Jima.

All of which contributes to the argument that the fine arts are to be classed with the bread of life, and not the cake Marie Antoinette is said to have suggested as a substitute to the starving peasants.

Images and Language Learning

Educators may ask whether and how art or the aesthetic experience contributes to the learning of other subjects in the curriculum.

That art helps children learn some school tasks is hardly a new discovery; it is a truism that a picture is worth a thousand words. The reason is fairly obvious, viz., a sensory image's meaning is direct and immediate; a word—with few exceptions, like "bang"—bears no resemblance to what it designates, it has to be translated. Relating words to things by means of pictures is a pedagogical ploy at least as old as Comenius, who in his day was famous for *Orbis Pictus*, a text that used pictures to facilitate the teaching of Latin vocabulary.

Research seems to indicate that imagery has an important role in the retention of school learning.[2] Bull and Wittrock note that how imagery functions in retention among children is not well understood, but seems to play a definite role.[3]

A study by Fries[4] provides another clue to the role of imagery in school learning. He found that among the prominent differences between the "vulgar" and "standard" uses of English was the "poverty" of the vulgar use. The word "get," for example, is employed ten times more often in vulgar than in the standard usage. Apparently there is a lack of imagery in the associative store relating to activities connoted by "getting." For if art is the making of images that expand the realms of feeling and understanding, then the perception of art is a major factor in constructing the allusionary store *with* which we think and feel; *with* which we learn the thoughts and attitudes of a civilization.

College students, I have found, do not cite "breathing across" in response to the word "transpire" or "breathing with" to "conspire." Latin study may not have an immediately practical use in our times, but without such study much of the significance of the imagery in English poetry is lost.

All poetry depends on imagery for its effect, but so does slang, the poetry of adolescence, and oratory, the poetry of politicians. Or consider the plight of the non-English speaker trying to construe the meaning of "We worked around the clock" or "I'll take the heat."

Imagery and Concept Learning

Kant put it bluntly when he wrote "Concepts without percepts are empty; percepts without concepts are blind." Some may regard this dictum as derogatory to both pure thought and eloquent art, but images of nothing amount to nothing; while "imageless" thinkers should refrain from admiring the "elegance" of a highly abstract mathematical proof. Even the mathematical symbol of equality, =, is an echo of the aesthetical principle of balance. What are light *waves*, electric *currents*, right and left-handed spin on a K meson, if not sensory images?[5] For F. W. Froebel, the originator of the modern kindergarten, the cube and the circle were the visible images of the Divine Unity.

When do images become messages? When do works of art become portraits of feeling? In the beginning, perhaps our remote forbears really sensed their blood as "boiling" and "the mouths of rivers" and the "teeth of ploughs" were not simply figures of speech. "Men sang before they spoke; they spoke in verse before they spoke in prose, as is made plain by the study of the kinds of signs and symbols they used, and the type of use they made of them."[6]

Images and Value Learning

Perhaps the most potent influence of art is on the learning of values, in large part because value experience is so largely an amalgam of ideas and emotion. Loyalty, honesty, divinity, sacrifice, democracy, justice are names of emotional states that accompany or induce action deemed appropriate to them.

Whence arise these notions of what ought to be? Presumably from the power of human minds to imagine what *might* be, but which in fact may not be the case. We do not attribute the tenderness of an animal mother to ideals, but to glandular responses. Human motherhood expands this glandular impulse to an extraordinary extrapolation of emotion and ideals. Drama, literature, dance, song, painting, sculpture portray these ideal possibilities and implicit demands for their realization.[7]

Perhaps the role of images in value education is most clearly illustrated by an example that occurs in *out of school* life. In walking along streets inhabited by "old line" families occupying very expensive "old line" mansions, one notes that there is a main front entrance to which leads a more or less ornate entry gate and path. At the side of the mansions is another pathway that curves to the rear of the main house leading to what may have been the coach house and is now used as a garage. Houses on less opulent streets in older sections of the town present the same approach to the passers by. The front of the house is dominated by the approach path to the front door. However, in the new sections of the town the frontage of the residence is not really in front of the house but to one side. A broad pathway leads to a double car garage from which a side path connects to the front door.

A ten-page essay on the role of the automobile in modern culture could not convey the change from the horse and carriage days more immediately and more vividly than the images afforded by the two streets. The images of daily life that appear in the popular media, in the work place, on the streets are far more potent than the refined images of art in the museum and in libraries. Formal schooling, especially the kind that makes up the curriculum of a liberal education, is an attempt to infuse the allusionary store with images that portray the high points in the value system of a culture. Art education is a potent factor in the process. Art education begins with bedtime stories and fairy tales, but we cannot afford to have it end there.

ART AS GENERAL EDUCATION

If the role of art in general education is accepted, it entails not only an acknowledgment of the part it plays in the culture and public education, but the feasibility of constructing a curriculum and a pedagogical methodology that qualifies it as a discipline on a par with the other disciplines in the required course of study.

To this end, W. Dwaine Greer and the faculty of the Getty Institute for Educators on the Visual Arts have put into place what has come to be known as Discipline-Based Art Education. It calls for a sequential curriculum incorporating production, aesthetics, history of art, and criticism. The summer institute conducted in Los Angeles and more recently at a number of other sites introduced classroom teachers to the skills and theoretical components of the curriculum. The summer institutes provide the classroom teacher with curriculum materials, background materials in art theory, and a method by which children can analyze the sensory, formal, and expressive properties of visual art objects.

The organization of the project entails the cooperation of the school district and frequent supervision and assessment of the project. Despite the criticism of some arts educators and a series of national conferences designed to scrutinize the philosophy and procedures of DBAE, there is little doubt that the project has demonstrated the feasibility of incorporating the visual arts in the curriculum and in the classroom of the public school.

It would be a mistake, however, to expect the effects of DBAE to be measured adequately by the familiar objective tests or even the most adequate supervision and observation. The expectation that school instruction's effects can be measured in this way practically insures the conclusion that formal schooling produces very little of the life-long results claimed for it unless special efforts are made to reinforce them more or less continuously through post-school experience.

In a number of publications and most extensively in *The Uses of Schooling*[7] I have distinguished among the replicative, applicative, associative and interpretive uses of schooling. The replicative use is simply the instantiation of a response as learned in school, e.g., the multiplication table, names and dates, etc. The applicative use, which is the most recently discovered "failure of the public school," requires the testee to use a principle or concept learned in school to solve a problem. Both of these uses require frequent reinforcement by more or less steady use to prevent forgetting. Thus well-educated professionals tend to forget theoretical learnings in which they garnered very good grades during high school and college, unless their work required the use of these facts and procedures. How many lawyers, for example, would score well on their high school or college examinations in chemistry? How many educated citizens can apply the principles of science to the repair of their automobiles, microwave ovens, television sets, and word processors?

Must it be concluded that these educated individuals wasted their high school and college years? Must we expect that courses in art history, art criticism, aesthetics and art production will be retained, as learned in school, by the citizen who does not use these courses in his or her daily life and occupation?

We would be constrained to reach such conclusions were it not for the fact that school instruction also functions associatively and interpretively. All instruction on which students pass examinations with good grades becomes part of their interpretive and associative store, i.e., their allusionary resources *with* which they think and feel. These uses differ markedly from our responses in fields in which we did not have formal instruction. And this is especially true for the role of the arts and arts education. Our course work in the literature, sculpture, music, and architecture of the Greeks and Romans is made manifest in our responses to the samples of these arts in museums and libraries or in our travels to foreign countries, even though we can no longer pass an examination in the course work which engendered them.

Much of what is now bewailed as cultural illiteracy may be attributed to tests that measure that amount of names, dates, places, events we have retained for replicative use or our ingenuity in doing high tone crossword puzzles. The advocates of liberal education in general and of the arts in particular would do well to invest time and intellectual effort in contriving adequate tests of the interpretive and associative result of arts education, especially if it is to become a solid citizen in the community of disciplines that constitute the curriculum of the public school.

The true test of such instruction comes in adult life when we are confronted by a painting in a museum, a drama, a building. Can we respond to the sensory, formal, expressive properties of these objects? Can we sense the feelings, concepts and values of which these works of art are the images? Or is our response limited to the descriptions in a catalogue or program note?

Notes

1. One dictionary lists 32 uses of the word "basic" all emanating from a primary image of one thing supporting another from below.

2. Allan Paivio, *Imagery and Verbal Processes* (New York: Holt, Rinehart, and Winston, 1971), states that "imagery is centrally important in facilitating long-term retention, at least for adults."

3. B. L. Bull and M. C. Wittrock, "Imagery in the Learning of Verbal Definitions," *British Journal of Educational Psychology* 43, no. 3 (1973): 289-293.

4. C. Fries, *American English Grammar* (New York: D. Appleton Century, 1940), p. 288.

5. Cf. J. P. Dougherty, "Substance as Controlling." In *Essays Honoring Allan B. Wolter*, ed. by W. A. Frank and C. J. Etzkorn (Saint Bonaventure, N.Y., 1985), pp. 117-129.

6. Isaiah Berlin, *The Divorce Between the Sciences and the Humanities*, 2nd Tykociner Lecture (Urbana, Ill.: Department of Electrical Engineering, University of Illinois, 1974), p. 2.

7. A systematic examination of these issues is to be found in my monograph, *The Role of Imagery in Learning* (Los Angeles: The Getty Center for Education in the Arts, 1987) and the *The Uses of Schooling* (London: Routledge and Kegan Paul, 1988).

GILBERT A. CLARK, MICHAEL D. DAY, AND W. DWAINE GREER

Discipline-based Art Education: Becoming Students of Art

This essay is about teaching art in schools and deals with a major shift in theory and practice in the field of art education that had its beginnings a quarter century ago. It is about a contemporary orientation to art education that presents a broad view of art and emphasizes art in the general education of all students from kindergarten through high school. This approach integrates content from four art disciplines, namely, aesthetics, art criticism, art history, and art production,[1] through a focus on works of art. The term *discipline* in this context refers to fields of study that are marked by recognized communities of scholars or practitioners, established conceptual structures, and accepted methods of inquiry. Decisions with respect to topics such as curriculum, instruction, learning, and evaluation are based upon the belief that art should be an integral part of general education. Art is viewed as a subject with content that can be taught and learned in ways that resemble how other subjects are taught in schools. Teachers are expected to teach their students by using written, sequentially organized curricula, and student progress is verified through use of appropriate evaluation methods. Goals, procedures, and evaluation are specific to the content of art but are consistent and compatible with those of general education. This approach has become known as *discipline-based art education* (DBAE).[2]

Theories in any field are built upon work of the past, and the theoretical construct presented here is no exception. This essay refers to scholarly contributions from the past two decades and recognizes the inclusion of many ideas from the professional literature of education. ... The explication of this theory and its identification by a recognizable and descriptive name are steps toward a general shift in the curricula and practices of art education.

This shift began during a time of general curriculum reform in the 1960s and was influenced by prominent ideas of that time. DBAE might be viewed by some as a belated application of old ideas, some of which subsequently have been discredited. The curriculum reform movement of the sixties emphasized the structure of academic disciplines in education in order to improve the nation's scientific, technological, and military capabilities. Contemporary critics of the curricula of that era have pointed out serious problems with content-centered, or discipline-centered, approaches that might conceivably be applied to the current discipline-based orientation in art education. The discipline-based art approach has taken twenty-five years to develop, however, and differs from the earlier movement in a number of significant ways. Clear distinctions can be made, therefore, between the content-centered approaches of the sixties and DBAE as outlined in this paper.

The content- or discipline-centered movement of the sixties was a comprehensive curriculum reform movement supported by the federal government and intended to influence the entire school curriculum. In contrast, DBAE has been generated from the field, funded by public and private agencies, and related particularly to art education. The sixties movement cast university scholars from the disciplines as curriculum developers and experts in matters of content to be taught.[3] Within DBAE, art curriculum specialists are recognized as experts in selection of art content appropriate for various age groups and in curriculum development. Figure 1 outlines major differences between the discipline-centered curriculum reform movement and the discipline-based art education orientation.

These differences are significant because they mark a shift in theoretical foundations for art education, and although the current effort has adapted ideas from the earlier curriculum reform work, development of the DBAE orientation has been marked by determined efforts to avoid misjudgments made in the 1960s. Within the discipline-centered reform movement, for instance, changing practice was a matter of installing "teacher-proof" programs. In contrast, DBAE uses a district-wide team effort by school board members, superintendents, principals, and teachers to bring about changes.

As a contemporary configuration of ideas, the DBAE orientation also differs significantly from the creative self-expression approach to art education that has dominated the field for forty years.[4] Within the creative self-expression rationale, art is seen as an instrument for developing what is assumed to be each child's inherent creativity and expressive abilities. In the early 1960s, at the height of the popularity of creative self-expression, several conferences were held in which art educators questioned fundamental assertions of the creative self-expression approach and suggested alternatives.[5] Since then, theorists, scholars, and

Sixties Discipline-centered Reform	Discipline-based Art Education
A general curriculum reform movement.	A specific effort to reform curriculum in art education.
Scholar-specialists as curriculum developers.	Art curriculum specialists as curriculum developers concerned with schools/ communities.
Attempted to make "teacher-proof" curricula.	Recognizes essential roles of teachers and administrators in curriculum implementation.
Focused on math, science, and foreign language.	Focuses on art in general education.
Implementation directed by federal funds granted to individual teachers for inservice training.	Implementation with public and private funds in cooperation with local school districts in local contexts.
Focused on structure of disciplines as content source.	Focuses on dynamic view of art disciplines including concepts, methods of inquiry, and communities of scholars.
Focused on purity and abstraction of disciplined knowledge.	Focuses on integrated understanding of aesthetics, art criticism, art history, and art production.
Model of learner as a discipline specialist.	Model of learner as a person with a well-rounded education.

Figure 1. Comparison of the Discipline-centered Reform Movement and Discipline-based Art Education

researchers have developed a body of literature that has moved the field consistently away from the creative self-expression approach.[6] It was not until the mid-1980s, however, that these early questions and suggestions, reinforced by twenty years of constructive criticism and scholarly writings, resulted in an alternative approach to art education.

The creative self-expression approach places great emphasis on art activities; DBAE, in contrast, requires a balanced art curriculum that emphasizes content from the four art disciplines. These differences reveal shifts in practice and curricula that distinguish the two approaches. Figure 2 compares differing conceptions about essential education topics held within each of the two approaches.

Creative Self-expression	Discipline-based Art Education
Goals	
Development of creativity; self-expression; personality integration; focus on child.	Development of understanding of art; art essential for a well-rounded education; focus upon art as a subject for study.
Content	
Art making as self-expression; variety of art materials and methods.	Aesthetics, art criticism, art history, and art production; art from world's cultures and eras.
Curriculum	
Developed by individual teacher; nonsequential, nonarticulated implementation.	Written curriculum with sequential cumulative, articulated, district-wide implementation.
Conception of Learner	
Learners are innately creative and expressive; need nurture rather than instruction; exposure to adult art images inhibits learners' natural creative development.	Learners are students of art; need instruction to develop understandings of art. Exposure to adult art images enhances learners' creative development.
Conception of Teacher	
Provides motivation, support; does not impose adult concepts or images; care not to inhibit child's self-expression.	Provides motivation, support; helps child understand valid art concepts at child's level; uses culturally valued adult art images; encourages child's creative expression.
Creativity	
Innate in child; develops naturally with encouragement and opportunity; lack of development is usually result of adult intervention.	Creativity as unconventional behavior that can occur as conventional art understandings are attained; untutored childhood expression is not regarded as necessarily creative.
Implementation	
Can be achieved on a single-classroom basis; coordination among classrooms and schools not essential.	Requires district-wide participation for full effect of sequence and articulation.
Works of Art	
Adult works are not studied; adult images might negatively influence child's self-expression and creative development.	Adult works are central to the study of art; adult images serve as focus for integrating learning from the four art disciplines.
Evaluation	
Based on child's growth and process of art making; evaluation of student achievement generally discouraged.	Based on educational goals; focuses on learning; essential for confirming student progress and program effectiveness.

Figure 2. Comparison of Creative Self-expression and Discipline-based Art Education[7]

A creative self-expression program, even with the addition of some art history and criticism for enrichment or motivation, still differs from DBAE because of fundamentally different philosophical foundations and different psychological orientations. . . .The ideas that describe and define DBAE. . . .are organized around the defining characteristics of a DBAE program (see figure 3).

Defining Characteristics of a DBAE Program

A. Rationale
   1. The goal of discipline-based art education is to develop students' abilities to understand and appreciate art. This involves a knowledge of the theories and contexts of art and abilities to respond to as well as to create art.
   2. Art is taught as an essential component of general education and as a foundation for specialized art study.

B. Content
   3. Content for instruction is derived primarily from the disciplines of aesthetics, art criticism, art history, and art production. These disciplines deal with: (1) conceptions of the nature of art, (2) bases for valuing and judging art, (3) contexts in which art has been created, and (4) processes and techniques for creating art.
   4. Content for study is derived from a broad range of the visual arts, including folk, applied, and fine arts from Western and non-Western cultures and from ancient to contemporary times.

C. Curricula
   5. Curricula are written with sequentially organized and articulated content at all grade levels.
   6. Works of art are central to the organization of curricula and to integration of content from the disciplines.
   7. Curricula are structured to reflect comparable concern and respect for each of the four art disciplines.
   8. Curricula are organized to increase student learning and understanding. This involves a recognition of appropriate developmental levels.

D. Context
   9. Full implementation is marked by systematic, regular art instruction on a district-wide basis, art education expertise, administrative support, and adequate resources.
   10. Student achievement and program effectiveness are confirmed by appropriate evaluation criteria and procedures.

Figure 3. Defining Characteristics of a DBAE Program

Conclusion: A Paradigm Shift in Art Education

In real-life experiences with art, those who have completed a discipline-based program should be able to respond comfortably and intelligently as they confront original works of art in galleries, museums, or other settings. They should possess the means to discuss and evaluate art as informed adults and should be able to understand unfamiliar or unusual works of art, including contemporary art or art from other cultures.

Because of their newly acquired aesthetic sensitivities, students' lives will be enriched as they experience works of art, the built environment, and the phenomena of nature. Educated adults will be able to discriminate between simplistic or insincere manifestations of the visual arts and those that are credited with high standards, pursuit of perfection, and lasting value. High standards among those who admire and purchase art as consumers should result in higher standards of artistic production.[8]

For some who have completed a discipline-based program, production of their personal art will hold a special place in their lives. Through artistic expression it will be possible for them to give form to their feelings and express their ideas with concrete visual materials. For others, the attraction of creative expression in visual media or the production of art criticism, art history, or aesthetics may result in the pursuit of an art discipline as a career. For many others, art will continue to be a meaningful and satisfying avocation. For perhaps the largest portion of high school graduates, knowledge of making art and understanding art will enhance their abilities to create art and to view the work of others with empathy and enjoyment. They are the ones who will support art education and art in society in the future.

This essay—which emphasizes the values of an art education that opens avenues of aesthetic experience, stimulates the mind, and provides students with a lens of the arts through which they can gain additional meanings from the world—acknowledges also that certain more practical values should be recognized. We live in a world in which the appearance of our clothing, the places where we reside, and the environments we create convey aesthetic attitudes and meanings. In our daily lives, we are virtually bombarded with influential messages conveyed through the arts. No other subject in school provides students with instruction in visual aesthetic discrimination and decision making. No other subject provides students with knowledge about the purposes and traditions of the visual arts that are necessary for informed choices. In the words of John Dewey, "Possession of this understanding broadens and refines the background without which judgment is blind and arbitrary."[9]

In a discipline-based art program, content of the art disciplines and the educational outcomes are emphasized to enrich the lives of individuals and benefit society. One need only imagine how our immediate environments might appear if all decision makers in our society had achieved the goals of DBAE or how the lives of so many might be enriched if they had developed the lens that would allow them to experience the world of the visual arts.

Notes

1. Throughout this essay, these disciplines are referred to alphabetically.

2. W. Dwaine Greer, "Discipline-based Art Education: Approaching Art as a Subject of Study," *Studies in Art Education* 25, no. 4 (Summer 1984): 212-18; Getty Center for Education in the Arts, *Beyond Creating: The Place for Art in America's Schools* (Los Angeles: J. Paul Getty Trust, 1985).

3. In their complete and cogent discussion of the discipline-centered curriculum movement initiated in the late 1950s and marked by the spending of hundreds of millions of dollars through the National Defense Education Act of 1958 and the National Science Foundation, Daniel and Laurel Tanner's *Curriculum's Development: Theory into Practice*, 2nd ed. (New York, Macmillan, 1980) list five realizations gained from successes and failures of the movement. These were that curriculum development requires consideration of (1) the nature and interests of the learner, (2) the problems of society, (3) the interdependence of knowledge, (4) the continuity between theoretical and applied knowledge, (5) the authentic function of general education as compared with that of specialized education, and (6) involvement of the whole school community, and not merely the scholar-specialist (p. 561).

4. Viktor Lowenfeld, *The Nature of Creative Activity* (London: Kegan Paul, Trench, Truber, 1939); idem, *Your Child and His Art* (New York: Macmillan, 1954); idem, *Creative and Mental Growth* (1947; reprint, New York: Macmillan, 1957); Victor Lowenfeld and W. Lambert Brittain, *Creative and Mental Growth* (1964; reprint, New York: Macmillan, 1982); Herbert Read, *Education through Art* (1945; reprint, New York: Pantheon, 1958); Victor E. D'Amico, *Creative Teaching in Art* (1942; reprint, Scranton, Pa.: International Textbook, 1966); Natalie R. Cole, *The Arts in the Classroom* (New York: John Day, 1940); idem, *Children's Art from Deep Down Inside* (New York: John Day, 1966); Henry Schaefer-Simmern, *The Unfolding of Artistic Activity* (Berkeley: University of California Press, 1948); Manuel Barkan, *A Foundation for Art Education* (New York: Ronald Press, 1955).

5. Edward L. Mattil, ed., *A Seminar in Art Education for Research and Curriculum Development* (University Park: Pennsylvania State University, 1966); Howard Conant, ed., *Seminar on Elementary and Secondary School: Education in the Visual Arts* (New York: New York University, 1965); Harlan E. Hoffa, *An Analysis of*

Recent Research Conferences in Art Education (Bloomington: Indiana University Foundation, 1974).

6. Manuel Barkan, "Transition in Art Education: Changing Conceptions of Curriculum and Teaching." *Art Education* 15, no. 7 (October 1962): 12-18; Elliott W. Eisner and David W. Ecker, eds., *Readings in Art Education* (Waltham, Mass.: Blaisdell, 1966); Michael D. Day, "The Compatibility of Art History and Studio Art Activity in the Junior High School Program: A Comparison of Two Methods of Teaching Art History," *Studies in Art Education* 10, no. 2 (Winter 1969): 57-65; Edmund B. Feldman, *Varieties of Visual Experience* (Englewood Cliffs, N. J.: Prentice-Hall, 1971); Ralph A. Smith, ed., *Aesthetics and Problems of Education* (Urbana: University of Illinois Press, 1971); June McFee, *Preparation for Art* (1961), 2nd ed. (Belmont, Calif.: Wadsworth, 1971); Elliott W. Eisner, *Teaching Art to the Young: A Curriculum Development Project on Art Education* (Stanford, Calif.: Stanford University School of Education, 1969); idem, *Educating Artistic Vision* (New York: Macmillan, 1972); Vincent Lanier, "A Plague on All Your Houses: The Tragedy of Art Education," *Art Education* 27, no. 3 (March 1974): 12-15; Arthur Efland, "The School Art Style: A Functional Analysis," *Studies in Art Education* 17, no. 2 (1976): 37-44; Francis Hine, Gilbert A. Clark, W. Dwaine Greer, and Ronald Silverman, *The Aesthetic Eye Project: Final Report* (Los Angeles: Office of the Los Angeles County Superintendent of Schools, 1976); Laura Chapman, *Approaches to Art in Education* (New York: Harcourt Brace Jovanovich, 1978); Gilbert A. Clark and Enid Zimmerman, "A Walk in the Right Direction: A Model for Visual Arts Education," *Studies in Art Education* 19, no. 2 (1978): 34-39; idem, "Toward a Discipline of Art Education," *Phi Delta Kappan*, 63 no. 1 (September 1981): 53-55.

7. This comparison contrasts two extreme theoretical positions for purposes of clarification. In practice, there are few school art education programs that completely exemplify either position. Many programs can be found that fall between the two positions on any of the topics of comparison.

8. Monroe C. Beardsley, "Critical Evaluation," in *Aesthetics and Criticism in Art Education*, ed. Ralph A. Smith (Chicago: Rand McNally, 1966), pp. 315-31.

9. John Dewey, *Art as Experience* (New York: Capricorn Books, G. Putnam's Sons, 1934), p. 312.

Elliot W. Eisner

What Is Discipline-Based Art Education?

> The arts tell the student about the significance of direct experience and of his own response. In this sense, they are complementary to the message of science, where direct experience must be transcended and the individual outlook of each observer counts only to the extent to which it contributes to shaping the common conception of the phenomenon under investigation.
>
> Rudolf Arnheim

There is a widely held view that children's development in art is best served by a kind of benign neglect. Each child is believed to have a particular genetically structured program that unfolds over time if the environment in which the child lives is not stunted. The plant, as it were, will become all that it can be if only a nurturant environment is created. The kindergarten—literally, a garden for growing children—has been the model that has influenced our view of what children need. In this view, the child develops essentially from the inside out, not from the outside in.

There is little question that all children, like all adults, are influenced by their genetic constitution: we do not enter the world as blank slates, nor are we endowed with identical aptitudes. But it is also true that the kind of environment in which a child lives influences the kinds of aptitudes he forms, the mental skills he develops, and the cognitive structures through which he perceives and interprets the world. The abilities that children come to possess are not determined at birth, nor are the aptitudes individual children possess identical to those possessed by others. We are born like all other people, like some other people, and like no other person.[1] The task of education is not one of standing by and letting nature take its course, but one of providing the conditions that will empower the young to shape their own development after leaving school.

For discipline-based art education, this means that we do not wait for children to learn simply by providing art materials they can manipulate, but that we provide supportive and encouraging instruction that guides learning. It means taking seriously the idea there is much of value in the visual arts—learning to see, to understand, to judge, and to create—and that teachers have a responsibility to help children have the kind of experience that will make what is valuable a part of their mental life. In sum, it means that those of us who share the ideals of discipline-based art education assume that children develop not only from the inside out, but from the outside in.[2] The outside—the only location available to any teacher—is the only place from which we can teach. It is true that much development is genetically determined, but what children do with their genetically determined capacities will depend upon the opportunities they have to learn. The school is the institution, and curriculum and teaching are the means, for creating and guiding those opportunities.

A second assumption is that the acquisition of artistic skills in the making and perception of art is complex and subtle in character. Complex and subtle skills are seldom acquired in single settings. They require time, repetition, exploration, and continuity of effort and practice. The goals of discipline-based art education are not likely to be realized by skipping about from material to material, task to task. Learning to perceive, create, comprehend and judge requires as much or more continuity of effort as do those less complex skills that can be learned and applied by following the rules.

HUMAN DEVELOPMENT

A third assumption in discipline-based art education is that learning in art is related to the course of human development. This means that developmental features define abilities that curriculum planners and teachers must take into account. One cannot profitably attempt to teach six-year-olds principles of aesthetic judgment or to develop forms of perception that exceed their developmentally determined capacities. If some who have focused upon the child and his or her development have underestimated the child's limits, those in discipline-based art education must not overestimate them. A child of seven is quite unlikely to be able to grasp historical concepts that require a level of cognitive development that has not yet emerged. An adult who has had a history of intimidating encounters with the arts of drawing and painting cannot be expected to relinquish these fears in a moment and to immerse himself joyfully in such tasks. Our developmental level and our personal biographies affect how we experience what we encounter. Discipline-based art education is predicated on the assumption that those who teach are sufficiently sensitive to the developmental and experiential aspects of their students to be able to teach effectively. In practice, this means that we cannot afford to either underestimate or overestimate what children and adolescents can do. The activities in which they engage must be challenging, not disheartening. They must be *appropriately* beyond their present competencies.

MATTERS OF MEANING

A fourth assumption in discipline-based art education is that the curricular tasks that children are asked to engage in must have meaning to them: intrinsic, not simply extrinsic, meaning.[3] Intrinsic meaning is necessary if what children learn is to become an internalized part of their intellectual and emotional life. There is so much in schooling that for children is largely a matter of going through mindless routines. Discipline-based art education does not aim at having children jump through hoops or otherwise engage in tasks that they do not understand or for which they receive little satisfaction. Activities in which children engage must yield benefits that transcend the limits of the classroom by being applicable to life outside of the classroom. One way in which this can occur is by teaching for transfer; that is, helping children apply what they have been taught in settings other than the one in which they were taught.

Another way to increase transfer of learning is to make what is taught relevant to children while they are learning. If new insights make sense to the child, or prove useful, what this child learns will not only be meaningful, the insights and skills acquired are likely to be applicable elsewhere. What we seek to provide in discipline-based art education are activities that can generate such meaning.

THE AIMS AND CONTENT OF DISCIPLINE-BASED ART EDUCATION: THE FOUR DISCIPLINES OF LEARNING IN ART

Educational values live their educational lives within classrooms. Classroom life, in turn, consists largely of what teachers and students do together around a body of ideas, skills, and activities. It is the curriculum and the quality of the teaching that mediates it that influence what children learn in the course of their schooling. And ultimately, it is the scope of the curriculum that defines the opportunities that children will have to develop their minds.

One essential task in all curriculum planning activity is the formulation of aims and the identification of disciplines relevant to the achievement of those aims. For discipline-based art education, there are four major aims that are central to its mission. These aims pertain to the four most important activities that one can do with the visual arts: One can create art, perceive and respond to its qualities, understand its place in history and culture, and make reasoned judgments about art and understand the grounds upon which those judgments rest.

In the adult world, the most sophisticated expression of these four activities is found in the work of artists, art critics, art historians, and aestheticians. Artists have the imagination, sensitivity, and skills to create expressive visual forms. Art critics know how to perceive the works they attend to and to describe and interpret their subtle and complex features. Art historians understand the place of art in time and culture. Aestheticians are sophisticated about the bases for judgments about art and about questions pertaining to its status as a form of knowledge or insight into the world.

These four disciplines—art making, art criticism, art history, and aesthetics—are the four major disciplines from which the content of discipline-based art education is drawn. We want children to experience the joys of creating visual images and to have opportunities to acquire the skills that make such joys possible. We want children to develop the visual sensitivity to see and describe the subtle and complex qualities of both visual art and the visual environment in which they live. We want children to understand the relationship of art to culture, the interaction between, for example, the technology and ideology of a period and the forms that artists create. Finally, we want children to learn how to participate in the perennial dialogue regarding the nature of art, the grounds upon which art can be appraised, and by which one's judgments about it can be supported.

We believe that these abilities and forms of understanding not only illuminate what artists have made, they are also critical for experiencing the visual world at large. Since the visual world is always present, the ability to "read" its qualities and to experience its pleasures is virtually always available as well. Discipline-based art education is aimed at developing the skills, understandings, and attitudes that are needed to secure such pleasures.[4]

Production

The educational significance of the four disciplines is not self-evident. Just what is it that makes work in these disciplines so important?

Consider the process of making visual art. The opportunity to convert a material into a medium—a vehicle through which the child conveys ideas, images, and feelings—enlists and develops a range of important cognitive skills. First, the child needs to conceptualize in some general way the kind of image he or she wishes to bring into existence. The problem, and it is a problem, is to somehow shape material so that what has been conceptualized is given some physical embodiment in the material.[5] The material carries the child's thought forward. To make a material function in this way requires not the application of a set of codified rules, but the creation of a set of expressive forms. To be able to do this, the child must develop sufficient skill to employ a technique in order to treat the material so that it will have a particular effect. Furthermore, the child has to organize the forms he or she has created. These forms must work, they must satisfy the standards the child holds for himself—all without the benefits of prescribed rules. No formulas can be used to determine the rightness of a visual solution to a visual problem. The child must exercise judgment, and judgment is dependent upon sensibility: the child cannot appraise what he or she cannot see or experience.

In working with materials in the context of an art problem, the child must do several other things that require sophisticated modes of thinking. The child must pay attention to nuance and to the complexity of the changing images while working. The child must plan ahead and be prepared to shift goals, that is, to be flexibly purposive. And the child needs to perceive the relationships of the parts to the whole, that is, to "decentrate," as a Piagetian might say. Because such cognitive tasks are demanding, they foster the child's ability to think about such matters and other related ones. Children have a wonderful way of learning to do what they are given an opportunity to do. The making of visual art provides opportunities not only to experience the pleasures and frustrations of creation, but also to practice and develop a valuable array of our most complex cognitive skills.

Criticism

Engaging in art criticism is significant in discipline-based art education because it provides children with the opportunity to learn to see and describe the visual world in another special way. Our most customary form of perception is one that is instrumental in character. We usually look in order to recognize, rather than to explore visually.[6] We look for visual information that satisfies our practical need to identify, to categorize, to locate ourselves in space. As a result, our attention to visual form is usually extended in time just long enough to accomplish practical tasks. These durations are often very brief. They are not only brief, they neglect vast arrays of visual information that are present in the world but that, with our instrumental orientation, we never see. In a sense, discipline-based art education expands our perceptual habits and teaches us how to look so that we may see more. The result is that children develop both the attitudes and the skills required to experience, analyze, interpret, and describe the expressive qualities of visual form, qualities found not only in works of art, but also in the forms we encounter in the environment at large. Compare the following two images.

The first is a bronze figure by the Italian artist Umberto Boccioni; the second, a marble sculpture by Jean Arp, a twentieth-century French artist. What do these two sculptures convey? How do they make you feel? And what is it about these images that creates the feelings you experience?

Perhaps the most striking and most obvious feature of the Boccioni is that the figure is one of a man, not simply a man, but a man in movement. It is not only a man in movement, but one possessing great force, a kind of soldier or Roman warrior. How has the artist invested a static

Umberto Boccioni, *Unique Forms of Continuity in Space*, 1913. The Museum of Modern Art, New York.

Jean Arp, *Human Concretion*, 1935, The Museum of Modern Art, New York.

image with virtual movement and tank-like power? Consider the way the forms are shaped. The trailing edge of this figure seems to flow as if driven by wind; the forward lean of the body further accentuates the drive that this image presents to us. The hard reflective surface, the sharp edges of the head, thigh, and hip, the nondescript combination of mechanical and animal face, the helmeted head and the strong widely spread blocks into which the legs are anchored give the image not only a strong, but an aggressive, driving character. The weight of these blocks confers not so much stability, but power. It would take much to withstand the strength of this image's forward thrust.

What we have here is an abstracted form of the human countenance, armless, faceless—almost reflecting a legacy of armless Greek and roman sculpture—that portrays aggressive strength. The artist shapes his material to shape our experience.

We turn to the work of Jean Arp. Here we find an image of soft curves, almost fetal in character, that gives us a sense of repose rather than of movement, but if of movement, then one of growth rather than of aggressive, forward thrust. In Arp's work, we see a large, smooth form almost hovering over two smaller ones that echo the larger one. Here we find a soft surface with no gloss, no reflection, no sharp features, but a kind of mellow skin-like quality that supports the organic character of the form itself.

The image as a whole has three sections whose creases meld into one another. The puffing out of the convex shape at the left and its repetition in a smaller scale at the right serve to create a kind of visual mass into which the central form is nestled. What we have here is an organic, almost biological image—one that seems to possess the capacity to grow.

Boccioni and Arp have orchestrated our vision, our feelings, and our consciousness because they were able to imagine, to see, and to create. The more we attend to their images, the more we see what they possess. The more we see, the more we feel. The area of art criticism in discipline-based art education is intended to help students participate in this chain of looking, seeing, and experiencing, and later to transfer what they have learned to do with art to the world at large.

The ability to see the qualities these sculptures possess is a means for shaping or, more correctly, creating our consciousness. The extent to which our senses are dulled is the extent to which our awareness is limited. Our imaginative capacities depend upon the content that an intellectually acute sensory system can provide.

History and Culture

History and culture constitute a third important area for learning in discipline-based art education. Here we are interested in helping children understand that art does not emerge in the proverbial vacuum. All art is part of a culture. All cultures give direction to art, sometimes by rejecting what artists have made and at other times by rewarding them for it. To understand culture, one needs to understand its manifestations in art, and to understand art, one needs to understand how culture is expressed through its content and form.

The austerity of a Shaker chair or table is a reflection of the religious convictions of the Shakers and how they thought life should be lived. The aggressive force and movement of futuristic artists in early twentieth-century Italy reflect powerful ideological beliefs about what Italian society should become. The pristine and lean qualities of the steel and glass skyscraper embody a view of the optimal relationship of man and machine. Such art forms in each period, each location, each culture mutually influence each other. Just as culture shapes art, art shapes culture. Our convictions, our technology, and our imagination shape our images, and our images, in turn, shape our perception of the world. One major aim of discipline-based art education is to help students understand these relationships by examining the interaction between art and culture over time.

Aesthetics

All people who look at art make judgments about it. Some of these are essentially statements of preference, statements that describe what pleases or displeases us. However, there are differences between what we enjoy and dislike and what we regard as artistically excellent. On what basis can we make judgments about the quality of works of art? Are there certain definable criteria that all good works of art must meet? Discipline-based art education is based on the premise that it is useful for children to become reflective about the basis of their judgments concerning the quality of works of art, as well as about the qualities of the visual world around them. The major intellectual resources for making such judgments are to be found in that branch of philosophy known as aesthetics. Aestheticians have developed a literature that addresses complex questions having to do with the nature of art, whether visual art provides knowledge, and the appropriate criteria for appraising quality in art. While discipline-based art education has no interest in "producing" professional aestheticians, it is interested in encouraging students to join in the continuing conversation about the nature and meaning of art in life. This conversation is most articulate in the field of aesthetics, a field that offers a basis for criticism in art.

Each of these four disciplines—the making of art, art criticism, art history and culture, and aesthetics—defines a major area in which learning activities are created and hence where learning is fostered. Collectively, they constitute a substantive set of resources for defining the aims and content for the design of discipline-based art education curricula.

A WORD ABOUT OBJECTIVES FOR DISCIPLINE-BASED ART EDUCATION

Thus far, we have described the aims of discipline-based art education and the four major disciplines for creating learning opportunities for children. Educational aims are those general statements of educational value that give direction to an educational enterprise. Aims are important as a kind of educational policy statement—they tell the world what is valued for a school or classroom.

In the process of curriculum development, aims are translated into goals, and goals into objectives. Educational objectives are statements of what students are expected to be able to do after they have engaged in a set of curricular activities. In years past, educators have often expected teachers to formulate hundreds of specific educational objectives in order to demonstrate that they were planning curriculum competently.[7] The result of this emphasis on specificity and detail was to burden teachers with requirements that did little educational good. Often, the result of such specific objectives was a curriculum that was fragmented and incoherent. Discipline-based art education does not attempt to reduce important educational aims to a trivial array of specific objectives: six to twelve objectives for a subject for any academic year may very well be adequate for guiding curriculum planning and assessing learning. Mechanistic and reductionistic approaches to curriculum planning have little virtue. What is important is that teachers and students understand the educational point of the tasks in which they are engaged, that they believe the aims and goals of the effort are worthwhile, and that the efforts they make to achieve them are satisfying. The teaching of art cannot afford to become a mindless or essentially lifeless routine that lacks spontaneity and pedagogical innovation.

The import of the foregoing is that school administrators must recognize that there will be times when teachers will need to shift objectives in process; one cannot predict everything that is of value in the classroom. It is the essence of truly skilled teaching to know when to alter one's objectives and to take advantage of new, unexpected teaching opportunities.

One final point needs to be made about the nature of objectives in discipline-based art education. In conventional approaches to curriculum planning, objectives are emphasized that specify the particular behavior a child is to be able to display after an instructional period. If, for example, the teacher's objective is for children to know the multiplication tables through nine, the teacher can determine with little ambiguity if his or her students have achieved it. Their behavior at the end of instruction and the specifications of the objective will, ideally, be perfectly matched. In the visual arts, particularly in the productive area, what is valued is often productive novelty, fresh ways of describing the world or of resolving visual problems. What one seeks, therefore, is not the kind of predictability that is desirable in mathematics and spelling, but diversity and surprise.[8] In a field where productive novelty is an important virtue, the teacher should not always determine the value of a child's art work or interpretation of art by matching it to a preconceived expectation, but instead, by appraising its unique features. In the visual arts, a static model of objectives is far less appropriate than it is where the educational aim is to help students learn standard conventions.[9]

Notes

1. This phrase is borrowed from Clyde Kluckhohn and Henry Murray's *Nature, Society, and Culture* (New York: Alfred Knopf, 1961).

2. The idea that children develop from the outside in as well as the inside out has been articulated most forcefully by Jerome Bruner in "The Course of Cognitive Growth," *American Psychologist* 19 (January 1964): 1-15.

3. For a lucid and trenchant discussion on the effects of rewards on children, see Mark Lepper and David Green, *The Hidden Cost of Reward* (Hillsdale, N.J.: L. Erlbaum Associates, 1978). In research conducted by the authors, they discovered that children who are given extrinsic rewards for tasks that would be otherwise intrinsically satisfying are less likely to engage in those tasks when the rewards are not provided.

4. Discipline-based art education is not solely concerned with enabling children to see what is referred to as "works of art," but the visual world generally. The skills needed to see the qualities of works of art are also applicable to seeing the qualities found in the environment in general. What is required, of course, is not only skills, but attitudes toward seeing. Discipline-based art education is interested both in skills and in attitude development.

5. For a more detailed discussion on the role of the senses in concept formation, see Elliot W. Eisner, *Cognition and Curriculum: A Basis for Deciding What to Teach* (New York: Longman, 1982).

6. In *Art as Experience* (New York: Minton, Balch, 1934) John Dewey distinguishes between seeing and recognizing as follows: "Bare recognition is satisfied when a proper tag or label is attached, 'proper' signifying one that serves a purpose outside the act of recognition—as a salesman identifies wares by a sample. It involves no stir of the organism, no inner commotion. But an act of perception proceeds by waves that extend serially throughout the entire organism. There is, therefore, no such thing in perception as seeing or hearing *plus* emotion. The perceived object or scene is emotionally pervaded throughout. When an aroused emotion does not permeate the material that is perceived or thought of, it is either preliminary or pathological" (p. 53).

7. For a critique of the use of objectives in the curriculum field, see Elliot W. Eisner, *The Educational Imagination: On the Design and Evaluation of School Programs*, 2nd ed. (New York: The Macmillan Co., 1985), chap. 6.

8. In the literature of educational psychology, this is referred to as divergent, rather than convergent behavior.

9. Eisner, op. cit.

Ralph A. Smith

DBAE: A Humanities Interpretation

> When we perceive the arts as "humanities" it is crucial that we inter-
> pret them as a demand that we pause, and in their light, reexamine our
> own realities, values, and dedications, for the arts not only present life
> concretely, stimulate the imagination, and integrate the different cul-
> tural elements of a society or of an epoch, they also present models for
> our imitation or rejection, visions and aspirations which mutely solicit
> our critical response.
>
> A. W. Levi

Albert William Levi's writings will serve as a theoretical foundation for
a humanities interpretation of DBAE. In summarizing his interpretation
I am not forcing educational relevance on ideas framed in academic re-
moteness from possible practical applications. Although Levi often addressed the problems of teaching the humanities in higher education,
he also indicated the suitability of his analysis for community college
humanities programs, humanities studies in a high school program
known as the International Baccalaureate, and aesthetic education
generally.[1]

Levi first recalls the extraordinary history of the humanities, a tradition that extends back to the Platonic Academy, was perpetuated by
the Romans, preserved by the monasticism of the Middle Ages, and then
celebrated by the Renaissance. Greek and Roman classics further proved
useful in John Locke's time in humanizing the law, and they are still
required reading in many liberal arts programs today. In his historical
survey, Levi identifies two alternating phases that are complementary
and an understanding of which is requisite for gaining insight into the
nature of the humanities. Both phases provide a convenient link to
discipline-based art education.

As a first measure, Levi takes the customary step of differentiating
between the sciences and the humanities or, to use his terms, between
the scientific chain of meaning and the humanistic complex. Unlike C. P.
Snow[2] whose distinction between the two cultures of scientists and

humanists placed emphasis on the ethical predispositions of the members of each culture, Levi finds their differences rooted in two divergent tendencies of the human mind. As these tendencies superintend the sciences and the humanities, respectively, they manifest characteristic purposes, methods, vocabularies, criteria of judgment, and products. The preeminent concerns of the scientific chain of meaning are true and false propositions, the problem of error, causality and scientific law, prediction and chance, and fact and matters of fact; whereas the humanistic complex addresses such matters as reality and appearance, the problem of illusion, destiny and human purpose, fate and fortune, drama and the dramatic event, and tragedy. The common thread running through the scientific chain of meaning is a commitment to objectivity and factuality, while that running through the humanistic complex is a commitment to human purposiveness and drama.

But as soon as Levi marks the distinction between the scientific and the humanistic domains, he is at some pains to qualify it. Adopting a maxim of Alfred North Whitehead's, he seeks simplicity but distrusts it. The sciences and the humanities, says Levi, "need to be seen as tendencies rather than as pure specimens or as subject-matter disciplines, and. . .the distinction between a science and an art probably indicates more a polarity than a disjunction."[3] The tendency toward factuality and exactitude and the tendency toward concern for human significance should thus be seen as forming separate and distinct radiating centers of intention from which impulses spread outward with diminishing intensity, making themselves felt in other circles that are dominated by different central interests. For example, while art historical scholarship has a scientific dimension, which is to say it betrays impulses toward factuality and objectivity, its reliance on imaginative reconstruction attests to its being an essentially humanistic discipline.[4] What is more, when art historians, or historians generally, assume as a function the need to renew historical memory for purposes of illuminating the present, they express a spirit germane to the humanities but foreign to the sciences. Similarly divergent impulses also occur in other disciplines.

Having concluded that there are no inherently scientific or humanistic subject matters, only scientific or humanistic treatments of things, it follows that both art and science can take persons, nature, and society as their subjects and submit them to alternative treatments. We have Wordsworth and Newton on nature, Rembrandt and Vesalius on man, Balzac and Durkheim on society. Yet in any given instance it is usually not difficult to tell which impulse, the scientific or the humanistic, predominates. We know, for example, the humanistic attitude is being taken when talk centers on the dramatic, the moral, and the sympathetic.

We should realize, however, that to define the humanities in terms of attitudes and treatments while denying the existence of inherently humanistic subjects is in effect to define them procedurally. Casting the humanities in this light has the advantage of putting us on guard against too rigid a compartmentalization of human capacity and expression, against erecting boundaries that excessively constrict and exclude. At the same time mere proceduralism is not sufficient.[5] Hence to teach only humanistic attitudes and strengthen humanistic impulses would leave students rudderless and prone to superficial learning. A substantive conception of the humanities must also be supplied, and this requires the specification of significant content.

In proposing a synthesis, Levi recalls the conception of the liberal arts that reigned from the sixth century until well into the fourteenth. The liberal arts were composed of the trivium (grammar, rhetoric, and dialectic) and the quadrivium (arithmetic, geometry, astronomy, and music). Although these arts were differentiated in terms of subjects or areas of study, they were essentially perceived as practical arts, as ways of doing things or organizing experience. It was the revisionism of the Renaissance that transformed these arts into subject matters and ultimately to a substantive understanding of the liberal arts that is still dominant today. Levi, a strong believer in cultural continuity, honors the legacy of the Middle Ages as well as that of the Renaissance by retaining what he deems best in both traditions, but with a difference. As a preliminary step he divides the liberal arts (the medieval contribution) into three categories: the arts of communication, the arts of continuity, and the arts of criticism. He then aligns these arts with subject areas (the Renaissance contribution). He assigns the arts of communication to languages and literatures, the arts of continuity to history, and the arts of criticism (critical reflection generally) to philosophy. In doing this Levi does not contradict his insistence that there are no inherently humanistic subject matters, if by "inherent" we understand yielding only to humanistic treatment and no other. But subjects like literature, history, and philosophy are preeminently suited to humanistic treatment. Put differently, the humanistic attitude and the three arts in which it expresses itself finds it purest and most rewarding exercise in these subjects.

It now remains to coordinate the three arts and their corresponding subjects with three of the disciplines in discipline-based art education and to make provisions for the fourth. It should be apparent that the arts of continuity, which have history as the characteristic arena for their exercise, are associated with the discipline of art history; that the arts of criticism, which have philosophy as their typical subject area, pair nicely

with philosophy of art or aesthetics. This leaves the task of accommo-
dating the arts of communication and the subjects of languages and literatures. Can they be assimilated to the discipline of art criticism? I think
it is possible if we assume that the visual arts communicate after their
own fashion. Questions about the propriety of construing art as a language notwithstanding, it is clear that works of visual art can be understood as artistic statements capable of enriching awareness by virtue of
their meanings and expressive qualities. Yet works of visual art of some
substance and complexity usually disclose their meanings only after prolonged probing, careful analysis, and astute interpretation by a percipient—or, as will often be the case, by a percipient under the guidance of
an art critic or tutelage by an art teacher functioning as a critic. Effica-
cious art criticism, then, is often needed to complete the act of artistic
communication. Accordingly, it is really not very different from literature as a liberal arts subject for there too much effort is spent on eluci-
dating the meanings or messages of literary works. In short, if we grant
the visual arts the power to communicate, and if we assign to art criticism the mediating task of preparing percipients for apprehending this
communication in its fullest and most rewarding form, then all three of
Levi's liberal arts—communication, continuity, criticism—can be accounted
for in a definition of discipline-based art education.

What about the discipline of artistic creation? Discipline-based art
education, it is clear, attaches importance to artistic creation. Levi in his
original analysis did not explicitly provide for creativity, but he approved
an emendation of his analysis that would. He subsumed artistic creation under the arts of communication simply by saying that because
art criticism would be impossible without works to be analyzed and
interpreted, creation is, in a sense, a preparatory phase for criticism. The
same could be said for art history and philosophy of art; neither could
get off the ground without prior creative activities that result in artworks.
We may therefore make artistic creation a fourth "c"—the arts of creation—in its own right. By granting artistic creation significant standing
with the other disciplines, we acknowledge what is in fact the case—
that through creative activities students learn much that will contribute
to a deeper, better-informed appreciation of works of art. In short, it is
possible to assemble, align, and place within the framework provided
by Levi the four disciplines of artistic creation, art history, art criticism,
and aesthetics, and their corresponding modes of making and inquiry.[6]

To avoid the impression that the disciplines in question and their
respective procedural and substantive aspects are distinct and do not

overlap, it will be well to recall Levi's radiation theory of definition. Such a notion of definition relies neither on Aristotelian essences of classes of objects nor on Wittgensteinian family resemblances. Rather, it suggests a "physical image of a dynamic center radiating outward like the ripples from a series of stones thrown into a pond and intermingling at their periphery with no blurring of the original sources of impetus."[7] This enables us to speak of the dominant radiating intentions of the four disciplines of discipline-based art education and to describe them as follows: in artistic creation the dominant radiating intention is the mak- ing of unique objects and is born of the human need to express ideas and feelings in visual forms; in the history of art it is to understand works of art under the aspects of time, tradition, and style and is born of the human need to be reminded of roots and to recall things worth remem- bering and experiencing; in art criticism it is the refinement of percep- tion and the rendering of qualitative judgments and is born of the hu- man need to perceive clearly and to separate the meritorious from the meretricious; in aesthetics it is the clarification of key concepts and ideas and is born of the quest for both reasonableness in our thinking about art and for avoidance of dubious assumptions.

In conclusion, a few words are necessary about the goals or objec- tives of the whole enterprise. And here we will notice again that what Levi says about the humanities applies in equal measure to discipline- based art education humanistically conceived. There is almost univer- sal consensus, says Levi, that the humanities are concerned with hu- man values and pursue this concern with an earnestness and concentra- tion found in no other field of inquiry. He notes that politicians, educa- tional theorists, humanists, and other interested parties all make remark- ably similar claims about the humanities; they not only teach values and judgment, they also reveal wisdom, help us to live well, and teach appreciation of the beautiful and the permanent.[7] What does Levi un- derstand by "values"? They are, first of all, concepts or ideas, but by being "affective" they engage our sense of approval and disapproval; and by being "volitional" they make claims on our choices to accept or reject. This means that teaching values involves more than acquainting the young with the humanistic meanings of works of art. It involves rational and persuasive argument that certain things are worthwhile and merit serious study and concern. To recall the words of the epi- graph of this essay, the humanities "present models for our imitation or rejection, visions and aspirations which mutely solicit our critical response."

Notes

1. See, e.g., *The Humanities Today* (Bloomington: Indiana, Indiana University Press, 1970); "History and Philosophy in the International Baccalaureate" in *Papers in Educational Reform*, Vol. 4 (LaSalle, Ill.: Open Court, 1974); "The Uses of the Humanities in Personal Life" (January 1976) and "The Humanities: Their Essence, Nature, Future" (Summer 1983) in *The Journal of Aesthetic Education*; and *Art Education: A Critical Necessity*, with R. A. Smith (Urbana: University of Illinois Press, 1992), which presents a humanities interpretation of DBAE.

2. C. P. Snow, *Public Affairs* (New York: Scribner's, 1971). Contains Snow's original essay on the two cultures and a second look. Cf. my discussion of the two cultures in *The Sense of Art* (New York: Routledge, 1989), pp. 146-56.

3. Levi, *The Humanities Today*, p. 44.

4. A good example is Erwin Panofsky's "The History of Art as a Humanistic Discipline" in *Meaning in the Visual Arts* (Chicago: University of Chicago Press, 1982), pp. 1-25. Originally published 1955.

5. For a criticism of proceduralism, which he terms educational formalism, see E. D. Hirsch, Jr., *Cultural Literacy*, updated and expanded version (New York: Random House, 1988), chap. 5.

6. It should not be supposed that I am redefining DBAE as the disciplines of creation, communication, continuity, and criticism. Rather I am saying how the disciplines of DBAE in their special ways address such basic human needs as those of creation, communication, continuity, and criticism.

7. Levi, *The Humanities Today*, p. 26.

Stephen Mark Dobbs

The General Characteristics of DBAE

Discipline-based art education is a comprehensive approach to instruction and learning in art, developed primarily for grades K-12, but also formulated for use in adult education, lifelong learning, and art museums. It is designed to provide exposure to, experience with, and acquisition of content from several disciplines of knowledge, but especially four foundational disciplines in art—art-making, art criticism, art history, and aesthetics. Education in these disciplines contributes to the creation, understanding, and appreciation of art, artists, artistic processes, and the roles and functions of art in cultures and societies.

Each of the disciplines provides a different lens or perspective from which to view, understand, and value works of art, as well as the world in which art objects are created. In the use of the word *disciplines*, several assumptions are operating: (a) that such fields constitute recognized bodies of knowledge or content, (b) that communities of professionals study and perform in each discipline, and (c) that characteristic procedures and ways of working exist that can facilitate exploration and study.

These disciplines are sources of knowledge about and experience in art. They are domains of knowledge and skill that have been and continue to be developed by individuals (artists, art critics, art historians, and philosophers of art) who conduct inquiry within the disciplines and who make contributions to their content. These disciplines reflect what practitioners actually do and say in their work. In fact, DBAE itself promotes inquiry into the foundational art disciplines.

But art disciplines alone do not furnish the exclusive content for DBAE. Additional fields that provide related resources include anthropology, archaeology, communication, cultural studies, educational assessment, linguistics, philosophy, and sociology. Current developments in these fields increasingly help us to understand art education more fully. . . .[H]owever, the focus is on the four foundational art disciplines noted above. It is the disciplines of art that provide the basic knowledge, skills, and understanding that enable students to have broad and rich experiences with works of art. Students can accomplish this in at least four ways.

- by *creating works of art*, through the skillful application of both experience and ideas, with tools and techniques in various media (art making);
- by *describing, interpreting, evaluating, and theorizing about works of art* for the purposes of increasing understanding and appreciation of works of art and clarifying the roles of art in society (art criticism);
- by *inquiring into the historical, social, and cultural contexts of art objects* by focusing upon aspects of time, place, tradition, functions, and styles to better understand the human condition (art history); and
- by *raising and examining questions about the nature, meaning, and value of art*, which leads to understanding about what distinguishes art from other kinds of phenomena, the issues that such differences give rise to, and the development of criteria for evaluating and judging works of art (aesthetics).

At the same time, although it is useful to define disciplines in order to grasp their principal roles and functions in encounters with works of art, these fields are also fluid, shifting, and intermingling with one another. Therefore, any closed definitions will eventually be shown to be insufficient, as the boundaries of the disciplines change and (usually) expand as related interests and new issues surface.

DBAE is a comprehensive approach to art education. DBAE programs, originally devised for but not limited to K-12 students, are based upon a rationale for art in general education. For example, works of art educate children about the world. Art helps us to understand how the many different communities of this increasingly interdependent world, both past and present, live and think and feel about their lives, their cultures, and their place in the world. In a comprehensive program, works of art provide the content for study, and teachers are encouraged to select works that will be meaningful for students. Thus no canon exists, no list of masterworks or indispensable items. The artworks studied depend on the audience in the classroom. Selected artworks need to be rich in meaning and interpretation, unique or interesting, and engaging for students.

A comprehensive approach employs specific strategies to deliver content in the classroom, such as inquiry-based experiences that engage students in making art, critical and historical investigation, and aesthetic inquiry. Talking about, writing about, and researching works of art are important strategies. For successful implementation, a comprehensive approach requires a support network of policy and administrative leadership, professional development, and a variety of curricular and community resources.

WHAT ARE DBAE'S GENERAL CHARACTERISTICS?

As DBAE has developed, it has acquired certain general characteristics that help to define and distinguish discipline-based art education programs from other models in art education. These features may be in place or in the process of being developed at sites throughout the nation:

- Students are engaged in the *rigorous study of art* derived from the four art disciplines.
- A long-range *program planning capacity* for art is in place, given impetus by the adoption by the local school district, university, or art museum of a policy statement and goals for student learning that include comprehensive art education.
- A *written art curriculum framework* exists, or is in the process of being developed, in which learning is sequenced within and between grades to reflect developmental and age-appropriate factors.
- Written, sequential lesson units and learning experiences engage students in balanced attention and study derived from the *content of the four foundational art disciplines*: art-making (also known as studio art or art production), art history, art criticism, and aesthetics (also known as philosophy of art).
- Art is *taught by certified teachers* who are provided opportunities for professional development to build their knowledge, skills, and understanding of DBAE. Art specialists and classroom or other subject teachers collaborate in planning and teaching.
- Students have access to *school-sponsored and community-based art experiences* and resources, such as frequent visits to art museums or to other public art settings.
- Assessment of *student learning* is conducted on a regular basis, with results reported to stakeholders, including students, teachers, administrators, policymakers, and parents.
- Art may be *integrated with the general curriculum* through application of the distinctive lenses acquired through study of the four art disciplines to content in other subject areas. Art may be integrated into other subject areas and vice versa.
- Art education is *for all students*, not just those who demonstrate talent in making art. Students with special needs are also identi-

fied and provided with art instruction at all levels. DBAE is for all students, not just those who are identified as "gifted and talented" and therefore favored with art instruction.

- The art program is appropriately *coordinated, administered, and supported at different levels*: by the faculty leader and principal within the school, and by the curriculum supervisor within the school district. The superintendent may assume responsibility for advocating and explaining the program to the school board, which in turn can support the program with parents and the community.
- *Technology is used to broaden art teaching and learning options.* Teachers and students have access to and use technology (a) to enhance production, creation, and/or design of works of art; (b) to communicate about art; and (c) to access and manage information about art.

WHAT IS NOT DBAE?

It may also be useful to list briefly some descriptions of what discipline-based art education is *not*:

- It is not a curriculum in the sense of being a stipulated series of learnings arranged in a prescribed manner. Rather, it is a conceptual framework or set of principles and an approach to teaching and learning in art based upon disciplines that contribute to the making and understanding of art.
- It is not a promotion of any one of the art disciplines over the others. Rather, it entails balanced attention (not necessarily equal or pro rata time for each of the art disciplines) to all of the foundational disciplines over a given period of time.
- It is not a monolithic system with a single conception of art, uniform notions of content, or a common prescribed set of practices. Rather, it is an evolving approach, one that is host to many variations of philosophy and practice within the basic commitment to comprehensive treatment.
- It is not intended for schools or other settings with identical specifications. Rather, it is flexibly configured to fit the needs and circumstances of local instructional goals, curriculum, and resources.
- It is not a single lesson. Rather, it is best presented as a unit of study taught over time, where each of the four discipline perspectives are covered in learning about works of art.

- It is not based on a conception of students as prospective scholars, artists, or discipline specialists. Rather, it is dedicated to meeting the needs of young persons and others for a general understanding of art as a basic form of human culture and as a basic means of human communication.

The DBAE disciplines are a means to an end—teaching kids about art.

NEEDS ADDRESSED BY DBAE

How Are the Goals of General Education Met?

In previous eras the neglect of reading, writing, and discussion skills as part of the art lesson contributed to a widespread perception among many school administrators, teachers, and parents that art did not contribute to general goals of schooling, such as teaching students how to think and learn to be problem solvers. Worse, the art lesson was often seen as outside the pale of the curriculum that mattered, a nonacademic activity in which no real "learning" took place, or at least none worth serious assessment.

The art lesson provided relief from the pressure of the academic curriculum; it was "tenderhearted" rather than "hardheaded," dealing with emotions and affect, which were considered extraneous to the real purposes of schooling. Art appeared to give students the opportunity to relax and not use their minds. Everyone (including students) knew that individuals were not promoted or graduated from school based upon their performance in classroom art activities.

By contrast, in DBAE the art lesson strongly supports general educational goals of the school, such as the goal of cognitive development. Students in art are challenged perceptually and intellectually as they learn a body of knowledge (art). They are encouraged to draw on their own ideas and feelings, their experience in the world, and the works of artists other than those presented in the classroom in order to know, understand, and create complex objects called works of art.

Such an approach nurtures student creativity, but does so while developing competence in perception, communication, imagination, judgment, and social understanding. The study of art is also a tool for developing problem solving and higher-order thinking skills, and for the acquisition and exploration of language and the development of visual literacy. School board credos and public opinion strongly endorse the basic mission of schools as teaching students to think, to become problem solvers, to develop their minds.

The DBAE approach also values flexibility and diversity in choice of curriculum content, selection of instructional resources, and respect for different student backgrounds. It taps different learning styles and is consistent with the maxim that there are many different ways of knowing and ways of learning. This includes forging successful study and work habits in both school and society. The art lesson alone cannot accomplish this, but together with other kinds of educational experiences, art can do much to help students function in a culture that is heavily dependent upon and dominated by visual forms of experience. In fact, the DBAE art lesson likely provides the very best (if not the only) place in the program of most schools where students have the opportunity to acquire the visual literacy that will empower them to function successfully in a visually saturated society. DBAE also acknowledges the contributions of art education to the behavioral and psychological well-being of students, nurturing such traits as self-esteem, patience, and rigor.

Practitioners function in domains that are richly intellectual, featuring such cognitive operations as perception, analysis, interpretation, and judgment. Skills of observation and problem solving are directly cultivated in a DBAE unit of study. The exercise of such higher-order thinking in art, as John Dewey observed more than 60 years ago, is as profoundly "intellectual" as the act of solving a quadratic equation. Such cognition is as familiar and commonplace to practitioners of DBAE as it is to practitioners of mathematics and other academic disciplines.

The theories of multiple forms of understanding and intelligence, explained by Howard Gardner and cognitive scientists, describe many different but related domains of mental functioning, revealing that artistic engagement is a mind-building experience. The concept of the "intelligent eye" also contemplates extensive mental functioning in the exercise of art, especially in looking at and thinking about images. This is contrary to the belief that art has little intellectual content and is primarily about feelings. There are methods moreover, teachable in schools, through which students can learn to see and understand the content in works of art that had been invisible to the untrained eye. David Perkins calls this making the invisible visible.

How Are the Goals of Art Education Met?

The goals of art education have been debated in the professional field for decades. Two general views may be outlined. One holds that art is a source of knowledge, beliefs, and values about ourselves and about our world, and that these are a critical and necessary part of the education of a citizen. Art offers access to knowledge, insights, and types of meaning that are not available elsewhere in the curriculum of most schools. For example, visual culture (paintings, drawings, sculptures, architecture, film, and so on) carries expressive content that can be learned, enjoyed, and utilized. Therefore, art should exist in the curriculum for what it provides, not for its subordinate or contributory purpose in advancing nonart kinds of knowledge. This is the essentialist argument (also called the noninstrumentalist or intrinsic-value argument) which holds that art provides a unique learning experience that is best addressed through a quality art education program.

The other view, which does not exclude the essentialist view, emphasizes the contributions that art makes to attainment and success in other subject areas and to more general goals of schooling. For a long time, the rationale for art in the curriculum was that it provided an outlet for children's feelings and "creative expression" that were not accommodated in the academic program.

Another rationale for art education is that the study of art promotes attention to perception and expression, and thus contributes to the building of language and communication, critical thinking, and problem-solving skills. If the policies of the local school board include the development of imagination or of awareness of a multicultural society, art might be enlisted in the service of these student outcomes as well. This is the instrumentalist (or utilitarian or extrinsic-value) conception of art's role in general education. It has often had to suffice because of the narrow chance that a school board or principal would appreciate or accept the essentialist rationale.

Both the essentialist and instrumentalist views have legitimacy for art education. On one hand, art education ought to merit its place in school programs because of what it uniquely and specifically provides for students. Art offers access to languages, experiences, and meanings that are understood and conveyed idiosyncratically through the expression and shaping of visual form. At the same time, no opportunity should be missed to embrace the collateral learnings and auxiliary educational payoffs that are a part of students' experience with art. Therefore, one routinely witnesses in DBAE classrooms exercises in perception, interpretation, and judgment based upon works of art that stimulate inquiry learning and lead to written and spoken language development. Essentialist and instrumentalist views alike are represented in a comprehensive approach to art. It is not one or the other. Art is important both for the distinctive and unique contributions it makes to learning and for the ways in which it serves general goals of schooling. This is manifest in the widespread activity over recent decades of setting goals for the field of art education that serve both views.

Goals for the field of art education are set at various levels: by national panels and commissions (such as those that developed the national standards), by state framework committees, by teacher education institutions and theorists in the field, by professional organizations of art educators, and by practitioners. For example, the National Art Education Association has promulgated in its "Quality Goals Statement" (1982) a conception of art and learners that broadly defines art education but clearly endorses a comprehensive approach. DBAE helps meet both essentialist and instrumentalist goals for art education.

How Are Societal Goals Met?

The United States is now the world's most multicultural society, and our culture is rapidly transforming itself. Demographic changes in U.S. classrooms have been accelerating throughout the past 10 years. DBAE supports the larger goal of creating a society in which there is opportunity and fulfillment for all citizens. It does this by providing a receptive and welcome place for cultural diversity in the school program. Indeed, works of art are one of the primary indicators of a nation's, culture's, or historical epoch's values, achievements, social structure, and faith traditions. By using a wide variety of exemplars of works of art from world cultures, educators can introduce students to the richness of cultural diversity. An increasing number of museums are seeking to attract more culturally diverse audiences by building collections and installing exhibitions of world art.

Schools now face the complex task of addressing the educational needs of an increasingly diverse population of millions of young people. America's classrooms routinely feature an array of racial, ethnic, national, linguistic, and cultural differences and traditions. The concept of the "melting pot" (all cultures blended into a single American culture) has been superseded by the metaphor of the "tossed salad" or "stew" (all cultures retaining some autonomy and legitimacy even while contributing to a common American culture). Assimilation into the American cultural mainstream is complicated by the debate over exactly what that mainstream culture may be. When this situation is prevalent in thousands of schools, pluralism translates into many new and provocative questions about the curriculum.

Studying the art of many cultures helps students to understand the people of those cultures, not just their artifacts. For example, the study of Chinese scroll paintings of the Sung Dynasty (960-1279 AD) reveals a reverence for nature in the form of meticulously drawn landscapes featuring magic mountains, lakes, and gardens. Scholars might unwrap a portion of such a scroll and discuss the meanings in that landscape. After viewing the work, they might actually take a walk in a garden to give texture and authenticity to their conversation and their experience. Thus studying the art of a distant time and place can help students understand and appreciate the people of such a culture and what was important to them, as disclosed by their art.

In fact, cultural diversity has helped to expand the range of curricular opportunities in art. The previous focus in the art disciplines on a primarily Western or Eurocentric tradition has shifted to global possibilities. The larger world stage provides educators with multiple occasions to introduce considerations and characteristics of culture that broadly affect what students are experiencing and learning in the four foundational art disciplines. This, in turn, supports the societal goal of building understanding and appreciation for the diverse communities that make up the United States.

Discipline-based art education welcomes and capitalizes upon these developments. The approach represents an emancipation, wherever possible, from the old boundaries of cultural thinking about sources for artists, works of art, and artistic traditions. For example, aesthetics offers a fertile context for understanding and appreciating multiculturalism. By examining the purposes and philosophies of art in various societies, students can begin to see the rich mosaic of the world from many perspectives.

Until recent times, an overwhelming emphasis on Western, and particularly European, art has been almost universal in school art programs, from kindergarten through college. But now there is recognition that other cultures, such as those of Asia, Africa, and South America, have been neglected as sources of rich imagery and ideas that can help students create, understand, and appreciate works of art. Therefore, a DBAE program might include exemplars of art and a range of types of art (such as folk art) from African, Asian, European, and Latin American cultures alike, ranging from the most ancient to the most contemporary. The eventual impact of such experiences on students in schools will play itself out in the larger society of which students are members.

Reading Suggestions for Part One

Arnheim, Rudolf. *Thoughts on Art Education.* Occasional Paper 2. Los Angeles: Getty Center for Education in the Arts, 1989.

Broudy, Harry S. *The Role of Imagery in Learning.* Occasional Paper 1. Los Angeles: Getty Center for Education in the Arts, 1987.

Chalmers, Graeme F. *Celebrating Pluralism: Art, Education, and Cultural Diversity*. Occasional Paper 5. Los Angeles: Getty Educational Institute for the Arts, 1996.

Dobbs, Stephen Mark. *The DBAE Handbook: An Overview of Discipline-Based Art Education*. Santa Monica, Calif.: Getty Center for Education in the Arts, 1992. The first Getty guide to DBAE.

Getty Center for Education in the Arts. *Beyond Creating: The Place for Art in America's Schools*. Los Angeles: Getty Center for Education in the Arts, 1985. The report that introduced the idea of DBAE to a wide audience.

Getty Center for Education in the Arts. *Discipline-Based Art Education: What Forms Will It Take?* Santa Monica, Calif.: Getty Center for Education in the Arts, 1988.

Greer, W. Dwaine. *Art as a Basic: The Reformation in Art Education*. Bloomington, Ind.: Phi Delta Kappa, 1997. The reflections of the director of the Los Angeles Getty Institute for Educators on the Visual Arts on art education and DBAE.

Smith, Ralph A., ed. *Discipline-Based Art Education: Origins, Meaning, Development*. Urbana: University of Illinois Press, 1989.

Southeast Center for Education in the Arts. *Discipline-Based Music Education: A Conceptual Framework for the Teaching of Music*. Chattanooga: Southeast Center for Education in the Arts, 1994.

Wilson, Brent. *The Quiet Evolution: Changing the Face of Arts Education*. Los Angeles: Getty Education Institute for the Arts, 1997. A description and assessment of the Getty regional institutes program.

Delacruz, Elizabeth Manley, and Philip C. Dunn. "The Evolution of Discipline-Based Art Education." *The Journal of Aesthetic Education* 30, no. 3 (1996): 67-82.

DiBlasio, Margaret K. "Reflections on the Theory of Discipline-Based Art Education." *Studies in Art Education* 28, no. 4 (1987): 221-26.

DiBlasio, Margaret K. "Harvesting the Cognitive Revolution: Reflections on *The Arts, Education, and Aesthetic Knowing*," *The Journal of Aesthetic Education* 31, no. 1 (1997): 95-110.

Duke, Leilani Lattin. "The Getty Center for Education in the Arts and Discipline-Based Art Education." *Art Education* 41, no. 2 (1988): 7-12.

Duke, Leilani Lattin, "Looking Back, Looking Forward," in *Keynote Addresses: National Art Education Association*. National Art Education Association: Reston, Va. 1999, 13-20.

Eisner, Elliot. "The Getty Education Institute for the Arts." *Studies in Art Education* 40, no. 1 (Fall 1998): 4-7. Remarks about the immediate origins of DBAE.

Greer, W. Dwaine. "Discipline-Based Art Education: Approaching Art as a Subject of Study." *Studies in Art Education* 25, no. 4 (1984): 212-18. Credited with having coined the term discipline-based art education.

Fleming, Paulette Spruill. "Pluralism and DBAE: Towards a Model for Global Multi-Cultural Art Education." *Journal of MultiCultural and Cross-Cultural Research in Art Education* 6, no. 1 (1988): 66-74.

Hamblen, Karen, A. "Neo-DBAE in the Nineties." *Arts and Learning Research* 10, no. 1 (1992-93): 132-40.

MacGregor, Ronald N. "An Outside View of Discipline-Based Education." *Studies in Art Education* 26, no. 4 (1985): 241-46.

McFee, June. "Art and Society." In *Issues in Discipline-Based Art Education: Strengthening the Stance, Extending the Horizons.* Los Angeles: Getty Center for Education in the Arts, 1988.

Reimer, Bennett. "Would Discipline-Based Music Education Make Sense? *Music Educators Journal* 77, no. 9 (1991): 21-28.

Schwartz, Katherine. "Improving Art Education in Alaska through Discipline-Based Art Education." *Alaska Journal of Art* 1 (1989): 16-21.

Silverman, Ronald H. "A Rationale for Discipline-Based Art Education." *NASSP Bulletin* 73, no. 517 (1989): 16-22.

PART TWO

The Disciplines of DBAE: Contexts of Understanding

Introduction

In the initial volume of the series Disciplines in Art Education: Contexts of Understanding, Albert William Levi, a distinguished philosopher of culture and the humanities, acknowledges the ultimate mystery of artistic creation. He believes, however, that insofar as the West is concerned, artistic creativeness is best characterized as the production of images saturated with feelings that derive from the artist's lived experiences, the effect of which on viewers is the augmenting of their powers of perception. After discussing the creation of art as act and message, Levi uses a Matisse still life to illustrate how artistic statements can be understood in light of two basic impulses, the Aristotelian (imposition of form on matter) and the Platonic (expression of uncontrolled forces). Without denying the possibility of judging artistic merit, Levi holds that seemingly contradictory artistic statements can nonetheless be valid as expressions of artistic truth. The excerpt reprinted here concentrates on the analysis of the Matisse.

The relations of art history and DBAE described by David Ebitz is part of a discussion that indicates not just what art history can contribute to art education but also what art education can contribute to art history. He reviews the evolution of the discipline since the Renaissance and describes three major specializations of contemporary art history: connoisseurship and iconography, social studies, and critical studies. He further remarks on the limitations of standard textbooks and content-centered instruction in contrast to inquiry-centered learning and recommends greater cooperation between art historians and art educators, especially with respect to multidisciplinary approaches such as DBAE.

In yet another volume in the Disciplines in Art Education series, Theodore Wolff, a practicing art critic as well as painter and author, foregoes theoretical explanation of criticism in favor of exploring the activities of critics and their characteristic styles, for example, diaristic, formalist, and contextualist, only the first two of which are discussed in the excerpt reprinted here. The third type, contextualist, subsumes art historical, psychological, and ideological criticism. As did his co-author George Geahigan (see Part Two, Curriculum), Wolff endorses open-ended inquiry into works of art from both the past and the present (which is to say art criticism is not restricted to contemporary art) for the sake of greater aesthetic understanding and self-realization, and he expresses the belief that art critics have an obligation rationally to support aesthetic judgments and critical evaluations.

There are many excellent explanations of the meaning of aesthetics as a discipline in the literature of aesthetics and aesthetic education. In an article intended to contribute to the literature of DBAE, Donald Crawford (see Reading Suggestions) points out how philosophic inquiry into the activities of creating, appreciating, and evaluating art, insofar as it involves consideration of basic human values, establishes the pedagogical relevance of aesthetics. Such inquiry encompasses five clusters of concepts—art objects, appreciation and interpretation, critical evaluation, artistic creation, and cultural context—of which teachers of art should have general knowledge. Assuming such an explanation of the discipline, Marcia Muelder Eaton indicates more specifically how the components of aesthetic experience—objects, makers, attendees, context—generate questions that help illuminate the nature, meaning, and value of art. What is more, Eaton favors expanding the notion of art education to that of aesthetic education, which would have the advantage of encompassing more than traditional art forms within the aesthetic purview. The excerpt reprinted here centers on the nature of aesthetic inquiry. In the remainder of the article, Eaton indicates that just as art and society change, so must the kinds of topics philosophers address. Examples are questions raised by an increased awareness of cultural diversity, the expansion of the meaning of art to include forms not usually regarded as art (e.g., quilts), and greater understanding of the relations of art and society in non-Western and indigenous cultures. Eaton discusses both the uses and limits of philosophic inquiry in the study of such matters.

Much of the literature focusing on the four disciplines of DBAE explains the nature of a particular discipline and how it can be taught (see Part Three, Curriculum) at levels appropriate for different ages. Thus we have recommendations for teaching art making, art history, art criticism, and aesthetics. Yet the early conceptualizers of DBAE never assumed that the four disciplines should be taught separately as disciplines. Rather it was believed that teachers should have a general knowledge of the ideas and methods contained in the disciplines and be able to integrate them in striving to attain the goals and objectives of DBAE. It is reasonable to hold that any teacher of art should have some sense of art history, a grasp of critical principles of judgment, a capacity to handle puzzling questions about the components of aesthetic experience, and practical experience in creating artworks.

In a discussion that could be placed under the topics of curriculum and professional development as well as that of disciplines, Anita Silvers raises questions about cognitive strategies by means of which teachers of art can discuss the special character of artworks. She emphasizes works embodying ideals of culture that transcend their time of creation as well as puzzling borderline cases that can stimulate students' individuality of response, their ability to integrate theory and application, and their awareness of interpretive frameworks. Silvers derives art's subject matter content from an institutional theory of art that posits an art world and its characteristic institutions, practices, and historical narrations. Accordingly, preparing teachers means preparing them to initiate the young into an art world, which presupposes an understanding of its various domains and activities, or what Eaton calls the components of aesthetic experience. Doing this requires the collaboration of those working in the four disciplines of DBAE. In contrast to those who have questioned the relevance of aesthetics to teaching art, Silvers clearly indicates its uses by showing how it can help set goals and select and organize content for DBAE.

In reading the literature of DBAE one finds reiterated that the teaching of art should be grounded in the disciplines of art making, art history, art criticism, and aesthetics. And so it should. Yet as the introduction to this collection points out, there is also a literature that advances social-science interpretations of DBAE, even to the extent of recommending the "anthropologizing" of the approach. Why then is no description of social-science disciplines included in this section? The omission is due in part to social-science interpretations being included in other parts of the collection, but also to the fact that the quartet of disciplines associated with DBAE have continued to be considered basic; and, as I say in Afterthoughts, there would be serious consequences for art education as a distinct field of study were it to assume the mantel of social science.

ALBERT WILLIAM LEVI

The Creation of Art

What I am after, above all, is expression. Sometimes it has been con-
ceded that I have a certain technical ability but that, my ambition being limited, I am unable to proceed beyond a purely visual satisfaction
such as can be procured from the mere sight of a picture. But the purpose of a painter must not be conceived as separate from his pictorial
means, and these pictorial means must be the more complete the deeper
is his thought. I am unable to distinguish between the feeling I have for
life and my way of expressing it.

Henri Matisse

Art is inescapably pluralistic. It thrives on diversity and knows nothing
of contradiction: all its opposite truths are equally true.

Jacques Barzun

The Act of Artistic Creation

Sometime around 1928, Henri Matisse arranged on an old green chest in
his studio a platter, a crumpled tablecloth, a blue-and-white pitcher, a
fruit knife, a glass two-thirds full of water, and five ripe peaches, and set
to work. The result is a lovely and serene work entitled *Still Life on a
Green Buffet*, in which the luna green of the buffet, the sky blue of the
wall behind, the white of platter and the pitcher, and the light blue
of the tablecloth form a rich color harmony against which stand out the
five rosy peaches, four on the white platter, one to the side of the light
blue tablecloth. The painting first passed into the hands of a private
collector but now is in the Museum of Modern Art in Paris, where it has
been a favorite of the many who visit that institution.

As Henri Matisse sits in his studio before the green chest and the
five peaches and other objects he has arranged upon the chest with his
blank canvas on the easel and his colors before him, what does he do?
Of course he dips his brushes in the pigments and transfers these pigments to the canvas, and slowly that previously white surface becomes
a colored surface that begins to resemble (but with some distortion and

not in the least photographically) the arranged objects on the green chest. It is clear that he has begun with "an idea," and that idea has something to do with that green chest and that platter and those five peaches and the way he has arranged them. He plans to make a statement about those peaches and their relation to the pitcher and to the blue tablecloth, and that statement is about objects in space. But he also plans to make a statement about the blue of the wall and its relation to the blue of the tablecloth and the relation of these two blues to the white of the platter and the green of the chest and the relation of all this to the pink-orange of the peaches. Naturally, those two statements are to be made not with words but with pigment upon canvas. Thus, to the idea implicit in the arrangement of his subject must be added the materials—blank linen canvas stretched tight on a wooden frame, pigments, oil, and brushes made of pig bristles or horsehair.

Now one tradition, which is as old as Aristotle, describes the creative process in these terms. It is an imposition of form upon matter, it is to begin with an idea and to express it in a medium. To the blank potentiality of the canvas Matisse gives an actuality of color and shapes that expresses his idea, and this process is equally true of the sculptor imposing form upon the unworked block of marble, the writer imposing form upon the possibilities of written language, the composer imposing structure upon the language of musical sound, or the filmmaker creating film form.

Naturally, the work of art has been pondered, thought about, brooded over before being made. Matisse found five peaches more to the purpose than three or six. Perhaps he spent some time in the arrangement of the subject to be painted, and surely he searched for the colors that would provide the proper contrast and the proper harmony. For the work was not to be a mere copy (and so no "imitation") of the objects he chose; it was to be a presentation of these objects in the light of his own imagination of their natures and ideal properties. All along, the emergence of the painting was controlled by the direction pointed to by his "idea."

The theory of artistic creation we are sketching recognizes that art as the imposition of form upon matter also requires technique, that is, great skill and mastery on the part of the artist. But although the artist must know how to use brushes upon the canvas or chisel upon the stone in order to produce a great and successful work, the "art" lies less in the skill than in the "idea" that the artist wishes to realize. Technical skill is in fact not the art at all, but the condition that removes the impediment of clumsiness, which might prevent the work of art from coming into

Henri Matisse, *Still Life on a Green Buffet*, 1928, National Museum of Modern Art, Paris.

being. True art lies in the mind and imagination of the artist. It is the artist's idea.

This view of artistic creation (which for convenience can be called the Aristotelian theory) is very intellectual. It makes the particular virtue of artists reside in their intellect, and it suggests that, since their control of their media is in the service of their intellectual vision, to lose that control is to condemn their art to mere sensuality and confusion. Of course, artists have feeling, and they must love what they are doing, but their love is a love of order, and the sort of order that they impose upon matter is the expression of a kind of artistic knowledge.

It is precisely this view of artistic creation that Plato denies. For him artists do not have knowledge, they have inspiration. When Matisse sits down before his easel and starts to feverishly paint the still life, which an unerring instinct has caused him to arrange in an instant, his mind is a blank, and it is his feelings that rush over him and into his work. He feels the reality of his pitcher and his peaches as if they were living things. They appeal to him with the immediacy of a child's appeal to its mother, and in his work he conveys to others, as a "medium" would, the way in which these objects "cry out." Sometimes he works smoothly and without error. On these days he has the sense that it is not he but some higher power that is guiding his hand, as if a creative force from outside were working through him and using him for its own inscrutable ends. On other days, the hand is clumsy, nothing seems to work, he throws down the brush with disgust, the green buffet seems ugly, and even the peaches, now over a week old, are unappetizing and slightly rotting fruit.

This is the modern version of Plato's theory of art as inspiration. Matisse creates because he is inspired and possessed. In making his work of art he is the loadstone or magnetic source of a feeling that, like a contagion, spreads later to the spectators of the work of art. And since this theory of "creation through emotion" is in opposition to the Aristotelian doctrine of an imposition of an idea upon matter, there is another consequence, too. It is that if you ask Matisse what he has been doing, or trying to do, he will be inarticulate. He will not really know. Or at any rate, he will only be able to point to what he has done and permit the art object to speak for itself. When Socrates asks Ion, the reciter of Homer, about his craft and about that very poet Homer, whom he interprets, Ion shows his intellectual weakness; he can make no critical judgments. And probably if Socrates would have been able to ask Homer himself, no answer, no aesthetic theory, would have been forthcoming.

Some years ago Sidney Janis produced a book of reproductions of paintings, *Abstract and Surrealist Art in America*. He asked the artists to explain their pictures, what they meant, what they thought they had been doing, and what their idea had been. One of the pictures was Georgia O'Keeffe's *White Barn, Canada*, a painting of a long, clean, rectangular barn with two large doors and a full, sloping roof. It was as serene and quiet a painting as Matisse's *Still Life on a Green Buffet* and presented its object with the same candor and straightforwardness. Many of the artists spoke of their pictures pretentiously, complicatedly, and glibly. But O'Keeffe's comment about hers was as stark and unadorned as the painting itself. "*White Barn, Canada* is nothing but a simple statement about a simple thing. I can say nothing about it in words that I have not said with paint."[1] Aristotle would have been disappointed with O'Keeffe's answer. But Plato would have been satisfied, for it would have confirmed him in his belief that creation is not intellectual but inspired and that artists cannot really know whence their inspiration comes.

Artistic objects are the product of the encounter between artists and their materials, and, whether one thinks of works of art in an Aristotelian way, as the imposition of form upon matter, or Platonically, as the expression of emotion through inspiration, the artists' relation to them ceases when they are created and sent out into the world. The act of artistic creation ends with the work of art. And with the work of art the act of artistic enjoyment begins. Yet the two phases of the artistic process are not as separate as one might think, and if I here consider the latter, it is less for its own sake than for the inferential light it throws on the act of creation: I mean the role of structure and organization as itself a part of the creative idea.

When as visitors to the Museum of Modern Art in Paris we stand before Matisse's *Still Life on a Green Buffet*, we are in the presence of a second encounter, this time between the spectator and the work of art. What is the nature of that encounter? And what is the effect upon the spectators? The very title that we have given to this encounter provides the first clue. It is an act of artistic enjoyment.

To say that the spectators "enjoy" the work is to say that the work gives pleasure, but it is not the same kind of pleasure as that which attaches to the satisfaction of the needs of the body. If Matisse's half-filled glass of water suddenly makes the spectators thirsty or if the five peaches make the viewers long to bite into their juicy flesh, then, whatever their enjoyment, it is not artistic enjoyment. For the pleasure that the peaches guarantee to the observers is a pleasure of the eyes and of the mind, a pleasure in roundness and solidity and in the contrast of orange-pink with blue and green, and the effect of this pleasure is not to arouse desire but to induce a certain calm and quietness in the observers.

There is obviously an important sensuous element in artistic enjoyment; for how else explain the appeal of forms and the lure of color? But it is a sensuous element abstracted and enjoyed for its own sake and not one that leads to anything beyond itself or to a bodily act. Thus, to the pleasure that initially defines the act of artistic enjoyment, we must now add two other characteristics: first, that it is a contemplative experience and, second, that it is an experience that points to nothing beyond itself, in short, that it is not a means to an end, that it is self-justifying. Such an experience is not come by easily. It makes heavy demands on spectators. They cannot take it lightly, finish it quickly, or give it only surface attention. To say that the act of artistic enjoyment is by nature pleasurable, contemplative, and self-justifying implies something about the quality of the attention that makes it possible.

The demands the work of art makes on the spectator are, although different in kind, hardly less than those it has made on its creator. For artistic appreciation and enjoyment require that the spectator both submit to the object and cooperate with it. This cooperation is intuitive. It means that the viewer (in the language of Bergson) does not so much "walk around" in the work of art as try to "enter into it." Knowledge on this level does not come without effort. It is like our acquaintance with persons, which begins superficially and may pass on to deep knowledge and even to love. The achievement of real artistic enjoyment requires time, and it probably requires us to return to the object again and again. But suppose that this condition is fulfilled and that the spectator of *Still Life on a Green Buffet* has an experience both pleasurable and contemplative. In what does the pleasure consist? And just what is it that is contemplated?

The Aristotelian theory of creation has an answer to both questions. For if the act of creation is the imposition of form upon matter and if the work of art is the expression of revelation of the artist's "idea," then the spectator's pleasure must be an intellectual pleasure derived from recognizing the form that the artist has imposed upon the work and from the spectator's contemplation of the "idea" revealed in it.

Attention to the formal structure *Still Life on a Green Buffet* shows it to be both complicated in design and extremely skillful in execution. The line formed by the front edge of the top of the buffet cuts the picture almost in two, with all the crucial objects—platter, peaches, pitcher, glass, and knife—placed on top of the buffet along the upper half. Yet two devices unify the two disparate horizontal segments of the picture plane. On the far left is a lavender vertical stretch of wood or wall running the entire length of the picture, and to the right of it the blue-checkered tablecloth both sits on the surface of the buffet and hangs over its edge far down into the bottom half of the picture.

But most remarkable of all is the way Matisse has given the objects on the buffet a perfect and almost symmetrical "Z" formation, the tablecloth being the downward vertical on the left, the platter and its extension in the knife forming a downward diagonal thrust from upper left to lower right, and the pitcher and glass forming an upper thrust on the far right, completing the nearly perfect "Z" figure. We know almost intuitively that the diagonal platter containing the four peaches, placed almost in the exact center of the upper horizontal of the picture, is the focus of Matisse's loving attention, his idea; but even if we did not, one other painterly persuasion would have forced our attention to this fact. The slightly open doors of the buffet are separated by a broad vertical jet-black line, and this line is like an arrow forcing our gaze immediately to the platter of peaches just above it. Matisse, the wise and sophisticated master of painterly structure, has manipulated our perceptual responses like the magician he is. Content is important, but it is form and structure that give a subject its unity and its life. There is nothing more difficult to achieve than a notable still life, for the objects are "dead," and all too often they confront one another in mute incongruity. It is to Matisse's great skill with structure that the success of this work is due; he has made of his miscellaneous items not a collection but a "family" of objects. And it is the appreciation of this formal element that provides the true artistic enjoyment. Thus, even from the standpoint of aesthetic reception we gain further appreciative insight into the creative process of the artist.

The two chief philosophic accounts of artistic creation that the Greeks provided, the Aristotelian concept of the imposition of form upon matter as having a distinctly intellectual source and the Platonic doctrine of inspiration under the force and direction of emotion, have both appeared in the rationalizations and the practices of Western artists, but not as equal influences. The Aristotelian view has, I think, become the established doctrine, with the Platonic position reemerging only at selected moments during the nineteenth and twentieth centuries. In fact the doctrine of artistic creativity as the imposition of form upon matter might be termed the "classic" position, while art as inspiration remains the contention of incurable romantics.

. . .

The Message of Artistic Creation

In the previous section I have tried to consider the creation of art with a few concrete instances as well as in the light of philosophic theory—namely, the Aristotelian theory of the imposition of form upon matter and the Platonic theory of emotional inspiration—the two that have dominated the thinking and the practices of artists in the West. But now I should like to turn to something much more ideological and problematic: that is, the concepts artists themselves have about the aims, ideals, methods, and mechanics of their own creativity. Here we are in the realm of complete pluralism, disagreement, and confusion, which can only be dealt with through such a principle of tolerance as the one Jacques Barzun expressed in the second epigraph heading this chapter: "Art is inescapably pluralistic. It thrives on diversity and knows nothing of contradiction: all its opposite truths are equally true."[2] The enormous quantity and diversity of the material here makes any exhaustive treatment impossible, but I wish to concentrate on a very small number of selected areas to indicate just a few other dimensions of the problem of creation in the art of painting.

About twenty-five or thirty years ago Josef Albers embarked upon an obsessive series of paintings that he somewhat misleadingly titled *Homage to the Square*. The title was misleading because Albers was not really interested in the square as a structural masterpiece. He had chosen it as a neutral and easily repeatable figure to support the experiments in color contrasts and color harmonies that were indeed the vital object of his concern. He should have titled his series of paintings *Homage to the Colors within the Square*.

The point is not of crucial importance, for the entrance of the square into modern art as a matter of ideological concern had already occurred just before and during the First World War. Malevich's "Supremacist" paintings, which feature the square, originated in 1913. And already in 1917 Theo van Doesburg and Piet Mondrian, joint editors of the art magazine *De Stijl*, were intensely propagandizing the centrality of the square as a structural element for painting. Van Doesburg proclaimed histrionically that "the quadrangle is the token of a new humanity. The square is to us what the cross was to the early Christians."[3] It is difficult to believe that there ever existed such foolish fanaticism among painters. Mondrian is of the same school, but somewhat more intelligible and more moderate. His attack on the forms of nature is at least better argued. "The new plastic idea cannot, therefore take the form of a natural or concrete representation, although the latter does always indicate the universal to a degree, or at least conceals it within. This new plastic idea will ignore the particulars of appearance, that is to say, natural form and color. On the contrary, it should find its expression in the abstraction of form and color, that is to say, in the straight line and the clearly defined primary color."[4]

Van Doesburg's espousal of the square, as Mondrian's of the straight line, already foreshadows the modern artist's dilemma of the conflicting claims on painterly commitment made by abstraction as opposed to representation, a conflict already partly mirrored in the more philosophical quarrel between the organic and the mechanistic approach to the world. Many years later Mondrian's Euclidian prejudices are to receive their angry response in the speculations of the talented Austrian painter Friedensreich Hundertwasser. "The straight line," says Hundertwasser, "is a heathen, immoral thing. The straight line is a reproductive and not a creative line. Neither God nor the spirit of Humanity resides in it." And then to assert his own counterclaim he states, "I regard the spiral as a symbol of life. I believe the spiral belongs where matter ceases to be such and begins to be a living thing. . . .My spiral is subject to vegetative growth."[5]

It is certainly true that Hundertwasser has the whole of Chinese culture on his side. Lin Yutang, in a fascinating book written over half a century ago, *My Country and My People*, made this abundantly clear. "We see everywhere in Chinese architecture," he says, "an effort to seek relief from straight lines through some form of irregularity suggestive of animal and plant forms."[6] And he instanced the sagging roof, probably the most distinctive and obvious characteristic of Chinese architecture; the round bridge, which harmonizes with nature because it is in a curve; and the pagoda, which tries to catch and incorporate the rhythm of nature and imitate its irregularity. And he even anticipates Hundertwasser's anger, referring to "our love for rhythmic or wavy or broken lines and our hatred of straight, dead ones."[7]

Hundertwasser's Chinese theory is, of course, only the philosophical expression of his painterly practice. And his marvelous landscapes, often with human faces embedded in them, are great undulating fields of paint, without a single straight line anywhere to be seen and simply appealing to us as some vast contour map of the organic imagination. It is impossible to imagine paintings more dissimilar, more "contradictory," than, say, Mondrian's *Composition in White, Red, and Blue* of 1933 and Hundertwasser's *Spiral Kopf* of 1965. Thus, theoretical opposition between the most Spartan means—namely, the straight versus the spiral or undulating line—becomes two "messages" of painterly creativity. Surely Mondrian and Hundertwasser present two completely opposite creative options, and the profound dissimilarity in their actual creativity mirrors and expresses their equally profound ideological differences. And so we are finally at the very center of the Barzun paradox. Mondrian's truth and Hundertwasser's truth are inescapable contradictories, and yet both of these opposite truths, I think we may say, are equally true.

The contrast between the straight and the curved line is an opposition at the level of the most elementary technical means. A similar opposition is to be found at the level of the source of creative inspiration. . . . [W]e have already had some experience of the Impressionist moment in France in the late nineteenth century, when painters like Monet, Renoir, Pissarro, and Sisley—all comrades at the Café Guerbois in Paris—forsook their studios in the capital city and flocked to Normandy, the English Channel, Provence, or the Midi to glory in the opulent tints and tones of the French countryside. Landscapists all, it was Monet who was their ruling prince. Unfortunately, this noble and gifted artist was all but inarticulate, and so it is rather to the voluminous letter writer Cézanne that we must turn for an articulation of the special source of inspiration to which this entire school paid homage. Of course, it is to Nature.

First, in a letter to Zola, Cézanne both describes the outdoor rationale and clearly associates it with nature as the creative source of artistic inspiration. "But you know all pictures painted inside, in the studio, will never be as good as the things done outside. When out-of-door scenes are represented, the contrasts between the figures and the ground are astounding and the landscape is magnificent. I see some superb things and I shall have to make up my mind only to do things out-of-doors. . . . I feel sure that all the pictures by the old masters representing things out-of-doors have only been done hesitatingly, for they do not seem to me to have the true and above all the original aspect lent by nature."[8] Further letters of the much later period of Cézanne's life bristle with a similar sentiment. "Couture used to say to his pupils: 'Keep good company, that is: Go to the Louvre. But after having seen the great masters who repose there, we must hasten out and by contact with nature revive in us the instincts and sensations of art that dwell within us.'" "The strong experience of nature—and assuredly I have it—is the necessary basis for all conception of art" (p. 18). "The Louvre is a good book to consult but it must only be an intermediary. The real and immense study that must be taken up is the manifold picture of nature" (p. 21).

There can be no question of Cézanne's turning to nature for sustained creative inspiration. And to a considerable extent this was also the resource for his Impressionist associates, including even that Postimpressionist van Gogh. Yet already in van Gogh doubts begin to arise, and an alternative source begins to surface—I mean the imagination. "The imagination," van Gogh wrote to Emile Bernard in April 1888, "is certainly a faculty which we must develop, one which alone can lead us to the creation of a more exalting and consoling nature than the single brief glance at reality—which in our sight is ever changing, passing like a flash of lightening—can let us perceive" (p. 31). Van Gogh's reference to the imagination was prophetic, because toward the end of the nineteenth century a new movement arose that rejected the naturalistic conception of art (Cézanne's) that had dominated the preceding generation. Artists now turned away from the external world and looked inward to their own feelings and imaginations as a new source of creative inspiration. Of course this new movement was at first literary rather than artistic: it began with the Symbolists—poets like Verlaine, Mallarmé, and Baudelaire—but it soon spread to the more iconoclastic painters also. In 1908 Edvard Munch was saying: "A work of art can come only from the interior of man" (p. 114), and a year or so later, Odilon Redon was also proclaiming that "there is a method of drawing which the imagination has liberated from those bothersome worries presented by the details of the exterior world" (p. 118).

Cézanne or Munch and Redon? The creative self looking outward to nature or inward to the imagination? Here again, in the matter of creative inspiration, as before in the case of the straight line versus the curve, we are in the presence of contradiction, of the copresence of two opposite truths. And how could anyone doubt that both are equally true? How can an artist definitely choose between the claims of nature and of the imagination? It would be like asking a philosopher to make a choice between the Realism of Aristotle and the Idealism of Kant.

Notes

1. Quoted in Sidney Janis, *Abstract and Surrealist Art in America* (New York: Reynal and Hitchcock, 1944), p. 42.

2. Jacques Barzun, *The Use and Abuse of Art* (Princeton: Princeton University Press, 1974), p. 90.

3. Quoted in Herschel B. Chipp, ed., *Theories of Modern Art* (Berkeley: University of California Press, 1968), p. 316.

4. Ibid., p. 32.

5. See the catalogue *Austria Presents Hundertwasser to the Continents*, 2d ed. (Glarus, Switzerland: Januara Ag., 1976), pp. 441, 490.

6. Lin Yutang, *My Country and My People* (New York: Reynal and Hitchcock, 1935), p. 318.

7. Ibid., p. 316.

8. Quoted in Chipp, ed., *Theories of Modern Art*, p. 16.

DAVID EBITZ

DBAE: Opening a Bridge Between Art History and Art Education

By adapting art production, art history, criticism, and aesthetics to the uses of education, DBAE can provide a multi-disciplined education in art. This interest in a multi-disciplined approach is not unique to art education. Multi-disciplined and interdisciplinary patterns of thinking are emerging as traditional disciplines are being called into question, recombined and replaced by entirely new disciplines in the sciences, social sciences, and humanities, as well as in the arts. Being an art historian, I am especially interested in the disciplines of art history. In particular, I hope to show what art history may have to contribute as one element of discipline-based art education, and what DBAE and art education in general may have to contribute to the practice and teaching of art history.

Today, art historians rarely talk with artists, critics, aestheticians, and certainly not with art educators, whether K-12 classroom teachers, museum educators or university professors. Unfortunately, our disciplines have become so separated, so distinct from each other, that they seem to be mutually exclusive. This separation of disciplines, however, is a relatively recent development. It would have seemed an odd state of affairs to the person who is generally credited as the father of art history, Giorgio Vasari. This 16th-century Florentine was a painter, architect, biographer, critic, modest aesthetician, and educator. In co-founding the Accademia del Disegno in 1563, in writing his *Lives of the Most Eminent Painters, Sculptors and Architects* (1550; 2nd ed., 1568), and in practicing his own arts of painting and architecture, Vasari combined a range of activities which today seem unusually comprehensive, from making art to criticizing it, from tracing its history and pondering its nature to teaching it. Vasari was even an administrator. For an account of his accomplishments, I recommend T. S. R. Boase, *Giorgio Vasari, The Man and the Book* (Princeton, N.J.; 1979). Vasari was what we admiringly call a "Renaissance man."

Much of Vasari's effort was directed to improving the social position of the artist. Hence he wrote biographies of great artists and he
extolled Michelangelo, a contemporary Florentine so extraordinary that
in Vasari's opinion he surpassed the ancients. Vasari was also a founding member of the Accademia del Disegno, an institution under the direct patronage of Cosimo I, the Medici Grand Duke of Florence. Though
the Accademia did improve the position of its artist members, its purpose was not entirely social. It had a practical educational program. As
in the guilds, which the Accademia and succeeding academies displaced,
the emphasis remained on art production, but art production informed
by history, criticism, and theory. This is the model which, very roughly,
has been proposed for implementation in our schools with discipline-
based art education. Might this multi-disciplined approach find a useful place again in our colleges and universities? And might the knowledge and practice of these disciplines, as they did for Vasari and his
contemporaries, strengthen the position of the art and museum educator within the world of art, within the hierarchy of education, and within
society at large?

What has happened since Vasari's day? Specialization. As an art historian, I can say that from the beginning of the 20th century specialization has increased the rigor, the intellectual and therefore the social standing of at least some of the disciplines in which Vasari engaged: art history, criticism, and aesthetics. But this specialization has compartmentalized experience and knowledge, going so far as to separate the kind
of knowledge that we acquire from reading—book knowledge—from
the experience we gain from actually doing something—the skills acquired by hand and eye. While in the 19th century most art historians
were also artists, as Vasari had been, my generation of art historians has
experienced little more than that single two-dimensional design course
taken as an undergraduate art history major. I remember my shock as a
graduate student when I saw a posthumous exhibition of watercolors
by Benjamin Rowland in the Fogg Art Museum at Harvard University.
Benjamin Rowland, my professor, had been one of the distinguished
faculty in art history at Harvard. That he was a painter as well seemed
to me then almost a contradiction in terms. I was fully indoctrinated in
the virtues of specialization. Rowland was one of the last of the art
historians who not only made art, but also asked some of the basic
questions of aesthetics and engaged in criticism.

If art history has dissociated itself from studio production, from art
criticism, and from aesthetics, of what relevance can it be to the contemporary understanding of art? This is one of several provocative questions

recently asked by Hans Belting in his book, *The End of the History of Art?* (Chicago, 1987 [1983]). It is no wonder that art educators find art history so unsatisfying, so inaccessible, so unteachable.

The situation of art history today and the problems that educators may encounter in trying to put it to use can be clarified, I think, if we briefly consider two issues: first, the primary role that texts have come to play in the art historian's approach to art, and, second, the tendency among art historians to focus on a content of knowledge rather than on the process of inquiry by which this content of knowledge is acquired. Texts and knowledge are intimately related, for all too often texts have become the sole source of the art historian's knowledge.

First, texts. In emulating its sister humanistic disciplines, an emulation that began with Vasari, art history has so come to rely on texts as its primary sources that there seems to be little place left for the art object or for the artist. As an educator and art historian working with actual objects in a museum I am particularly sensitive to this. Words too often overwhelm visual experience as the art historian studies the iconography or subject matter of a painting examined in a black-and-white reproduction, for instance, or seeks to reconstruct the social, political, economic, and religious contexts of the time in which the work was made by studying the relevant written documents. It is also texts, the texts that we publish, which inform the next generation of art historians in schools and colleges in the United States where students have so little access to original works of art.

My second issue is the primacy of received knowledge over the process of inquiry. Again, in emulation of history and other humanistic disciplines, art historians have come to concentrate on the content of what is known and transmitted to us, on tradition, rather than on how we go about acquiring knowledge, the new questions we could ask, and the skills we could apply to answer them. This distinction is not just between whether we should teach K-12, undergraduate and graduate students the facts of the history of art, or whether we should teach them the processes by which these new facts come to be. This distinction between facts and processes is at the center of any discipline with a tradition. Are we to relish what we know and increase this body of knowledge by adding more of the same kinds of information, that is to say, focus on the content of the history of art? Or are we as scholars and educators to change our frames of reference, ask new questions, go about our jobs in other ways, think about how we are thinking, face the ambiguities of the art object directly, not through the simplification of reproductions and words? Words are necessary, I have no doubt, but they are not sufficient, certainly not for the artist, not for the critic, not for the art historian, and perhaps not even for the aesthetician. And what is the educator to make of all this talk and writing?

Having spoken in the abstract about art history, I should take my own advice and be specific. What is art history? It consists of a number of independent sub-specializations that can be roughly divided into three groups: those that concentrate on the object, the work of art; those that concentrate on the artist and his or her context of production; and those that concentrate on the changing perception or reception of the object and artist over time.

First, the art object is the direct focus of the connoisseur, who attends to when, where, and by whom it was made. It is also, if only briefly, the starting point of the iconographer, who seeks to identify its subject matter by reference to the appropriate contemporary texts. Connoisseurship and iconography are the most venerable methods of inquiry of the professional art historian.

Second, the artist and his or her social context are the focus of the biographer, who may use the tools of psychology and psychoanalysis, and the focus of the social historian, who takes into consideration such conditions of production as the social, economic, political, religious, scientific, cultural, and intellectual life of the time.

Third, the changing perception of the art object and the critical reception of the artist over time are the recent focus of scholars who have brought to art history frames of reference from other disciplines. These frames of reference include such approaches as the psychology of perception, structural analysis, semiotics, the sociology of knowledge, reception theory, and Marxist and feminist history.

Taken as a whole, art history is a discipline of extraordinary breadth and complexity, a discipline made up of many disciplines, but unfortunately there are few art historians today with the sweeping grasp of the 19th-century cultural historian Jacob Burckhardt, or, in the 20th century, with the profound learning of Erwin Panofsky, the overarching psychological explanations of Sir Ernst Gombrich, or the insight into the relation of form and content of Meyer Schapiro. Art history generally functions at a more modest level as a discipline divided into specializations by specialists who do not speak to each other, much less to practitioners of other disciplines, not even to artists, critics, and aestheticians. Lack of communication breeds prejudice. The iconographer is suspicious of the intuitive methods of the connoisseur, and the connoisseur complains that the iconographer never looks at original works of art. Both agree that the social historian, especially if a Marxist of feminist, ignores art altogether. And every one complains uncomfortably of the jargon of the semiotician.

This multiplicity of specialized approaches and the internal lack of communication among art historians may explain in part why art educators either find it difficult to understand what art historians are up to or simplify the richness of art historical practice to one or two approaches and a set of facts. These are promptly criticized by art historians as inadequate. It would help, then, if art historians were willing to write introductory surveys to use in the schools. But with the prominent exception of H. W. Janson (with Samuel Cauman and Anthony F. Janson, *History of Art for Young People*, 2nd ed. [New York]) and Sir Ernst Gombrich (*The Story of Art*, 13th ed. [Englewood Cliffs, N.J.; 1978]) we have shown little inclination to do so. This is symptomatic of our specialized patterns of thought, emphasis on scholarly research, and the low value we place on education. By default, the high school texts are being written instead by educators, such as Gene A. Mittler (*Art in Focus*, 2nd ed. [Mission Hills, Ca.; 1989]) and Gerald F. Brommer (*Discovering Art History*, 2nd ed. [Worcester, Mass.; 1988]).

Art history has only of late begun to wonder what it is doing, here and there to review its own history, and to examine the assumptions under which it operates. By comparison the level and kinds of questioning we see in art education and now in museum education are lively indeed, the evidence of enthusiasm in youthful disciplines seeking both to understand their nature and to justify their existence. Art history has not seen anything comparable since the beginning of the 20th century. But it too is now entering a period of renewal. Evidence of such renewal is found in the comprehensive surveys of art historical method by W. Eugene Kleinbauer (*Modern Perspectives in Western Art History* [New York, 1971]) and with Thomas P. Slavens, *Research Guide to the History of Western Art* [Chicago, 1982]), in Mark Roskill's *What Is Art History?* (New York, 1976), and in recent intellectual histories of art history of the late 19th and first half of the 20th century by Michael Podro (*The Critical Historians of Art* [New Haven, 1982]) and Michael Ann Holly (*Panofsky and the Foundations of Art History* [Ithaca, 1984]). Moreover, since the early 1980's, sessions at College Art Association conferences, where both art historians and studio artists gather annually, have increasingly focused attention on basic methodological questions. This past year one session addressed the teaching of art history in the United States at the turn of the century. . . . We have just been given the first glimpse of the art historian at work in *Object, Image, Inquiry, The Art Historian at Work*, published by the Getty Art History Information Program and the Institute for Research in Information and Scholarship at Brown University (Santa Monica, 1988). I hope to see more attention given to this matter of how we learn and how we work.

But we have yet to see an adequate examination of art history as a practice, as a profession that is learned and taught, functioning within a historical and social context. Few scholars have addressed the education of the art historian, and the influence this has had on his or her practice. As art historians, for example, we take the comparative method for granted and so we assume that projecting two slides on the screen at the same time is the natural and only way to teach. Clearly this practice has a profound effect on our thinking. The practice began with Heinrich Wölfflin at the beginning of this century. The history of art is still intellectual history. In light of this, it is not surprising that few art historians have considered their social responsibility as teachers, especially in the United States where the university establishment provides some security from unpleasant social realities. In contrast, there is greater awareness of social issues in Great Britain, where art historians have more difficulty earning a living, witness the lively essays, some on teaching, edited by A. L. Rees and Frances Borzello in *The New Art History* (London, 1986).

The nature of knowledge is under review on so many fronts that the still dominant, complacent assumptions of art history will not survive. At the very least the facts of art history—those facts which comprise the bulk of what is taught in the classroom and the art museum, from the fifth grade to graduate school—will have to be seen in new light, if they continue to be regarded as the relevant facts at all. Anthropologists, Marxists and feminists, for example, are disabusing us of the not-so-innocent assumption that the only relevant focus of attention is fine art created by men living in western Europe during historically documented periods.

As we reexamine within our discipline what we mean by the history of art, I hope, first, that we will improve relations with our sister disciplines, and, second, that we will develop new models for what can be taught by educators in the classrooms and art museums of this country. Art historians should get together with historians, literary theorists, and semioticians, with anthropologists and scientists. In fact, some of us are doing so with enthusiasm. But we must also knock down the walls that separate art history from the disciplines immediately adjacent to our territory, disciplines intimately engaged with art, the other disciplines in DBAE. We should begin to give thought to what we can learn from at least talking to artists, if not from making art. We should introduce with critics the issue of quality into our discussions, and clarify with aestheticians the nature of what we study and the assumptions underlying our approaches to it. If art history is to say anything useful about the art of the past, it must come to terms with the practice, criticism and understanding of art today.

As we inquire into what we do and why, I hope that this process of inquiry will come to be recognized as the most effective means by which to teach art history in schools, colleges, and museums. A chronological presentation of slides in a darkened room is an inadequate education for a college student, and a useless model for the teaching of art history in the schools. No wonder art history finds so little place in the curriculum. But art history understood as a process of inquiry has greater promise. Mary Erickson has been telling art educators this for some time in a series of articles and presentations (for example, "Teaching Art History as an Inquiry Process," *Art Education*, 36, no. 5 [1983], 28-31). But the college art history professor remains largely oblivious to this pedagogical approach, choosing rather to transmit information to a passive audience roused only by the professor's enthusiasm for the knowledge imparted.

If we let students into the workshop, to participate in the process, the teacher can become a facilitator for new discoveries rather than just the transmitter of received knowledge. Vasari, in his *Lives*, remarked on the difficulties of his task of gathering and verifying information, and he said what he thought of his material. We could do the same.

As art educators and art historians we have much that we can learn from each other. To do so, however, we will have to bridge a separation that goes back to the beginning of this century, a separation institutionalized in the National Art Education Association, on the one hand, and the College Art Association, on the other. Discipline-based art education may open this bridge. Art history and the other disciplines of DBAE provide necessary if not sufficient models for art education. Art education has an equally important, though as yet unrealized contribution to make to the practice and teaching of art history.

The potential contribution of art education to art history lies in three areas. First, the multi-disciplined approach being explored by art educators may remind art historians that art history was once integrated with the production of art, with criticism and with aesthetics. Without understanding these disciplines, art history cannot provide an adequate history of *art*.

Second, with its focus on art history among the other disciplines, discipline-based art education can give high school students, perhaps even grade school students, a first taste of the methods and pleasures of art history. This could increase the number of undergraduates interested in art history and better prepare them for college art history courses. It could also increase the number of knowledgeable and skilled visitors to art museums. If art education in the schools becomes as good as it should be, this preparation will not be limited to knowledge of art historical facts, useful as they may be. This preparation will foster an awareness of art history as a process of inquiry, an appreciation for the kinds of multi-disciplined thinking necessary to the study of art and other subjects in the curriculum, visual literacy, a broader grasp of the humanities, and greater tolerance for cultural diversity.

But there is a third, more fundamental contribution that art education can make to the practice of art history. Art educators by the nature of their task have to face their responsibility to society in a manner that art historians are not called upon to do. Educators must attend to students, and justify their actions to principals, school boards, parents, press, and state and federal government. To do so, educators must establish general goals and specific objectives for their teaching and face the recurrent responsibility of evaluating their success in meeting them. Though I certainly do not advocate giving up academic freedom, I am convinced that art historians working in universities and museums can find models here for thinking about why, what and how we teach, for teaching to objectives, for evaluating success, and for examining the overall enterprise of art history within a larger social context in which we have more responsibilities than we may realize or care to admit.

THEODORE F. WOLFF

Types of Art Criticism

In the very broadest sense, there are three basic types of art criticism: diaristic (also known as emotive, impressionistic, or autobiographical criticism), which features the subjective sensations and personal impressions of a critic; formalist (also known as internal, intrinsic, or aesthetically autonomous art criticism), which features the properties and qualities of artwork; and contextualist (also known as art historical, psychoanalytical, and ideological criticism), which stresses the factors or forces responsible for a work's assuming a particular shape or having a special meaning. When reading art criticism it is helpful to know whether a critic is talking about his or her personal feelings, in which case we may learn a great deal about the critic but not necessarily about the work under discussion; about the work of art itself, that is to say its sensuous, formal, expressive, and symbolic aspects; or about the conditions responsible for bringing a work into being, whether historical or psychological. In practice, these kinds of criticism are often not rigidly separated. No critic practices one or another exclusively, and even the most doctrinaire critic must, at times, incorporate elements from the others into a critique. Each type of criticism has historical precedents, but I will concentrate on examples from the nineteenth and twentieth centuries.

Diaristic Art Criticism

Diaristic criticism is the most common and the most informal kind and in many ways the most difficult to write. If not well done, it tends to be quite loose, overly personal, and even given to gossip. But when well managed it can read like a detailed entry in a diary or like a warm, perhaps impassioned, letter from one friend to another. A key to the character of diaristic criticism is the use of the personal pronoun *I* to establish identity and credibility and justify the highly subjective nature of this kind of writing. At its most casual, a diaristic critique may begin by saying, "I finally got out of my apartment and walked over to West Broadway to see what Mary Boone is showing in her gallery these days." Or, "I saw some mind-boggling canvases at the Guggenheim Museum this afternoon." Much art reviewing seldom rises above this level of writing. But in the hands of a sensitive critic, a personal, impressionistic approach can be both effective and rewarding, attracting readers to the deeper and more significant goals of art criticism.

Diaristic criticism arose in the nineteenth century as a reaction to criticism that concentrated too exclusively not only on the biography and personality of the artist and the social and historical conditions of art but also on a style of criticism that abided by the strict rules of the official artistic academics of the time. In contrast to official criticism, which any intelligent critic can apply once the rules are known, critics such as Oscar Wilde, Anatole France, and Walter Pater emphasized the subjectivity of criticism. Writing against standards of objectivity in criticism in favor of emotive expression, Wilde observed that what critics require "is a certain kind of temperament, the power of being deeply moved by the presence of physical objects." Anatole France echoed a similar sentiment when he said that criticism consists of describing "the adventures of one's soul among masterpieces." And Pater asked perhaps the central question of emotive criticism: "What is this song or picture, this engaging personality presented in life or in a book, to me? What effect does it really produce in me? Does it give me pleasure? And if so, what sort or degree of pleasure?" That diaristic criticism is a perennial and basic form of criticism is evident by the statements of a number of contemporary art critics. Donald Kuspit, for example, thinks a critic's task "is to try to articulate the effects that the work of art induces in us, these very complicated subjective states"; Robert Pincus-Witten stresses the need of critics for empathic identification with artists and believes that a critique of a work of art is as much a work of art as the work being criticized; and Joanna Freuh, a feminist critic, sets store by the importance of intuition and bodily sensations.[1]

The two examples of impressionist criticism that follow stand for many others; one is by Pater and the other is by Pincus-Witten.

Pater was associated with the Pre-Raphaelite movement in Great Britain, a secret brotherhood that rebeled against the stereotypical medievalism and dry subject matter of the academic painting of the period. He became known as an apostle of aestheticism, a doctrine that places great importance on the enjoyment of aesthetic experience. This is evident in his discussion of Leonardo da Vinci's *Mona Lisa*.

> Hers is the head upon which all "the ends of the world are come," and the eyelids are a little weary. It is a beauty wrought out from within upon the flesh, the deposit, little cell by cell, of strange thoughts and fantastic reveries and exquisite passions. Set it for a moment beside

one of those white Greek goddesses or beautiful women of antiquity, and how would they be troubled by this beauty, into which the soul with all its maladies has passed! All the thoughts and experience of the world have etched and molded there, in that which they have of power to refine and make expressive the outward form, the animalism of Greece, the lust of Rome, the mysticism of the middle age with its spiritual ambition and imaginative loves, the return of the Pagan world, the sins of the Borgias. She is older than the rocks among which she sits; like the vampire, she has been dead many times, and learned the secrets of the grave; and has been a diver in deep seas, and keeps their fallen day about her; and trafficked for strange webs with Eastern merchants: and, as Leda, was the mother of Helen of Troy, and, as Saint Anne, the mother of Mary; and all this has been to her but as the sound of lyres and flutes, and lives only in the delicacy with which it has molded the changing lineaments, and tinged the eyelids and the hands. The fancy of a perpetual life, sweeping together ten thousand experiences, is an old one; and modern philosophy has conceived the idea of humanity as wrought upon by, and summing up in itself, all modes of thought and life. Certainly Lady Lisa might stand as the embodiment of the old fancy, the symbol of the modern idea.[2]

Art criticism has had no better aesthete than Walter Pater. But the diaristic tradition continues in the contemporary writing of Pincus-Witten. Especially noteworthy are the entries in his journal, selections from which appear in a volume representing twenty years of his criticism. Here is an entry dated October 10, 1982, about the painter Julian Schnabel.

> *The Raft* is a huge plate painting, crockery silvered over to represent the shimmer of water. A cast bronze Christmas tree (and how complex was the gating for that pour?) stands as proportionately high off the surface as Duchamp's bottle cleaner from the background of his *Tu'm*. *The Raft* echoes with the violence of Géricault, as well as its realism, and the independent American-mindedness of Twain—Life on the Mississippi. Its single bronze tree invokes the three Christmas trees of Beuys's incarcerated Russian winters—as seen in *Snowfall*, the great work preserved in Basel.
>
> The other relief painting is an untitled altar—a huge antlered bronze cross manacled to a painted backdrop. The work is too carbuncled. The imagery, such as it is, is indecipherable—intensifying the Carolingian book cover-like character of the work. Religious intention it has—what with a triptych-like composition and altarpiece organization. This is the part of Schnabel that exalts Michael Tracy: Schnabel as decorator. But sincerity is invisible.
>
> Apart from these works, Schnabel is attempting a kind of fever-dream painting of liberated unself-consciousness, dredging paint and

image together. By moments he attempts to keep color fresh (often unsuccessfully), as fresh as his desire to ride out his heated jet of inspiration. Colors go murky owing to frenzied revision—painting under fire—painting hovering just at the edge of respectability. It is a kind of dizzying aerial gymnastic, not so much as without a net below as wanting the very wire above—though this thread may be the disguised untrammeled verge-imagery itself.[3]

The combination of informality, gossip, pointed observation, apt association, and metaphor is characteristic of diaristic criticism. Although I do not always agree with Pincus-Witten's judgments (especially about Schnabel) and have misgivings about his belief that a critique is as much a work of art as the work that inspired it, I am sympathetic to his sentiment that critics should know artists and try to understand their concerns and intentions as much as possible. I prefer to leave gossip to the gossip columnists. To repeat, in the hands of accomplished writers who have clear insight into art, a knowledge of its history, and a flair for perceiving relations, diaristic criticism provides an alternative to art reviewing that merely skims the surface of works and reveals little of the quality of a critic's experience of a work.

The chief drawback of diaristic criticism is its tendency to draw attention away from the artwork to the critic, whose literary account often upstages the work being discussed. Moreover, by eschewing principles of judgment and explanations of why given works are particularly meritorious, it opens the door to the expression of mere opinion. In doing this, diaristic criticism loses much of its educative value, that is, the disciplinary value inherent in coming to terms with the complexity of works of art. Granted that criticism has numerous functions, it is reasonable to expect that a critic will at least point out what is actually in a work to enjoy.

Formalist Art Criticism

It was because of their greater appreciation of art objects that formalist art critics gained increasing influence in discussions of modern art. Attempting to counteract excessive historicizing and psychologizing, critics such as Roger Fry and Clement Greenberg insisted that the form in which a work is conceived and realized is of utmost importance. Such conception and form determine artistic quality and significance, and art criticism that doesn't do justice to the formal quality of artwork is a failure. This is particularly true of writing about modernist works from roughly the mid-nineteenth century on, which heralded a dramatic change in artistic expression. Formalist critics maintain that modern art from Cézanne and Seurat to the Cubists and Abstract Expressionists and on to the geometric and reductive painters of the mid-twentieth century cannot be discussed properly without a detailed analysis of form.

They also insist that structural analysis must lie at the heart of criticizing not just work reflecting strict formalist ideas but work mirroring the wildest excesses of the imagination. In fact, if a work resists formal analysis, that in itself can be taken as proof that it certainly isn't art. Compare a finger-painting by a chimpanzee with a superficially similar abstract-expressionist canvas by Hans Hofmann and the chimp's picture will rapidly prove to be structurally incoherent— hence not art— whereas the Hofmann will reveal the presence of both intention and method behind the apparently undisciplined wildness of the artist's paint handling. Intention and method count most here. The former, activated and given form by the latter, proves the existence in artists of a level of intelligence and concern dramatically higher than that evidenced by the chimpanzee. Form thus becomes the prime clue to the nature and depth of artists' creative intentions and to the vision, feeling, idea, or experience they wish to shape and communicate. To formalist art critics, therefore, Hofmann's formal method not only represents the artist's perceptions of the nature and meaning of life but is also a personal, finely honed verdict on reality.

Small wonder then that formalist critics place so high a premium on the ways artists "package" their ideas. And small wonder that Roger Fry, the distinguished English art critic and writer who did so much to explain modernism to a skeptical British and American public during the early decades of this century, placed such great emphasis on "significant form" in his writings about modern artists. Form, if it wasn't always everything, was close to it for writers such as Fry, Clive Bell, Clement Greenberg, and Erie Loran, whose *Cézanne's Composition* (1943) caused an entire generation to rethink Cézanne in terms of how he constructed his paintings.[4] Examples of the critical commentary of Fry and Greenberg will convey the character of formalist criticism.

Fry was the leading critic of the first third of the twentieth century. His career included, in addition to critical writing, the study of science, the holding of a museum directorship, and the editing of a magazine. Kenneth Clark has said of Fry that insofar as the taste of an era can be changed by any one man, it was changed by Roger Fry.[5] At point here is Fry's discovery of the art of Cézanne, which persuaded him that the defining features of visual art were its plastic and formal qualities. Such qualities are highlighted in his description of Cézanne's *Card Players.* Fry writes that Cézanne

> seems to have carried the elimination of all but the essentials to the furthest point attainable. The simplicity of disposition is such as might even have made Giotto hesitate to adopt it. For not only is everything seen in strict parallelism to the picture plane, not only are the figures seen in almost as strict a profile as in an Egyptian relief, but they are symmetrically disposed about the central axis. And this again is, as it were willfully, emphasized by the bottle on the table. It is true that having once accepted this Cézanne employs every ruse to render it less crushing. The axis is very slightly displaced and the balance redressed by the slight inclination of the chair back and the gestures of the two men are slightly, but sufficiently varied. But it is above all by the constant variation of the movements of planes within the main volumes, the changing relief of the contours, the complexity of the color, in which Cézanne's bluish, purplish and greenish greys are played against oranges and coppery reds, and finally by the delightful freedom of the handwriting that he avoids all suggestion of rigidity and monotony. The feeling of life is no less intense than that of eternal stillness and repose. The hands for instance have the weight of matter because they are relaxed in complete repose, but they have the unmistakable potentiality of life.[6]

Fry further remarks that the gravity of *The Cardplayers* is reminiscent of some monument of antiquity or of the monumentality achieved in the paintings of the Renaissance master Giotto. And particularly relevant to our current situation in culture is Fry's appreciation of the formal qualities of Cézanne and the Postimpressionists resulted in his developing a fondness for African and Asian art, a fact that multicultural critics of Fry's formalism usually fail to point out.

For another example of insightful formalist criticism consider the observations of Greenberg, a contemporary American critic whose influence in persuading others to see the qualities of modern and contemporary art rival Fry's accomplishment in educating viewers to the values of Postimpressionist painting. To dip into Greenberg's collected essays and criticism is to be reminded just how insightful and effective good art criticism can be and of how clearly and unpretentiously it can be written. Just as important, Greenberg shows us that it is possible to be both brief and to the point. His November 1942 account of a Morris Graves exhibition is exactly 154 words long, beginning with: "Gouaches. At the Willard Gallery. Graves's works almost exclusively in gouache on paper. He takes most of his motifs from zoology and embroiders them decoratively—birds, snakes, rodents and the like." And his last sentence sums up one attribute of this particular artist clearly and precisely: "He generates power out of lightness and fragility—that is, in his best work."[7]

Nothing could be simpler or shorter, and yet this brief essay says just about everything that could be said about Graves in 1942. Most of what we know of Graves today, especially his profound commitment to Eastern thought and religion, didn't become clear until later. Besides, Greenberg, a formalist art critic, would have paid little attention to Graves's metaphysical subject matter, no matter how important it was to Graves or to his collectors. Thematic content, Greenberg would have argued, has no real bearing in matters of artistic judgment. It is a purely subjective and irrelevant element and thus plays no significant role in art criticism, which must at all times remain objective and focused on formal matters.

Readers may have noticed, however, that this particular piece reads more like an art review than like a piece of art criticism. It is primarily descriptive, and although it does, elsewhere in the essay, predict a great future for Graves, it does so casually and without clearly defined critical justification. I selected this example, however, more for its brevity, simplicity, and straightforwardness than for its demonstration of a particular critical principle. Considering that Graves's work has always tempted critics into overwriting, Greenberg's cool and somewhat detached approach is especially noteworthy. Compared to the majority of his longer and more critically incisive writings—especially those on the abstract expressionist and color field painters—this is a very minor example. And yet it accomplishes precisely what it set out to do and in exactly the number of words needed—no more and no less.

One might argue that Greenberg's formalist approach is totally inappropriate for an analysis of Graves's profoundly subjective, even elusive, paintings and drawings. These, as I have written elsewhere, "seem more to have sprung spontaneously into being, or to record fragile evidence of the passing overhead (or within) of intangible but profoundly real and mysterious forces, than to have come about as the result of professional artistic concerns." If that is so, and if it is also not incorrect to say "Graves hunts and fishes for evidence of the divine,"[8] then how can a formalist art critic like Greenberg possibly understand or have anything worthwhile to say about an artist like Morris Graves?

Greenberg can write perceptively about Graves because he probes beneath the surface drama or attractiveness of a work to what he considers its objective, definable core, its purely formal identity, and then examines it strictly in the light of how successfully impulse and idea were translated into expressive form. In Graves's case, Greenberg obviously realized that even that artist's most elusive and ephemeral paintings were grounded in sophisticated formal realities and that he was an artist of significant form as well as provocative themes.

A somewhat more formal analysis is found in Greenberg's critical essay on Piet Mondrian, which appeared on March 4, 1944:

> Mondrian's painting. . . takes its place beside the greatest art through virtues not involved in his metaphysics. His pictures, with their white grounds, straight black lines, and opposed rectangles of pure color, are no longer windows in the wall but islands radiating clarity, harmony, and grandeur—passion mastered and cooled, a difficult struggle resolved, unity imposed on diversity. Space outside them is transformed by their presence. Perhaps Mondrian will be reproached for the anonymity with which he strove for the ruled precision of the geometry and the machine in executing his paintings: their conceptions can be communicated by a set of specifications and dimensions, sight unseen, and realized by a draftsman. But so could the Parthenon. The artist's signature is not everything.9

Beautifully put—and so succinctly written. Whether or not one agrees with Greenberg's theoretical position—and his more recent writings have been come under severe attack since the 1970s—the main body of work still makes most other critics appear woolly and unclear. Even for those who cavil at his critical judgments, his place in mid-twentieth-century American art history is secure. More than any other writer, he has kept American art critics on their toes.

Although formalist criticism can be extremely helpful in discerning the structural qualities of works of art, its chief limitations are twofold. In slighting the subject matter of works of art, it fails to take into account what attracts many people to art in the first place and gives insufficient attention to the ways the interactions of medium, form, and subject matter contribute to the content and expressive power of a work. These limitations were the consequence of the formalist's project to return interest to the object, a project that was in effect a protest against types of criticism that showed more interest in contextual considerations than in aesthetic values.

. . .

Observations

The types of criticism are never as clearly defined nor as precisely differentiated in real life as they have been in these pages. Only the most narrowly dogmatic or orthodox critics would insist that all art must be judged by one set of rules and standards.10 Fortunately, such critics are extremely rare. Most practice an open, pragmatic approach toward the diverse and often complex thematic, formal, and technical aspects of art. Without in any way lowering their standards, they engage works of art with a broad range of critical criteria drawn from all categories of art criticism. Everything that helps illuminate the issues of a given work is grist for their critical mill. Only after the evidence is in and the analytical and shaping process begins do they reveal themselves by drawing conclusions that will identify them as primarily diaristic, formalistic, or contextualist. The resulting synthesized criticism may disappoint purists of various persuasions, but it is generally more insightful and informative and brings art to life on the printed page much more vividly than narrow doctrinaire and dogmatic criticism.

More open-minded and pragmatic critics, on the other hand, place as much emphasis on the richness and life-enhancing nature of art as on its precisely defined significance and worth. Their objective is as much to convey the dynamic, generative aspects of a work of art as it is to determine its merit as an art object or cultural icon. This willingness to approach art openly and without prejudice or predisposition, to examine it carefully and respectfully before deciding by which set of rules it shall be assessed, is a welcome indication that American art criticism is coming of age. It also suggests that art criticism is beginning to educate the public to a deeper understanding of the purposes and procedures of art. This is an encouraging development.

Pragmatic, eclectic art criticism is not easy to write. In addition to a broad and deep understanding of art, it requires a keen insight into the ideas and issues of the day, a thorough knowledge of the available kinds of art criticism, and the ability to distill complex thoughts and feelings into words and sentences that induce comprehension rather than confusion. As one writer has said, "If you could teach people to be critics, you could teach them to be human."[11] Difficult and challenging as this may be for the professional critic, it's obviously even more so for those who lack the necessary background and experience. Art teachers, although they have no interest in writing art criticism professionally, can usefully apply the insights and methods of the discipline in their classrooms.

Notes

1. For a discussion of Impressionist criticism and references to Oscar Wilde, Anatole France, and Walter Pater, see Jerome Stolnitz, *Aesthetics and Philosophy of Art Criticism: A Critical Introduction* (Boston: Houghton Mifflin, 1960), 475-78.

Donald Kuspit is quoted in Terry Barrett, *Criticizing Art: Understanding the Contemporary* (Mountain View, Calif.: Mayfield Publishing, 1994), 16.

2. Walter Pater, *The Renaissance* (London: Macmillan, 1924), 129-30; quoted in Harold Osborne, *The Art of Appreciation* (New York: Oxford University Press, 1970), 258. Appendix 3, "Reflection of Attitude and Interest in Critical Writing" in Osborne's book, contains a number of excerpts from art-critical writing.

3. Robert Pincus-Witten, *Eye to Eye: Twenty Years of Art Criticism* (Ann Arbor: UMI Research Press, 1984), 193-94; cf. Sun-Young Lee, "The Critical Writings of Robert Pincus-Witten," *Studies in Art Education* 36 (Winter 1995): 96-104.

4. Erie Loran, *Cézanne's Composition* (Berkeley: University of California Press, 1943). Loran's book, in fact, helped popularize the formalist approach to criticism, especially with art students, and upgraded Cézanne at the expense of the Impressionists.

5. See, for example, the dedication to Fry in Kenneth Clark's *Looking at Pictures* (New York: Holt, Rinehart and Winston, 1960).

6. Roger Fry, *Cézanne: A Study of His Development* (New York: Macmillan, 1927), 72-73, quoted in Jacob Rosenberg, *On Quality in Art: Criteria of Excellence, Past and Present* (Princeton: Princeton University Press, 1967), 110; cf. the discussion of Fry in A. W. Levi and R. A. Smith, *Art Education: A Critical Necessity* (Urbana: University of Illinois Press, 1991), 94-100.

7. Clement Greenberg, *The Collected Essays and Criticism*, ed. John O'Brian (Chicago: University of Chicago Press, 1988), 1:126.

8. Theodore E Wolff, *The Many Masks of Modern Art* (Boston: Christian Science Monitor Books, 1989), 100.

9. Greenberg, "Obituary of Mondrian," *Collected Essays*, 1:126.

10. For example, in *Out of the Whirlwind: Three Decades of Art Commentary* (Ann Arbor: UMI Research Press, 1987), Dore Ashton observes, "I don't have a critical method—common or otherwise. I am a fusion of many methods" (315).

11. Francis Sparshott, "Basic Film Aesthetics," in *The Philosophy of the Visual Arts,*. ed. Philip Alperson (New York: Oxford University Press, 1992), 335.

MARCIA MUELDER EATON

Philosophical Aesthetics: A Way of Knowing and Its Limits

Philosophical aesthetics is the study of the nature and components of aesthetic experience. This simple statement is, of course, a not-very-helpful gloss, for it immediately provokes the question, Just which experiences are aesthetic and who has them? And, in particular, Do children have them and, if they do, can they recognize them sufficiently to study them? I think there is ample evidence that children do have aesthetic experiences (though, of course, they may not call them that). A much tougher question is how we decide which experiences are aesthetic, that is, which experiences we want to study.

Perhaps the easiest way to distinguish aesthetic experiences from non-aesthetic ones is by considering the objects of those experiences rather than by trying to discover some commonalties in the experiences per se. Individuals and social groups, after all, respond and behave in very different ways when they have what they identify as aesthetic experiences. Is there some *one* way you always feel and feel only when you have what you identify as an aesthetic experience? Or think about what goes on when people listen to music. Some sit quietly with their eyes closed; others sit erectly on the edges of their seats; still others tap their feet, shake their shoulders, and generally exhibit lots of movement—all in response to the very same sounds. Similar behavioral variations are evident in the presence of literature, painting, dance, film, and so on.

But suppose we do give up on a behavioral definition of aesthetic experience and turn instead to the objects of those experiences—to the artifacts and natural objects that we refer to as "aesthetic objects." Again we face a vast array: symphonies, sonnets, sunsets, serigraphs, and so forth. Since anything, it seems, from coffee mugs to urinals, can be objects of aesthetic experience, one finds oneself immediately confronted with a puzzle if aesthetic experience is to be identified by its objects, not by some inner state or behavioral set, and if anything can be the object of aesthetic experience, then how can one ever distinguish aesthetic from nonaesthetic experiences? And if aesthetics is the study of aesthetic experience, how, then, can one know if one is doing aesthetics or not? This is the point I made in the first paragraph: as soon as one begins to *talk* about aesthetics, one is forced to *do* it!

This realization can make one's head spin. But at least one knows, then, that one's head is *working*, and this is a major goal of philosophical aesthetics. The admonition to include aesthetics in art curricula is a direct result of the belief that one crucial element of artistic activity is thinking about it. Too often art has been taught as if it were exclusively production or expression, as if, to use current pop-psychology lingo, it were exclusively a "right-brain" activity. We have been warned that too much thinking and talking about art stifles creativity. My own view is that this position is dead wrong. Quite the opposite is true: thinking and talking about art stimulate and reinforce creativity. Introducing aesthetics into art curricula recognizes that as important as manipulation and investigation of media and expression are, the value of art derives at least in part from the fact that it engages the left side of the brain as well. Reflecting upon our aesthetic experiences and their components is an important and rewarding discipline in itself; it can also be instrumental in drawing students into more rewarding productive activity.

But we are back at the problem of identifying aesthetic experiences. Fortunately for the purposes of incorporating aesthetics into art education, the problem of deciding which experiences are of interest to us is a bit easier to get a handle on than one might initially think. For the class of *objects* that are of interest is already bounded to some extent, namely to *art objects*. Thus the study of the nature and components of aesthetic experience is directed at the nature and components of the experiences people have when they pay attention to artworks. (Later I shall indicate ways in which I think we might extend attention beyond artworks.)

One general way of approaching the nature of aesthetic experience is by asking what goes on when people look at paintings or read literature or listen to music or watch dances or films. But these activities are so diverse and complex that I prefer another approach. Many theorists have agreed that more specific questions can be directed at certain core components of these experiences:

A. the objects that are the focus of attention (artworks)
B. the makers—persons causually responsible for the objects' existence (artists, performers)
C. the attenders (readers, listeners, viewers—in general the audience)
D. the context of the experience (the art world or the society in which it is located)

Questions about each of these components individually and questions about the relations between and among them are at the heart of philosophical aesthetics.

Individual philosophers have emphasized one or more of these components, and for each of them many questions can be and have been raised. And various answers have been suggested. Many of these answers are elegant and exciting and intrinsically worthy of detailed study. But the most important part of philosophy is articulating clear questions and encouraging students to develop their own positions; and this will, of course, involve some study of what people who have addressed them seriously and intelligently have contributed. Young people at different stages of development will formulate questions differently, but as soon as they begin to ask "Why?" (which we all know is *very* young), they are able and willing to engage in philosophy, for the why-question is at the heart of philosophy, and the readiness with which it is asked is the sure sign that all human beings are philosophers by nature. When "Why?" is directed at artworks, students are able and willing to do philosophy of art or philosophical aesthetics. (In addition to "Why?" there are, of course, other questions that both philosophers and nonphilosophers ask: "What?", "When?", "Who?", and even "Who cares?"—a question that often takes the place of "Why?" when the natural curiosity of people is stifled too long.)

Students at different levels will also, of course, find the contributions of philosophers more or less helpful. Five-year-olds will not read Plato, but some fifteen-year-olds will find some of his writings exciting, if challenging. The latter group love to debate the issue of whether art is "real," and even some five-year-olds are able to think about whether pictures of beds are "as real" as the bed they sleep in. Teachers will discover for themselves which questions work and which philosophers' answers are accessible.

Each of the components A to D above has particular questions traditionally associated with it. (Students may come up with their own and should certainly be encouraged to do so.) These perennial questions are a good starting point. I cannot provide anything like a comprehensive list here, but I hope the following will be suggestive.[1]

A. *Objects*: What is art? What is beauty (or aesthetic properties such as gracefulness, harmony, unity)? Which properties of objects serve to represent, express, convey ideas, act as symbols? What is the metaphysical status of the work: is there only one of its kind (as the *Mona Lisa*) or several (as *Hamlet*)? Is there a difference between form and content? What role does each play? Is there a difference between art and craft?

B. *Makers*: What is creation? What is creativity? What role do artists' intentions play in descriptions and evaluations of their work? How is what a work expresses related to the artist—if a painting is sad, must the artist have been sad when he or she produced it? Is artistic activity primarily intellectual or emotional?

C. *Attenders*: What is an aesthetic experience? What is the role of aesthetic scanning? Why is it important?[2] What is the role of emotion? What is the role of intellect? What is the role of taste? To what extent is aesthetic experience removed from or connected to everyday life? What is the nature of criticism? Are some interpretations of works better than others? Why are aesthetic experiences valuable? If one thinks a work is beautiful, must one also enjoy it? Does criticism affect aesthetic response?

D. *Context*: How is aesthetic value related to other values, for instance, economic, religious, ethical, political, ecological? How does culture determine which objects are art or which objects have aesthetic value? Is censorship ever justified? What role do traditions and history play in creation, interpretation, evaluation? What should public policies be with respect to art? What institutions play primary roles in shaping aesthetic experiences?

Again, teachers can "translate" such questions to accommodate different levels of student development. For example, the question Which properties of objects serve to represent ideas? may for beginners (and there are beginners of all ages—some fifty-year-olds have had very little experiences with sustained questioning about art) take the form of asking what colors can be seen, or whether the music is fast or slow, or whether one can hear rhyming words. One can go on to ask what the colors or speed or rhymes have to do with specific objects or ideas that are represented. Much later, as students become more adept at description and interpretation, more general philosophical issues can be raised: what does color (or tempo or rhythm) have to do with representation in general?

Another way to understand what aesthetics is, is by comparing and contrasting it with art production, art history, and art criticism. Although I believe one cannot separate these activities precisely from one another, one can see differences in emphases. Consider, for example, representation and expression. (Although these examples come from the visual arts, they can be "translated" into other arts forms.)

Representation:
1. Production: Make a pencil drawing of a horse.
2. History: Study the ways horses have been represented in different periods.
3. Criticism: Decide whether this is a good drawing of a horse and give your reasons.
4. Aesthetics: What does Plato say about the role of representation in art? Furthermore, since 1, 2, and 3 all play an important role in aesthetic experience, and since aesthetics raises general questions about this experience, there are philosophical questions that can be raised about each. For example:
    4.1 What makes x a representation of a horse? Fill in the blank "X is a representation of a horse if and only if _____."
    4.2 How is historical context relevant to determining whether a particular representation of a horse comes from one century rather than another, from one country rather than another? Does an artist's intention make something a representation of one thing rather than another?
    4.3 What makes something a good reason in support of an interpretation or evaluation? Do facts settle questions about whether works are good or bad representations? Is the fact that a given work is a representation of a horse rather than a pig relevant to its evaluation?
Expression:
1. Production: Make a sad papier mâché mask.
2. History: How has sadness been expressed in different periods and cultures?
3. Criticism: Is this a successful expression of sadness?
4. What is Tolstoy's expression theory of art?
    And again, play-offs from 1, 2, and 3:
    4.1 What makes this sad rather than happy? Fill in the blank "X expresses y if and only if _____."
    4.2 Does one have to know something about the artist's life or culture in order to know that a mask is sad?
    4.3 Is sadness relevant to evaluation? Could a mask that the artist intends to be sad but that makes us happy be a good mask?

There will always be overlap when art educators think of what they are doing as "whole-brain" activity. Evaluation—asking, "What makes a good x?"—will not only require studying how individual philosophers have answered this question, but will also require thinking about how x's are made, whether people in other cultures and times have also made x's, why members of a culture do or do not bother to make x's, and so on.

Including aesthetics in art education can have two different thrusts: asking philosophical questions in the context of artworks for the sake of asking itself and asking philosophical questions as a way of directing attention to specific artworks. Both are valuable, though of course as a philosopher, I will be more apt to find the former satisfying. One may ask, "What is art?" because the question is interesting in itself or because dealing with it sheds light on important developments in twentieth-century Western art. I favor an *aesthetic education* that includes art education rather than vice versa. For one thing, I think there are important aesthetic issues—aesthetic problems having to do with the environment, for example—that students should be made aware of. How do people's landscape preferences differ from culture to culture, region to region? How can different preferences be handled by public policies? Are ecologically sound environments more beautiful than those which are unhealthy? I believe aesthetic education could meaningfully be extended to cover such issues.

Notes

1. There are several introductory books. I recommend George Dickie, *Aesthetics: An Introduction* (New York: Pegasus Books, 1971); Anne Shepard, *Aesthetics: An Introduction to the Philosophy of Art* (Oxford: Oxford University Press, 1987); and, of course, Marcia Muelder Eaton, *Basic Issues in Aesthetics* (Belmont, Calif.: Wadsworth Publishing, 1988).

2. Too often, "aesthetics" has been *defined* as "aesthetic scanning." As this essay will show, I think aesthetics involves much more than the description of a work's properties.

Anita Silvers

The Art World and the Disciplines of DBAE

Some say that nothing short of a time machine to transport American education back to its purported Golden Age could satisfy the current educational reform movement. The message broadcast by a multitude of reforming commissions and best-selling authors like Allan Bloom and E. D. Hirsch has appeal because it promises that we can retrieve an ordered, purposeful curriculum and world. Nor should we too hastily assume that the past is impossible to recreate, especially when the past's most desirable features are its ideals.

After all, the attraction of ideals lies in their being sought, not necessarily in their being attained. But to be realistic in pursuing ideals, we must comprehend how what is essentially abstract nevertheless is learned concretely. We need to understand how the direct, concrete perception of an ideal instance or paradigm or key image can communicate what is general, and consequently can have significance beyond the immediate moment. To the extent we master this crucial cognitive strategy, we can improve how we train teachers to teach tradition and values, as well as how we teach them to teach art.

For many reasons—among which is the affinity of contemporary psychological theories with the nineteenth-century romanticism that celebrated artistic creativity—the shift from teaching common content to developing individual potential proved fertile for education in art. Departing from their academic predecessors, twentieth-century art educators displayed reluctance to rely on the masterworks of the field as guides, even though the appreciation of modern and postmodern art incorporates essential references to historical masterworks. But perhaps because of the critical linkages of art to its own history, art studies did not beat as hasty a retreat from subject-matter content as happened elsewhere in education.

Nothing could diverge further from the approach of an art educator like Joshua Reynolds, founder of the Royal Academy, than John Dewey's approach to education in art. Post-Deweyan art educators avoided in-hibiting students by imposing paradigms of great art. For shared im-ages, shared tradition, and shared values, they substituted appeals to students' common psychological development to justify a curriculum. Despite them, Dewey himself observed, learning about art remains part of learning about cultures. So art education can play a very special role in conveying tradition from past to present.

Whereas we cannot directly encounter events or persons from the past, art objects available to past persons can be equally available to us. Through direct, concrete perception of the objects our ancestors also perceived, informed by the narrative and theoretical frameworks through which they looked at these same objects, we can share appreciation of Raphael's paintings with Vasari, Joshua Reynolds, and Clive Bell, and appreciation of Chartres with Henry Adams as well as with its Gothic builders. In so studying art, we can look directly at the perceived ideals, visual paradigms, or key images of present or past persons or societies. Thus, to master the subject-matter content of art is to possess at least partial mastery of tradition and culture.

What is the subject-matter content of art? A way of answering this especially attuned to Postmodernism is what aestheticians call "the In-stitutional Theory of Art." This theory posits a special kind of world, the art world, as a fundamental explanatory concept. The art world has a special kind of history, methodologically different from the history of events. The art world is delineated by certain institutions constructed out of characteristic practices informed by commonly acknowledged, but not necessarily commonly accepted, narrative histories and evalua-tive theories. The art-world institutions define, at any time and place, what objects are included in the collection of works of art. Consequently, mastery of the subject matter of art requires participation in the art world's institutions, which means skillful engagement in the art world's institutional practices, which in turn presumes facility in furnishing and framing narrative histories and evaluative theories, so as to be able to distinguish between art and nonart in producing and in appreciating aesthetic objects.

A corollary of the institutional account is that mastering the disci-plines of art making, art historical narration, art criticism, and aesthetics is central to participating in the art world. To teach teachers to devise concrete learning activities for engaging students in the art world re-quires collaboration among the practitioners of the art studies' disci-plines. The special character of the art world prohibits divorcing instruc-tional strategy from content. This is an implication of one of the romantics' important insights: that art cannot be constrained according to rules. Because each work, and each style or period, is the ultimate arbiter of which theories or principles illuminate it, one cannot understand what teaching strategies effectuate learning about a work, style, or period prior to understanding the work, style, or period itself.

To be concrete about what teachers would be taught, let us explore a concrete instance of what they should teach. The following example of a DBAE lesson was adapted from an article in the *Los Angeles Times Magazine* (1985) to serve to introduce the essay "Becoming Students of Art," by Clark, Day, and Greer *(The Journal of Aesthetic Education,* Vol. 21, No. 2, Summer 1987).

> The fourth-grade students examine the face of a woman projected on the wall in their classroom. The face is expressionless and the children describe it, noting the kinds of lines and colors used by the artist. The image changes as another face is projected. The woman has a different expression; her eyebrows are knit and her mouth takes a dive. After mimicking her attitude by pulling their own faces into dramatic frowns, the children agree. This is not a face that expresses joy.
>
> Lights snap on and the children go to work drawing and painting expressive faces. After assessing their own artwork, the children see a picture of a sculpture by German artist Wilhelm Lehmbruck and hear that his melancholy bronze figures reflect his depression about World War I. So ends a session on the shape of human emotions.
>
> "Bring me a van Gogh, a Homer, and a Renoir," the teacher suddenly instructs the boy in her class. Reacting as though these are his best friends' names, he quickly extracts reproductions of the artists' paintings from a large bin of prints. "Who painted this picture?" the teacher asks elevating a Vincent van Gogh Self-Portrait. Several hands shoot up. Having dispensed with artistic identification, the youngsters analyze the painting's swirling strokes, intense color, and, again, the sadness of the face.
>
> The class moves on to Winslow Homer's *Snap the Whip,* noting the artist's penchant for dramatic movement, and then to a sunny French Impressionist landscape by Pierre Auguste Renoir. Wildly waving a hand until he's called upon, a dark-haired boy offers his interpretation of Renoir's painting "Oh, you do love the Impressionists" laughs the teacher.

During this lesson, the fourth graders have engaged in various activities that might be elements of developing their mastery of art:

1.   They have *attributed expressive properties* to drawings of the human face by identifying the lines and colors constitutive of pictured expression and by associating the looks of the drawings with the looks on their own faces when they express emotion.

2. They have *given meaning* to a sculpture by connecting its expressive properties with both the feelings and the historical situation of the artist who made the sculpture.
3. They have *evaluated* new works of art.
4. They have *recognized the styles* of various artists.
5. They have *interpreted* some well-known works.

Or have they?

A skeptic might claim that these fourth graders are mimicking, rather than mastering, the appreciation of art. Suppose that their identification of van Goghs, Whistlers, and Renoirs results from their having memorized who painted each painting, much as they memorize the multiplication table, rather than from their recognizing stylistic characteristics? Suppose what they mean when they attribute expressiveness to the drawings is simply that the drawn faces reproduce the looks typically adopted when humans emote, so that their reason for saying that Hals's and Cassatt's portraits of elderly women express happiness is merely that both paintings depict smiling faces. If this is the case, how can they perceive pictures without faces as expressing happiness? Suppose that, having heard Lehmbruck's story (i.e., the story *about* him), they decide his sculptures must be melancholy before they see them. If these are the sorts of reasons that guide children's activities, the skeptic might charge that their teacher's approach inhibits rather than improves their competence to deal with the aesthetic domain.

From the *Los Angeles Times* account, we cannot tell whether the youngsters are genuinely studying art, or whether they are misled into thinking that learning about art is just like learning math and social studies. While I have no quarrel with those who contend that the classroom activities depicted in this account may be effective introductions to art, I am sure that a crucial test of how effective such introductory studies are lies not in whether children learn to deal with clear cases, amenable to noncontroversial resolutions, but in how they respond to cases in which rote learning, rules, and recipes do not suffice.

For one thing, such puzzling cases probably are more reflective of the high points of art study than are unchallenging ones. In attributing, interpreting, assessing, and in other characteristically aesthetic activities, we enjoy artworks for their individuality by rendering their idiosyncrasies intelligible. It is in appreciation of the uniqueness of art that our most memorable aesthetic enjoyment lies.

Also, challenging cases invigorate the process of reason-giving. Puzzle cases are intriguing in virtue of their omitting, or violating, conditions otherwise assumed, relied on, or taken for granted in clear cases.

As a result, we must puzzle out what we see in the absence of some of the reasons and cues usually available to inform our perception. In so doing, we attend more reflectively to those features of the work that remain available to serve as illuminating reasons.

Pedagogically, puzzling out and thus developing conclusions affords two related benefits. First, typically overlooked features, those obscured in straightforward instances by the very clarity with which the cases are resolved, have a chance in puzzling cases to receive their appreciative due (this phenomenon is taken advantage of in much postmodern art). Second, reason-giving itself becomes a more explicit and reflective process, more masterfully commanded by the reason-giver.

As instructional strategies and subject-matter content are inextricably intertwined, so mastery of appreciative skills is inseparable from knowledge of art. This promotes a curriculum in which challenging cases occasion students to acquire a knowledge of art, to exercise skills in creating interpretive and evaluative conclusions, and to prompt reflection on the aesthetic concepts and methodologies invoked during these processes. Such a course could suit both the general-education and teacher-education curricula, particularly if it were designed and taught collaboratively.

Here is a sample college class that is structured somewhat unrealistically so as to parallel the fourth-grade class. It is essential to this class's success that the course or curriculum in which it is embedded has given students foundational learning in the history and theory of art. Only when on a firm foundation of knowledge are students secure enough for puzzles to be productive for learning.

> The college students examine the face of a woman projected on the wall in their classroom. The face is expressionless and the students describe it. The image changes as the same face, now thickly covered with white makeup, is projected. The students consider whether the second picture is more expressive than the first. Da-wei, who accompanies his grandfather to performances of Chinese opera, proposes that the second picture reveals the subject's craftiness. Tanya, who has recently seen Walt Kuhn's *The White Clown*, agrees that the second image is more expressive than the first, but she attributes an expression of sadness to it. The students discuss whether they are contradicting each other when one says the face expresses craftiness because it is white and the other says it expresses sadness because it is white. One of them wonders whether the paleness of the face portrayed in Roger van der Weyden's *Portrait of a Lady* makes the lady seem sad or crafty.
>
> "Bring me a David, a Chardin, and a Fragonard," the teacher suddenly instructs. A student quickly extracts reproductions of the artists'

paintings from a large bin of prints. "Who painted this picture?" the teacher asks, elevating a copy of the portrait of *Mademoiselle Charlotte du Val d'Ognes*, which was bought by the Metropolitan Museum of Art in 1922 to represent the work of Jacques-Louis David in its collection. Several hands shoot up. Having dispensed with artistic identification by noting the 1951 discovery that the work probably was painted by David's student Constance Charpentier, one of the students quotes a critic of the 1950s to prove that the Met's curator had been negligent or incompetent in attributing the painting to David: "Its poetry, literary rather than plastic, its very evident charms, and its cleverly concealed weaknesses . . . all seem to reveal the feminine spirit." The students argue about whether interpreting the painting as poetic and feminine is the cause, or the effect, of attributing it to a woman painter. They compare its charm, its femininity, and its weaknesses to the other pictures pulled from the bin: Chardin's *The Young Governess*, David's *Madame David*, and Fragonard's *A Young Girl Reading*.

Next the students see a picture of Veronese's painting titled *The Feast in the House of Levi* and hear that its original title was *The Feast in the House of Simon*, i.e., the Last Supper. Veronese was accused of heresy because he included a figure whose nose is bleeding, another who flourishes a toothpick to clean his teeth, and St. Peter carving while the apostle next to him holds out his plate impatiently. The judges of the Inquisition believed these images mocked church doctrine and gave Veronese three months to revise the painting by eliminating them. Instead, Veronese renamed the painting *The Feast in the House of Levi*, and it no longer struck the inquisitors as expressing scorn of the church. The students consider whether Veronese's painting is still a painting of the Last Supper, whether changing the title could change what the picture expresses, and why Veronese took the risk of revising only the title but not the painted surface.

The class moves on to Leonardo da Vinci's *Mona Lisa*, noting the artist's penchant for ambiguity, and then on to some variations on the image: Duchamp's and Dali's mustached paintings, an ad for Levelor blinds, a reproduction of da Vinci's painting on which one of the students has painted a pink and green punk hairdo and a spike necklace. Wildly waving a hand until he's called on, a pink-and-greenhaired boy insists that all the versions of Mona Lisa are equally art. "Oh, you do love Postmodernism," laughs the teacher.

How is the college lesson advanced beyond the fourth-grade one? The college students engage in the same characteristically aesthetic activities that the younger students do. They attribute expressive properties, recognize styles, interpret, give meaning, and evaluate. But, unlike the fourth-grade lesson, the cases that constitute the college-level lesson do not admit of a single clearly correct response, nor could any student

Anita Silvers

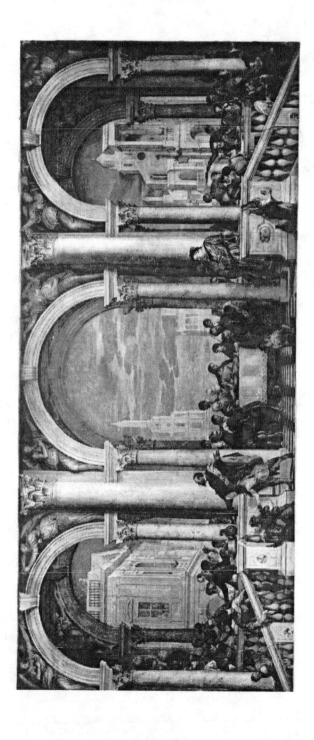

Paolo Veronese, *The Feast in the House of Levi*, 1573. Galleria dell' Accademia, Venice.

succeed with a simple yes or no. Addressing any of the cases convincingly is a complex cognitive activity requiring the giving of reasons of various kinds, all of which derive their relevance by appeal to implicit or explicit art historical, art critical, or aesthetic narratives or theories.

What point is there in worrying about whether Veronese's painting glorifies the sacred or the profane or profanes the sacred? If we were teaching biology or French, it probably would be an instructional error to present students with complex or borderline examples until their mastery had become sophisticated. But the subject-matter content of art is unlike that of naturalistic studies. We bring students to appreciate nature by revealing the lawlike operations and systems and reiterated regularities that underlie what may first appear chaotic and unorganized. In contrast, we bring students to appreciate art by revealing the novel or original method of effecting intelligibility in what may first appear chaotic and unorganized.

In the Veronese case, confusion is exacerbated by the insouciance with which Veronese changed the painting's name. Veronese's action appears to rule out our taking the painting to depict a historical event, because changing the reference to a depicted event did not require changing the picture. Often, titles are relied on to provide evidence of what paintings depict, and what a painting depicts indicates what the picture means. Here, this kind of clue is eliminated. We can identify the referents of at least some of the figures (for instance, Christ and the apostles), but the title change obscures our identifying the depicted event.

Without clearly recognizing the event, can we determine how the pictured sacred and profane figures relate to one another from internal evidence alone? What is the composition of the work, and in what patterns does it draw the eye? What is the function of the architecture in the composition? These questions, although they are internal, are illuminated by contrasting Veronese's painting with other treatments: Veronese's overcrowded dinner compared with Leonardo's less populated one, Raphael's imposition of unifying geometrical shape upon architecture and gesture compared to Veronese's more distracting uses of the same shapes. Successful comparisons enhance our perception of whatever is compared, and we come to perceive Veronese against the contrast of his predecessor painters.

Art critical and art historical reason-giving effectively draws attention to, rather than abstracts from, the directly perceived properties of the works themselves. Even that part of the process that might be thought to direct our perception away from the Veronese to other paintings actually helps us see more about each painting, including the Veronese. Does the Veronese have a crowded, chaotic look, or is it dense but organized? How does it appear when considered as a successor to Raphael's *School of Athens*? How does it appear when considered as a predecessor of Frith's *Paddington Station*?

And in looking at and thinking about this puzzle, do we not also address another, more abstract puzzle: the interfacing of the sacred and the profane in the physical world? By struggling to resolve this puzzle as it appears in the case of the Veronese painting, we can retrieve understanding and revitalize experience of abstractions that are crucial elements of culture and tradition. We bring our mastery of the skills and knowledge of art criticism and art history to bear to adopt or construct a conceptual or philosophical framework that places this Veronese painting in perceived relationships that expand our aesthetic and cultural appreciation.

To reflect the individuality of appreciative experience, to promote the integration of application and theory, and to stimulate sensitivity to the conceptual framework itself (for Kant and Coleridge, a key element in aesthetic experience), treatment of challenging cases is crucial to the curriculum. I have used a college-level class to illustrate the mastery we should expect from our preservice students. The skills acquired in such a challenging college course can be used with advantage to create appropriately similar challenges for younger students. Here the experience of art educators is particularly important. To provide the foundation on which students can engage art puzzles, art historians, critics, and aestheticians can use guidance in sequencing their presentations of foundational knowledge. For example, we are inclined to introduce art history to adults chronologically because its methodology is so profoundly evolutionary, but this may not be the best pedagogical sequence to employ for children.

Because art studies cannot abandon the concrete, they are anchored in immediate perception and consequently are suited to children's cognitive abilities. For children as well as adults, the process of unlocking key images can retrieve or recreate crucial cultural principles and occasion comprehension of abstractions that have informed cultures of the past. This potential permits art educators to respond to the reform movement's call for education that retrieves and revitalizes tradition and culture. If art educators accept the challenge, the growth art education enjoyed during the shift away from core curricula can be maintained now that education is shifting back.

Reading Suggestions for Part Two

Art Making (Artistic Creation)
Brown, Maurice and Diana Korzenik. *Art Making and Education*. Urbana: University of Illinois Press, 1993. A volume in the series Disciplines in Art Education.
Feldman, Edmund B. *The Artist*. Englewood Cliffs, N.J.: Prentice-Hall, 1982.
Zurmuehlen, Marilyn. *Studio Art: Praxis, Symbol, Presence*. Reston, Va.: National Art Education Society, 1990.

Burton, Judith M. "Once More with Feeling: The Discipline of Art/The Art of Discipline." In *Discipline in Art: An Interdisciplinary Symposium*, ed. Thomas Ewens. Providence: Rhode Island School of Design, 1986, 89-114.
Emshwiller, Ed. "Inside, Outside Inside, Out." In *Inheriting the Theory: New Voices and Multiple Perspectives*. Los Angeles: Getty Center for Education in the Arts, 1996, 3-4. Seminar summary of remarks.
Goldyne, Joseph. "The Uniqueness and Overlap among Art Production, Art History, Art Criticism, and Aesthetics: An Artist's Viewpoint." In *The Preservice Challenge: Discipline-Based Art Education and Recent Reports in Higher Education*. Los Angeles: Getty Center for Education in the Arts, 1988, 163-69.
Greer, W. Dwaine. "Hospers on Artistic Creativity." *The Journal of Aesthetic Education* 20, no. 4 (1986): 62-64.
Korzenik, Diana. "The Studio Artists." In *Coming Together Again: Art History, Art Criticism, Art Studies, Aesthetics*, ed. Eldon Katter. Kutztown, Pa.: College of Visual and Performing Arts, Kutztown University, 1984, 17 pp.
Richmond, Stuart. "In Praise of Practice: A Defense of Art Making in Education." *The Journal of Aesthetic Education* 32, no. 2 (1998): 11-20.
Spratt, Frederick. "Art Production in Discipline-Based Art Education." In *Discipline-Based Art Education: Origins, Meaning, Development*, ed. Ralph A. Smith. Urbana: University of Illinois Press, 1989, 197-204. A book made from a special issue of *The Journal of Aesthetic Education* 21, no. 2 (1987) on DBAE.
Wilson, Brent. "Studio-Based Scholarship: Making Art to Know Art." In *Collected Papers, Pennsylvania's Symposium III on the Role of Studies in Art Education*; ed. Joseph B. DeAngelis. Harrisburg: Pennsylvania Department of Education, 1989, 11-20.

Art History

Addiss, Stephen, and Mary Erickson. *Art History and Education.* Urbana: University of Illinois Press, 1993. A volume in the series Disciplines in Art Education.

Bakewell, Elizabeth, William O. Beeman, and Carol McMichael Reese. *Object, Image, Inquiry: The Art Historian at Work.* Santa Monica, Calif.: J. Paul Getty Trust, 1988.

Collins, Bradford R. "What Is Art History?" *Art Education* 44, no. 1 (1991): 53-59.

Ebitz, David. "The Uniqueness and Overlap Among Art Production, Art History, Art Criticism, and Aesthetics: The View from Art History." In *The Preservice Challenge: Discipline-Based Art Education and Recent Reports on Higher Education.* Los Angeles: Getty Center for Education in the Arts, 1988, 156-62.

Erickson, Mary. "Styles of Historical Investigation." *Studies in Art Education* 26, no. 2 (1985): 121-24.

Janson, Anthony F. "The Personal Importance of Art History." *The Journal of Aesthetic Education* 25, no. 4 (1991): 121-25.

Kleinbaurer, W. Eugene. "Art History in Discipline-Based Art Education." In *Discipline-Based Art Education: Origins, Meaning, Development,* ed. Ralph A. Smith. Urbana: University of Illinois Press, 1989, 205-15.

Levi, Albert William. "Kunstgeschichte als Geistesgeschichte: The Lesson of Panofsky." *The Journal of Aesthetic Education* 20, no. 4 (1986): 79-83.

Rice, Danielle. "The Uses and Abuses of Art History." In *Collected Papers: Pennsylvania's Symposium II on Art Education and Art History,* ed. Joseph B. DeAngelis. Harrisburg: Pennsylvania Department of Education, 1989, 7-14.

Simmons, Sherwin. "Art History and Art Criticism: Changing Voice(s) of Authority." *Controversies in Art and Culture* 3, no. 1 (1990): 54-63.

Smith, Ralph A. "The Tradition of Art: Art History." In *Art Education: A Critical Necessity,* by Albert William Levi and Ralph A. Smith. Urbana: University of Illinois Press, 1991, 54-86.

Art Criticism

Barrett, Terry. *Criticizing Art: Understanding the Contemporary.* Mountain View, Calif.: Mayfield, 1994.

Feldman, Edmund B., *Practical Art Criticism.* Englewood Cliffs, N.J.: Prentice-Hall, 1993.

Wolff, Theodore and George Geahigan. *Art Criticism and Education.* Urbana: University of Illinois Press, 1997. A volume in the Disciplines in Art Education series.

Anderson, Tom. "The Content of Art Criticism." *Art Education* 44, no. 1 (1991): 16-24.

Barrett, Terry. "Description in Professional Art Criticism." *Studies in Art Education* 32, no. 2 (1991): 83-93.

Geahigan, George. "Art Criticism: An Analysis of the Concept." *Visual Arts Research* 9, no. 17 (1983): 10-22.

Meynell, Hugo. "On the Nature of Art Criticism." *The Journal Aesthetic Education* 20, no. 4 (1986): 94-99.

Risatti, Howard. "Art Criticism in Discipline-Based Art Education." *The Journal of Aesthetic Education* 21, no. 2 (1987): 217-25.

Schulze, Franz. "The Uniqueness and Overlap among Art History, Art Criticism, and Aesthetics: The View from Art Criticism." In *The Preservice Challenge: Discipline-Based Art Education and Recent Reports on Higher Education.* Los Angeles: Getty Center for Education in the Arts, 1988, 170-73.

Smith, Ralph A. "The Critique of Art: Art Criticism." In *Art Education: A Critical Necessity* by Levi and Smith. Urbana: University of Illinois Press, 1991, 87-123.

Vallance, Elizabeth. "Art Criticism as Subject Matter in Schools and Art Museums." *The Journal of Aesthetic Education* 22, no. 4 (1988): 69-81.

Wolff, Theodore F. "The Values and Work of the Art Critic." In *Art Criticism and Education* by Theodore Wolff and George Geahigan. Urbana: University of Illinois Press, 1997, 33-66.

Aesthetics

Kaelin, E. F. *An Aesthetics for Art Educators.* New York: Teachers College Press, 1989.

Lankford, Louis. *Aesthetics: Issues and Inquiry.* Reston, Va.: National Art Education Association, 1992.

Moore, Ronald E., ed. *Aesthetics for Young People.* Reston, Va.: National Art Education Association, 1994.

Parsons, Michael J., and H. Gene Blocker. *Aesthetics and Education.* Urbana: University of Illinois Press. A volume in the series Disciplines in Art Education.

Smith, Ralph A., and Alan Simpson, eds. *Aesthetics and Art Education.* Urbana: University of Illinois Press, 1991.

Battin, Margaret P. "The Contributions of Aesthetics." In *Research Readings for Discipline-Based Art Education,* ed. Stephen Mark Dobbs. Reston, Va.: National Art Education Association, 1988, 126-29.

Best, David. "Aesthetics: Theory and Practice." In *Dialogues with British Art Educators: Teaching Aesthetics, Art History, and Art Criticism*, ed. Al Hurwitz. Baltimore: Maryland Institute College of Art, 1987, 20-38.

Eaton, Marcia Muelder. "Context, Criticism, and Art Education: Putting Meaning into the Life of Sisyphus." *The Journal of Aesthetic Education* 24, no. 1 (1990): 95-110.

Eaton, Marcia Muelder. "Philosophical Aesthetics: A Way of Knowing and Its Limits." *The Journal of Aesthetic Education* 28, no. 3 (1994): 19-31. Also in Ronald Moore, ed. *Aesthetics for Young People*, 19-31.

Hagaman, Sally. "Philosophical Aesthetics in Art Education: A Further Look Toward Implementation." *Art Education* 43, no. 4 (1990): 22-24, 32-40.

Hamblen, Karen A. "Approaches for Aesthetics in Art Education: A Critical Theory Perspective." *Studies in Art Education* 29, no. 2 (1988): 81-90.

Parsons, Michael J., and H. Gene Blocker. "Aesthetics, Art, and the Aesthetic Object." In *Aesthetics and Education* by Michael J. Parsons and H. Gene Blocker. Urbana: University of Illinois Press, 1993.

Smith, Ralph A. "The Philosophy of Art: Aesthetics." In *Art Education: A Critical Necessity* by Levi and Smith. Urbana: University of Illinois Press, 1991, 124-52.

Silvers, Anita. "Vincent's Story: The Importance of Contextualism in Art Education." *The Journal of Aesthetic Education* 28, no. 3 (1994): 47-62. Also in Ronald Moore, ed. *Aesthetics for Young People*, 47-62.

Van de Pitte, M. M. "Discipline-Based Art Education and the New Aesthetics." *The Journal of Aesthetic Education* 28, no. 2 (1994): 1-14.

PART THREE

Curriculum

A. Teaching and Learning

B. Implementing and Evaluating

Introduction

A. Teaching and Learning

The task of making selections from an extensive literature is especially difficult when it comes to addressing the topic of curriculum, which here subsumes teaching, learning, implementation, and evaluation. What I've chosen is representative, but several other choices could have served equally well as readers who follow up some of the reading suggestions will discover. All the selections on teaching and learning stress inquiry learning in one form or other, perhaps to the point of underestimating the value of good didactic instruction. But it is clear that, as interpreted by major writers in the field, inquiry learning presupposes significant knowledge about art on the part of teachers. What is more, the grounding of DBAE in experiential learning is fully justified.

The importance of experiential learning and its relation to theoretical knowledge is discussed by Richard Lachapelle. While it may seem obvious that knowledge plays a part in any kind of worthwhile activity, Lachapelle refers to writers who not only claim such relations are important and necessary but also indicate how they can be construed in DBAE, for example, in art making, art history, art criticism, and aesthetics. He further refers to research to support his own model of the aesthetic encounter.

While the selections of Part One on the nature of DBAE's disciplines often discuss their relevance to teaching and even provide some recommendations, the writings selected for this section concentrate specifically on pedagogy and describe ways in which the content and methods of the disciplines can help achieve the goals of art education. Hence, Stuart Richmond discusses how art making can contribute to the basic goal of appreciation. In doing so he not only describes the nature of artistic process and how the young can be introduced to its practices, he also draws attention to statements by artists that support his contention. In addition to the value of the intrinsic gratification afforded the young in the creation of artworks, Richmond further addresses the intellectual, social, and moral aspects of art making.

In contrast to Richmond's discussion of the value of creative activities in cultivating aesthetic appreciation, Maurice Brown, in an excerpt from *Art Making and Education* (a volume in the Getty-sponsored series, Disciplines in Art Education: Contexts of Understanding), provides examples of his own efforts to involve students in acts of artistic expression. He also discusses attitudes toward the idea of creativity, current issues in the art world, and the relations of art making to the disciplines associated with DBAE. In doing so, Brown reveals the depth of his cultural literacy and its bearing on his work as a teacher and painter.

If Richmond and Brown talk about the role of artistry in reaching the goals of art education, David N. Perkins emphasizes critical inquiry into works of art as a way to develop what he calls the intelligent eye. In a Getty occasional paper that stresses learning to think by looking at art, Perkins covers topics ranging from the nature of art and intelligence to various knowledge and intelligence gaps and traps. All this is done with a view to developing reflective thinking, a capacity of mind that implies patience, open-mindedness, concern, commitment, persistence, and a spirit of investigation. The excerpt reprinted here explains why works of art are especially conducive to developing such thinking.

A good example of how inquiry learning has influenced the theory and practice of DBAE is Mary Erickson's distinction between art history and the history of art and art history as art-historical inquiry or process. Recommending the latter for its pedagogical benefits, she illustrates how various interweaving aspects of the art-historical process—reconstruction, description, attribution, interpretation, explanation—can be used to help students develop histories on their own, if not of major periods in the history of art, then of histories of art in their own communities.

In *Art Criticism and Education*, another volume in the series Disciplines in Art Education, Theodore Wolff and George Geahigan both provide pedagogical suggestions for teaching art criticism. Wolff's understanding is that of a practicing critic, Geahigan's that of an educational theorist who understands criticism as inquiry into the meaning and value in works of art. Geahigan indicates not only how art criticism can be translated into an instructional practice that aims to cultivate personal response to works of art but also how concept acquisition and student research can be construed as playing a role in teaching criticism.

Once more, although philosophies of art have often mentioned the bearing of aesthetics on pedagogy—for example, the writings of Ronald Moore, H. Gene Blocker, Marcia Muelder Eaton, Margaret Battin, and Anita Silvers—I have selected an article by Marilyn Galvin Stewart who has successfully applied the writings of aestheticians to teaching the young. Rejecting opinions that aesthetics is too difficult or irrelevant to art education, she discusses program rationales, learning goals, and instructional strategies that involve critical inquiry into the nature, meaning, and value of art. Statements of learning outcomes stress the acquisition of knowledge, inquiry skills, and appropriate dispositions. Instructional strategies consist of posing significant questions and using puzzles and case studies to stimulate discussion about a range of topics, aesthetic value among them. The excerpt reprinted here stresses learning outcomes.

Among the successful methods used for developing aesthetic literacy in DBAE workshops and institutes is one called aesthetic scanning, the purpose and scope of which, however, has often been misunderstood. As Broudy points out in the appendix to his Getty occasional paper, *The Role of Imagery in Learning*, aesthetic literacy *begins* with learning to perceive the sensory, formal, and expression properties of aesthetic images, but it does not stop there. Making an informed aesthetic response also involves historical criticism, imaginative apprehension of artistic meaning, and critical evaluation. Consistent with the theme of this section, aesthetic scanning is understood simply as aesthetic inquiry by another name. In terminology borrowed from Kenneth Clark's *Looking at Pictures* (New York, 1960, 71) aesthetic scanning may be said to consist of the kind scrutiny that follows the initial impact of a work and fuels further reflection.

B. Implementation, Evaluation, and Interdisciplinary Study

One consequence of the Getty venture in art education has been an increased concern with the nature of implementation and evaluation. A number of efforts have produced models and results such that it is now possible to speak of a substantive literature on these topics, although debate continues about what should be evaluated and with which methods.

The topics are well introduced by Michael D. Day who highlights the character of DBAE by means of an imaginary guided tour through a school with a DBAE program in place. Visitors, he writes, could not fail to notice that the art program is an essential component of the general curriculum, that art is taught regularly in strong courses in studio art as well as others emphasizing combinations of content from the disciplines associated with DBAE, that students who study art at advanced levels can choose courses concentrating on these disciplines and receive career counseling, and that in most courses numerous art images are used during instruction. This is only a sample of Day's significant contributions to DBAE. His *Discipline-Based Art Education: A Curriculum Sampler*, co-edited with Kay Alexander and listed in the reading suggestions, is a major document of DBAE.

The first major effort of the Getty Center to implement and evaluate efforts to reform the teaching of art in the elementary schools according to the principles of DBAE was the work of the Los Angles Getty Institute for Educators on the Visual Arts, directed by W. Dwaine Greer from 1982 to 1989. Emphasizing staff development, school teams of administrators, principals, and teachers, institutional change through curriculum development, and summer inservice programs, the evaluation concluded that successful implementation is a function of substantive teacher training, district-mandated written curricula, adequate resources, and committed leadership. The excerpt reprinted here is taken from Chapter 7, "Conclusions and Discussions of Problems."

Building on the findings of *Improving Visual Arts Education*, Brent Wilson and Blanche Rubin recall the second major Getty effort to reform art education, reported more fully in Wilson's *The Quiet Evolution: Changing the Face of Art Education*, an account of the first seven years of the activities of several Getty-supported regional institutes. Wilson and Rubin, who were the principal evaluators for the report, address a range of considerations involved in effecting change, in particular the problem of meshing the efforts of several relevant communities. The authors describe the mission of the regional institutes, interacting forces, descriptions of DBAE schools, the place of the disciplines in DBAE, instructional forms, and the values that informed their assessment.

Today any discussion of curriculum design and implementation must address questions of pluralism and cultural diversity, or multiculturalism generally. F. Graeme Chalmers's reflections on the topic are presented in a Getty occasional paper written from an essentially anthropological point of view. He believes this standpoint to be congruent with demographic projections, a functional definition of art, the evolution of DBAE, and a social reconstructionist interpretation of schooling that would have teachers of art encourage students to address pressing social problems. The excerpt reprinted here concentrates on the context, design, and implementation of a multicultural art education curriculum.

By definition DBAE implies some kind of interdisciplinary teaching and learning. The content and methods of the disciplines associated with DBAE must be selected and integrated in order to achieve goals and objectives. The purpose of a cooperative study of the Getty Center and the College Board was to discover if DBAE could further contribute to the integration of the curriculum generally, particularly with regard to strengthening its cognitive and substantive character. The initial report of a five-year study written by Bruce Boston describes the project and the role of cross-disciplinary studies in achieving stated outcomes. Assumed was that disciplinary competence is a precondition of cross-disciplinary competence.

A. Teaching and Learning

RICHARD LACHAPELLE

Experiental Learning and Discipline-based Art Education

For Clark, Day, and Greer (1987), works of art are at the center of experience-based learning in the visual arts. "Placing works of art at the center of DBAE provides a natural means for integrating learning from the four disciplines. In DBAE students should emerge with an integrated view of the visual arts based on *learning experiences* offered in their classrooms" (p. 170) (emphasis added). Smith (1987) also addresses the important role that experience plays during aesthetic encounters with works of art. He reminds us that text-based knowledge about a work of art is not a good substitute for the kinds of knowledge that are acquired during an actual encounter with the work.

> What is important to appreciate is the distinction between *knowledge about* art and *knowledge of*. The distinction implies that one may have substantial information about a work of art—information, say, about its origins, meaning, and influence—without ever having really experienced its expressive presence." (p. 6)

Smith quotes Frank Sibley to support and develop his argument: "Merely to learn from others, on good authority, that the music is serene, the play moving, or the picture unbalanced is of little aesthetic value; the crucial thing is to see, hear, or feel" (Sibley, 1965, p. 6). Smith then qualifies his stance: "Ideally, of course, relevant knowledge about a work should help one to experience it in the way indicated by Sibley, and most of the writing discussed in this essay assumes in one way or another that knowledge does indeed have an important bearing on both our interest in and experience of art" (p. 7).

Knowledge: The Complement of Experience

Smith has touched upon an important notion. Knowledge does have a key role to play in the way we undergo and understand our experiences and how we learn from them. In the published proceedings of the

1987 Getty Center for Education in the Arts National Invitation Seminar, art historian David Ebitz, like Smith, further expressed a concern for the need to integrate knowledge about art with the experiencing of art. In the Getty Center's summary of his address, he is reported to have said that: "specialization has created a gulf between intellectual knowledge and direct emotional experience. The art historian has become too dependent on the text as the primary source for understanding and knowledge of art; current modes of learning stress the 'content of knowledge' rather than the 'practice of inquiry'" (The J. P. Getty Trust, 1988, p. 19). Ebitz later reiterated this position: "This specialization [of the art disciplines] has compartmentalized experience and knowledge, going so far as to separate the kind of knowledge that we acquire from reading—book knowledge—from the experience we gain from actually doing something—the skills acquired by hand and eye" (Ebitz, 1989 b, p. 11).

Artist Joseph Goldyne (1988) examines the same concern from the artist's point of view; he proposes the notion of connoisseurship as an explanation of the interdependence of knowledge and experience during an aesthetic encounter with a work of art.

> What specifically does the connoisseur do that should interest a proponent of DBAE? The connoisseur looks first and enjoys looking carefully. But his looking is not that of a hedonist, as too frequently has been the allegation rendered by those who sense a weak academic base to the activity. Nothing should be further from the truth, for what one observes must, at once, be filtered through a considerable fund of both visual and historical data to rank as connoisseurship. When what the connoisseur has seen is in some way related to this data, a connection is noted. When enough connections are established the connoisseur will propose them as a new piece of knowledge—an attribution, forgery, relationship, or chronology. (p.167)

The process that Goldyne's connoisseur uses for investigating works of art resembles in some respects the "practice of inquiry" to which Ebitz refers. Both visual art experts are commenting on the complementary roles of knowledge and experience within the process of aesthetic experience. Ebitz talks in terms of "intellectual knowledge" and "direct emotional experience" while Goldyne uses the terms "visual and historical data" and "careful looking." The art historian and the artist may be using different terminology, but they are in agreement about the importance of both of these components in aesthetic understanding.

Csikszentmihalyi and Robinson (1990) have also examined the problem of the relationship between knowledge and experience within aesthetic experience. They bring to this discussion a different perspective, one from cognitive psychology.

> Despite the obvious importance of knowledge and education [in shaping aesthetic experiences], there is more at stake than the mere application of knowledge. . . . *Informed experience* is a good term to characterize the process by which exposure to works of art gradually transforms the nature—and the experience—of aesthetic interactions. Informed experience involves developing the ability to see as well as developing understanding. Many of the interviewees [in our study] saw the two processes as intimately related. . . . Knowledge means educational experience combined with seeing. (pp. 152-153)

Once again, two components are identified as the essential elements of aesthetic experience. In coining the term "informed experience" Csikszentmihalyi and Robinson have managed to encapsulate the very essence of aesthetic experience: aesthetic experience is the coming together, through a process of interaction, of the two key constituents, information and experience.

A Harvard researcher, David N. Perkins (1994) has examined how human intelligence is manifested in aesthetic responses to works of art. Perkins has concluded that the "intelligent behavior" evident in a person's aesthetic response involves three different types of intelligence: "neural intelligence," "experiential intelligence," and "reflective intelligence." Neural intelligence consists of "the contribution of the efficiency and precision of the nervous system to intelligent behavior." Experiential intelligence is "the contribution of intuitively applied prior experience to intelligent functioning." And reflective intelligence is "the contribution of mindful self-management and strategic deployment of one's intellectual resources to intelligent behavior" (pp. 13-14). Perkins uses the construct of "the intelligent eye" (pp. 7-11) to explain how the three intelligences described above come together during the course of an encounter with a work of art.

> The intelligence of the "the intelligent eye" lies in more than the reflexive work of eye and mind represented by experiential intelligence. The missing ingredient is reflective intelligence. In essence, reflective intelligence is a control system for experiential intelligence. By cultivating awareness of our thinking, asking ourselves good questions, guiding ourselves with strategies, we steer our experiential intelligence in fruitful directions. This steering function is reflective intelligence. (p. 15)

Reflective intelligence fulfills its steering function by compensating for the gaps that exist in our experiential intelligence. According to Perkins, the gaps in experiential knowledge that we are most likely to encounter during the course of an aesthetic experience are gaps in the "background knowledge" required to understand specific works of art and gaps in our "knowledge of art" itself.

The way in which Perkins has conceptualized the aesthetic encounter in terms of three different types of intelligence seems compatible with the thesis I have been developing in this discussion. His concept of "experiential intelligence" is sympathetic to my notion of "experiential learning." Furthermore, the function of Perkins's concept of "reflective intelligence" is essentially the same as that of "theoretical learning." As in the case of reflective intelligence, theoretical learning is an activity in which learners engage in order to fill gaps in their knowledge about the work of art, and its historical and social contexts.

During the course of my own research with adult museum visitors I have begun to understand that, for the viewer, each new encounter with a work of art is in fact a learning experience. Based on actual observations of adults' responses to selected works of art, I have developed a hypothetical model that has become the focus of my current research. *The Model of Aesthetic Understanding as Informed Experience* (Lachapelle, 1994) examines the process of aesthetic experience from the educator's perspective: it identifies the kinds of knowledge involved in aesthetic encounters with works of art, as well as the types of learning that occur in each stage of the process that leads to aesthetic understanding. Three theories informed the development of the model; these were: the *Model of Aesthetic Experience by Interaction* (Csikszentmihalyi & Robinson, 1990), the *Model of Learning as the Integration of Knowledge* (Artaud, 1989), and the *Model of Experiential Learning* (Kolb & Fry, 1 975; Kolb, 1984).

In *The Model of Aesthetic Understanding as Informed Experience*, the process of viewing and understanding a work of art is conceptualized as a two-phased type of informed experience. In the first phase, the viewer encounters the work of art through a process of experiential learning. During the second phase, a theoretical learning process is employed by the viewer as a means to confront a related body of theoretical knowledge. This two-phase process of learning results in a reconstruction of knowledge about the art object. Use of the two learning processes in tandem not only permits the viewer to expand his or her understanding of the work of art, it also favors aesthetic growth and development. During each new encounter with a work of art, the interaction of experiential and theoretical learning results in an expansion of the viewer's background knowledge in art, resulting in better preparedness to encounter the next work of art.

As I noted earlier in my reference to Smith, when it comes to appreciating and understanding a work of art there can be no substitute for an actual encounter with the work of art. Likewise, without some prior knowledge on the viewer's part about art in general and about the context and possible interpretations of the work of art in question, it is doubtful that the encounter between viewer and art object would ever take place. Those scholars whose work has been discussed here, all refer to the fact that aesthetic understanding requires two types of knowledge: experiential knowledge and theoretical knowledge. The viewer encountering the actual work of art learns about it through actual experience of it. However, no viewer ever approaches a work of art with an empty mind. Prior knowledge is necessary for a successful aesthetic encounter. Such knowledge can sometimes be acquired from the experiences provided by previous encounters with works of art. However, the greatest proportion of the prior knowledge we bring to our aesthetic encounters is theoretical in origin, acquired by studying the text-based work of art experts: art educators, art historians, art critics, and philosophers. These texts act as a source of information to guide and further the understanding of works of art.

Text-based or theoretical learning can take place either before the encounter with the art object or after it. The latter commonly occurs when a viewer does a little reading or research after seeing a work of art in order to seek answers to questions that arose during the course of the initial encounter. Theoretical knowledge, then, is knowledge about the work of art and about the historical, social, and aesthetic contexts that surround its creation. It usually exists in the form of printed text, but it can also be transmitted by other means such as verbal communication, or films and video. Such knowledge is the result of the work of art experts and, therefore, it is the product of discipline-based inquiry.

Experiential and Theoretical Learning Within the Four DBAE Disciplines

An adequate curriculum in aesthetic education needs to be modeled on the actual activities undertaken during the course of successful aesthetic experiences, both in the studio and in the art museum. In other words, students need to learn the skills that will allow them to engage favorably in these activities.

Experiential and theoretical learning interact in the context of art criticism activities. There can be no question that art criticism, for example, requires an actual experiential encounter with the work of art, and that the learning this involves is both challenging and rewarding.

Furthermore, there is no doubt that without the insight provided by external sources of information about the work of art, the student's appreciation of the work of art will not proceed beyond limited, idiosyncratic understanding. Student learning in art criticism requires both experiential and theoretical learning.

Can the same be said for the other three disciplines: art production, art history, and aesthetics? Is learning in each of these disciplines enhanced by the interaction of experience-based and theory-based learning?

The activity of responding to works of art is a key factor in all four DBAE disciplines. One of the ten defining characteristics of a DBAE program, as proposed by Clark, Day, and Greer (1987), is that "works of art are central to the organization of curricula and to integration of content from the disciplines" (p. 135). The visual and critical analysis of works of art is a major component of the process of inquiry used in art criticism and figures prominently in the processes of inquiry that are specific to the study of art history and aesthetics. Not surprisingly, visual and critical analysis is also a key element in the process of making works of art. Since the disciplinary practices specific to each of the four disciplines require that the student engage in aesthetic encounters with works of art, we can conclude that, inasmuch as those aesthetic encounters are concerned, the process of inquiry of each discipline requires the use of both experience-based and text-based sources of knowledge.

However, each discipline provides its own specific opportunities for experiential and theoretical learning. There can be no doubt that studio art provides ample opportunities for experiential learning. This has been the very foundation of art education practice for decades. Students learn the skills required for drawing, painting, sculpture, ceramics, photography and video by engaging in activities which require that they hone different aspects of these skills. Making art, however, is not just a question of technique and craft.

> Producing art, from conception to conclusion, involves a range of human processes that include thought, perception, feeling, imagination, and, importantly, action. Exercise of these processes contributes to their development and can lead to the sophisticated judgment and critical sensitivity needed to deal with today's complex visual stimuli and multimedia statements. (Spratt, 1987, p. 199)

In Spratt's terms, art production is a very complex activity, one that involves all facets of intelligence. For this reason, the development of many of the skills required in art production can be assisted, up to a point, by learning experiences that are text-based. For example, students can hone their skills in the use of color by reading and studying color theory. They can learn about the basic chemical formula required for making new glazes for use in ceramics by studying the theory of glazing. Students and teachers regularly turn to books for answers to problems of a technical nature in photography, printmaking, sculpture, and other media. Accordingly, in the study of art production theoretical learning is an essential complement to the experience-based learning involved in art making.

Art history can provide ample opportunities for both experiential and theoretical learning.

> Art history is the branch of knowledge or learning that involves the investigation and interpretation of works of art. . . . Concerning themselves with objects of aesthetic creativity made in the past and physically existing in the present, [art historians] seek to discover the historical niche that a work of art occupies and to assess that work in the light of its unique position. They therefore set forth to identify its physical properties, creator, and time, as well as to relate it in a historically meaningful way to other works of art of the same creator, school, period, and culture. At the same time they attempt to remain sensitive to its essential aesthetic individuality. (Kleinbauer, 1987, p. 209)

A student need not learn about art history only from books and slides. A creative teacher will devise art history assignments that encourage students to become involved actively in historical inquiry. A work of art, whose author and origins are kept hidden from the student, can become the starting point for the student's own investigation of the object. By visiting the local art museum, by researching different archives, by perusing the production of related artists and art movements, the student will find the visual evidence needed to provide a classification and, perhaps, an attribution for the work of art in question. In a second phase of inquiry, the student can proceed with text-based research to verify findings about the work of art and, in a written exercise, justify and defend his or her conclusions.

The study of aesthetics provides additional interesting avenues for combining experience-based and theory-based learning in attempts to maximize outcomes.

> Philosophy, then, is not simply reflection but critical reflection, the assessment chains of reasoning (or "arguments," as they are called) in the attempt to gain insight into our beliefs and values. It aims at understanding our ideas, clarifying them for ourselves and others. Thus, Hospers [1969] introduces the problems of aesthetics by stating that philosophical inquiry or reflection on the arts is concerned "to clarify the basic concepts we employ in thinking and talking about the objects of aesthetic experience." (Crawford, 1987, p. 228)

The creative art educator will devise student assignments that promote active investigation of issues in aesthetics based on a process of inquiry similar to that used by philosophers. A classroom reenactment of the 1927 U.S. Customs Court Trial pertaining to Brancusi's *Bird in Space* provides such an opportunity. At issue in this trial was whether or not Brancusi's abstract bronze sculpture was indeed a work of art and, therefore, qualified for duty-free entry into the United States. Customs officials maintained that the object was nothing more than "manufactured metal and therefore taxable at 40 percent of its value under paragraph 339 of the Tariff Act" (Adams, 1976, p. 37). By using a trial such as this as a case study, students can be brought to investigate such issues as the definition of an art object and the differences that exist between a personal appreciation of the work of art and its critical evaluation within the context of the art world. In the example presented here, students could begin their investigation of *Bird in Space* by writing about their own personal understanding and appreciation of the object. Afterwards, in a reenactment of the trial, they could assume the roles of the various participants in the trial: artist, art collector, lawyers for the defense, custom officers, lawyers for the state, expert witnesses for both sides, and jurors. During the reenactment, students could develop and present an argument in support of the point of view of the characters whose roles they have assumed. Following the end of the trial, students could be invited to reflect on their experience by studying the account of the trial presented in the second chapter of Laurie Adams's (1976) book *Art on Trial: From Whistler to Rothko*. Students might compare the arguments they have developed with the actual events and outcome of the trial. Finally, the art teacher could conduct a debriefing exercise that leads to the identification and elaboration of the key points in aesthetics encountered before, during, and after the reenactment.

The Interaction of Experience and Knowledge Leads to Understanding

I have argued that experiential learning is an essential component of a Discipline-based Art Education pedagogy and maintained that theoretical learning is its necessary counterpart. I have also argued that the interaction of these two types of learning assists the student in constructing a new, more complete, and integrated understanding of the art material being studied.

According to psychologist Gerard Artaud (1989), profound changes in the very structure of personality result from a learning process where experiential and theoretical knowledge come together to generate a new body of integrated knowledge.

[Use of] the word integration [to designate this new knowledge] means precisely that this new knowledge can only take form by being integrated into the very structure of personality and, thereby, modifying it. ... The learner—who has thus acquired a new vision of his world, who has attained a more profound understanding of the phenomena that, before, were hidden from him or her—can no longer remain as before: his or her attitude has changed. There is every reason to believe that he or she will not be able to behave in the usual way. The goals of learning have been reached: by its interaction with scientific knowledge, experiential knowledge has not only broadened and consolidated itself, it has been transformed into a whole new way of being, which is the essential condition for a new savoir faire. (1989, p. 141) (author's translation)

Evidently, the aesthetic encounter is a common feature of the four DBAE disciplines, and requires both experiential and theoretical learning. Furthermore, each discipline—art production, art criticism, art history and aesthetics—is a locus for the interaction of such learning. Therefore, we can conclude that a pedagogical approach based on the integration of experiential and theoretical learning is compatible with a Discipline-based Art Education program. DBAE programs that integrate the four disciplines are particularly suited to provide opportunities for the integration of experience-based and text-based learning.

References

Adams, L. (1976). *Art on trial: From Whistler to Rothko.* New York: Walker and Company.

Artaud, G. (1989). *L 'intervention educative.* Ottawa: Les Presses de l'Universite d'Ottawa.

Clark, G. A., Day, M. D. & Greer, W. D. (1987). Discipline-based art education: Becoming students of art. *The Journal of Aesthetic Education,* 21(2),129-196.

Crawford, D. W. (1987). Aesthetics in discipline-based art education. *The Journal of Aesthetic Education,* 1(2),227-242.

Csikszentmihalyi, M & R. E. Robinson (1990). *The art of seeing: An interpretation of the aesthetic encounter.* Malibu: The J. Paul Getty Trust.

Ebitz, D. (1989). The uniqueness and overlap among art production, art criticism and aesthetics: The view from art history in *The preservice challenge: Discipline based art education and recent reports on higher education.* Seminar Proceedings from A National Invitation Seminar Sponsored by the Getty Center for Education and the Arts, Snowbird, Utah, 158-163.

Ebitz, D. (1989). DBAE: Opening a bridge between art history and art education. *The Alaska Journal of Art,* 1 (1),10-18.

Goldyne, J. (1988). The uniqueness and overlap among art production, art criticism and aesthetics: An artist's viewpoint in *The preservice challenge:*

Discipline-based art education and recent reports on higher education. Seminar Proceedings from a National Invitation Seminar Sponsored by the Getty Center for Education and the Arts, Snowbird, Utah, 163-170.

Kleinbauer, W. E. (1987). Art history in discipline-based art education. *The Journal of Aesthetic Education,* 21(2), 205-215.

Kolb, D. & Fry, R. (1975). Towards an applied theory of experiential learning. In M.T. Keeton & P. J. Tate (Eds.), *Learning by experience: What, why how.* San Francisco: Jossey-Bass.

Lachapelle, R. (1994). *Aesthetic understanding as informed experience: Ten informant-made videographic accounts about the process of aesthetic learning.* Doctoral Dissertation. Concordia University, Montreal.

Perkins, D. N. (1994). *The intelligent eye: Learning to think by looking at art.* Santa Monica, CA: The J. P. Getty Trust.

Sibley, F. (1965). Aesthetic and nonaesthetic. *The Philosophical Review,* 74(2). 135-159.

Smith, R. A. (1987). The changing image of art education: Theoretical antecedents of discipline-based art education. *The Journal of Aesthetic Education,* 21(2),334.

Spratt, F. (1987). Art production in discipline-based art education. *The Journal of Aesthetic Education,* 21 (2),197-204.

STUART RICHMOND

In Praise of Practice: A Defense of Art Making in Education

My basic belief is that all art education is education for appreciation. By appreciation I mean the sustained perception, understanding, and appraisal of a work's form, meaning, and value, undertaken mainly for the sake of the experience in itself. An appreciative response, at once contemplative, affective, yet disinterested, is an aesthetic response: one attuned to the way that the stylistic, formal, and expressive qualities, thematic aspects, subject matter, and images in a work are organized and treated, that is, typically with fluency, competence, insight, imaginative freshness, particularity, and compositional coherence. The usual venue for appreciation is the study and contemplation of existing artworks. But appreciation is also closely connected to art making whose purpose it is to produce artifacts that will reward aesthetic attention. As a result, the process of art making is filled throughout with moments of heightened perception and judgment, both being necessary for a work to advance, and for this reason the endeavor can be described as a worthwhile aesthetic activity. Involvement in art making also makes students appreciate more directly the compositional and creative challenges faced by the artist and the pleasures and benefits of firsthand productive experience. Whether through creative engagement or response to finished art, the point of art education is to increase students' capacities and appetites for the rich appreciative experience of art.

Artistic Process

The practice of art is exciting to a child (as it is for people of all ages). Satisfying the universal urge to create, make a mark, and thus leave a reassuring trace of one's existence, it speaks of pleasure in using materials and tools, the senses, and the physical body. It is active and constructive, real and concrete, and for students it is work that they can claim as their own. Indeed, it is difficult to convey on the printed page the sense of purpose and energy to be found in a well-run art room. For many, art making is valuable for the experience of process itself; for the doing, exploring, executing, inventing, and manipulating; for the challenge in finding precisely the right way to give form, shape, and presence to an idea or subject. This involves discipline, close concentration, and persistence. To work at art is to be engaged in living one's life at a level of intense interest and effort that is sometimes rewarded by a successful aesthetic outcome. Students learn early, or they do if the program is authentic, that practical work in art is really more a stream of attempts than the regular outcropping of finished masterworks. Nevertheless, the doing of art, successful or not, provides many opportunities for learning.

To be initiated into a world of practice—be it in drawing, painting, sculpture, claywork, photography, printmaking, or any other art form—is to acquire skills and techniques, to become familiar with certain standards, values, and problems, and to be compelled to make an almost endless series of decisions and interpretations throughout the creative process. In speaking of the creative process I do not wish to imply anything fixed and sequential. On the other hand, the realities of art production can be pretty unromantic: there is a job of work to be done. Pissarro, for example, gave Cézanne some very detailed and unequivocal advice about which colors to use, how to develop light-dark contrasts, painting only what he saw in nature, covering the whole canvas at once with paint, and so forth, which that artist went on to adopt to great advantage.[1] Ansel Adams held that it is by means of absolute technical mastery, the visualization of a finished photograph, control of composition, exposure, filter, development and presentation, that a photograph, as a piece of creative art, gets made, and "made" was Adams's operative word.[2] Adams produced photographs widely accepted as the finest art, yet he was not the least bit precious or mystical about the craft side of his art. In working at their own art, students learn from the inside how art is brought into being, how it is structured, what the material difficulties are, what works best in certain situations, what the compromises of intent and possibility are, what is excellent technically. They experience the inherent satisfactions and frustrations of art making and in the process gain an appreciation of and respect for the achievements of artists generally.

Learning to See

David Hockney in a recent book remembers how, for him, conceptualism in the seventies made art arid, lacking in sensuality, and alien.[3] Art, it can't be said often enough, is about looking. It is about making meaning out of the fluid nature of our visual impressions. A training in art is a training in ways of seeing, which is why realism is the centerpiece of art. Picasso didn't develop cubist and abstract interpretations by default. These approaches grew out of his draughtsmanship, various influences of the time, and his mastery of forms, especially those pertaining to the human figure. This is no less true for Georgia O'Keeffe's abstract landscape and flower paintings and the forms of nature. In this sense, art essentially seeks the truthful representation of appearances. In an age of easy relativism, subjectivism, and the ubiquity of ready-made media imagery, it is all the more crucial to point out the need for students of art to strive for an objective response, to get beneath habit and cliché in order accurately to represent the complex and changing patterns of reality. If there is an artistic model *par excellence* for this kind of effort, his name is Cézanne. Patrick Heron in his article on the 1996 Tate Gallery exhibition of Cézanne's work remarks upon the amazing freshness and relevance of Cézanne for art today. The important point to be borne in mind for education is that, as Heron puts it, "when Cézanne resolved visual realities into countless groups of delectably ordered *strata* of brush strokes lying parallel to one another, he was magnifying something seen,"[4] even as he was abstracting out of the myriad possibilities that compose the visual world. We see and picture the world by means of forms and patterns we help constitute. This is the great creative challenge for artists and is the reason why art is different from literal illustration or pure self-expression. It is also the reason why good art is so powerful an educator. Through its images we learn how the world can be seen. The many still lifes, landscapes, figure studies, and portraits by Cézanne serve as a reminder that it is by means of imagination and the patient, insightful, ordering intelligence of perception that artists and viewers in particular, and people generally, are enabled authentically to connect with the tangible world.

As a consequence, the core of art making in education must consist in learning to observe and depict one's surroundings for oneself. Through a language of forms—ways of picturing things—the various features, shapes, textures, colors, tones, and relationships associated with a subject are distinguished, organized, and rendered in a medium. Kimon Nicolaides's book *The Natural Way to Draw*,[5] a fifty-five-year-old classic of art schools that is still in print, is a perfect example of how drawing can be taught systematically but sympathetically. Sustained effort through countless exercises that focus on gesture, contour, structure, anatomy, technique, modeling, composition, and light and shade, especially in relation to the human figure, lie at the core of Nicolaides's program. Teaching any art form, however, requires a diffident touch by the instructor. Always the point must be to work toward the student's own emotional grasp and interpretation of medium, subject, and image-making possibilities. But, as Nicolaides points out, "the first step in drawing is an objective step—the observation of facts as they exist. And that is the surest way toward the development of subjective power, which is after all the power of an accumulated real knowledge."[6]

Art making in education, it should be pointed out, need not be limited to realism. There is room for a broad range of approaches and traditions; for eclecticism, experimentation, and work in the crafts. My argument, however, is that the ability to represent the visual world remains at the heart of all practice in art education. The making of a good clay pot depends on an understanding of form principally derived from the organic shapes of the natural world. Painting a protest poster takes skill and knowledge of many shapes and figures.

Being trained in careful observation makes students more aware of the richness and variety of the visual world. They notice, for example, the presence and qualities of different kinds of flowers, trees, birds, and landscape environments, the visual and aesthetic complexity of street and courtyard in light and shadow, views through windows, and people's physiognomies; and they become aware of all manner of opportunities for visual appreciation in daily life. The pleasure and insights to be gained from such experience feed back into art as a realization that everywhere the artist is surrounded by amazing subject matter. The development of sharpened perceptual abilities enables students better to engage with existing artworks which, in their turn, complement, inspire, and inform ongoing artistic practice.

Artistic Practice: Social and Moral Implications

In his monumental philosophical treatise *Sources of the Self*, Charles Taylor articulates the role of art in the formation of human identity. We become full human agents, he argues, by acquiring artistic languages of expression (among others) through which we engage in a dialogical relation with the world. We understand the world through these languages, and in making an artistic response we are at the same time making manifest aspects of our inner selves.[7] This is another way of saying that as artists interpret experience through their art, so their aesthetic preferences and personality become apparent in the work. In response to Taylor, Mette Hjort argues that Taylor's modernist view of art as creative, expressive, disinterested, and aesthetically rich, though key to his arguments about self-formation, is elitist and ignores the social construction of taste cultures that are established through the use of power structures to enhance social prestige. In short, according to Hjort, he leaves no room for the social and pragmatic functions of art and hence he ignores popular art in his analysis. In Hjort's view, art is a game the playing of which confers status in the social hierarchy. The player learns "good" taste according to the rules of the game; these rules, and not any qualities in art itself, determine the worth of art.[8] In his counterargument to Hjort, Taylor points out that as soon as concepts of art and judgments of taste are *wholly* explained in terms of the struggle for social distinction,

> the account leaves us incapable of understanding why taste can ever serve to distinguish. Unless art has some independent power for humans, in some way interpellates and commands our attention, then we couldn't possibly use it to enhance our position by defining our taste. . . . But if art has this independent power, then it follows that not all rankings can be games of distinction.[9]

There remain, therefore, possibilities for exploring the meaning and value of art in people's lives through art itself, which is what I am currently attempting to do. Hjort also makes the point against Taylor that disinterested attitudes belong in the domain of the privileged, since they make little sense for people trying to meet their basic needs.[10] But even if this claim is true, it is not an argument against the good of aesthetic interest in itself. Nor is it the case that a disinterested attitude toward art necessarily implies a lack of moral concern generally, as is often imputed. I shall return to this point later. I believe that whatever the inequities of the world, the contemplation of art and beauty can help sustain the human spirit, if not satisfy physical needs and appetites, and that, surely, is a worthwhile end.

The idea that art exists mainly to embrace and advance chosen causes or nonaesthetic functions is, however, very common. In Paul Duncum's view, for example, art study should enable students to detect and critically analyze meanings of social importance in art. The underlying intent in this perspective, which includes images of every kind, is the development of a visual literacy that helps students determine those images that can best serve their interests. In this way art education, conceived as a politics of visual communication and social criticism, is said to contribute to a more democratic society.[11] Suffice it to say for my purposes that in his single-minded emphasis on analysis and the social sciences, Duncum has made art, in any material or aesthetic sense, virtually disappear from the educational landscape.

Contemporary art provides many examples of art seen as social activism. Suzi Gablik describes projects ranging from the cleaning up of rivers to the public thanking of garbage men.[12] Through photomontage, often involving large letters of text, Barbara Kruger sets about disrupting viewers' responses to images that purportedly shape ideas of power, gender, and consumerism, while she eschews notions of aesthetic intent. Without doubting the sincerity of activities such as the above, I do question their artistic credentials and note that, by comparison, artists who continue to work at more traditional aesthetic projects unfortunately risk being accused of escapism and social irresponsibility.

What I find interesting in debates concerning the social role of art is the attitude of artists in the former Soviet Bloc. An example is Václav Havel, the well-known playwright and President of the Czech Republic whose plays, essays, and books had been banned for two decades and who was imprisoned by the Soviets. He remembers with conviction that in his early work in the Czech theater, during the famous Prague spring, his group didn't try to instruct audiences or promote theses; rather their work was more of the *l'art pour l'art* kind. Nevertheless, according to Havel, the work done at that time still managed to express the "genuine drama and genuine ineffability of life, things as fundamental as despair, empty hope, bad luck, fate, misfortune, groundless joy."[13] A similar attitude can be seen in the writings of Milan Kundera, a Czech novelist who speaks of the "radical autonomy"[14] of the novel. He argues that it is precisely this autonomy that allows the writer or artist to explore and express aspects of the human condition beyond the scope of social and political thought. John Berger, an English artist, novelist, and critic with strong leftist leanings, explores the tension between the social and aesthetic duties of the visual artist in his novel *A Painter of Our Time*, set in the mid-fifties. The protagonist, an Hungarian Marxist expatriate painter with a strong commitment to art, writes in his diary after much soul-searching, "You can't work for anything under the cover of art. . . . You can only work for something else under the cover of non-art. Art does not cover—it reveals."[15] And later, "Do not demand Socialist Art. . . . Demand Socialist propaganda when it is needed and encourage art. . . . Do not ask for Socialist works of art to be judged by Socialist standards. The standards will be untrue and opportunist."[16] There was a good example of opportunist standards at work in Hollywood in recent years when actor Tom Hanks received an Academy Award for his performance in a wholly predictable film about a business executive who gets AIDS. For artists constrained by committees and ideologies the freedom to work according to their own vision and imagination is the obvious ideal.

All too obvious moral lessons and politically correct subject matter do not guarantee either good art or a high moral ground. As Octavio

Paz points out, the saddest thing about the committed art of Latin America after the Second World War was not simply its aesthetic poverty but its loss of moral and political tension,[17] which I assume is the inevitable result of removing ambiguity and uncertainty from human situations. The main concern in putting art in the classroom at the service of moral or political causes, besides doubt about the maturity of students, is the question of who decides the selection of causes and who determines the appropriateness of student response. It is one thing for the teacher to instruct students on artistic matters, quite another to teach and evaluate art on the basis of particular sets of beliefs about the social good.

To speak of the autonomy of the artist, however, need not imply moral indifference. Indeed, a defensible connection between artistic practice and morality, I would argue, lies in the artist's attempt to see and represent the world truly and impersonally. This is difficult, given the many distracting influences on perception, but with adequate education it is not impossible. To contemplate the world in a disinterested and unbiased manner entails a necessary diminishment of self-interest. It is to accord respect to the intrinsic being of the other, encountered in its rich particularity, qualities, and identity, as an end rather than as a means. For Iris Murdoch, realism, understood as the just and compassionate perception of that which exists independently from ourselves, stands as a moral achievement. She argues that the more a person is seen as separate and unique yet with needs similar to one's own, the harder it is to treat that person as a thing.[18] British painter Lucien Freud, for example, explores unflinchingly the many faces of human desperation. His work shows the psychic and unlovely pain of sad and alienated people. Beyond superficial resemblance yet deeply naturalistic, his paintings reveal the tormented emotions of his subjects, devoid of media hype. Freud shows us with focused and expressive intensity what life is like for some people. We see human pain and anguish without ulterior motives, that is, with the kind of affective though impersonal understanding that supports a humane and sympathetic response. I would want, however, to extend Murdoch's arguments to include the whole of nature. The more an old-growth forest, for example, is experienced and appreciated for its intrinsic qualities, the more difficult it becomes to accept its degradation and destruction, for whatever reason.

Concluding Remarks

In referring to the work of Taylor earlier I drew upon his argument that to be of value art must have some qualities that stand apart from socially derived rules of taste. The source of that value is the aesthetic presentation of subject matter having human significance. Content or idea alone is insufficient for art. The locus of pedagogical effort under this view is found in the making of art that embodies such value.

The practice of art in education involves students in skill development, use of materials, and creative process. Students begin to understand what it means to respond to the world artistically, and in so doing they become aware of the attractions, difficulties, and satisfactions of creative work.

Art making develops powers of perception and understanding of visual form, which constitute a very potent way of making sense of, and communicating, the meaning of experience. Far from being idle play, art is a fundamental language of understanding and one that calls upon the resources of the whole person. Art making involves students in the difficult balancing act of fusing feeling, imagination, perception, and skill; qualities that, together with knowledge of tradition, form the genesis of style and originality in art bearing universal significance.

While learning to see clearly and realistically and to construct images that convey truths about humanity and the visual world, students often struggle to understand and portray matters concerning individual existence, relationships to others and the world at large, and matters of value—aspects of life that lie at the core of the moral domain. Thus moral understanding is inherent in, and can result from, artistic work that attempts to do justice to the visible world.

Finally, art making requires all manner of judgments, and judgment is the basis of appreciation. What is being sought is a thoroughgoing practical education in art that values the aesthetic character of both process and outcome, and this is something that is best revealed in student work itself.

Notes

1. Ilrike Becks-Malorny, *Paul Cézanne: Pioneer of Modernism*, trans. Phil Goddard (Cologne: Benedikt Taschen, 1995).

2. Jonathan Spaulding, *Ansel Adams and the American Landscape: A Biography* (Berkeley and Los Angeles: University of California Press, 1995).

3. David Hockney, *That's the Way I See It*, ed. Nikos Stangos (San Francisco: Chronicle Books, 1993).

4. Patrick Heron, "Solid Space in Cézanne," *Modern Painters* (Spring 1996):17.

5. Kimon Nicolaides, *The Natural Way to Draw* (Boston: Houghton Mifflin, 1941).

6. Ibid., p. 122.

7. Charles Taylor, *Sources of the Self: The Making of the Modern Identity* (Cambridge, Mass.: Harvard University Press, 1989).

8. Mette Hjort, "Literature: Romantic Expression or Strategic Interaction?" in *Philosophy in an Age of Pluralism: The Philosophy of Charles Taylor in Question*, ed. James Tully, with assistance of Daniel M. Weinstock (Cambridge, U.K.: Cambridge University Press, 1994), pp. 121-35.

9. Charles Taylor, *Philosophy in an Age of Pluralism*, ed. James Tully, with assistance of Daniel M. Weinstock (Cambridge, U.K.: Cambridge University Press, 1994), p. 242.

10. Hjort, "Literature: Romantic Expression," pp. 121-35.

11. Paul Duncum, *Beyond the Fine Arts Ghetto: Why the Visual Arts Are Important in Education* (Geelong, Australia: Deakin University Press, 1993).

12. See, for example, Suzi Gablik, *The Reenchantment of Art* (New York: Thames and Hudson, 1991), for arguments in favor of activist art.

13. Václav Havel, *Disturbing the Peace: A Conversation with Karel Hvízdala*, trans. and intro. Paul Wilson (New York: Alfred A. Knopf, 1991), p. 52.

14. Milan Kundera, *The Art of the Novel*, trans. Linda Asher (New York: Harper and Row, 1988), p. 117.

15. John Berger, *A Painter of Our Time* (New York: Pantheon Books, 1959), p. 72, originally published by Secker and Warburg in Great Britain in 1958.

16. Ibid., p. 147.

17. Octavio Paz, "A Literature of Convergences," in *Convergences: Essays on Art and Literature*, trans. Helen Lane (New York: Harcourt, Brace, Jovanovich, 1987).

18. Iris Murdoch, *The Sovereignty of Good* (London: Ark Paperbacks, 1985), originally published by Routledge and Kegan Paul in 1970.

MAURICE BROWN

Art Making and the Classroom

We still do not quite accept as a rich and equal educational source the actual processes of the artist, with their possibly childish, even sordid turns and confusions. Although we are reluctant to associate our most serious enterprises with those of the artist, we seize the artist's product, capitalize it (in every sense), and ponder its utility and what it implies about our condition, past and present. But the studio, like the workshop, laboratory, or library, is among society's soulful repositories, not an "ivory tower." The artist in Harold Rosenberg's remark is not of another planet. It is indeed an individual who continues while shots ring outside, but it is also a culture whose "salvation" lies in the continuity of that and similar processes. A society unable to recognize itself or find value in the *making* must question the depth of its judgment about the *work* of art.

I am addressing, of course, the usual separation of more or less sanitized art and its more or less problematic makers and making. "Learning about art," says a commentator, "is entirely different from learning to make or experience it. There is . . . some tension between the two activities."[1] I agree, although it is important that the two can strongly augment, if not call for, each other; that there is little reason so quickly to interrupt the early, generally productive cohesion of the two with that later, more sophistical "tension." There can be reason and integrity in approaches to learning that genuinely, fully include or definitely exclude the "hands-on" or experiential. The difficulties begin when the inclusion is only weak or nominal. Unless educational access to the fullest, most serious levels of these phenomena is as usefully prized as it is anywhere else, "making and experiencing" in particular will yield fewer relations to other disciplines and confirm either their relative insignificance or sphinxlike isolation.

I do not mean to suggest that correction of this "usual separation" necessarily depends on Artists-in-the-Schools programs, especially as they have come to be known over the past two or more decades. One of the worst of many bad things about such programs was the whisper within the phrase itself: two alien forces joined! Many have noted with amusement that during that time everyone became an "artist," but only the very specially prepared can be teachers. Even so, "artists," why-ever they are so called by whomever, are no more certain than "accredited teachers" to handle "making and experiencing" in such a way that creation and its interrelations with other disciplines are of a high, syncretic quality. In the terms in which this issue is most often examined, my view poses difficulties, no doubt, but I identify rather than isolate "artist" and "teacher," at least insofar as together they form a "middle entity" on which the highest, long-term functions of both art and education have always depended.

Argument on these matters seems to boil down to two broad approaches. One is based in the belief that art in the schools is best used frankly and directly as an instrument in establishing certain values; the other is based in the belief that these and other values are eventually best served when art itself—its craft, unpredictable creation, and apprehension—is given priority. Although the two approaches may not seem necessarily to exclude each other, in practice the wilder, disinterested spirit and helpful insights of art are more often lost to the first approach than social or other concerns are ignored in the second.

If, as I believe, it is the artist who encounters the whole of human history in his or her lifetime, it follows that anything having to do with the serious transmission of art's information, practices, or values will be a many-particle fusion. It will include the craft of making and making as expressing that which "cannot be put in harness to any but spiritual uses."[2] It will include or be directly informed by its many aspects, aesthetic, psychological, historical, and otherwise. However anomalous their preparation, however many hyphens in their titles, the individuals who present "making and experiencing" in this light will be comfortably, prolifically, and contemporarily based in it.

We may all be regarded as having at least a logical effect on the future. But it is the broader, somewhat less uncertain significance of it that Henry Adams had in mind in his famous speculation that the teacher's effect is infinite.[3] If this is correct, then even an art teacher's technical concentration cannot be separated from potential personal, intellectual, or social significance. Enlightenment through creation is universal currency. To assist in it, the teacher, like the artist, may choose from the full scope of human learning and employ whatever subversion or elaboration of theoretical programs is necessary. Both may control as well as follow and be the source as well as the medium of enlightenment.

In offering the following suggestions for the classroom, I am aware of the odds against saying anything that might practically and often enough apply to every level of students. I have taught several age groups, young and old, and helped raise two sometime apprentices, a daughter and a son, but most of my instructional experience has been at the college graduate and undergraduate levels. Of my students who went on to teach, most are K-12 teachers. A few are art directors of school districts. From this experience and the reports of these former students, I think I can emphasize a few things that may be considered in most situations.

Though lectures are often appropriate, the majority of the time in art sessions is spent at work with various materials and evaluations of it. This fact alone explains the piecemeal, opportunistic, individual, reactional nature of most such instruction, however loose or tight the planning and however central or peripheral the teacher's style or presence. The rest of the time is divided between demonstrations and presentations of one kind or another. All of these are not only distinct options of equal potential but overlapping choices that may suddenly evolve from one another, depending on circumstances to which the teacher's purposes and sensitivities must be tuned.

Demonstration is critical. Apart from its obvious purpose to show how "this thing is possible," the demonstrator's competence is emphatically connected with a recognized pursuit that consumes time and thought beyond school age and has its own methods while being, like mathematics, widely applicable. The demonstration says, "This belongs not only to an already granted abstraction with its real center elsewhere, but is something actual and here as well, something that can be yours." Even the flaws, humorous difficulties, and odd occurrences can serve, perhaps not as well as the successes, but as grounds for other insights, observations, and projects. In this sense, demonstration cannot irretrievably fail.

Here is an example of a basic painting demonstration meant more dramatically to convey, among other things . . . a flexibility of medium so free and inexhaustible that any objective may benefit from any event without being prevented.

While discussing all sorts of technical matters, I begin a large painting. Gradually, after several configurations and many additions and subtractions to show different surfaces, relations, and so on, I turn the painting on its side. Together, we discuss its possibilities. Most see it as a developing landscape, let us say. Next, each student is given a chance to affect the work in any way (depending on their number I have limited them to a few moves or several minutes of work). As one might imagine, a good deal about the image and the students may be revealed. Sometimes a single configuration is cooperatively developed. More often, new directions rise up, or the whole "history" is suddenly lost in playfully total, energetic, even purposely destructive effects. Always there are beautiful, intriguing developments and a marvelous running commentary; always there are sighs of regret at what is lost and expressions of amazement at what has suddenly come about through casual effort. Eventually, I return to the painting and, perhaps deceptively discussing other matters, begin to work with whatever is there. If lucky, I can seem for quite a while simply to be bringing out what was "submerged" there—which is not entirely untrue. Soon, though, my contribution becomes strange, then a plainly purposeful overlay, even though I am also *relying* on the accumulated shapes and colors. As students begin to frown or bend sideways for a different orientation to the painting, I turn it back to its first position. The image is now obvious, and I add a few touches. Finally, I ask the first-arriving student to whom I had given a sealed envelope to tear it open and read aloud the contents. "In a room with a window open to a night sky," reads the student, "a woman wearing a large, dark hat holds a basket of bright flowers"—a preconceived description that fits the haphazardly gotten painting.

Yes, it is a shameful stunt, but for only moments does it seem magical or to have been about my performance. In spite of often stunning coincidences, that part of it burns away in the students' growing realization of how easy it was—of how forgiving and cooperative the medium can really be.

One may make many variations on this demonstration. In one, the "window ... woman" (or some such) description is given as an assignment to one class. Meanwhile, a second class is taken through many "blind detours" (swapping canvases, turning them upside down, and so on) before being given the same assignment and only a minute or two to achieve it on the same surface. Each class is shown all of the work from both and, without explanations until later, preferences are discussed. Practically always, the works of the second class are preferred (discussing why they are or are not leads easily to other concerns). In any case, a highly suggestive difference is apparent, and it is the source of this difference *in their assumptions,* instead of the crazy mechanics of the second class, that becomes the real topic. Works from the first class tend to be anemic versions and show careful, uniform effort only toward what was mentioned; those of the second reveal a far wider, "undirected" range of qualities not specifically mentioned in the assignment but in rich extension and support of it.

The "presentations" I mentioned above mean anything from visiting teachers, students, and specialists to field trips and slide shows. However, I would like to comment on reproductions in general, because films, slides, and other electronic means offer many possibilities and are increasingly used.

What we know and feel about certain works, and about painting in general, comes from much varied experience and information, only a small part of which is study of the actual object. Most of us, I expect, wish it could be a larger part. For some, the shortcomings of reproductions are a small price to pay for an increased range of knowledge and familiarity. I cannot argue with them, but I would say unequivocally that it is a bargain of dangerous benefits for anyone, but particularly for the artist.

I value my books and collections of reproductions and turn to them often; however, they are also copies of works in their own right. Having necessarily loose relations to their sources, they are examples of another kind of discrimination as graphic art—a printed medley of designed intervals, shapes, sizes and continuity. There are the works of Kurt Schwitters, for example, and then there is the "meta-Schwitters" of the books, posters, and magazines. (He came to mind because so many of his collages were composed of pieces of posters, newspapers, and magazines.)

I am nevertheless aware of the realities of schools, where the need to provide valuable information and visual experience for large numbers of students is met in part with reproductions. Aside from a wide range of the highest quality available, there are ways to increase their value. Several quite different slides of the same work immediately remind the student of the relativities at play. Where feasible, some effort to make the projected image of slides the same dimensions as the actual work is revealing and worth the trouble. A very few actual, exemplary paintings will lend their substance to many reproductions.

However, nothing so increases the value of such aids as the frank teacher who discusses this topic and does not take reproductions or their uses for granted; whose use of them admits the many distortions of the actuality. In addition to the utter impairment of size's import, there is a critical difference between looking at a light bulb through a slide, or the ink of a bookplate, and looking at the tissues and materials of the real surface. The identifying "face" is there in the print, betrayed in some degree, but the "body" of the impelling and irreplaceable object is missing. Nevertheless, sensing what a reproduction may withhold in what it provides—seeing it as a "meta-work" of interest and a flawed substitute—further trains the imagination and the senses.

In addition to all that goes into good teaching in art, there is a general approach or attitude that is particularly favorable, and I would like to end with a rough characterization of it. It has to do with an active and delving (though of course not exclusive) interest in visual perception.

The activities of the mind are always related to the world received by the senses.[4] Therefore, one of art's firmest connections with the rest of the curriculum is its purposeful manifestations and study of appearance. (I mean, of course, any appearance, not only art—and any art, not only that which sets out to copy or represent appearances.) Whatever else art classes may be about, they benefit from a teacher's willingness at every opportunity to become involved with the data, habits, and characteristics of perception.

The involvement—or rather, consciousness of how fully one is already involved—does not come easily. Perception is taken for granted, and our routines help it to forget itself in being functional. We are willing to grant that there are physiological differences in vision or theoretical features due to unusual conditions and cultural or social causes, but we are reluctant to look further into the fundamental, equally circumstantial quality of our own "everyday" visual conditions. That is, although we rarely note it (and then as triviality), the relativity of vision is accepted in principle, but only up to a point. Beyond it, the profusion is "read" largely in constant, already received, and unexamined ways. In denying informal investigation of this as a gainful study in art, or even the connection between vision and art as marginal at best, some would unknowingly undercut the central experience of making and apprehending art and what it provides as preparation for other fields of study.

There will be moments when these opinions are persuasive, but they and other, perhaps material problems are effectively balanced in the moments of simply beginning. One gains confidence from the fact that visual relationships, oddities, artlike phenomena, unifying cues, and other possibilities for study and comment are literally always and everywhere present. One must acknowledge for oneself that what is seen or not seen can be important; that visual pleasure and acuteness can be increased; that avidly and studiously looking is a profound adjunct to thinking, or can be another form of it; that what one knows, feels, and does is based in some measure on what one sees and has seen, the importance given to it, and the interpretations one made of it.

Vision is conditional, paradoxical, and eclectic. Appearances expose and reveal, but they also conceal and are complicated. The role these effects play in making and seeing art has been a subject for many commentators, from da Vinci to E. H. Gombrich, Anton Ehrenzweig, Maurice Merleau-Ponty, and many others of our time. Eventual familiarity with such studies is important; more essential, however, is the teacher's own first, faltering but instructive beginnings, in which these effects are engaged ad hoc, with no specific reference or goal.

The beginning may be or become narrowly technical or general and philosophic. Color, where Cézanne said the brain meets the universe, will perhaps be a center of engagement or subconsciously near by. Pasting a square inch of each of ten colors against a larger but contrasting field of the same colors easily shows what *is always* taking place: their relations alone create more than the ten colors of the paper, paint, or whatever is used. Regardless of different medium, size, subject matter, or historical period, art can bridge over such differences in the way it looks; therefore, one way of providing students with a sense of the "common bases" . . . is an examination of the similar form and appearance of otherwise very different art. Computers can now deal more quickly with data than can humans, but we are unparalleled in our ability to recognize, imagine, and manipulate patterns,[5] another possible entry point to perception. By "doctoring" slides, slyly cropping one side of some famous paintings, for example, I once set off a chain-reaction that continued in unpredictable but productive forms for a year. However, perception opens up to ever more speculative issues. When we see, we go out as well as take in, we collect *and* project—nature is inside us, said Cézanne; yet, it is obviously a major channel of learning. "Vision alone makes us learn that beings that are different, 'exterior,' foreign to one another, are yet absolutely *together*, are 'simultaneity,'" wrote Merleau-Ponty.[6] Perception both demonstrates and undermines the "tremendous power of factional belief over the freedom of the mind."[7]

What distinguishes classes in which the beginning is made, helping to insure their connection with many other interests, and these with art, is the multiplex nature of that engagement—the descriptions, explanations, comparisons, analyses, guesses, random observations, verbal inventions, admissions, hands-on trials and experiments, pondering, and vital staring that takes place when how and what we see (and the causes and effects in art and life) are subjects in an art room environment.

I belong to the first generation of artists forced to witness the unquestionable, dawning possibility in fact of Nietzsche's century-old prediction, "The artist will soon come to be regarded as a splendid relic." I suppose he left us and himself some breathing room: being regarded as a relic is yet different from being one. Besides, we are harmed by too greatly disliking our own time, and I have tried to convert even my negative feeling for that dawning and its causes to positive sources of work. Although I take some satisfaction in what I have actually accomplished (downcast as I have also been at not having realized more), I greatly value the sense of awareness and capability from which it came. Like the ratio of many scattered shreds to fewer Presentable Works, the artist's capacity exceeds the work. The work, no matter how good or numerous, is also an indication of how much dies with us. It is the tip of the proverbial iceberg. A proper view of creativity will always include technique as but part of a much larger, life-size "excess." (Teachers, too, inhabit an "excess" that students are rarely encouraged or enabled to "use up"; however, the students and *their* work are in part its proof.)

Even so, I agree that the tale instead of the teller, the work, not the artist, must be looked to. Misfortune for an artist is when sense of self and theory outstrip performance. My separable work and self are brought together only by me and in the flow and backflow of creation. For me, the best work always requires fluent relation with that "excess," no part of which is, once and for all, superfluous. But the work is the objective. Only its realizations justify. Every other benefit may be gotten some other way.

Personal accounts of creating sooner or later bump, or are thought to bump, against pride. Whether or not I am guilty of it, I do not regard the tendency and its loftier symptoms as "romantic," the charge with which the current "un-arting" protects itself—which I find ironic because of the romanticism of *that* quest. I regard the tendency as another often mistaken aspect of our topic. It is mistaken, first, due to a confusion of "loftiness" with yearning for an unattainable happiness or integration; then, second, to seeing even measured happiness as naive blindness. Injustice, the grimness of daily prospects, and the gloomy estimates of our globe's health are surely plain. But whatever it may finally send out, I cannot see the *act* of creation as mournful. Making enacts a frame of mind so prone to the remedial and possible that it never fails to inch away from the sorrowful as well as the joyful in order to consider its effects, uses, and sources. Whether this is seen as inhuman detachment, a prideful rebuke of misery's company, or a harmless home-movie of denial, it is actually but another operation in that mindframe's refusal of all that might keep it from the Whole, whether squeamishness before the dirty facts or fear of heights.

Although it has no recipes, creation seems born of a compulsion that can support as well as be at odds with "the present." If one of its demands is a base in the present, we should consider how it also helps to qualify that present, to define what is in the present, and how it occupies the present. If there is no past or future in art, as Picasso said, or if, as William Faulkner wrote, "the past isn't dead, it's not even past," it must mean that, whatever else creation consists of, it is possessed by the idea Delacroix noted in his journal, that "what has been said has still not been said enough." To say it well and again requires a continuing belief in the transcendence of re-mulling and chewing existence in order to make the other existence that is art. It requires toughness of a particular kind: burning without being consumed, remaining vulnerable to heartbreak, staying open to any knowledge while closing it unremittingly in one's medium, and beholding bottomless time's losses while steadfastly anticipating how one will continue and succeed against all odds at making something that recreates, validates, and celebrates the way we are.

Notes

1. Edward C. Banfield, *The Democratic Muse: Visual Arts and the Public Interest* (New York: Basic Books, 1984), 125.

2. *The Notebooks of Samuel Butler* (New York: AMC Press, 1968), 293.

3. Henry Adams, *The Education of Henry Adams* (New York: Modern Library, 1931), 20.

4. Hannah Arendt, *The Life of the Mind: Willing* (New York: Harcourt Brace Jovanovich, 1978), 143.

5. James Fallows, "Wake Up America," *New York Review,* 1 March 1990, 15.

6. Maurice Merleau-Ponty, "Eye and Mind," *The Primacy of Perception and Other Essays,* ed. James M. Edie (Evanston: Northwestern University Press, 1964), 187.

7. Richard Mitchell, *The Leaning Tower of Babel and Other Affronts from the Underground Grammarian* (Boston: Little, Brown and Company, 1984), 275.

8. In *Human, All-Too-Human,* quoted in Bernard Yack, *The Longing for Total Revolution* (Princeton: Princeton University Press, 1986), 341.

9. Walter Pach, trans., *The Journal of Eugene Delacroix* (New York: Viking Press, 1972), 88-89.

DAVID N. PERKINS

Building the Mind through Art

Art as an Occasion of Intelligence

"I can resist everything except temptation," wrote Oscar Wilde.[1] A real problem, when there are so many temptations to resist. And surely one of the most insidious is far from what we usually think of as temptation. It is the temptation of stereotypes.

For a case in point, consider looking at art. The temptation is to treat art as yielding up all to a glance, at least most of the time. The idea seems to be that the work of art is a kind of SWAT team of color, form, and line, put together to prove itself by its sensory assault on the viewer. The work asserts, the viewer beholds.

This notion is an insult to the intelligent eye. Although it has often been challenged, let us take a few moments to remind ourselves of the basic argument as formulated here. The stereotype of the passive viewer fails on two counts. First of all, looking at art demands what I called experiential intelligence. Recall that this means the intelligence of experience, what we gain from a rich range of knowledge and a multitude of encounters with diverse aspects of life. To the extent that we have considerable lived experience, know something of the past, speculate about the future, have some familiarity with source cultures, and a stock of general and particular knowledge of different kinds of art, we are readier to see what is there to be seen.

While seeing what art offers calls for experience of the world in general and some experience of the world of art, seeing what art offers also demands reflective intelligence. Experiential intelligence, remember, specializes in the quick take. It thrives on the expected. It honors the predictable over the adventurous, and the simple over the subtle. To bundle this in a quartet of quandaries, the output of our experiential intelligence can all too easily be "hasty, narrow, fuzzy, and sprawling."

By definition, reflective intelligence refers to the knowledge, skills, and attitudes that contribute to mental self-management. When we stand in front of a work of art, we need not respond willy-nilly. We can prompt our experimential intelligence, cajole it, aim it, redirect it, to arrive at more varied and deeper readings of the work before our eyes.

At the broadest level, this controlling role of reflective intelligence can be viewed as a matter of dispositions—the disposition to give looking time, to look broadly and adventurously, to look clearly and deeply, and to look in an organized fashion. These four dispositions counter one-on-one the four unfortunate dispositions that come part and parcel with the power of experiential intelligence. When we put together the deliberative and managerial powers of reflective intelligence with the quick and flexible response mechanisms of experiential intelligence, then we truly have the intelligent eye.

Art is emblematic here. What is true of art holds for many other facets of life as well. Experiential intelligence working alone gets us by in familiar circumstances, where the quick take and the steady habit serve. But in the face of subtlety and novelty, those four intelligence traps of narrow, hasty, fuzzy, and sprawling thinking snap shut. We need the countervailing dispositions of reflective intelligence to make the most of experiential intelligence, to see better, to think better, and to act more wisely.

The Opportunity of Art

Now back to Oscar Wilde. The trouble with resisting temptations is that no sooner have you resisted one, than another is likely to pop up in its place. If we can resist the temptation of a stereotypical view of art, what next? Next is the lollipop wrapped in these pages, the idea that art is a tasty way to build better thinking. What a curious strategy!

Is it too good to be true? Should we dampen our hopes and sharpen our skepticism? A curmudgeon might well gripe as follows: "Lovely, I'm sure, all these experiences in front of paintings and sculptures. But what's so special about them as far as thinking is concerned? Why not build thinking through history or mathematics? And maybe better!"

The curmudgeon has at least part of a point. Any domain affords rich opportunities for the development of human thinking. But art offers something special. In several ways, looking at art is a particularly supportive platform for building thinking dispositions.

Take, for instance, *L.D.*, a 1937 drawing by the French artist Henri Matisse. Suppose you want to look at it, talk about it, and learn something from it. Something about art. And something about thinking. How might *L.D.* help you?

Sensory anchoring. Discussion is usually woven of words and memories—about baseball scores, presidential candidates, or yesterday's picnic,

Henri Matisse, *L.D.*, 1937. Pen and india ink, 14 3/4 x 11 in. © 1993 Succession H. Matisse/ARS, New York.

and, in classrooms, about the causes of the Civil War or the concept of a mole (chemistry or biology, take your choice). It's all too easy for attention to drift with nothing but a lattice of language and recollections to hang in on. And all too hard to check judgments directly. Here immediately a work of art is special. It or a reproduction can be physically present as you think and talk, providing an anchor for attention over a prolonged period of exploration. It's easy to spend a while with *L.D.*

Instant access. L.D., or any other work, also helps out with "instant access." You can check something with a glance, point with a finger. "Look how lost in her own world she seems," you say. "You know, the tilt of the head does a lot of that." You point to the tilt. "Look at the line of the eyebrows." You point to them. "Imagine that her head wasn't tilted, her eyebrows level. She'd look a lot more alert instead of lost in thought."

If instant access seems too obvious to mention, remember how different discussing last night's sitcom or short story is. The sitcom lies in the past, the short story sprawls across several pages and several minutes of reading. You have to check judgments by memory or riffling pages. *L.D.* is here and now.

Personal engagement. Works of art invite and welcome sustained involvement. Perhaps you resonate sympathetically to the pensive *L.D.*, recalling bemused moments of your own. Or perhaps it makes you furious: "The daydreaming of this pretty woman reflects the typical male artist's treatment of women as pretty things." This is personal engagement, too, just as visceral although far from what Matisse had in mind. While there will always be some neutral responses, by their very nature, works of art are likely to stimulate one kind of spasm or another.

Dispositional atmosphere. All this plays well into the dispositional character of thinking. I have emphasized that thinking is a passionate enterprise. Giving thinking time, thinking broadly and adventurously, and so on, are uses of the mind that call for concern and commitment, spirit and persistence. In an atmosphere of heightened affect, the dispositional side of thinking seems more at home. For instance, L.D. herself might be giving thinking time—musing about an old lover or a new one, or recalling how on her eighth birthday she flew a kite so high it almost disappeared.

Wide-spectrum cognition. Building thinking around a work of art guarantees the involvement of multiple sensory modalities. *L.D.* puts to work your pictorial and spatial perception on the one hand and more verbal analytical kinds of thinking on the other. It encompasses what Rudolf Arnheim calls visual thinking as well as other modes of cognition.[2] It addresses the range of symbol systems Nelson Goodman writes of in his *Languages of Art*. All this suits well the character of real-world thinking. By and large, we reason about things we see and on which we can lay our hands, into which we can project ourselves physically and emotionally—whether to buy this watch, accept that job, dare a ride on the carnival Tilt-a-Whirl. Central to experiential intelligence is its experiential character, its roots in our sensory world of actions and reactions. Real-world thinking is almost always wide spectrum in character, rarely just a play of words or symbols. So with art: In thinking about Matisse's *L.D.*, we *meet* L.D. However they grow and branch, our thoughts cling around the trellis of that perceptual reality.

Multiconnectedness. What is *L.D.* in the end? A study of grace in line. A symbol of male artists' reduction of women to pretty things. An intense evocation of day dreaming. An oddly distorted image (why is *L.D.*'s forehead so short, her cheekbone on the right so protuberant?).
An exercise in weight and balance (notice that architecture of *L.D.*'s arms, hands, and chin, creating a tilted structure that, like the Leaning Tower of Pisa, nonetheless stands up). And many other things too. In other words, there is no "in the end." Art tends to be multiconnected. We can

find links with many things—social issues, aesthetic concerns, trends of the times, personal commitments, even science and mathematics sometimes. Art is generally richly connected culturally and historically. The connections range from ones easily accessible to most human beings to arcane references only penetrable by a scholar of the place and time of origin. The multiconnectedness of art creates an opportunity to bridge thinking dispositions across to diverse other contexts explored in tandem with the work of art.

As Oscar Wilde reminds us, temptation is hard to resist. But thankfully not all temptations need to be resisted. The above catalogue makes it clear that many of the temptations of cultivating thinking through the arts are more than just lures—they are good reasons for doing so.

The Challenge of Transfer

L.D. today, smarter decision making tomorrow. Art builds better thinking, right?

That depends. We cannot expect even thoughtful experiences of looking at art to spill over and make our thinking better elsewhere unless we work hard to make it happen. Here is why.

It all turns on one of psychology's most central ideas about human learning, the concept of transfer. By transfer is meant the impact of learning in one context on performance in other significantly different contexts. For example, you learn to drive a car. Later, moving your household, you rent a small truck and find that you can drive it fairly well. That's transfer. Or, for example, you enjoy playing chess. Later, entering a local political race, you find that principles of chess, like "strive for control of the center," help you in your strategizing. That's transfer as well. Or you study French in college. Later, planning a trip to Italy, you study Italian and find that some things you learned in studying French spill over and help you—some specific vocabulary but also a heightened awareness of syntax, certain tricks for memorizing, and the confidence that you can handle the learning of a language. That's transfer too.

The catch is this. Considerable research tracing back to the beginning of the twentieth century argues that, very often, the transfer we want simply does not occur. Learners do not carry over what they learn in one context to other contexts. For example, while almost anyone would make the car-to-truck transfer mentioned above, the chess-to-politics transfer is much less likely. After all, sitting behind the wheel of a truck reminds you of all your car-driving skills, which apply well to the truck context. But politics does not necessarily remind you of chess. It's easy to miss useful connections.

So bleak a picture has been presented by the long history of research on transfer that some educational psychologists have come close to concluding that transfer is a lost cause: Except in circumstances quite similar to one another (the car-to-truck case), we cannot expect much transfer. Each skill, strategy, fact, attitude, and concept has to be learned in its own context.

If this were true, it would be bad news for the enterprise of building thinking through the arts, or in any other general way. It would say that people have to learn to think better situation by situation. The hope of developing generally helpful thinking dispositions, or anything else helpful over a diversity of circumstances, would be slim.

But the prospects of wide and fruitful transfer are not as grim as they might seem from the story so far. While many studies of transfer have yielded negative results, a few have shown positive ones. It's critical to understand what factors make for success when it happens. My colleague Gavriel Salomon and I have proposed a model accounting for both the successes and the failures.[3] According to this model, transfer is a finicky phenomenon. Transfer has generally not occurred because the conditions needed for transfer were usually not present.

However, the conditions for transfer can easily be engineered into instructional situations. We will get transfer when we teach for transfer. In particular, transfer depends on building certain conditions into the instructional experience. According to the view of Salomon and Perkins, there are two alternative approaches:

1. *Abundant and diverse practice.* Well-mastered skills are more likely to stand up in new contexts. And diverse practice prepares the mind for a variety of future applications. Unfortunately, in most school settings, skills and knowledge are underpracticed, or practiced only in a narrow range of circumstances. Or . . .

2. *Reflective awareness of principles and deliberate mindful connection making.* These encourage seeing the common principles that bridge disparate contexts. Unfortunately, in most school settings, skills and knowledge are learned in a rote rather than a reflective way, with little attention to mindful connection making.

Of course, both of these approaches can be used at the same time. Salomon and I call the first of these the "low road" to transfer, because it depends on automatic triggering of prior learnings. We call the second the "high road" to transfer, because it depends on mindful reflection and active connection making. The moral: If we want far-reaching transfer, we can have it. But we have to build in abundant and diverse practice for the low road, or reflective connection making for the high road, or, better yet, both.

What does this mean concretely? Suppose you are a teacher. What can you do around Matisse's *L.D.* to teach for transfer? Here are some possibilities:

- Make Matisse's *L.D.* part of a much larger program. Over a number of weeks, take up varied works of art representing different cultures and periods. Look at them all with attention to the four dispositions. This exercises the "low road," plenty of diverse experience. But what kinds of experiences? Read on . . .

- Welcome personal connections. What are your experiences of bemusement? How akin do you feel to *L.D.*? This makes connections to everyday life.

- Provoke reflection around those experiences. What do you think of daydreaming? Does it have a function? Is it a waste of time? This is a piece of the "high road," abstract reflective thinking.

- Raise the feminist issue if it does not come up. It connects Matisse's work to other dimensions of life. More high road reflective thinking.

- And throughout all this, promote good dispositions for looking and for thinking alike—giving looking and thinking time, making looking and thinking broad and adventurous, clear and deep, and organized. Explicit recognition of these dispositions takes the high road, dealing in articulate abstractions that help us to connect across different contexts of thinking.

Many teachers and some students might be alarmed at all this. Does it not reach too far beyond the work of art itself? Are we not losing sight of *L.D.* in its specificity? It's all a question of balance. No one is suggesting we spend all our *L.D.* time thinking about other things altogether. But if the rectangular boundaries of the drawing itself are never violated, the dispositions cultivated in looking at the work are likely not to spill over and inform learners' abilities and attitudes more widely.

Besides, in large part, works of art resist being kept within their frames. They reach out by design. We have to be ready to reach with them to partake of what they offer.

Art and the Wide World

The world of art as youngsters usually meet it is a narrow one. Art means studio art and often the most trivial versions of it—pumpkin cutouts for Halloween, turkey cutouts for Thanksgiving, the perennial parade. Of course, this cutout mentality cuts out most of the richness in the art.

Part of making art a more meaningful pursuit and connecting it to a wider world consists in making the world of art itself wider. This concern sounds clearly in the Getty Center for Education in the Arts' emphasis on discipline-based art education. The Center has advocated art studies as a distinct and worthwhile discipline that should take its place alongside the other disciplines taught in today's schools. Moreover, the Center has pressed the case for a multifaceted approach that recognizes diverse perspectives on art. As described by Elliot Eisner and by Stephen Dobbs, a well-rounded program includes attention to art production, art criticism, art history, and aesthetics (issues of value and interpretation).[4]

While this discussion has emphasized art criticism, clearly all four of the Getty themes feed one another. Moreover, all four invite attention to the thinking dispositions so central to the good use of one's mind. In the studio as well as in front of *L.D.*, one can give thinking time, make thinking broad and adventurous, clear and deep, and organized. In understanding historical perspectives on art and struggling with deep issues of aesthetics, we need to exercise persistent, adventurous, deep, and organized thinking. All in all, the four pillars of discipline-based art education define a spacious atrium where thinking dispositions can thrive.

However rich the wide world of the arts, the wider world beyond the arts issues even more of an invitation to powerful dispositions of thinking. From choosing a site for a holiday to selecting a school, from puzzling over a math problem to pondering for whom to vote, from programming a computer to planning a political campaign, circumstances call for thoughtfulness. While our routine habits of thinking may satisfy our needs 90% of the time, we need the 10% solution, the thinking dispositions of reflective intelligence to manage the best deployment of our experiential intelligence.

Nowhere is this message more called for than in educational reform. After all, schools, more than any other single element of society, have the potential to cultivate thoughtfulness and contribute more critical and creative graduates to the future. In my recent *Smart Schools*, I argue that today we have an understanding of teaching, learning, and the nature of intelligence ample to transform education into a much more thinking-centered process than it usually is. We can organize education effectively for the enhancement of understanding and thinking. Central to such a vision is the cultivation of key thinking dispositions.

In all this, art has a distinctive role to play. The liberal borders of art help us to carry good thinking dispositions nurtured in the context of art to the wider world. Art is an extrovert. Art connects because artists make it connect, because artists strive to express not just the anatomy of bodies but the anatomy of the human condition and of the universe that impinges upon it. If most disciplines dig moats, art builds bridges.

Notes

1. From O. Wilde, *A Woman of No Importance*, Act I (1983 ed).
2. R. Arnheim, *Visual Thinking* (Berkeley: University of California Press, 1969).
3. D. N. Perkins and G. Salomon, "Transfer and Teaching Thinking" in *Thinking: the Second International Conference*, eds. D. N. Perkins, J. Lochhead, and J. Bishop (Hillsdale, NJ: Lawrence Erlbaum, 1987), 285-303. D. N. Perkins and G. Salomon, "Teaching for Transfer," *Educational Leadership*, 46 (1) (1988): 22-32. G. Salomon and D. N. Perkins, "Rocky Roads to Transfer: Rethinking Mechanisms of a Neglected Phenomenon," *Educational Psychologist*, 24 (2) (1989): 113-142. For a practical classroom guide to teaching for transfer, see R. Fogerty, D. N. Perkins, and J. Barell, *How to Teach for Transfer* (Palatine, IL: Skylight Publishing, 1991).
4. See S. M. Dobbs, *The DBAE Handbook: An Overview of Discipline-Based Art Education* (Santa Monica, CA: Getty Center for Education in the Arts, 1992). E. W. Eisner, *The Role of Discipline-Based Art Education in America's Schools* (Los Angeles: Getty Center for Education in the Arts, 1988).

MARY ERICKSON

Teaching Art History as Inquiry

Two distinct types of art historical inquiry can be undertaken in the classroom; replicative and generative. Replicative inquiry is rediscovery of accepted knowledge. Generative inquiry is inquiry that has never before been undertaken.[1] Both can be valuable processes within an art history program. The classic high school term paper is a prime example of replicative research. Students are asked to locate, read, analyze, ponder, and synthesize what others have concluded about a subject, and then they are asked to share their conclusions and synthesis in the form of a written or oral report.

Interesting activities have been developed by teachers to help students come to understand traditionally accepted information in art history. A high school art teacher concluding a lesson on Renaissance painting shows pairs of slides contrasting High Renaissance and Baroque paintings. The students are asked to compare and contrast the two sets of slides. Actively analyzing and comparing, they reach conclusions about general characteristics of painting in the two periods. This exercise is a marvelous way to engage students actively in thinking about art history. The students' conclusions are predictable, like the results of a chemistry "experiment" following procedures outlined in a high school laboratory manual.

Another example of replicative inquiry in art history instruction involves sorting reproductions into stylistic groupings and placing them in chronological order. The students "discover" styles and sequences that are well accepted in the field of art history. If a student "discovers" that Impressionism occurred after Cubism, the replicative "experiment" went wrong. Replicative inquiry is an excellent instructional method for teaching art history. Although new information is not generated, established information is introduced indirectly.

Generative inquiry in art history leads into the unknown and is therefore generally more difficult but potentially more rewarding. The process is engaging and participatory, and the results are not predictable. In generative inquiry, students are challenged to ask new questions about artists and artworks of the past,[2] or they are challenged to inquire about more familiar, less studied visual artifacts such as advertising design, fashion, local art, or popular art.

Is teaching generative art historical inquiry a worthwhile goal within an art program? Is the acquisition of information sufficient for a complete understanding of art history? Is history adequately taught if students are unable to raise historical issues? Is science adequately taught without experimentation? Education is more than the acquisition of knowledge. Skills and attitudes are also part of the content of education. . . . The axiom "one is never to believe experts without thinking for oneself" holds not only for art historians but for all of us.

Students should learn to think for themselves about art history for several reasons. First, they will have an inaccurate understanding of the discipline if they understand nothing of its methods. Minimally, students should come to realize that the art historical information presented to them was established as a result of the curiosity and investigation of art historians.[3] Art historians think for themselves and sometimes disagree with each other to reach conclusions. Their thinking and disagreement help us all to better understand artworks from the past and from other cultures.

Students should also learn to think for themselves about art history simply to meet the general goals of education. Art historical inquiry requires higher-order thinking skills that are too seldom present in the elementary and secondary curriculum. Authentic generative inquiry is intrinsically more interesting and can therefore be a means of increasing student motivation. Understanding the method, not only the information, that characterizes a discipline can empower students to move beyond the limitations of their curriculum. When planning instruction in a discipline that is as information intensive as art history and in courses that are as short on instructional time as art courses, fostering inquiry is doubly important. When tough choices must be made about which artworks, periods, and cultures to study, encouraging art historical inquiry can enable students to investigate neglected areas independently. This empowering may instill in the students an encompassing curiosity about visual objects and an interest in how people of other times and other places saw the world. It can also serve them outside the formal structures of schooling as they face their own worlds.

Three Categories of Inquiry

Art historical inquiry can be defined as establishing facts, interpreting meaning, and accounting for change.

These statements make different sorts of claims. Much of what art historians attempt to do is to establish basic facts about works. They make claims about what an artwork looked like when it was produced; about how an artwork was made, what subjects are depicted, and how the work is formally organized; and about who made the artwork, for whom, when, and where. All such claims are factual claims. An artwork either did or did not have certain qualities when it was made; it was either made by a certain process or it was not; and so forth. We know that art historians have sometimes been wrong in their factual claims. However, what they attempt to establish are matters of fact.

One might categorize art historians' basic factual claims into three groups: imagined restoration, description, and attribution. Imagined restoration is the process of determining how an artwork appeared when it was produced. Description is the process of examining an artwork in great detail and reporting one's findings. Attribution is the process of examining evidence in and outside the work that leads to a conclusion about who produced the work, for whom, when, and where.

Art historians make additional claims that are interpretive, not factual. Art historical interpretation is the process of making sense of an artwork within its own context. Art historians must learn to remove themselves from the here and now and to imagine themselves there and then to interpret an artwork. An art historical interpretation states what an artwork was about for the artist who made it, for contemporary viewers who saw it, and within the context of the culture in which it was produced. Art historical interpretations include claims about the contemporary meaning or significance of an individual artwork that are not factual but are inextricably involved with human values. Interpretive claims are judged on their comprehensiveness and credibility.

Art historians also make claims that may be called accounts or explanations. With the accumulation of many factual and interpretive claims, patterns and divergences emerge among artworks of different times and places. Art historical styles are identified in order to describe similarities and differences. Art historical accounts attempt to explain why these differences and similarities occurred. Some accounts focus on particulars, as narrative art histories do. Other accounts focus more on generalizations, as theoretical art histories do. There have been and will continue to be multiple art historical accounts of the same historical or cultural changes. . . .

Stephen Addiss describes his own art historical inquiry process as he studied the art of Kameda Bosai, a Japanese artist and calligrapher of the Edo period.[4] In the factual category, Addiss writes about three parts of his research in Japan. He calls one of those parts "seeing artworks," which serves as a basis for descriptive notes of "original impressions." He describes Bosai's calligraphy as having been given "a sense of rhythmic life by [his] alternations of heavier and lighter strokes, thicker and thinner lines, and straight and curved shapes." He describes the subject matter of a Bosai painting as "a scholar-poet crossing a bridge beneath high mountains, with a lonely pavilion near the peak." Addiss uses his descriptive notes of original impressions when he compares photographic reproductions of Bosai's work. In addition, Addiss establishes basic facts about a number of works. By studying signatures and seals, he is able to attribute some works to Bosai and to identify others as imitations of Bosai's work.

To prepare himself to interpret Bosai's work historically, Addiss did background reading in Japanese history, culture, and the art of the Edo period before leaving the United States. In Japan, he retraced the route of a journey made by Bosai, stopping at farms where Bosai might have stopped and passing mountains and rivers that might have "encouraged" Bosai in his landscape painting. Addiss learned much about Bosai's life and world that led him to conclude that Bosai's work "is deeply embedded into the values of traditional Japanese literati culture." In the exhibition catalog that was the culmination of his inquiry, Addiss wrote comments that he intended to be helpful for viewers attempting to understand or interpret Bosai's work.

Addiss also explains changes in Bosai's work over time. His narrative account of Bosai's life and work includes, for example, an explanation of the effects of Bosai's journey on his calligraphy and painting. Art historians do not always draw conclusions about facts, interpretation, and explanation in all their studies, nor does inquiry in these three categories need necessarily to be pursued in the sequence presented here. Addiss has done some work in each category, working back and forth from one type to another as he studies the life and art of Bosai.

Teaching through Establishing Facts

Teachers might engage students in generative art historical inquiry in their own classrooms. As noted earlier in this chapter, some art historians challenge the selection of objects that can be considered appropriate for art historical investigation. Donald Kuspit characterized the present state of art historical scholarship this way: "If [the discipline of art history] is to develop, to get a move on, the distinctions between the art historical and the extra-art historical, what is proper and improper art history, must give way. . . . The whole decorum and topography of art history must change. It must understand itself to exist in a field of humanistic operations, as one of many cross-fertilized investigations."[5]

Art teachers are not as bound by "decorum and topography" as art historians are, and in many cases, they have established traditions of broadened "topography." In art classrooms, crafts, advertising, package design, and product design are commonly studied alongside the more traditional painting, sculpture, and architecture. In their continuing search for ways to relate art to the lives and interests of students, teachers have broadened the range of objects studied in art classes. However, this focus is usually taken only in art production classes. Jewelry, magazine ads, album covers, containers, book illustrations, and other objects are used to stimulate production of similar objects. They are seldom exploited as objects for art historical inquiry.

Factual investigations might be undertaken with ordinary objects such as toys, books, and clothing. To appreciate the task and significance of imagined (or real) restoration, students might be given an old doll, a broken toy car, or a worn-out baseball cap. They might speculate on how the object appeared when it was new. This is the same process that art historians must undertake when they study the Parthenon as it appears today. Before drawing conclusions about Van Eyck's *Arnolfini Wedding Portrait*, art historians must be confident that it has not deteriorated or been altered through the centuries.

The skills of detailed observation can be practiced with ordinary objects. Students can list any subject matter they find, identify the materials from which it is made, speculate about how the parts were put together, and list the object's colors, shapes, textures, and use of space. As observations are put into words, students are learning to be descriptive. Description is a basic skill of art historical investigation. As art historians begin their studies of artworks, they make detailed observations. Tiny details, like the fruit on the window sill or the decoration on the mirror in the Van Eyck painting, are carefully considered.

Attribution, or the establishment of basic information about a work, can also be undertaken with ordinary objects. Students might attempt to date a magazine advertisement by talking with older people or making comparisons with other ads from dated magazines. Old toys, kitchen utensils, or children's books might have original packaging materials, labels, or title pages that give clues about who manufactured an item or when and where it was made. Evidence might be available in the form of other artifacts, old documents, or memories of contemporary witnesses.

Jan van Eyck, *The Arnolfini Wedding Portrait*, c. 1390-1441. National Gallery, London.

Art historians attribute works to particular artists and establish dates of production through examination of similar evidence. Some paintings long assumed to have been painted by Rembrandt have been "de-attributed" in recent years by renewed art historical inquiry. The history of ownership of the *Arnolfini Wedding Portrait* helps determine when and under what circumstances the painting was produced.

Teaching through Art Historical Interpretation

The skills of art historical interpretation can be practiced with everyday objects. For example, the regalia of a full-fledged hippie couple of the 1960s might seem absurd to today's young people. How could anyone have ever thought that sandals, leather-fringed jackets, love beads, handmade muslin dresses, and macrame vests were "cool"? What sort of statement did hippies make as they put together their look? These are questions for art historical interpretation. They require that today's young people set aside today's fashions and values and attempt to place themselves in the sixties. They must come to understand that the parents of hippies were the World War II generation and that many young people of the time were breaking traditional taboos about sex, careers, drugs, and music. This was also a time when Americans were sharply divided on the Vietnam war. Just as the 1980s yuppie "dress-for-success" look was intended to communicate upward mobility, the 1960s hippie look was sometimes a declaration of independence with antiwar overtones. Supposedly, the sixties look is coming back into fashion as a nostalgic look of rebellion. This neo-hippie fashion revival will surely complicate the task of interpreting the clothing styles of that era—just as during the Italian Renaissance or the French neoclassical era, when interpreting ancient Greek and Roman art was made more complex by their contemporary revival.

Popular culture shifts rapidly—no current example will be current for long. Perhaps studying the white shoes and polyester suits of the 1970s disco look can provide a genuine challenge for young people's historical interpretation skills. Are there symbols to be found in the disco look? Students must use the same skills if they are to come to understand historical artworks. If students are unable to step out of the here and now and imagine themselves there and then, they will see Van Eyck's *Arnolfini Wedding Portrait* as a picture of a man and a pregnant woman in funny clothes with their pet dog. . . . The significance of the dog, mirror, bed, woman's figure, and clothing will be lost on students without some skill in art historical interpretation.

Teaching through the Development of Art Historical Explanations or Narratives

As with art historical attribution and interpretation, students can learn to account for visual change by using familiar objects. A collection of old soda bottles, sheet music, neckties, costume jewelry, or children's books can exemplify a visual change through time that demands explanation. . . . Many young people are collectors, and their own collections might be studied. Others are connoisseurs of visual change in their own areas of interest, such as skateboard stickers or MTV videos. Students can look for style groupings within their chronologically sequenced collections. They can invent names for and establish basic characteristics of each style. They might investigate whether there have been any revivals through the years. They might discover when change is gradual and when it is dramatic. They might also find that, during some time periods, more than one style exists.

After describing visual change, some attempt can be made to explain it. Art historical explanation cannot be undertaken without some knowledge of the times in which the objects were produced. Reading assignments, social studies classes, and conversations with parents and neighbors can provide some of that knowledge. Students might report their findings as general principles of visual change or as event-to-event narratives of change. Arnold Hauser accounts for changes in art through the millennia by tracing changes in society. Heinrich Woefflin explains changes in styles of painting by proposing a theory of alternating baroque and classical tendencies. Hans Belting cautions that the scholar's conception of art history may dictate that scholar's interpretation of historical events.[6] Students will be better prepared to appreciate the significance of changes in art history if they are made aware of the notion of change closer to home.

Sources of Art History Content

When we think of what can be taught about art history, we tend to think first of teaching information. In the preceding section I have attempted to show that students can also learn inquiry processes. Information and inquiry are interrelated. As we gain information, we are able to ask new questions that lead to further inquiry. This often yields new information that in turn leads to new inquiry.

Identifying what is to be learned in the area of art historical inquiry requires that we identify not only information but also skills and attitudes. If students are to learn the process of art historical inquiry, then they need to be able to carry out certain tasks—that is, they need to learn skills. Such skills include describing and contrasting visual change, supporting conclusions, imagining life in another time or culture, constructing historical interpretations, and proposing explanations that account for change. There are also attitudes associated with art historical inquiry—inclinations, tendencies, beliefs, values. Some attitudes that might be encouraged in art history instruction are appreciating the views of others; valuing art as a realm of human accomplishment; and valuing one's own ability to make sense of the visual world. . . . The educational content that might be drawn from the discipline of art history is broad indeed. As art history is made part of the art curriculum, many factors must be considered.

Notes

1. The examples and persistent interest of Thomas Laudenslager, art teacher at Palisades High School in Doylestown, Pa., contributed to the formation of this distinction.

2. Virginia Fitzpatrick, "Teaching Art History as Inquiry," *Ohio Art Line* 14, no. 3 (1989): 12.

3. Kerry Freedman, "Recent Theoretical Shifts in the Field of Art History," *Art Education* 44, no. 6 (1991): 40-45.

4. In Stephen Addiss and Mary Erickson, *Art History and Education* (Urbana: University of Illinois Press, 1993), chap. 4.

5. Donald Kuspit, "Conflicting Logic: Twentieth Century Studies at the Crossroads," *Art Bulletin* 69, no. 3 (1987): 117.

6. Arnold Hauser, *The Social History of Art* (New York: Alfred A. Knopf, 1951); Heinrich Woelfflin, *Principles of Art History: The Problem of the Development of Style in Later Art* (New York: Dover Publications, 1932); and Hans Belting, *The End of Art History?* trans. Christopher S. Wood (Chicago: University of Chicago Press, 1987).

GEORGE GEAHIGAN

Art Criticism and Art Education

Art criticism means different things to educators in the visual arts. First, the term is used to denote a set of critical functions, tasks, or activities that critics perform: describing, analyzing, interpreting, explaining, evaluating, and judging. In formulating models of criticism for schools, educators translate these activities into tasks that students will perform in criticizing works of art. Educators also use "art criticism" to refer to a discipline or field of inquiry. Criticism as a discipline is an evolving social institution marked by certain intellectual aims or goals, traditional types of problems, methods of inquiry, and groups of investigators. Finally, educators use "art criticism" to refer to certain outcomes of instruction. They sometimes speak of fostering critical skills or critical dispositions, of teaching students how to criticize and to criticize works of art. These skills, attitudes, and habits are not things students do; they are more correctly thought of as states of mind or dispositions to do certain things.

Although the latter two meanings of the term are relatively unproblematic, there is often a troubling ambiguity in educators' attempts to explicate criticism as a set of instructional activities. Many conflate the idea of critical inquiry—criticism as a set of activities performed to enable critics to determine the meaning and value of works of art—and critical discourse, criticism as a set of speech acts (and the resultant product of such acts, critical statements).

This problem has its roots in the philosophical literature. Philosophers explicate criticism principally in terms of critical discourse, for they are primarily interested in such things as the nature and verification of critical statements and the types of the arguments critics use when they talk or write about works of art. Yet they often go beyond explications of critical statements and critical arguments to offer observations about such things as aesthetic perception, critical reflection, and the working methods of practicing critics, concerns that reveal a more encompassing interest in critical inquiry as a whole.

Within these texts it is often difficult to separate observations about perception and critical reflection from concerns with critical discourse. One reason for this is that words such as *describe, analyze, interpret, evaluate,* and *judge* are used ambiguously. They are used not only to refer to acts of speaking or writing but also to ways of thinking. Such shifts indicate a fundamental uncertainty about how the discipline of art criticism is to be explicated. A similar uncertainty can be found within the philosophy of science, where philosophers have long been divided about whether their professional concerns rest solely with explicating science within a "context of justification" or whether they encompass a "context of search and discovery" as well. Clearly, observations about critical perception and reflection reflect a concern with search and discovery, whereas explication of speech acts, different kinds of critical statements, and their methods of verification, reflect a concern with justification.

In relying upon such accounts to inform their conceptions of criticism, educators imported a similar conflation of these two ideas into the models of criticism devised for classroom instruction. They are never separated clearly; instead, ideas about perception and critical reflection are embedded within an overall framework principally devoted to explicating certain types of critical statements. Words such as *description, analysis, interpretation,* and *evaluation* thus acquire two kinds of meanings. They are defined explicitly in terms of the performance of certain kinds of speech acts and are also used ambiguously to refer to perceptual or cognitive processes.

This unconscious conflation has had unfortunate consequences. Critical inquiry encompasses both a context of search and discovery and a context of justification. Yet because the activities of art criticism were defined explicitly in terms of the performance of certain kinds of speech acts, the larger concern was reduced to a more narrow focus upon certain types of critical statements and their verification or justification.

Translating Art Criticism into Instructional Practice

Despite some rhetoric about inquiry in the literature, the models of art criticism that educators developed are actually models of critical discourse rather than critical inquiry.[1] Nevertheless, because of the conflation of these two ideas, teachers and curriculum designers were inevitably led to identify inquiry into the meaning and value of works of art with a certain kind of structured discourse. Critical inquiry thus became equated with various procedures for talking or writing about art.

It is not hard to understand the appeal of such procedures for educators faced with the difficult task of designing classroom instruction.

In presenting an account of what art criticism is, models of art criticism seemingly offer answers about how to structure teaching and learning. Yet some reflection will reveal that these models are not as promising as they might initially appear.

Despite frequent references to dialogue and discussion in the educational literature, for example, the models come nowhere near to being an adequate conceptualization of classroom discussion. One reason is that they fail to capture the enormous range of statements that one could reasonably expect to be made when students and teachers speak to one another about works of art, a fact that has begun to attract the attention of a number of educators. A few have noticed that teacher-student discussions, for example, will inevitably include questions or statements about personal reactions to a work of art. These types of statements, however, are typically not included in the models of criticism educators have proposed.[2] Another reason is that the models overlook the unpredictability and dynamism typical of class discussion. Dialogue or discussion does not proceed in a step-by-step fashion. To propose a rigid sequence of steps (describing, interpreting, evaluating, and so forth) for criticizing works of art would be to stifle meaningful discussion rather than promote it.

There is only one plausible way of interpreting these models: as a recommendation for another traditional method of instruction: student recitation. Unlike discussion, recitation is a structured form of talk or writing in which students proceed in a linear fashion through a series of discrete steps or stages. Whether educators intended their models of criticism to be construed in this way is an open question. Nevertheless, it has been the most common way of translating them into instruction. Most teachers believe the way art criticism is to be taught is to place students in front of a work of art and have them describe, analyze, interpret, and evaluate what they see.

If one construes art criticism in this fashion, the question of how to teach criticism seemingly does not arise because a workable method for criticizing works of art in the classroom appears to be readily at hand. Yet it is doubtful whether such a hope can be sustained. Educators have begun to question the practicality of the recitation format. Is it reasonable, for example, to have every student exhaustively describe a work of art when classmates are able to view it for themselves? Do teachers really want every student to go through exactly the same procedure for each and every work of art? That would be tedious and time-consuming. Some students will be bored with listening to other students talk, just as they might be with listening to a lecture. They almost certainly will grow tired of the same instructional activity being monotonously repeated. And do educators want students to acquire the habit of responding to works of art in some mechanical fashion?

Teachers are faced with not simply the problem of involving students and structuring novelty and variety into their classes, although these are real concerns. They also have to consider the great range of students whom they hope to teach: students who differ in their ages and backgrounds, in their academic abilities and attitudes toward schooling, and in their life interests and career goals. It is unreasonable to expect that one and only one method of instruction will be effective with all students in all teaching situations. If recitation provides a possible answer about what to do in teaching art criticism, it also leaves teachers with the disquieting problem of how to retain student interest over the long term as well as how to meet individual needs.

The feasibility of recitation as a method for enabling students to understand and appreciate works of art can also be questioned. Some educators have begun to notice that there is a formalist bias in current models of criticism. Formalism is a view that treats the work of art as a self-sufficient entity and assumes that viewers can gain adequate understanding of a work of art through careful scrutiny alone without recourse to information about the artist or the context in which a work of art was produced. That there is such an assumption underlying many models of art criticism seems readily apparent, for classroom recitation, in and of itself, makes no provision for moving beyond the work to acquire information about its artist or cultural context.[3]

What is disturbing about a formalist approach is its unduly constricted notion of what actually constitutes meaning in a work of art. In attempting to deal with what can be confirmed only through study of the object itself, formalists have tended to limit the boundaries of critical relevance to directly perceptible properties. Formalists have traditionally given short shrift to the iconography and symbolism in a work of art, for example, surely an important dimension of appreciation. Formalists have also overlooked the personal reactions of viewers. For many theorists of criticism, these have come to be seen as unwarranted limitations. They would argue that art criticism needs to recognize a much broader range of human concerns.

Critical theorists have also come to dispute formalist assumptions about how viewers come to understand art. Historically, formalism developed as a reaction against biographical criticism and its preoccupation with information about the artist. In attempting to redirect critical attention to the art object itself, formalists argued that consideration of an artist's intentions had no relevance to a work of art's meaning. Many theorists now dispute this. Formalist strictures against consideration of artistic intentions, they contend, rest upon a basic misconception of artistic intentions as purely private events in the mind of the artist. They argue that artistic intentions are something else entirely. Seeking to determine what an artist intended—a central concern of critics—is a fundamental way of coming to understand a work of art. In pointing this out, theorists have reaffirmed the relevance of biographical and contextual information to critical practice.

Critical theorists have also taken exception to formalist views about aesthetic perception, which they view not as passive reception of a work of art's properties but as an active effort at obtaining meaning and shaped by an observer's cognitive repertoire. That being the case, simply observing a work of art is no guarantee that a person will thereby gain a full understanding of what is seen. Viewers lacking the appropriate cognitive background are more likely to be puzzled or prone to misinterpreting the work. Formalists seem to be mistaken in believing that observation alone is sufficient for obtaining understanding.

Clearly, an impasse has been reached in thinking about how art criticism can be applied to educational practice. Models of criticism in the educational literature traditionally treat it as a form of discourse, a set of linguistic activities defined in terms of the making of characteristic kinds of critical statements. In applying these models to educational situations, many teachers are led to equate critical inquiry with student recitation. If recitation seems to have initial promise as an educational method, it also leaves educators with some troubling concerns. It seems to be impractical as a method for meeting the needs of different students in different classroom situations and over extended periods of time. It also commits educators to a formalist view of art criticism. Formalism, which in recent years has come in for a great deal of criticism, distorts the nature of aesthetic perception and critical meaning and fails to recognize the central role of background knowledge and contextual information. In relying upon a recitation as an instructional strategy, educators seem to be denying students the kind of learning they want them to attain.

Art Criticism as Critical Inquiry

The way out of this impasse lies in a reconsideration of the basic categories with which art criticism has been conceptualized. In the classroom, it is best construed not as a form of discourse but as a form of inquiry.[4] Critical inquiry can be identified with efforts to determine the meaning and value of works of art, the central goals of art criticism as a discipline. Critical inquiry may be defined, therefore, as the pursuit of meaning and value in works of art.

How should this search be undertaken in the classroom? Instead of advocating a single method or procedure for criticizing, educators should think in terms of three sets of instructional activities: personal response activities, concept and skill instruction, and student research activities. All emphasize determining the meaning of works of art rather than identifying value and other goals of professional critics.[5] This does not mean that critical inquiry in the classroom is to be restricted to this focus, however. The pursuit of meaning inevitably raises issues and concerns about the aesthetic and moral value of works of art, about the artist and the viewer, and about the contexts in which the work of art is created and appreciated. Nevertheless, determining the meaning of a work of art is the initial concern of any viewer, and for this reason it must be given priority in planning and implementing classroom instruction.[6]

Personal Response to Works of Art

Critical inquiry starts with the personal experience that students have with a work of art and with reflection upon the adequacy of that experience. Reflection, in turn, begins when students confront what John Dewey called a problematic situation. Works of art are potentially problematic because they can be understood and evaluated in different ways. The challenge to reflection often goes unrecognized, however. If students are sometimes puzzled by a work of art and realize that they lack relevant understanding, more often than not they believe that what they observe is the only way to see and understand that work. If merit can be assessed in many different ways, students typically base evaluations upon a narrow set of value criteria.

Critical reflection can be promoted in the classroom in three ways. First, teachers can have students exchange observations and opinions about a work of art. In doing this, they provide opportunities for students to test the validity of their reactions to works of art and to gain insights from the experiences of others. Second, teachers can have students compare and contrast related works of art and so provide opportunities for them to overcome the limitations of their preconceptions about works of art as simply imitations of reality. And third, teachers can confront students with provocative and controversial works of art. In doing this, they provide opportunities to experience works that challenge their own ideas and values.

All three strategies can help promote critical reflection. In using them teachers function both as facilitators and as collaborators, assisting and working with students to determine the meaning and value of works of art.

Concept and Skill Instruction

Personal response activities necessarily predominate in any curriculum devoted to critical inquiry, but they do not exhaust the kinds of instructional activities needed if students are to arrive at more adequate determinations of meaning and value. Teachers also need to plan for the acquisition of relevant aesthetic concepts and skills. Knowledge of aesthetic concepts enlarges and refines response, provides strategies for viewing works of art, and often increases enjoyment. Teaching concepts and skills requires a teacher to assume the role of an authority in providing knowledge rather than functioning as a facilitator or collaborator in the search for meaning and value.

Student Research

In addition to conceptual knowledge and skills, students also need to acquire biographical and contextual knowledge, which enhance a viewer's ability to find meaning in works of art. Sometimes it is appropriate for teachers to provide such knowledge through lectures or assigned readings. It is usually better, however, to have students acquire this knowledge through independent research projects. Topics for such projects can be derived from questions that arise from prior encounters with works of art. In student research activities teachers function as mentors and guides in helping students plan projects and assisting them in conducting library research.

These three types of instructional activities define the parameters of critical inquiry in the classroom. This approach to art criticism differs in fundamental ways from other proposals for criticism in the educational literature. First, it does not assume that students can adequately understand or judge a work of art through observation alone. Instead, it assumes that works of art present problems of meaning and value. Second, it does not rely simply upon exposure to the work of art for student comprehension. Instead, it recognizes that students may need to be taught concepts and skills and that they may need to go beyond the confines of a work of art in order to seek background information. And, third, it does not rely upon a single method of instruction but rather countenances the legitimacy of many kinds of instructional activities, including class discussion, lectures, and other modes of teaching and learning.

Notes

1. For a discussion of this problem, see George Geahigan, "Conceptualizing Art Criticism for Effective Practice," *The Journal of Aesthetic Education* 30 (Fall 1996): 23-42. What would a model of critical inquiry be like if actually constructed? I think it would have to be formulated along the lines of Dewey's well-known theory of reflective thinking. In Dewey's theory, reflection starts with the existence of a problem or felt difficulty. In the case of art criticism, this problem would bear upon questions about the meaning and value of a work of art. Following this phase is one in which the problem or felt difficulty is intellectualized into a problem to be solved. That phase, in turn, is followed by the formulation of a hypothesis to guide further observation. Following this, the thinker reasons about the consequences of the hypotheses through observation or imaginative action. See John Dewey, *How We Think* (Boston: D.C. Heath, 1933). I have chosen not to explicate art criticism in terms of such a model because educators historically have had a tendency to misinterpret Dewey's model as a procedure for acting.

2. The absence of statements such as these is but one indication of the oversimplified view of language reflected in current models of art criticism. Models of criticism in the educational literature reflect ideas about language that were prevalent during the 1940s and 1950s. During that period philosophers thought that ordinary discourse (hence critical discourse) could be adequately categorized into a few types of critical statements (description, interpretation, evaluation, and the like). Since that time, however, philosophers have come to realize that ordinary discourse is immensely more complicated. Instead of a handful of critical statements, they now estimate that there maybe upward of a thousand or so different types of statements in ordinary language, most of which can be expected to appear in critical discourse and in class discussions about works of art. See J. L. Austin, *How to Do Things With Words* (Oxford: Oxford University Press, 1962). A lack of awareness of the full complexity of ordinary language is one reason why educators have been prone to confuse student recitation with class discussion.

3. It is ironic that such an assumption runs counter to what many authors of current models of criticism may believe about art and aesthetic response.

4. This does not mean that critical discourse is irrelevant to the concerns of educators, however. Speaking and writing are some of the ways in which critical inquiry is undertaken, and they are the ways that the findings of critical inquiry are conveyed to others. Educators, therefore, are legitimately concerned with critical discourse when seeking to understand classroom interaction and evaluating student learning. Typologies of critical discourse, in and of themselves, cannot be used to structure instructional activities in the classroom, however.

5. The discipline of criticism embraces many goals quite apart from determining meaning and value. Critics, for example, are sometimes interested in social criticism and promoting the careers of certain artists. Determining the meaning of works of art, however, is a necessary prerequisite to achieving these larger goals.

6. Professional critics are paid to make value judgments about works they are criticizing. Students in the classroom, on the other hand, are under no such obligation. Although concerns about the merit of a work of art will frequently enter into the study of works of art, it is by no means necessary that students decide upon the value of a work of art while studying it. Determining the meaning of work of art, however, is always a concern of viewers.

MARILYN GALVIN STEWART

Learning Outcomes in Aesthetics

It is a mistake to think of aesthetics as one more burdensome component to be squeezed into an already tightly packed art program. Philosophical issues and questions arise naturally and invite serious attention when students are actively engaged in the study of art—creating and reflecting upon their own artworks and considering cultural, historical, and art critical issues associated with their own art and that of others. Teachers need to recognize that philosophical issues may arise without their planning for them and be prepared to address them. In addition, there are concepts, skills, and attitudes associated with the discipline of aesthetics which, once learned, can contribute to a student's overall understanding of and fulfilling engagement with art. Learning outcomes in aesthetics can be identified in general terms for a K-12 program. These outcomes can be stated with increasing specificity as one moves from the program level to the grade, unit, and lesson levels of study. In an attempt to provide experiences in aesthetics as an integral part of the study of art, teachers can plan units and lessons in which issues in aesthetics become the major focus of or a component of a unit or lesson. The following general learning outcomes for aesthetics, which include knowledge of concepts, skills, and attitudes, are posited for consideration.

Generally, students will know that

1. individuals tend to wonder and ask questions about the nature significance, and experience of art and beauty;
2. individuals develop beliefs about the nature, significance, and experience of art and beauty;
3. careful use of words, statements, and reasons can help individuals reflect, talk, and write about their questions and beliefs;
4. careful reflection can result in beliefs being changed;
5. philosophers explore questions about art and beauty and their experiences with them and construct explanations, or theories, to address these questions.

With respect to skills of philosophical inquiry, students generally will know how to

1. reflect upon their beliefs about the nature, significance, and experience of art and beauty;
2. listen carefully to others' points of view;
3. select and evaluate carefully the use of words, statements, and definitions to make general statements about the nature, significance, and experience of art and beauty;
4. carefully present and evaluate reasons in support of their positions;
5. use the above skills to engage productively in philosophical inquiry alone or with others.

Given knowledge of the above, students will have certain attitudes, tendencies, and propensities, such that they will be inclined to

1. inquire into the nature, significance, and experience of art and beauty;
2. value their own beliefs and reasons for holding these beliefs;
3. appreciate the enterprise of offering and assessing reasons;
4. seek and respect alternative views about philosophical issues.

Drawing from these general outcomes, teachers can formulate specific learning objectives for integration with units and lessons of study.[1] These objects should take into account the developmental capacities of children, their prior knowledge of, experiences with, and questions about art, as well as other considerations of sequence—what parts of the whole might logically follow others.[2] Knowing how to listen carefully, for instance, is a prerequisite for reflecting upon the statements made by others. Teachers can design strategies grounded in art content that help students develop their listening skills. In the early years, teachers might give the students rough categories drawn from distinctions made by philosophers and others, which serve as ways of helping students to reflect upon and organize their own thinking. Over time, students are provided opportunities to examine these distinctions, critically assess their appropriateness, and develop new ones believed to be more appropriate. With careful sequencing, students will progress in their ability to analyze and construct distinctions, definitions, and value statements and can be encouraged to develop theoretical perspectives of their own. Although familiarity with the theoretical perspectives of particular philosophers or other theoreticians ought not be seen as an end in itself, it can serve as a catalyst for refinement of the students' own perspectives. When considered holistically, the inclusion of aesthetics in the K-12 curriculum provides students opportunities to construct and test their own ideas about key philosophical issues raised, encountered, and addressed within the study of art.

Instructional Strategies for Teaching Aesthetics

Perhaps the most important way in which teachers can help students construct frameworks through which to understand their art-related experiences is to establish an environment where inquiry is valued. Teachers need to encourage rather than suppress discussion of philosophical questions as they emerge. They must also help students learn how to reflect upon and present their own views and to consider the views of others. In addition to allotting time and establishing an appropriate environment for the discussion of philosophical issues, opportunities for the development and refinement of critical thinking skills must be provided.

In an environment in which questioning is valued, students will feel comfortable raising philosophical questions. The challenge for the teacher often is to determine when it is appropriate to engage the whole class or possibly a small group of students in a philosophical discussion.

Spontaneous Questions and "The Big Questions Chart"

The art classroom is often full of activity, with students working on various studio projects, requiring assistance as they go about their work, and with the teacher moving around the room, attempting to address the various needs of students as they emerge. At other times, small and large groups of students are engaged in critical and historical inquiry. When students are engrossed in making and thinking about art, they are apt to think about their experiences in general terms. Philosophical questions which emerge rarely can be adequately addressed with simple, clear-cut answers. Ideally, a teacher would take advantage of the interest evidenced by such thinking and questioning and provide opportunities for students to sort through problems or issues as they arise, but it is not always practical to do so. When time and other constraints preclude discussion at the moment a question is raised, philosophical questions might be placed on a "Big Questions" chart on display in the room. This chart serves as a reminder that there are important questions to consider about our experiences with art. Further, having such a display might encourage students to consider one or more of the questions alone or in small groups in or out of class. Time can be set aside at a later date to conduct a class discussion about issues noted on the chart. While not addressed immediately, the philosophical question is validated as a serious one, one that merits consideration. As students become experienced in adding philosophical questions to the list, the chart helps to create and maintain an environment hospitable to inquiry arising from a serious study of art.

Planned Discussions

Employing a variety of strategies, teachers can plan for philosophical discussions within the curriculum. In addition to arranging for time to address questions remaining from other class times, teachers can plan for discussion of questions or issues associated with a particular unit of study. Teachers can anticipate questions or issues stemming from engagement in art-making activities or from engagement with certain artworks or themes. The lesson in which students in [one teacher's] class considered computer-generated images of *American Gothic*, for instance, was tied to a series of lessons in a unit on Regionalist art and a previous unit on computers and art and a series of discussions prior to completion of a worksheet. Games, role-playing, worksheets, and other familiar strategies can be employed to elicit responses to philosophical questions. In addition, teachers can plan for discussions by employing strategies such as those which follow.

1. *The Use of Philosophical Puzzles.* Philosophical issues are often at the heart of community debates about public art, specific exhibits, or special events. The installation of the Viet Nam Memorial in Washington, D.C., for example, spurred a flurry of nationwide discussion about whether public art, or war memorials in general, should be representational or not. The large black wall was offensive to some who believed that the Memorial should look like the many other war memorials found on county courthouse lawns across the country. The widespread and prolonged interest in the appropriateness of the Memorial is but one indication that real-life situations can be philosophically puzzling. Teachers and students can look to the media for evidence of such debates and for associated philosophical problems. Editorials and letters to editors contain opinions based upon a variety of assumptions about the nature of art and its role in society. These assumptions can be noted and can serve as catalysts for discussion.

While the real world offers a wealth of philosophically interesting issues, teachers and students can create hypothetical situations that raise philosophical questions. The invention of such situations, or "cases," is a long-standing practice in philosophical inquiry and in the teaching of philosophy, and one that has been highlighted by several philosophers as a viable strategy for art educators wishing to engage students in the discussion of aesthetic puzzles.[3]

2. *Great Debates.* An effective format for philosophical discussion is one in which students assume different positions relative to a particular issue. Issues for debate might stem from engagement with themes or concepts or from real or hypothetical "cases." Students argue for their own positions about the issue or for positions assigned to them in role-playing situations. Assuming roles of members of a museum board of directors, for instance, students might offer reasons for or against including a particular object or work of art in the museum collection. To aid students in presenting various points of view, teachers might distribute role cards upon which different beliefs or theories are explained. Role-playing also is effective when students are divided into groups in which all members of each group assume the same position. In role-playing, as students attempt to persuade others to accept the positions associated with their respective roles, they sometimes will be challenged to argue for points of view that are not necessarily their own. In the process of developing arguments, they will become more aware of their own views and develop an appreciation for the views of others.

3. *"In-Out-Maybe" Activities.* Commercially produced or handmade items of all types can be brought before the class as students consider whether these items have aesthetic value (In) or not (Out). After discussion, it may be determined that some items may have aesthetic value under certain conditions (Maybe). As with all group discussions, students must provide reasons for their views. This activity is especially intriguing when similar items are considered. For example, a piece of pottery made from a mold and found in great volume in a local discount store, a piece of pottery that is handmade but made in great volume for the tourist trade, and a piece of pottery that is handmade and unique will prompt discussion of such notions as originality, uniqueness, use, and intention when each is considered relative to its aesthetic value. "In-Out-Maybe" can be planned as a small- or large-group activity, can be used in conjunction with role-playing, or can take the form of an ongoing discussion centered on a bulletin board or display case upon which items or pictures of items are periodically placed.

Whether philosophical discussions are conducted spontaneously by addressing questions or issues that emerge during class or are prompted by returning to a question placed on a growing list, by arranging for classroom debates or other game-like situations, or by presenting students with real or hypothetical puzzles to consider, teachers need to recognize the classroom discussion as a pedagogical strategy in and of itself. As such, it requires serious consideration, not only in terms of getting it started, but also in terms of guiding it as it progresses and bringing it to a satisfactory end.

Facilitating Philosophical Discussions

Art education preservice programs have not always emphasized the role of the art teacher as discussion facilitator. Experienced teachers who are highly skilled in organizing studio activities often are hesitant, due to lack of experience in this area, to enter in class discussions. Although skill in facilitating discussions develops with practice, some remarks about conducting and providing closure to philosophical discussions are in order.

The teacher as the facilitator helps students formulate well-reasoned views about philosophical issues. The facilitator requires that students provide reasons as they state their positions and asks others to respond to what has been offered. Facilitating often involves summarizing the positions stated and offering related questions for consideration.

Good reasoning skills are modeled by the teacher who helps identify underlying assumptions, asks for clarification of terms, requests that students provide examples when necessary, and helps them make distinctions. There is no predetermined pattern for philosophical discussions, and sometimes the direction will shift away from the original question posed. New issues may be raised and addressed. The facilitator must judge when it would be or not be appropriate or helpful to move into another area for discussion. Judgments also must be made regarding appropriate closure.

Because philosophical discussions can be lively and engaging, it is often the case that the end of the class period comes before a "natural" end of the discussion. In order to address the pedagogical concern for providing closure, the teacher can help the students review the discussion as far as it has developed, noting the original questions, how the discussion progressed, what positions were taken, what new ideas were presented, and what new questions were raised. If there are two or more clear positions, these should be noted. The facilitator should emphasize that rational discussion can result in opinions being changed, and when they are not changed, participants can be more aware of their reasons for holding them. Students can be helped to understand that there are times when it is reasonable to agree to disagree—that some issues cannot be resolved because they are rooted in deeply held beliefs that do not seem able to be changed.

Reflection upon Philosophical Discussions

While every student is encouraged to enter into group discussions, it is likely that some students will remain quiet. All students should have the opportunity to reflect upon the discussion and upon their own views, regardless of the extent to which they were noticeably involved in it. In a journal devoted to "Thoughts about Art," for example, students can be asked to consider the discussion, noting statements made with which they agree and those with which they disagree. Students can be asked to indicate questions that they still have regarding issues addressed. If students know in advance that they will be required to write in their journals, they will likely listen more carefully. In addition, these journals provide a record of their own views and changes in these views over time.

Teaching Specific Concepts and Skills

Students learn the use of good reasoning during dialogues with the teacher who serves as a model and who, through questions comments, requires the students to think carefully. Teachers also can teach reasoning skills directly, by providing activities and worksheets designed to address them. As part of its series of novels and dialogue suggestions, the Philosophy for Children[4] program includes worksheets and exercises for developing reasoning skills. The increasing focus in the literature on critical thinking has resulted in a proliferation of materials for teaching thinking skills. Teachers can adapt these materials to art-related activities that help students learn to identify assumptions, clarify and evaluate the use of words and statements, and construct and evaluate arguments. The task for art educators is to design activities such as these with a focus upon aesthetic issues. At times, art specialists and classroom teachers can work together to provide opportunities for students to learn the skills that will help them engage in philosophical inquiry. Again, sequencing objectives and instructional strategies in aesthetics is crucial toward the development of a substantive, balanced discipline-based curriculum in art.

The Role of the Aesthetician

It is useful for students to learn something about philosophers and what they have said about art, about making and responding to art, about the role of art in society, about issues in criticism, and about aesthetic experience. Views of philosophers can be summarized for students to consider. Philosophers might be invited to meet and talk with students about their views and about aesthetic issues in general. The emphasis here is upon the aesthetician as a real human being who is interested in the kinds of questions students have when they engage in the serious study of art.

Conclusion

It is precisely because wondering about philosophical questions and issues is central to what it means to be a real human being who is exploring the meanings inherent in the activities of making and responding to art that aesthetics should be included as an integral part of the art curriculum. In planning an art curriculum that includes aesthetics as an area of inquiry, we can formulate learning outcomes at the program, unit, and lesson levels, and these outcomes can comply with most state and district general outcomes. Learning in aesthetics should be specified and sequenced throughout a K-12 program in art, while at the same time connected to inquiry in the other discipline areas of art production, art criticism, and art and cultural history.

Notes

1. For sequenced objectives and strategies for instruction and evaluation, see Mary Erickson, Eldon Katter, and Marilyn Stewart, *The BASIC Curriculum for Art* (Kutztown, Pa.: MELD, 1988).

2. Insights into how children develop beliefs about art can be gleaned from Michael J. Parsons, *How We Understand Art: A Cognitive Developmental Account of Aesthetic Experience* (New York: Cambridge University Press, 1987).

3. Margaret P. Battin, John Fisher, Ronald Moore, and Anita Silvers, *Puzzles about Art: An Aesthetics Casebook* (New York: St. Martin's Press, 1989).

4. For an account of the work conducted by the Institute for the Advancement of Philosophy for Children, see, for example, Matthew Lipman, Ann Margaret Sharp, and Frederick Oscanyan, *Philosophy in the Classroom* (Philadelphia: Temple University Press, 1980); Matthew Lipman, *Philosophy Goes to School* (Philadelphia: Temple University Press, 1988).

HARRY S. BROUDY

Aesthetic Scanning

Briefly, if imagery affects life and learning to the extent this essay claims, then the skills of perceiving aesthetic images should be a major focus of instruction in the elementary grades in conjunction with performance skills. The reasons for this are (1) proper aesthetic perception, unlike the ordinary variety, has to be especially attentive to the sensory content of the image and (2) the skills of perception can be taught to all normally educable pupils by classroom teachers after a relatively short training period. Given the skills of perception, the historical and critical materials (especially by way of exemplars) can be introduced and amplified at appropriate times.

The question is raised: Is aesthetic perception aesthetic education? And how does it relate to aesthetics? Aesthetic perception is comparable to reading a text where the text is an image or a set of images. It construes these images through what Susanne Langer called "presentational" symbols, rather than through the "discursive" symbols of written language.[1] Aesthetic literacy begins with learning to perceive the sensory, formal, and expressive properties of aesthetic images—that is, those that convey human import.

The skills of aesthetic perception may be summarized as follows:

1. Perceiving the vividness and intensity of the *sensory* properties in the work. These features convey the affective qualities of the object by means of colors, gestures, shapes, textures, and so on.
2. Perceiving the *formal* qualities of the object, its design or composition, the arrangements that provide unity in variety through balance, repetition, rhythm, contrast, and so on.[2]
3. Becoming familiar with the *technical* merits of the object, the skill with which it has been carried out.
4. Perceiving the *expressive* significance of the object, its import or message as aesthetically expressed.

There is no mystery about teaching these skills of aesthetic impression, nor is there in devising tests to assess progress in sensitivity in the perception of these properties. Experience in the Getty Institute for Discipline-based Art Education and in Project Heart in Decatur and Champaign, Illinois, can supply evidence for these claims. Furthermore, there is reason to believe that elementary classroom teachers, given a relatively short period of inservice instruction, can master what has been called "aesthetic scanning" and teach it to their pupils. . . . The basic ground rule for these exercises is that pupils be ready to point to something in the object by virtue of which they are willing to assert that it has this or that property or characteristic. What could be more behavioral? There is also nothing to prevent the teacher from having the pupils make their own aesthetic objects to serve as targets for perception. In this way performance training and perception training coalesce. The performer and the maker use perception from moment to moment to test whether the effects they desire are being achieved.

For example, the distinction between sensory and formal properties can be brought out more clearly if we vary one dimension at a time. We can arrange six spots of red in a number of ways, or we can take any one of the patterns and give it a variety of colors or color combinations. Melodies can be held constant while rhythms are changed; rhythms can be held constant while the orchestration is varied. Sometimes works of art can be selected to bring out these distinctions. The plethora of collections of art reproductions now available in the various media makes the task of selecting materials for the study of the various dimensions of the aesthetic experience far easier than it used to be.

The teaching situation changes when we come to the expressive dimension of aesthetic properties. We can still use the perceptual approach, but we can no longer say with confidence just what it is that is to be perceived. Colors and shapes are fairly public objects, and given normal sense organs, there is little difficulty in getting agreement on whether a given area of color is red, green, or violet. The same, of course, is true in the fields of sounds and gestures. But suppose that a seascape is said to depict an angry sea or a melody is said to be cheerful and spritely or a poem melancholy. To what in the aesthetic object do we direct the attention of the observers as evidence for our characterization?

It makes sense to answer that the image as a whole provides that evidence, but sensory and formal properties may also be expressive. Colors and sounds and shapes can be expressive. They can be bright and sharp, serene or agitated. The way unity is achieved depends on aesthetic responses to formal properties. The criteria and language enumerated in the scanning chart (see Appendix) can be applied to the sensory and formal properties of the work as well as to the work as a whole.

And we can be true to the principle of phenomenological objectivity—namely, that whatever is being perceived must *be perceived as being in the object*—while not insisting that it is *ontologically* in the object.[3]

Appendix

Making an Informed Aesthetic Response[4]

I. *Aesthetic Perception*
    A. *Sensory Properties.* First, carefully look and/or listen; note what actually exists within an object or event and then identify as completely as possible the character of its sensory properties (qualities that can be seen, felt, or heard):

    In art, identify the nature of elements such as shapes (square-round), lines (thick-thin), values (dark-light), textures (coarse-smooth), colors (bright-dull), size (large-small), space (deep-shallow), etc.

    In dance, observe body gestures (curved-angular), movements (fast-slow), space (open-contained), etc.

    In drama, observe elements such as vocal qualities (cadence, quiet-shrill), body movements (fast-slow), costumes and sets (sober-bold, realistic-abstract), etc.

    In music, identify the nature of aural qualities such as pitch (high-low), tempo (fast-slow), duration (long-short), dynamics (loud-soft), etc.

    B. *Formal Properties.* Second, respond to ways in which sensory properties are organized within an object or event by identifying the character of its formal properties (try to answer the following questions as the work is experienced):

    To what extent is each element necessary? What is the nature of the movement (real or imagined) from one part to another, which thereby contributes to a sense of evolution and unity? How is the sense of unity maintained, even though elements may vary? How is unity in variety achieved?

    Are there some elements that are more dominant than others— a hierarchy of elements? Which elements appear to be most dominant, thereby contributing to the major theme? How is variety achieved in the repetition of these elements, so that thematic variation results?

    How is equilibrium maintained between and among both similar and diverse parts, so that a sense of balance is created?

What rhythmical qualities are created when mode of balance and thematic variation are combined?

C. *Expressive Properties.* Third, reflect upon both the nature of the existing sensory properties and the ways they appear to be organized and then speculate about the possible meanings of an object or event by identifying its expressive properties. Aesthetic objects and events possess presentational (faces, trees, environmental sounds, familiar movements, etc.) and/or metaphorical-symbolic characteristics that evoke responses from one's storehouse of images and, when combined with sensory and formal properties, translate into pervasive qualities, such as:

Mood language—nuances of feeling describable in terms such as *somber, menacing, frivolous,* etc.

Dynamic states—arousing a sense of tension, conflict, relaxation, etc.

Idea and ideal language—interpretations of social or psychological events and beliefs, and/or expressions of courage, wisdom, etc.

D. *Technical Properties.* Finally, one can also be attracted to an object or event and attempt to identify how it was created because of the significance of its technical properties. Attending to the extraordinary surface texture created by an impasto application of paint or the richly patterned sounds produced by the pizzicato plucking of violin strings are examples of reacting to the technical aspects of art forms. Knowing how something is made is often important to aesthetic perception; however, aesthetic responses and judgments can be made without such awareness if other properties are considered.

II. *Aesthetic Criticism*
A. *Historical.* Determining the nature and expressive intent of works of art within their historical context and in relation to school, period, style, and culture.
B. *Recreative.* Apprehending and relating imaginatively what the artist has expressed in a specific work.
C. Estimating the value of works of art in relation to other works using three criteria: degree of formal excellence, truth, and significance.[5]

Notes

1. S. M. Langer, *Philosophy in a New Key* (Cambridge, Mass., 1942); idem, *Feeling and Form* (New York, 1953).

2. From D. H. Parker, *The Analysis of Art* (New Haven, Conn., 1926); reproduced in M. Rader, *A Modern Book of Esthetics*, 3rd ed. (New York, 1960), pp. 323-31.

3. See H. S. Broudy, *Enlightened Cherishing: An Essay on Aesthetic Education* (Urbana, Ill., 1972), chap. 2, pp. 75-76.

4. Prepared by H. S. Broudy and R. Silverman.

5. Adapted from T. M. Greene, *The Arts and the Art of Criticism* (Princeton, N. J., 1940), reproduced in M. Rader, ed., *A Modern Book of Aesthetics*, 3rd ed. (New York, 1960), pp. 323-331.

B. Implementing and Evaluating

MICHAEL D. DAY

The Characteristics, Benefits, and Problems Associated with Implementing DBAE

High school graduates probably know Madonna, the pop singer, but are they able to appreciate a *Madonna* by Raphael, the great painter? They probably are more familiar with Kermit the Frog than with Rodin's *The Thinker.*

Is the popular culture, so readily absorbed through the mass media, sufficient for the education of our students? Or do the schools have a responsibility to provide access to the best images artists of the world have produced?

Should students learn to express their thoughts and feelings in visual form? Should students be able to experience the wonder of Van Gogh's *Starry Night*, the calm mood of introspection conveyed by an Indian Buddha, or the powerful emotional quality of an African mask? Should the high school years prepare students to understand the role of the visual arts in their everyday lives through the mass media, advertising, fashion, and product design? Should they learn that art speaks to us in ways that words cannot; that art reflects the values of cultures and peoples; and that the visual arts communicate eloquently across time as a revealing mark of civilization?

Current recommendations for art education call for a comprehensive view of the visual arts that fosters skills in creative expression, understanding of the nature of art, the ability to respond deeply to works of art, and comprehension of the roles that art plays within historical and cultural contexts. This approach has come to be known as discipline-based art education (DBAE) because content for curriculum and instruction is derived from the art disciplines: art production, art criticism, art history, and aesthetics.

More and more school districts across the country are recognizing the value of art education and are implementing discipline-based art programs. What are the characteristics of this approach; what are the benefits; and, what are the problems associated with implementation of discipline-based art education? In order to investigate these issues from the perspective of concerned educators, we will accompany two hypothetical secondary school principals on a visit to a high school that is involved in DBAE.

A Visit to Central High School

Fred and Myrna are high school principals from different sections of the country attending an education convention in another state. Both are looking for ways to evaluate the art programs in their respective schools and have specific questions in mind.

What are the current practices in art education? How can one recognize quality in the art program? Should the art program serve the entire range of students, college-bound as well as potential dropouts? Should art be viewed as a special subject for a few interested students or as an essential component for the general education of all students? What about occupations and careers in art for which students might prepare?

The conference program features visits to schools in the area with programs of particular interest. Myrna, Fred, and a few of their fellow principals choose to visit Central High School, noted for its up-to-date art program.

They are greeted in the Central High main office by Rebecca, a mid-career principal who was assigned to this school nearly six years ago. "Welcome to Central High. I know that you are especially interested in our art program, which we think is excellent."

The principal explains that this is not an art magnet or other art specialty school, and that Central provides a comprehensive curriculum of which they are proud. According to Rebecca, this district is not a wealthy one, although the schools are adequately funded. The district serves a mid-sized urban community with some suburban students. The district has developed a very current art program from kindergarten through the high school, and administrators are accustomed to hosting visitors interested in art education. She invites the group of visiting principals to ask questions at any time.

Fred responds immediately, "How is it that you can have an exemplary art program in a school that does not specialize in art? Many of us come from schools in which art is only an elective offering and is often vulnerable to budget cuts."

This question is central to the philosophical justification for art in education that distinguishes the discipline-based approach. Art is viewed as an essential component of a balanced education for all students, not just as a nicety that will enrich the education of a few who are particularly interested in art.

Rebecca explains that the district's board of education has endorsed art as a regular part of the instructional program, not only as an elective or a so-called "frill." The board has studied the state curriculum guidelines and recommendations from other respected professional sources and has supported art as an essential.

Myrna asks, "Do you mean that art is required for graduation?"

"Yes, it is," explains Rebecca. "Every student is required to take one of the art offerings during their four year program at Central."

State Graduation Requirements

According to the National Art Education Association, she says, 26 states currently have art requirements for graduation. Central High, as other high schools in the country, has developed courses that address this requirement and that appeal widely to students who are not necessarily interested in art as a career. The studio art offerings remain central to the program but, as Rebecca explains, the view that art is an important academic subject influences the content and instruction in studio courses as well.

"I'm anxious to see what you are talking about," says Fred. "It sounds like you have an unlimited budget."

"Not at all," replies Rebecca. "Let's move over to the art area and you can see what the students have done and meet Bill, the head of our art program."

As they walk through the school, the group notices a number of impressive art displays. A large bulletin board near the art room is filled with a range of student work. One display is based on the study of Cubist painting and includes reproductions of works by Picasso, Braque, and Gris, three prominent Cubist artists. Historical information about the artists and the Cubist style is included in the display, along with material about the intellectual and cultural influences of pre-World War Europe. Student still life collages, obviously influenced by the Cubist style, are displayed with lettered signs which identify art concepts that were studied and applied by the students.

Rebecca points out to the group the selection of the display that depicts African masks and presents information about the African cultures that produced them. The influence of these masks is evident in a reproduction of a painting by Picasso.

Fred is concerned that the approach is too academic for most students. "Do the students understand these concepts? Aren't they bored with the historical part? I would think that they have enough of that in their history classes."

Comprehensive Art Education

"Let's ask Bill," says Rebecca, as they move into the art room where Bill is waiting to be introduced.

After the formalities, Bill leads them on a tour of the art room. "There are other high schools that have better facilities than we do, as we are not a large school. In the studio area we offer courses in drawing and painting, ceramcs, printmaking, graphic design, and photography. We have the tools and equipment to offer a crafts course occasionally, depending on student demand. We also offer a general art history and appreciation course for students who want to learn more about art, but who do not want to specialize."

The Central program offers two art history courses for students interested in advanced study or the Advanced Placement program for college-bound students, Bill explains. But the artwork on display is from the foundation history and appreciation course that fulfills the graduation requirement in art. Some art history is included in every studio class as well. Cultural and critical content is integrated with studio activities in ways that students seem to enjoy.

"Well, that appears to be one of the unique aspects of your art program at Central," says Fred. "You seem to teach art history with everything else."

Bill explains that the Central High program is patterned after the approach to art education that is generally known as discipline-based (Clark, Day, and Greer, 1987). It is a balanced, comprehensive approach that focuses on helping students to understand the roles that art plays in their lives and in cultures of the past and present.

One of these roles, of course, is personal artistic expression. Although there is some debate about terminology, this approach is recommended by the National Art Education Association (1986), the National Endowment for the Arts, the College Board, the Getty Center for Education in the Arts (1985), many state departments of education, and numerous school districts.

Fred appears impressed, but not totally convinced by Bill's explanation. "Is this something new? If it is so highly recommended, why isn't DBAE taught in more schools?"

Rebecca responds, "You know how demanding it is to keep up with educational innovation in all the subject areas as well as with technology, such as computers." This approach is an educational innovation in the area of art, she explains, and it represents a major change in the way educators think about the role of art in general education and as a foundation for advanced study and career choice.

A discipline-based art program provides excellent opportunities in the area of higher levels of thinking, a major concern in general education.

The basic ideas of the discipline-based approach have been in the professional literature for decades. Many teachers, schools, and districts across the country implement parts of the DBAE program. Major changes in education often occur slowly, however, so that to date relatively few districts have fully implemented the approach.

There is currently a significant amount of activity in this direction at the regional, state, and local levels. Evidence of this change can be seen in the content of state art frameworks and guides, in the topics on agendas of state and professional meetings of art educators, in the professional literature, in the significant increase in published support materials for art instruction, and in district art guides.

Instructional Materials

The principals in our hypothetical group move around the art room, viewing the displays and the facilities. They are attracted to a display of Chinese landscapes balanced with a dozen sensitive student landscapes in watercolor. They note a magazine rack with titles such as *American Artist, Art in America, ARTnews, Ceramics, Art Education, School Arts, Art and Man,* and others. A number of art books are found on a shelf next to the magazines.

Rebecca and Bill, major players in the development of this high school discipline-based art program, continue to lead the tour and explain the theory on which the program is founded. The visiting group learns that visual instructional materials are necessary for this approach and that the art room features a modest resource area in the storage room with trays of slides, sound filmstrips on various art topics, and large mounted art prints labeled and stored for easy access.

In response to the question of budget Rebecca explains that, since art is considered a regular subject in the curriculum, it receives the same priority for instructional supplies as math, science, history, or physical education. She notes that visual materials, like textbooks, can last for years when they are properly cared for. Slides and prints of artworks do not become outdated, but can be purchased with each year's budget to form a significant collection. And, because some of the courses emphasize the critical and historical dimensions of art learning, fewer expendable art supplies are needed.

Rebecca conveys her belief that the discipline-based approach, because it deals with a wide range of content and learning activities, accommodates a range of student learning styles. For example, art production requires the making of qualitative decisions as well as skills of rendering. Concepts, ideas, and ideals can be conveyed by students in visual form through the process of artistic expression. Art history can be verbally demanding while requiring students to make fine visual distinctions. Research and writing skills can be developed in relation to visual content.

A discipline-based art program provides excellent opportunities in the area of higher levels of thinking, a major concern in general education. As they talk and write about exemplary artworks, students apply visual concepts, recognize stylistic characteristics, discover expressive content, and interpret meanings in visual forms. As they examine fundamental questions about art, such as what art is and what determines value in art, students are engaged in aesthetics, or philosophy of art. They learn to formulate questions and issues about art, develop supportive arguments, and recognize valid alternative arguments on the issues.

Studio Production in DBAE

Fred looks up from the art book that he is examining. "But, aren't you concerned that you have de-emphasized personal expression and made art too much like every other academic subject?"

Bill, who considers himself a serious artist, responds. "I was concerned about that myself in the beginning. But our studio courses enroll about the same number of students as they did before we initiated this approach.

"Now we are also reaching students who want to study art, but not as artists. The interesting thing is that our studio students produce better work because they are more aware of ideas and options for their own expression as a result of becoming aware of what other artists have done.

"For example, they understand the various ways that space is manipulated by painters from various times and cultures, as you noted in the bulletin board displays of Cubism, African art, and Chinese painting. This provides them with a range of ways that they can deal with space in their own drawings and paintings. Our advanced studio students get involved with expressing ideas in their work. I might add that they are very successful in student art competitions and with Advanced Placement exams."

As a typical art teacher, Bill indicates his interest in the futures of his advanced students. "We are satisfied that we can meet the needs of a broader population of students as well as those especially interested in art. We are thinking also of the range of art careers for which our students might want to prepare." The range of art careers is much broader than the traditional role of the fine artist, he explains. Included are such occupations as art teaching, art museum education, and art curatorial work. Some students might decide to become art historians, critics, or aestheticians, or maybe even gallery directors, art administrators, or art dealers. Some students who specialize in studio production will want to go on to art school or study in a college art department. Others will consider the wide range of applied arts such as illustration, graphic design, architecure, or fashion design, to name a few. Or, they might decide to become exhibiting fine artists who make a living from their creative works.

The discipline-based program, Bill believes, provides advanced students, even those who are primarily interested in art history or criticism, a fair understanding of their options for careers and occupations in art. Counseling is essential to inform students of the many art career options, the various possibilities for advanced study, and to assist them to make career choices.

Because the range of content in a DBAE program is broad, art teachers find themselves engaged in a variety of instructional activities, Rebecca explains. They demonstrate art production skills with brush and paint, lecture with projected slides of artworks, lead discussions about art, supervise research projects, and help students talk and write about specific artworks including their own.

Art teachers who use this approach become versatile as instructors as they are called upon to teach a greater variety of content. This versatility allows a small art staff to present a range of courses that focus on art history and appreciation, aesthetics and criticism, and studio production. It also encourages the integration of art discipline content within all classes.

Content from the four art disciplines is included in all art courses and presented in an integrated fashion, but the emphasis on a particular discipline will vary with each course. Art history courses, for example, will engage in studio production sparingly, usually as a means to reinforce a historical understanding such as the use of cartoons by the great Renaissance muralists.

Studio courses continue to focus on developing expressive competencies in students. Study of great works of art and the reasons for their greatness is presented to assist students in their own work. When they understand purposes and ideas associated with various artistic styles, students gain additional control of their own creative expression. And they are introduced to ideas and methods that otherwise might not have occurred to them.

In courses required for all students, an attempt is made to present a more balanced emphasis of content from the art disciplines, but the studio part takes a larger share of class time. Content from more than one discipline is often considered simultaneously, as when students critique their own work. At a basic level content from the disciplines often merges, as when students apply critical judgment in the course of painting a canvas.

Evaluation of Student Progress

Rebecca leads the way to the ceramics room as she discusses the role of evaluation of student progress in arts courses. Evaluation in art is treated very much as in other subjects, except that different methods are necessary to accommodate differences in subject matter and types of learning. The breadth of content and variety of instructional methods require a range of evaluation methods as well.

The purposes of evaluation efforts are to validate student progress and assess effectiveness of the art program. Common devices can be used, such as questionnaires, tests, performance assessments, essays, and interviews with students. Some evaluation procedures are unique to art, such as identification of artworks and artistic styles, and judgment of aesthetic qualities in students' art production. A variety of methods can be applied to determine profiles of student progress and also for grading purposes. Such obvious items as participation in a project or class discussion or completion of an assignment are part of typical evaluation efforts.

Bill adds, "We feel that we can discuss their progress with each student and point out their strengths and where they might need more effort. We believe that this approach encourages students, especially those who have some difficulties with art production or with writing, for example. They realize that they can build on their personal strengths and that their success in class will not be determined solely by a specific ability in which they might be weak."

Myrna listens to this discussion with a somewhat perplexed look on her face. "I don't think that my art teachers will go for this approach.

They are interested in art production and view themselves as artists, modeling this behavior for the students. They like to focus on creativity and artistic expression rather than on educational concerns such as curriculum development and evaluation strategies."

Rebecca and Bill agree with Myrna that this can be a problem. Bill has experienced this preference among colleagues around the state. "It is not surprising that some experienced teachers are uncomfortable when introduced to the DBAE approach. It appears to require additional art background and teaching skills in order to bring in the cultural and critical components."

The purposes of evaluation efforts are to validate student progress and assess the effectiveness of the art program.

This situation is changing, as many of the colleges and universities that educate teachers currently advocate the discipline-based approach and present a balanced program for prospective art teachers with significant course requirements in art history and at least one course in aesthetics and art criticism. In these programs undergraduates are informed about methods of instruction, curriculum, and evaluation and are made aware of commercially available art curricula and curriculum materials.

However, other teacher education programs, either because of philosophical differences or hesitancy to change, continue to prepare teachers with an almost exclusive emphasis on studio production. Many art teachers enter art education because of love for painting or sculpting, and most have a strong studio emphasis in the undergraduate program. It is not uncommon that certified art teachers have no coursework in aesthetics or art criticism. And too often art history at the college level is taught in ways that would be uninteresting for high school students.

"What is the answer to this problem, then?" Fred joins the discussion. "How do you convince art teachers to accept this notion?"

Changing to DBAE

"First, we need to recognize that many fine art teachers will not choose to change their programs in this direction. We realize that DBAE is an alternative approach to teaching art, and we see quite a few benefits to adopting it here at Central. Other districts might want different outcomes, however, and choose to implement art programs that focus exclusively on studio production. We realize also that some programs attempt something in between the discipline-based program and exclusive studio orientation."

"However," she continues, "for teachers who are interested in changing to this approach, we have noticed a rejuvenation in some of their careers. One of the teachers on our staff is an example of this. After teaching for fifteen years she had begun to feel burned out and was considering retiring from teaching.

"When she decided to give DBAE a try she started reading the current art journals and other art history sources and visiting art galleries and museums more often. From some of the art education literature and a demonstration she saw at the state art education conference, she learned a model for engaging students in critical discussion of artworks.

"The result is that this teacher is excited, not only with her own learning, but with the skills that she can now share with her students. She has restructured her courses considerably and finds that she now enjoys teaching very much. She seems to be ready for another fifteen years."

Myrna appears especially interested in the change process with respect to the art program. "Considering what we all know about implementing new educational programs or curricula, it doesn't seem realistic to think that you could develop this art program merely by asking your art teachers to read some articles and attend a couple of demonstrations."

"Of course you are right," Rebecca says with emphasis. "I mentioned earlier that this approach has been adopted by the school board and it has been implemented on a district-wide basis from kindergarten through high school. This was accomplished with considerable effort and support within the regular district process for implementation of any curriculum change."

One recent study on implementation of discipline-based art education (McLaughlin and Thomas, 1985) stressed the broad support from community, top school administration, art educators, and teachers that is required for successful implementation. Support came, in one case, from a state college professor who understood this approach and worked with the district as a consultant. Another district received assistance from the art person at the state department of education.

Any strong implementation effort requires regular inservice time to provide education for all teachers from elementary, middle, and high schools who are responsible for teaching art. Districts most often experience success when implementation of art programs is conducted according to regular implementation procedures that have worked for new programs in reading, math, and other regular subjects.

A Discipline-Based Art Program

Another hour is spent by the group in discussion and observation of students' paintings, ceramics, and other art objects, applied design such as illustration and graphics, critical commentary written by students, brief essays on aesthetics topics, and research papers on art historical subjects. After appropriate expressions of appreciation and farewells, the group of school administrators return to the convention headquarters.

During their visit they learned that the discipline-based art program at Central has the following characteristics:

1. Art is considered an essential component for a balanced general education for all students.

2. Art is taught regularly to all students in the elementary and middle grades in the school district. The high school art program assumes this prior learning and begins at relatively advanced levels of instruction.

3. The art program offers strong courses in studio art production and also features art courses that emphasize a combination of content from the disciplines of art history, art criticism, and aesthetics.

4. All students take at least one art class during their four years of high school. Many take a course in art history and appreciation that includes some studio production, but does not require high levels of studio proficiency. Others take beginning-level studio courses, such as drawing or painting. These courses also include considerable historical and cultural art content related to the studio emphasis.

5. Students who desire to study art at advanced levels can choose from courses that emphasize art history, aesthetics and art criticism, and a selection of studio courses.

6. All the art courses at Central are written in syllabus form with goals, objectives, vocabulary, lists of materials, content derived from the art disciplines, suggested activities, and evaluation. The written syllabus also contains lists of artworks that students will see during the course. Historical information such as name of artist, country or culture, date or period, medium of the work, style or tradition, and relevant contextual commentary is included.

7. All courses in the Central art program feature numerous art images used during instruction. These are in the form of slides, prints, filmstrips, books, and magazines.

8. Evaluation of student progress is an integral part of each art course. Evaluation is taken as seriously here as in the math or science programs. Assessment procedures are appropriate for the unique content of art.

9. Students who choose to take advanced art courses at Central are provided with up-to-date counseling about potential careers in art and about art schools and colleges that can provide the types of education required for various career choices.

References

Clark, Gilbert, Day, Michael, and Greer, Dwaine. "Discipline-Based Art Education: Becoming Students of Art." *The Journal of Aesthetic Education*, Summer 1987.

Day, Michael. "Evaluating Student Achievement in Discipline-Based Art Programs." *Studies in Art Education*, Summer 1985.

Getty Center for Education in the Arts. *Beyond Creating: The Place for Art in America's Schools*. Los Angeles, Calif.: J. Paul Getty Trust, 1985.

McLaughlin, Milbrey, and Thomas, Margaret. *Art History, Art Criticism, and Art Production: An Examination of Art Education in Selected School Districts*. Vol. III. Executive Summary. Los Angeles, Calif.: Rand Corp., 1985.

National Art Education Association. *Quality Art Education: Goals for Schools*. Reston Va.: NAEA, 1986.

W. Dwaine Greer

Improving Visual Arts Education

The literature of school change is replete with accounts of the frustrations of reformers who have attempted to change the status quo. Projects that have attempted to introduce new methods of instruction or to change curricula have often been short-lived. The open classroom and team teaching movement are two examples of such efforts that have had little lasting effect.

The Institute has had outcomes different from these earlier efforts. Given the presence of five necessary components identified in the Institute research—substantive training of teachers and principals, use of a written curriculum, consistent district leadership, adequate funding and resources, and commitment and enthusiasm of district leaders—many classroom teachers have been able to establish DBAE as part of their districts' regular instructional programs. Though not without problems, the Institute was successful in effecting this change in art education, from marginal status to an essential part of the general curriculum, because of the following elements in its approach:

1. Art instruction, previously viewed by school staffs and community leaders as a special activity and not part of the basic curriculum, became seen as a discipline-valid part of general education.
2. Staff development activities enriched teachers' understandings of art, presented instructional strategies for conducting discipline-based art instruction, and focused on use of a written DBAE curriculum.
3. Implementation of the DBAE approach was established as a long-range team effort that involved all levels of district personnel.
4. Evaluation was used to refine both staff development and implementation efforts in relation to discipline-based ideas.

ESTABLISHING ART AS A PART OF GENERAL EDUCATION

The Bases for Program Change

That art should be a part of the general education of all students seems to be a reasonable expectation. Persons presented with the discipline-based rationale for art in general education—how art builds the allusionary base by which language is built and how it contributes to the set of structures that provide lenses for understanding the world and form the bases for critical thinking[1]—are quick to recognize the void that would exist if the study of art were eliminated. This concept of what is lacking in a student's education when the serious study of art is not included proved very appealing to parents, school board members, and administrators.

Institute participants quickly realized that art education that addresses the understanding and appreciation of art is a desirable part of the school curriculum. Concepts from the four art disciplines provided them with a structure for defining and describing what students can learn in their art program. Content is embodied in a curriculum, and the curriculum is the foundation for a districtwide program that can be evaluated.

At the classroom level, what emerges from adopting DBAE as an approach to art education is the shift from a focus on studio activities to a greater balance of instruction in the four art disciplines. The motivation for teachers to change their classroom art programs came from a variety of sources: the recognition of and decision to act consistently with their own values, the observation of their students' powerfully positive response to DBAE, and, in some instances, the imposition of their administrations.

Administrators see the narrower interpretation of studio art as teaching a special subject to a special group of students, those who are talented and who may become artists. They believe that there is a place for special programs for the gifted and talented, but also that most students are not future artists. Because it is the general student who will constitute the audience for art, these district decision makers see the balanced instruction of DBAE as better serving all students.

Cautions and Constraints

Even as the success of discipline-based ideas as a foundation for art in general education is seen, there are notes of caution. At the outset of the Institute, DBAE theory had been set forth in the field of art education in very general terms.[2] It was well enough articulated to serve as a basis for beginning staff development efforts, but it was very quickly apparent that there were few curriculum models available and little history of classroom practice in disciplines other than art production. As the Institute staff developed each succeeding summer program, art educators who were working on materials in art history, aesthetics, and criticism brought their ideas to the participants. The materials that were prepared for these disciplines have become a part of the literature of DBAE and have been widely circulated and used. Nonetheless, a substantial need remains for the development and testing of additional DBAE curricula and materials.

In addition to the preparation of staff development and classroom materials for the various disciplines, refinement and further articulation of the DBAE theory itself was necessary. Over the course of the Institute's efforts, theoretical work by many in the field has continued, and the increasing amount of professional literature provides a rich source for those who are interested in DBAE theory.[3]

At the same time, the ongoing development and refinement of theory does create problems for those interested in using a DBAE approach. Written materials and both preservice and inservice training must also continue to change as the theory is developed. The ongoing changes require that the materials used and the background of teachers already trained need to be continually updated. This need for ongoing reeducation and refinement of practice often creates funding problems. Not only must art compete with other subjects afforded higher priority, but schools are not accustomed to continuing staff development costs in any one subject area, much less art, over a sustained period. Training in one subject area is likely to be of short duration, and funds are then switched to another subject, until the next curriculum adoption cycle comes around. Only when the general benefits of discipline-based art education have become apparent and are accepted can we expect a level of commitment in any district that will ensure the ongoing staff development required for successful districtwide DBAE implementation.

STAFF DEVELOPMENT FOR TEACHER ENRICHMENT AND IMPROVED INSTRUCTION

The twin components of staff development and curriculum implementation were designed so that they took into account the many variables that are necessary for educational change to take place. The Institute staff development program provided rich encounters with art and presented the major ideas of a subject that few teachers were ever required to study. For many participants this personal enrichment was a major factor in their acceptance of DBAE and in revitalizing their teaching.

Practice lessons and introduction to curriculum resources were also significant for many teachers, who wanted to take something back that they could immediately apply in their classrooms. When teachers returned to their classrooms, it was the Institute's curriculum focus that accounted for much of their success in changing instruction. The requirement that participating districts adopt a written, sequential curriculum as the basis for implementation was a strength of the model. This requirement, however, is also one of the areas where problems arose and remain.

Cautions and Constraints

As teachers gain new levels of background and expertise in art, they look for ways to use their newly acquired skills. Successful implementation programs must allow for new ways for teachers to apply what they have learned.

It follows from the logic of the DBAE approach that the strength of the program rests in large part on the quality and comprehensiveness of the curricula adopted by districts. While many teachers are willing and able to add to a curriculum to ensure that it covers all the components of a discipline-based approach, most quite logically expect to achieve the goal by simply teaching the curriculum well. The limitations of commercially available curricula remain a major problem for those who are attempting to implement DBAE—that is, many curricula fail to incorporate aesthetics, have limited visual examples, or emphasize production almost exclusively. Unfortunately, when districts set about writing their own curriculum in response to their needs, the challenges of developing sequential and cumulative curricula become apparent. Unless there are sufficient resources and enough people with DBAE expertise assigned to the task of curriculum development, the results are likely to be less than satisfactory.

IMPLEMENTATION AS A LONG-RANGE TEAM EFFORT

Choosing an approach that could bring about change in the way art is taught presented a major challenge to the Getty Institute staff. Many earlier attempts in education to change school practice were either top-down impositions managed by administrators or bottom-up efforts focused on retraining teachers. Neither approach had proven successful.

In addition, most efforts in specific subject areas followed a six- or seven-year curriculum cycle designed to give periodic attention to each subject area in turn. Art would come up for attention every six or seven years and receive special attention for one year. In the interim, art could be safely ignored. The Los Angeles Getty Institute was designed to address both these problems.

The Team Concept

The Institute did not assume that any one level of personnel involved in the introduction of DBAE would be the key to change. The project required that individual school teams be composed of at least two teachers plus the principal. Special events and information sessions were provided for all levels of district administrators and for board of education members. The concept was to create leadership teams that would be able to work with all aspects of the system. To ensure districtwide attention to DBAE, the Institute staff sought leaders or champions at all levels, from classroom teachers to school board members. When champions emerged, the Institute staff supported those leaders with advocacy materials and ongoing training as they worked with their district teams to implement DBAE. The district inservice resource team and school leadership team system provides a way to effect change throughout a district. It is an approach that can be used with any subject, and some participating districts have begun to build inservice resource teams for other subjects, adapting the model used in art.

The Five-Year Implementation Model

Earlier studies of educational change showed that leaders in the change process frequently made mistaken assumptions, such as that once innovation was introduced and initial training had taken place, teachers and principals would be able to put the idea into practice. Little attention was given to the kind of effort required to achieve institutionalization. Knowing that the establishment of DBAE had to be a long-term process, the Institute asked districts to make a five-year commitment.

The first set of teams trained in each district initiated the planning process that guided the implementations. As teachers returned to their classrooms to begin implementation, the Institute established a support system to encourage and sustain their efforts. Leadership teams were given training in leadership skills and strategies for bringing about district change. Training sessions were held for school board members, district-level administrators, and principals. Each group told evaluators how effective the approach was. School board members, for example, commented that this was one of the few times when they were really informed about a new program.

Attending to individuals in the change process is important, but attention to the institutional character of the schools is equally crucial. It is apparent from project results that using an approach congruent with the way schools deal with other subjects was a factor in the Institute's success. Because the DBAE approach called for building knowledge and skills based on content from recognized art disciplines and was based on the use of a written, sequential curriculum and included the expectation of accountability, those responsible for major curriculum decisions recognized that art instruction could be managed in the same manner as other curricular areas. Art could join the rest of the subjects in general education.

Cautions and Constraints

The inservice resource (IR) team is a powerful way to introduce change into a district. Once the team is in place, however, there are considerations that require attention. To maintain the team, new members have to be trained and team members require ongoing renewal and update. In addition, the team has to feel useful. Team members need to have meaningful tasks to perform that make use of their training, or their interest wanes. They need adequate district support to continue their efforts. New superintendents and board members bring with them new priorities, and they need to be persuaded that the district's DBAE program is an important part of the general education curriculum and must be supported.

Inevitably, as in many human endeavors, personal and political agendas can create friction and even sabotage the best of programs. For this reason, careful district selection of participants, sensitivity of Institute staff members, and high-quality leadership training are important factors in combating potential problems.

Solidifying membership in IR teams between the third and fourth summers of a five-year program appears necessary, first to allow natural leaders to emerge and then to provide them with recognition and a position from which they can influence district DBAE implementation.

Two desirable outcomes for IR teams to seek are the annual provision of DBAE orientation for all new teachers in their districts and the placement of DBAE inservices on their districts' annual master calendars. These steps help DBAE implementation to move from its status as a new program to a natural, accepted component of a district's educational plan.

It was recognized that teachers, team leaders, and administrators tend to have an insatiable need for support in their attempts to institutionalize a new program. Finding a balance between what the Institute staff could provide and what needed to be provided by district personnel, district resources, or other outside experts proved to be a delicate issue.

Follow-Up

Two years after the Institute significantly decreased its support of DBAE in the 21 districts, the districts' IR teams were visited to assess the status of their programs. The following conclusions were drawn:

- Teachers trained by the Institute were still teaching art in a discipline-based approach and had probably improved with experience and the renewal efforts provided to them. They had been won over, and their commitment remained strong.
- The remaining teachers in the districts, having received less training or none at all, were probably not providing much in the way of DBAE because training expectations for some IR teams had not been met.
- All the IR teams that had met their training expectations had district administrators and/or principals as members. IR teams staffed only with teachers had not been nearly as effective, because they had little influence in setting priorities.
- The more the district administration was involved, the more likely it was that the DBAE program was functioning and expanding.

Based on these conclusions, an evaluator recommended that if the IR teams were to be strengthened, especially in light of impending budget problems, the following efforts were necessary:

- The commitment of trained teachers would have to be fortified with renewal activities, and new teachers would have to be provided with introductory training.
- Training for principals would need to be intensified so that principals could make DBAE happen at each site.
- The commitment of administrators and board members, most of whom serve finite terms within their districts, would need to be recaptured continually.

Without these efforts, many teachers and administrators anticipated that their DBAE programs would show significant decline by the following year and would thereafter be little more than the classroom efforts of individual teachers, of whom there would be fewer with each passing year. On the assumption that the Institute's strategy for changing art education was basically appropriate and efficient, the conclusion seemed to be that such changes cannot be initiated and then maintained on their own. Promoters of such changes need to provide maintenance on a continuing basis.

EVALUATION IN RELATION TO DBAE THEORY

Very few educational projects undergo the extensive evaluation that marked the Los Angeles Getty Institute. Outside evaluators offered a level of objectivity that gives special credence to the findings of this research and development project. The formative nature of the evaluations provided impetus for the evolving nature of the Institute. The model, with its focus on staff development, curriculum implementation, and goals for each component of the project, provided criteria against which progress was measured regularly. Evaluation studies, particularly those relating to measures of teacher attitude change and effectiveness of staff development presentations, also served subsequent Getty Center projects.

Cautions and Constraints

The lack of consensus about the content of art curricula causes ongoing problems in the area of student assessment. The use of criterion measures that are curriculum specific seems to be the most effective strategy available at the present. Further refinement of the theory and delineation of content from each of the disciplines in relation to each grade level remain as major contributions to the field yet to be made. It may well be that the current call for accountability in the arts will hasten the day when there are student learning outcomes that can be addressed by several different curricula, all leading to a deeper, more complete understanding of the world of art.

Notes

1. Harry S. Broudy, *The Uses of Schooling* (New York: Routledge, 1988).
2. W. Dwaine Greer, "A Discipline-based Art Education: Approaching Art as a Subject of Study," *Studies in Art Education* 25, no. 4 (1984): 212-18.
3. W. Dwaine Greer, "Developments in DBAE: From Art Education toward Arts Education," *Studies in Art Education* 34, no. 2 (1992): 91-101.

BRENT WILSON AND BLANCHE RUBIN

DBAE and Educational Change

In reforming art education, it is deceptively easy to think that since teachers are responsible for delivering art instruction, reform initiatives should be directed primarily toward elementary and secondary school art teachers and elementary classroom teachers (who teach art in approximately half the nation's schools that function without art specialists). After all, as conventional wisdom tells us, they are on the firing line and if they don't change, nothing will change. Conventional wisdom, however, ignores the fact that change must occur simultaneously throughout an entire community, and that activating one group within a community seldom changes the whole. What is the community in which Getty-sponsored DBAE evolved and how did it function?

The first lesson from the Regional Institute programs, building on the early findings of the Los Angeles Institute, is that the reform of art education cannot be left to teachers alone; if left just to art and classroom teachers, the effort will fail. Ironically, however, if teachers are not at the center of educational reform, the effort will also fail. Expansion of the number and types of individuals and institutions responsible for "shaping" art instruction is one of the most important factors associated with the development of DBAE in Getty-sponsored institutes.

The original request for proposals for Regional Institutes called for programs to "adapt or replicate or provide new models for staff development and curriculum implementation." The evaluation team perceived that newly appointed Regional Institute directors were uncertain regarding the extent to which they could depart from the DBAE model developed in Los Angeles. After the issue was raised and discussed, it was resolved that the new institutes were research and development projects, free to develop new forms of DBAE. The charge to develop new forms of DBAE was a second factor that distinguished the Regional Institutes from the Los Angeles initiative. But who was to do the developing?

In addition to receiving the charge to develop new forms of DBAE, each Regional Institute was expected to create a consortium consisting of:

(1) a central organization with directors, advisory boards, staff members, institute faculty members and facilitators, consultants from the arts and academic disciplines, advisers, and evaluators,
(2) school districts that entered into agreements with the Regional Institutes to participate in discipline-based professional development programs and to support DBAE program implementation In district schools—both administratively and financially,
(3) colleges and universities and their departments of art, education, art education, literature, philosophy (and in some instances, music and theater) including faculty members, administrators, and students,
(4) state departments of education and, in some instances, educational service units and other subdivisions of departments of education, bringing educational services to groups of local school districts,
(5) museums and art centers,
(6) state and local arts and humanities agencies and organizations, and
(7) professional educational associations of teachers and administrators, charitable foundations, and grant-giving organizations.

Prior to the establishment of the Regional Institutes the theory and practice of Getty-sponsored DBAE programs had been in the hands of relatively few art educators and discipline consultants associated with the Los Angeles Institute. When literally thousands of stakeholders in the various consortia took the principles of DBAE and shaped them to their individual needs and interests, the DBAE initiative changed drastically. It evolved from a top-down to a top-down/bottom-up reform initiative.

We will describe just a few of the interacting change forces[1] that functioned within the emerging DBAE consortia. In summer professional development programs—often held in museums—artists, art historians, critics, and philosophers of art brought the modernist/postmodernist debates about issues such as feminist art history and anti-formalism to the study of DBAE. Museum educators presented their permanent collections and special exhibitions as the primary content of DBAE. Classroom teachers brought with them already established practices such as "whole language" instruction and already-constructed interdisciplinary instructional units "ready" for art to be infused. District administrators established the expectation that a new art program was to be developed and implemented; if they didn't, district-wide DBAE programs seldom flourished. School principals developed five-year plans for organizing school curricula to include art and sometimes even centered on art. When they didn't, schoolwide programs seldom developed. Art educators brought to the table their conventional conceptions of how to teach art—such as curricula based on the elements and principles of design—as well as a desire to broaden their art teaching to include history, criticism, and aesthetics, and they struggled to resolve contradictions. Students enriched DBAE theory and practice by adding ideas or fresh insights their teachers may not have considered and by initiating activities that suggested new procedures for developing portfolios. In our role as evaluators we were able to observe the results of the interactions of these forces—some positive and some negative. Conventional approaches were pitted against innovation, and change forces contended with desires for the status quo. While all of this brewed, the summer Regional Institute staff development programs functioned like rites of passage to new forms of art education. Theories and principles of DBAE were handed to practitioners and through their experiments and applications to classroom practice, DBAE evolved from an initiative designed by a small number of individuals to one shaped by thousands. The consortia became change communities consisting of interactive networks for the development, transmission, and exchange of ideas, both within a single consortium and throughout the seven consortia. At first, existing theory led practice. Then, through the work of practitioners, new forms of DBAE had to be accounted for theoretically. Practice sometimes guided theory.

Just as the regional consortia became change communities, so did some individual school districts and schools. Effective districtwide DBAE implementation programs were invariably led by district administrators and their staffs. In a variety of ways district leaders informed school administrators that each school was to develop a DBAE program: they appointed curriculum leaders, provided resources, and established district professional development programs in DBAE. Art specialists and classroom teachers committed to the arts assumed new leadership roles. Some of these programs were highly effective. For example, in a survey of one outstanding school district[2] we found that nearly 90 percent of the teachers involved with the DBAE Program believed that "one of the best things about the DBAE change initiative is that everybody from teacher to university art education professor, museum educator, and discipline expert is expected to contribute to the development of DBAE." Over two-thirds of the same teachers indicated that sometimes even students have an opportunity to have a significant influence on DBAE theory and practice. All of the teachers agreed that DBAE had provided the opportunity for collaborative development of discipline-based instruction within and among schools.

Members of the evaluation team found that they could recognize a DBAE elementary school within a few minutes of entering a school building. Students' works, artists' works, and students' writing about artworks (artists', and their own), share hallway display space. Every classroom features displays of artists' works and students' artworks. Labels around artworks indicate that the themes and ideas associated with artworks are interwoven with instruction in the arts and language arts, social studies, science, and mathematics. DBAE schools result from teachers and administrators developing one-year and five-year plans for art in their schools. Schools such as those we have just described are indeed communities that have been changed by art. The changes are the result of efforts of a vast consortium of individuals and institutions functioning within and beyond the schools.

The dramatic transformation of education through the visual arts that we have just characterized occurred in perhaps as few as five or ten percent of the schools that set out to implement a DBAE program. In other schools, anywhere from one or two teachers to most members of the staff adopted the new art program. When programs did not fully succeed, generally it was because district and school administrators did not seek the assistance of the complex consortium formed to serve their schools and districts, or did not have the vision to create local change communities.

We return to our initial point: DBAE is not just something that art and classroom teachers present to students. It is a systematic collaboration of many individuals working together within a change community that they have created. The Regional Institute programs demonstrated the vast array of factors that must be in place and functioning if a change initiative is to fully succeed.

The Place of the Art Disciplines in DBAE: Primary Content or Primary Means?

As its name implies, discipline-based art education has been defined by the content and inquiry processes of artists, art historians, critics, and philosophers of art—and possibly by the related disciplines of anthropologists, archeologists, sociologists, and cultural critics. During the time in which DBAE was being developed in the Regional Institutes, the art disciplines were themselves undergoing rapid change. Artists experimented with various forms of environmental, installation, and performance art. Critics, philosophers, and historians viewed contemporary artworks from new theoretical, aesthetic, political, and social perspectives—as well as from the vantage point of thoroughly established forms, theories, and practices associated with the disciplines. Art educators involved in the reform initiative were themselves subjected to different and sometimes conflicting sets of influences. As they experimented with DBAE and the content of their art instruction they had to struggle with points of conflict between new forms of art education and older forms reflected in state and school district curriculum guides, textbooks, and their own existing instructional practices.

Members of the evaluation team took the position that if art and the art disciplines were continually transforming themselves, then DBAE, if it were to remain true to its basic principles, would also continue to change. In our research we set out to:

(1) determine the structures and practices of different forms of DBAE,
(2) compare them to various aspects of content and inquiry processes found within the art disciplines,
(3) determine whether the different versions of DBAE contained within them sound conceptions of education,
(4) judge whether those conceptions would lead to the achievement of valid and enlightened art educational goals, and
(5) assess the prospects for improving the way art is taught in schools.

In short, we asked the question: did the forms of art instruction we observed in the Regional Institutes meet the promises implicit within this new and comprehensive conception of art education?

A Variety of Instructional Forms

When DBAE was introduced, art educators undertook detailed investigations of what aestheticians, artists, art critics, and art historians do. Consequently, the art disciplines came to be seen as the new content of art education. In "Becoming Students of Art," Clark, Day, and Greer (1987), for example, state that "content for [art] instruction is derived primarily from the disciplines of aesthetics, art criticism, art history, and art production" (p. 135). This first source of content for DBAE is followed by a second: "a broad range of visual arts, including folk, applied, and fine arts from Western and non-Western cultures and from ancient and contemporary times" (p. 135). We think that these two statements show the tension that existed at the outset between disciplines-as -

content and artworks-as-content. This tension was reflected in the variety of approaches to DBAE taken in the Regional Institute programs. We will characterize several of those forms, beginning with versions that we found problematic and ending with models we believe have promise.

Disciplines Disregarded. For over a half-century, the elements and principles of design have composed the content of most art programs. Curriculum guides and art textbooks present lessons based on line, shape, color, texture, balance, and emphasis as features common to all works of art. Did DBAE offer another instructional paradigm, and could art educators develop and use it? In DBAE staff development programs we watched art historians and critics, aestheticians and artists demonstrate their inquiry methods and content usually with little or no mention of the elements and principles of design. Then we watched art educators present instructional models (lessons, unit plans, and curricula) labeled DBAE, but organized around the elements and principles of design. The response of many art teachers was predictable: "if this is DBAE, I've been doing it all along." A considerable amount of space in our evaluative reports was taken up with analyzing why presentation of the elements and principles of design (or sensory and formal properties) as the primary content of instruction, is basically incompatible with DBAE. We have contended that the formal qualities of artworks should be presented as just one aspect of content among many others. Only when the elements and principles of design cease being used as the foremost organizational structure for art instruction does DBAE take on a character distinct from traditional practice.

Disciplines as Content. In many DBAE summer institute programs considerable emphasis was placed on the distinctive characteristics of the art disciplines, not on their common features. The disciplines themselves—their histories, theories, and methods—were viewed as the content of DBAE. Instructional schemes were devised to assist kindergarten through high school students to act in increasingly sophisticated ways in each of the disciplines. Learning about the individual art disciplines and how to use them was the principal objective of some early forms of DBAE. It would not be uncommon, for example, to hear lectures on the history of aesthetics or varying definitions of art with scant reference to actual works of art. Artworks created and studied through the art disciplines had an uncertain status; sometimes artworks were shown merely to illustrate what it meant to engage in disciplined inquiry. In our evaluative reports we contended that the disciplines provide a means to an end, that they are not ends in themselves. We proposed, alternatively, that the goals of DBAE reside in the knowledge and insight into oneself and one's world derived from the themes and content of artworks created and studied in school.

Artworks as Primary Content and Disciplines as Means. Through the efforts of many individuals, discipline-based art education became what might be viewed as artwork-based art education. Individuals working in the various Regional Institutes selected artworks of a surprising variety and placed them at the center of comprehensive instructional units. The four art disciplines were used as lenses to create and reveal themes, issues, and ideas associated with the works studied. When artworks become the focus of attention, the disciplines are employed as means, used when they are needed, when works "call out" to be studied or created in particular ways. The art discipline lenses may be combined so that they overlap. In many instances during DBAE instruction it seems unnecessary, for example, to distinguish between art historical and critical interpretation. Sometimes a "large" discipline lens is employed along with three "smaller" lenses—depending upon what the creation and study of particular artworks seem to need. As the artworks are studied in their historical and social contexts, they are connected to works from literature, the humanities, sciences, and the other arts. Other lenses associated with these works are added to the means available for disclosing the meanings of artworks in relationship to other human creations. Paraphrasing Roland Barthes (1985), in essence, DBAE students and teachers are provided opportunities to write and rewrite the texts of these artworks into the texts of their own lives. The meaningful content and vital ideas contained within the artworks become foremost, acquiring critical significance and personal, social, and cultural relevance for the individual.

A Brief Meta-Evaluation

We have had the space to touch on only a few conclusions derived from our evaluation studies of the Getty-sponsored Regional Institute programs. If we were to step back and view the things we have just written as opportunities for reflection—not just as analyses and interpretations of what happened in regional consortia, but also as opportunities to examine our own values and biases— what would be revealed? How might our beliefs, which developed and deepened during the evaluation process, be summarized?

In our observations (what we chose to see) and conclusions (what we came to believe), we placed great value on interactive systems and the collaborative efforts of individuals within a system. We saw DBAE not just as an approach to instruction, but as an educational reform initiative based on a consortium of change communities. We concluded that the DBAE enterprise is a model for educational change in general, wherein thousands of individuals working within hundreds of cooperating institutions are given the opportunity to create and recreate new forms of education. What we do not know, however, is whether or not a consortium change model can be sustained without continued funding from an entity such as the Getty Education Institute, or whether such consortia can even be organized initially without external intervention.

As evaluators, we understood that we value the rights and opinions of all individuals within DBAE change communities. We believe that all stakeholders, including students, should have a voice in shaping DBAE. Indeed, we were as delighted when students added new content to DBAE instructional units and assessment procedures as when art educators and art discipline consultants devised new theoretical formulations for DBAE. We think that a dynamic change community should recognize, indeed should insist upon gathering and incorporating into the initiative the contributions of all stakeholders. We value the continual interplay of practice and theory—the way they reshape one another.

As evaluators, we placed a high priority on the creation of rich, meaningful learning environments and instructional activities for students. We recognized and valued the excitement and enthusiasm that both teachers and students experienced when immersed in DBAE inquiry-based programs.

As evaluators, we came to see artworks and the art disciplines as inseparable. Like Arthur Danto, we believe that art objects become artworks by virtue of being interpreted (Danto, 1986). Art educates as artworks are created and interpreted. The kinds of human themes, issues, ideas, feelings, interests, and concerns that might be revealed through the creation and study of particular works provides the basis for selecting the artifacts to place at the center of instructional units. DBAE provides a means for transforming art materials and objects into works of art. The obverse is that when artworks are studied merely to reveal their formal features, we question the educational adequacy of those instructional activities. When the art disciplines are employed merely to show their character and the way they function, we question the relevance of such activities. We value most the use of the art disciplines when they are sensitive to the needs and even the rights of artworks—the right to be created, interpreted, and judged holistically—

not from a predetermined point of view. We value most those instructional activities that, as Richard Rorty (1992) has stated, treat works of art as "honorary persons" which have the potential to change us and thus change our lives.

As evaluators, we came to value art-in-the-making as much as art-already made. We realized the value of art that was local as much as art that was universal, art of our time and place as much as that of other times and places, art of lower status as much as that of high status. These values were shaped as we observed individuals in DBAE change communities addressing the meaning and significance of objects in their own communities as well as world communities. In our evaluative reports we spent considerable time analyzing the challenges of applying the art disciplines to artworks that had not yet received attention from critics, historians, and aestheticians. We recognized that we valued the insights and interpretations of students and teachers as much as we valued the insights of artists, historians, critics, and philosophers.

As evaluators, we came to understand that we valued integration over separateness. We valued instruction in which the art disciplines were employed simultaneously as much as when they were employed individually. Even more importantly, we valued instruction in which artworks were studied within their social, cultural, and historical, and aesthetic contexts, and when they were studied in relationship to other artworks, artifacts, documents, texts, and other school subjects. We valued art instruction that was integrated into students' and teachers' lives, when it was connected to their lives within and beyond school.

Before we began our evaluation of DBAE as it evolved in the Getty-sponsored Regional Institutes, surely we must have held some of these values. Nevertheless, we could not have written these declarations of value—certainly not in the way we have just written them, without our experiences in the Regional Institutes. Were it not for the DBAE reform initiative we have had the privilege to observe and evaluate, we probably could not have stated our values with this degree of clarity and sharpness.

Notes

1. We have borrowed this phrase from the title of Michael Fullan's (1993) book, *Change Forces: Probing the Depths of Educational Reform*. London: The Falmer Press.

2. These data are from a survey conducted in the Grand Island, Nebraska school district in the summer of 1996.

References

Barthes, R. (1985). Day by day with Roland Barthes. In *On signs*. M. Blonsky (Ed.), (pp. 98-117). Baltimore: Johns Hopkins University Press.

Clark, G. A., Day, M. D., & Greer, W. D. (1987). Discipline-based art education: Becoming students of art, *The Journal of Aesthetic Education*, 27(2),129-193.

Danto, A. (1986).*The philosophical disenfranchisement of art*. New York: Columbia University Press.

Rorty, R. (1992).The pragmatist's progress. In U. Eco (S. Collini, Ed.), *Interpretation and over interpretation*. Cambridge: Cambridge University Press.

Wilson, B. G. (1997). *The quiet evolution: Changing the face of arts education*. Los Angeles, CA: The Getty Education Institute for the Arts.

F. GRAEME CHALMERS

Designing and Implementing a Curriculum for Multicultural Art Education

The National Art Education Association, in its publication *Quality Art Education: Goals for Schools*, states that all schools should provide "a *sequential* program of art instruction that is balanced to include the study of aesthetics, art criticism, art history, and art production" (emphasis added). Although not as rigidly as implied by the drawing books of the late nineteenth century, art education has gradually been returning to stronger notions of sequential curricula and moving toward national standards for what young people should know and be able to do in the arts at particular points in their schooling. A developmental and incremental approach to art education is central to DBAE and should contribute to conceptual foundations for the thematic study and practice of art in multicultural societies. However, to think about scope and sequence only in terms of content, as is frequently done (e.g., covering the art of a few cultures in the primary grades, a few more in intermediate and middle school or junior high grades, with the art of a final few cultures "covered" in senior secondary grades), is extremely naive and shows little understanding of either the purposes of multicultural art education or the stages of human growth and development.

In art education there is a rich heritage of developmentally focused research in art making (some of it cross-cultural), as well as a growing interest in both how students begin to understand history and how they may move through various stages in responding to art (see Addiss and Erickson, 1993; Parsons, 1987). Curriculum developers should make use of this material in determining the readiness of students to study and to make art in ways that reinforce the tenets I have set forth in this discussion. Currently, relatively sophisticated students are able to see artworks as "cultural artifacts" and as parts of sociocultural systems (Parsons, 1987). However, if educators deliberately teach toward this goal, as I am suggesting they do, there is absolutely no reason such realizations should be the exclusive accomplishment of students at higher grade levels. In a multicultural society, art educators at all grade levels should teach about the functions and roles of art across cultures, and thus such contextual perceptions should occur among students at earlier ages. As I have suggested, students at various levels can be asked to find, research, and discuss cross-cultural examples of art by makers who have become ascribers of meaning and/or status, catalysts of social change, enhancers and decorators, interpreters, magicians, mythmakers, propagandists, recorders of history, sociotherapists, storytellers, and teachers. Some of these activities, such as looking cross-culturally at artists as decorators, interpreters, and storytellers, can certainly begin in kindergarten. I suggest some possible starting points below.

Level 1 (Primary Grades/Lower Elementary)

By the age of 5, children have formed attitudes about themselves and their peers, and they are beginning to develop cultural awareness (Smardo and Schmidt, 1983). Children quickly learn the prevailing social attitudes toward ethnic and other differences. Beginning in kindergarten, it is important for students to learn that art is made by women and men in all cultures, and that this has been true throughout history. Even very young children can, to some extent, contemplate and imagine the functions and roles of art in various societies. Children in the primary grades typically enjoy making and looking at art, and appreciate art works in personal and concrete ways, e.g., favorite color, appealing subject matter. . . . Although their interpretations of art can be insightful, their grasp of artistic symbol systems . . . [may be] too limited [for them] to . . . engage in complex aesthetic inquiry. (Lankford, 1992, p. 37; based on Gardner, 1990; Gardner and Perkins, 1989).

According to Parsons (1987), students at this level hold nonjudgmental, nondiscriminatory views of art. Consequently, although their views can be highly personal, young children may be very open to considering the art of many cultures, particularly if it is not too historically remote. What is known, local, and familiar is a good starting point. For some time, public school art educators have believed that young children should work with a wide variety of art media and experience a number of ways to make art. Young children should also have opportunities to talk about many different kinds of art, from a variety of cultures and many time periods. Kindergarten children are certainly not too young to spend some time studying different artists and the contexts in which they work, especially at the local level.

Primary-age students can listen to stories about art and artists from a variety of cultures and can make their own art to tell and to illustrate stories. Multicultural approaches to art education may both challenge and make use of Piaget's developmental concepts. For example, Egan (1979) questions the notion that children need to begin with what is known and move outward. He believes that development moves in the opposite direction, with the self being known last, and he posits that it is the most abstract of ideas that appeal to children in early childhood— opposites like good and evil, weak and strong, cowardly and courageous. Egan asserts that this "mythic state" should be what characterizes the early childhood curriculum. Accordingly, teachers would teach through stories, experiences, and narratives that engage children's interest in these abstract bipolar opposites, which are reflected in the art of many cultures. Like Piaget, Egan places the motivation for learning within the child. He wants to regain the imaginative and the poetic as part of the foundation for future learning (see Egan, 1991). As we are beginning to see in some young children's picture books, looking for the imaginative and the poetic in the art of other cultures can provide a fascinating introduction to art education.

Young children can also learn some basic art terms and concepts that can be used across cultures and can begin to distinguish and recognize works from a variety of cultures in different media. Broad-based social understanding becomes possible as children begin to understand that diverse groups of people make art for a similar variety of reasons.

Primary-age students can see and describe what is obvious or intrinsic in the art being discussed: subject, color, texture, and so on. McFee and Degge (1980) suggest that young children, and also older students, should "describe how artists [from a variety of cultures] repeat sizes, colors, shapes, or forms and textures to make order in an art work" (p. 376). They also suggest that primary-age children should be able to "describe how objects with similar uses are made differently by people from different cultures" (p. 379).

It is always important for children to draw and otherwise take note of cultural objects. Also, as they progress in their art education, they should be visiting museums and other places where they can have many different encounters with art (broadly defined).

Level 2 (Intermediate and Upper Elementary Grades)

Parsons (1987) has noted that by the time they reach the upper elementary grades, European American students value skill, realism, and beauty. Little work has been done, however, with students from other cultural backgrounds of similar ages. Lankford (1992), again relying on research reported by Harvard University's arts education-related Project Zero (Gardner, 1990; Gardner and Perkins, 1989), posits that upper elementary students are aware that art can express ideas and emotions and that they are capable of pondering artistic motives. He suggests the use of "vivid cases" (e.g., puzzles and imaginary scenarios) to get older elementary students "thinking about the concept of art and about the nature of artistic expression" (p. 43).

At this level, students can make art for a purpose and thus identify with other artists in all cultures who use art for rather similar reasons. They can be encouraged to ask conceptually oriented questions about art from many cultures. How was something made? Why was it made? Fitzpatrick (1992) suggests that children at this level must be guided by teachers "who know which answers can be found by students in material kept in the classroom or in simple conversations with artists" (p. 37). Upper elementary students can take notes at talks given by artists and others; use publications, films, and tapes for research on arts; interview community members about art; make short verbal presentations and write paragraphs or summaries about artworks; and make bulletin board displays showing commonalities in the roles and functions of art and artists in a variety of cultures.

Level 3 (Junior Secondary Grades)

Students in the lower secondary grades are more aware of various aspects of aesthetic experience than are younger children. They may also accept differences of opinion more easily. Lankford (1992) cites research showing that young adolescents are especially concerned with the ways in which their own and others' artworks are able to convey meaning. They are increasingly able to recognize artistic styles and to relate art forms to various historical and cultural contexts, and can interpret symbols and compare and contrast ideas. Also, particularly useful from the perspective of multicultural education, they can speculate about origins and consequences, make suggestions and inferences, and consider alternatives. McFee and Degge (1980) suggest that students at this level are more visually aware than younger students and can identify differences and similarities in artistic styles. These students can recognize that artists and designers in different cultures organize and emphasize particular elements of design for particular purposes.

By the time they reach this level, students are increasingly able to use photography and video as research tools for observing and describing the art forms of many cultures. They can become visual anthropologists, and, in addition to observing and describing, they should be able to consider the meanings of particular artworks and be able to modify their ideas about art as it functions in a variety of cultures. At this level, teachers should encourage more independent research and build upon students' curiosity. As Wilson notes, the tastes of middle-class high school students are broad. He describes an innovative and gamelike approach to collecting and understanding artworks that has been implemented at Colerain High School in suburban Cincinnati. The students seem not to be prejudiced against art from other cultures, as they actively seek to add reproductions of African, Hispanic, and Asian work to their collections.

Many students at this level are able to utilize relatively sophisticated art-related publications, and some may build impressive visual files (Fitzpatrick, 1992). These students may produce radio and television talk shows about aspects of art in a multicultural society, curate multicultural and thematic in-school museum exhibitions and produce accompanying catalogs, or produce video documentaries about various local art cultures.

Level 4 (Senior Secondary Grades)

By the senior grades, aesthetic inquiry intermixes with historical, ethical, and political perspectives (Lankford, 1992). Students at this level question more and argue specific cases as lawyers might do in a courtroom. These students are increasingly able to use originating groups' standards when evaluating works of art. They are more capable than younger students of assuming the position of the other.

By this stage, McFee and Degge (1980) suggest, students can make more sophisticated written, oral, and/or visual seminar presentations to "analyze the role of the artist in different societies and see how the cultural values encourage the reward the artist" (p. 380). Students at this level can study the connections among art, artists, cultural organizations, and the roles and functions of various types of museums (Fitzpatrick, 1992). Increasingly, they can use out-of-school primary sources as they investigate what is common about art in a variety of contexts. As they develop, they become better "able to see and report more remote relationships among things" (McFee and Degge, 1980, p. 374). Students at this level are also increasingly able to maintain their independence when discussing the art of other people, despite peer pressure to conform.

Some students at this high grade level will be able to use their own art as communication and to address an audience. They may use murals, videos, illustrated publications, and group theme shows both to document the status quo and to move art education into the arena of social reconstruction.

Learning Styles

Because prior experience conditions the ways in which a person learns, it is important for teachers and others to acknowledge and accommodate a variety of learning styles—particularly in a multicultural classroom. However, educators must also understand that all students from a particular ethnic group will not necessarily learn in a particular way. Culture is not defined only by ethnicity; it is much more complex than that. Reminiscent of McFee's (1961) early work is the following characterization of a possible art student provided by Stuhr et al. (1992): "A student may be five years old, female, Chinese (Taiwanese), hearing impaired, wealthy, and Buddhist" (p. 18). As McFee points out, such combinations of factors affect not only students' performance in the art classroom but how they approach learning in general—their learning style.

Cornett (1983) defines learning style as a consistent pattern of behavior in three areas: cognitive (concerned with processing, encoding, storage, and retrieval of information), affective (concerned with attention, motivation, and personality), and physical (concerned with perceptual modes, energy level, time preferences, and preferred learning environment). Rowntree (1982) defines learning style as "a student's habitual manner of problem-solving or thinking or learning, e.g., serialist or holistic, reflective or impulsive. The student may not be conscious of his style and may adopt different styles for different learning tasks or circumstances" (p. 155). A student's learning styles or learning strategy, then, consists of "the student's general approach to a variety of learning tasks or . . . to his chosen way of tackling a particular task" (p. 155).

Collier and Hoover (1987) and others have identified and labeled a number of different learning styles that may certainly be found in multicultural classrooms. However, being able to label a particular learning style is not very important by itself. What is important is that educators recognize that members of some cultures and subcultures employ out-of-school teaching styles to develop certain interests and aptitudes in children, so that instead of ignoring these influences, they can reinforce and utilize students' home-based and culturally unique learning and communication styles. When teachers attempt to impose learning styles on students, schools can too often become institutions of social adaptation rather than education.

McFee (1961, 1966; McFee and Degge, 1980) and Stockrocki (1990) have made extensive studies of cross-cultural learning styles and their implications for art education. Their work has been based upon findings from the social and behavioral sciences that show each person's potential to learn is unique and depends upon past and present opportunities to use this potential. McFee pays significant attention to the influence of culture in all of her work, but she also stresses that we should attend as much to individual as to group differences. There is a fine line between being aware of some potential effects of ethnicity on learning styles and expecting a student from a particular ethnic group to behave in a particular way. Educators should not view any person as a cultural or ethnic stereotype, but should respond to each learner as an individual for whom ethnicity is only one of many personal characteristics. However, research into the characteristics of particular ethnic and cultural groups can help educators to become more sensitive to their students' needs and values. For example, information on different cultures' views of the appropriateness or significance of silence, eye contact, and emotional display, as well as differing perceptions of time, can be useful to the art teacher. Educators also need to acknowledge cultural change. As Spruill-Fleming's (1991) research shows, numerous social and demographic changes have conditioned learning styles in all cultural groups by greatly enlarging the number of "urbanized, TV-addicted, fast-food/fast-paced/fast-times oriented youngsters" (p. 8).

Longstreet (1978) asserts that there are three factors teachers must address if they wish to embrace and acknowledge diverse learning styles: classroom atmosphere, relevance of information, and appropriateness of materials. Much of this discussion has addressed the need for art teachers to be less ethnocentric in their definitions and understanding of art. Individual teachers also need to be aware of their own learning styles, which in turn affect their teaching styles, because these too have been conditioned by ethnicity, education, life experiences, religion, economic status, personality, and so on. Kendall (1980) suggests that teachers can find out about their own learning styles by examining the same behavioral patterns in themselves that they would examine in a student to identify the student's learning style. Through such awareness, teachers can recognize their own tendencies toward ethnocentrism and can examine their willingness to adapt their teaching styles to match the learning styles of their students.

Knowledge about art is important, but implementing any of the theory presented here requires a skilled teacher: one who asks good questions and is open-minded, diplomatic, confident, patient, organized, flexible, and able to interest and enthuse students. The teacher needs to be able to create a supportive learning environment for each student. Citing recent research, Hernandez (1989) posits that now, perhaps more than in the past, "most teachers intuitively employ multiple teaching approaches, and students demonstrate flexibility and adaptability in dealing with . . . modes of instruction" (p. 129). Although this may be more a desirable goal than a true reflection of current practice, it is a situation that seems particularly possible in an art classroom where the four disciplines (production, aesthetics, art criticism, and art history) encompass a variety of modes of instruction.

Certainly, as schools become more culturally diverse, art teachers need to consider alternative means of enabling students to learn and to express understanding in ways appropriate to their own cultural backgrounds and personalities. A discipline-based approach is ideal, because it allows students, individually and in groups, to learn about art in a variety of ways, using a variety of learning styles. They may use words, sort pictures, draw, or take photographs to describe, define, analyze, and classify art from many cultures. DBAE also provides opportunities, particularly through art making, for students to reflect, imagine, and construct personal meaning in other ways. For example, they might illustrate facets of "character" in the art they are studying through music, dance, or mime. We need to present students with opportunities to learn about the broad themes and functions of art within and across cultures . . . in terms of their own experiences and through a variety of different media and learning activities.

Conclusion: Evaluating Our Approaches to Multicultural Art Education

As designers and implementers of multicultural approaches to art education, we need to ask a number of key questions about ourselves, our students, the curriculum, and the environments in which we teach (Etlin, 1988; Hernandez, 1989; Mehat, 1990).

For example, *what do we know about ourselves and our attitudes and beliefs about art*? Have we confronted prejudice and inequality? Are our views ethno- and/or egocentric? What do we know about the aesthetic attitudes and values of others who are different from us? How are these attitudes, values, and beliefs manifested when we teach children or interact with other educators? Do we celebrate diversity in art and in life, or does an acknowledgment of cultural pluralism appear to be tacked on, as an afterthought, to the things that we do, say, and believe? Do we demonstrate respect for cultures and backgrounds that are different from our own and firmly acknowledge that all groups can produce and define cultural artifacts that are "excellent," and that, despite the many variations, in all cultures art is socially constructed and can exist for rather similar reasons? Are we committed to behaviors, dispositions, outlooks, and values that are multicultural?

Have we made genuine attempts to make visual art education relevant to all students? Do we provide classroom atmospheres in which our students' cultures and their art forms are recognized, shared, and respected? Are we knowledgeable about, and sensitive to, students' differing cultural backgrounds, values, traditions, and learning styles, and do we give students and community members opportunities to teach us what we don't know or understand about the arts of their cultures? Are *we* prepared to be students? Do learning and teaching operate in both directions in art classrooms and in galleries and museums? Do we involve parents and other community members in art learning activities? Whether we are teacher educators or teachers in schools or museums, we all need to ask: Who are our students? What are their cultural backgrounds? What do our students or museum visitors know about the art of others who are different from them? If we teach students from only one cultural group, this does not mean that we can ignore multiculturalism. In our increasingly global society, multicultural approaches are for everyone.

In our curricula, are the arts viewed as socially constructed? Are questions about art raised and framed in ways that encourage us to see that the arts may serve somewhat similar functions and roles in diverse cultures? For whom are the art curriculum and support materials we use designed? Is our instruction appropriately sequential and developmental? What attitudes and beliefs do particular art materials instill? Where are the gaps in terms of multicultural learning about the arts, and are they being addressed? What more can be done to reflect multicultural attitudes, help us see similarities, and build tolerance for diversity in the arts? Are we developing and actively encouraging the development of multicultural art curricula materials that are neither limited nor biased?

And, finally, *how is the art classroom learning environment constructed?* What is the emotional and psychological climate in the art classroom? Whose work is displayed? What student needs are attended to? Whose art is dominant? Why?

References

Addiss, S., and Erickson, M. 1993. *Art history and education.* Urbana: University of Illinois Press.

Collier, C., and Hoover, J. J. 1987. *Cognitive learning strategies for minority handicapped students.* Lindale, TX: Hamilton.

Cornett, C. E. 1983. *What you should know about teaching and learning styles.* Bloomington, IN: Phi Delta Kappa. Educational Foundation.

Egan, K. 1979. *Educational development*. New York: Oxford University Press.

Egan, K. 1991. *Primary understandings: Education in early childhood*. New York: Basic Books.

Etlin, M. 1988. To teach them all is to know them all. *NEA Today* 6 (10): 10-11.

Fitzpatrick, V. L. 1992. *Art history: A contextual inquiry course*. Reston, VA: National Art Education Association.

Gardner, H., and Perkins, D. (eds.) 1989. *Art, mind, and education*. Urbana: University of Illinois Press.

Gardner, H. 1990. *Art education and human development*. Los Angeles: Getty Center for Education in the Arts.

Hernandez, H. 1989. *Multicultural education: A teacher's guide to content and process*. Columbus, OH:

Kendall, F. E. 1983. *Diversity is the classroom: A multicultural approach to the education of young children*. New York: Teachers College.

Lankford, E. L. 1992. *Aesthetics: Issues and inquiry*. Reston, VA: National Art Education Association.

Longstreet, W. S. 1978. *Aspects of ethnicity: Understanding differences in pluralistic classrooms*. New York: Teachers College Press.

McFee, J. 1961. *Preparation for art*. Belmont, CA: Wadsworth.

McFee, J. 1966. Society, art, and education. In *A seminar in art education for research and curriculum development*. University Park: Pennsylvania State University.

McFee, J. K., and Degge, R. M. 1980. *Art, culture, and environment: A catalyst for teaching*. Dubuque, IA: Kendall Hunt.

Mehat, I. 1990. Four approaches to multicultural education. In *Symposium on the fine arts in education—music, visual art, dance—prompted by the new British Columbia schools curriculum the year 2000*. Burnaby, BC: Simon Fraser University.

National Art Education Association: *Quality in art education: Goals for schools*. n.d. Reston, VA.

Parsons, M. 1987. *How we understand art: A cognitive development account of aesthetic experience*. New York: Cambridge University Press.

Rowntree, D. 1982. *A dictionary of education*. Totowa, NJ: Barnes and Noble.

Smardo, F. A., and Schmidt, V. 1983. Developing multicultural awareness. *Children and Today* 12(3): 23-25.

Spruill-Fleming, P. 1991. *Multicultural education and discipline-based art education: Toward a visionary future*. Unpublished manuscript (prepared for the Getty Center for Education in the Arts), California State University, Fresno.

Stockrocki, M. 1990. Issues in multicultural education. In E. W. King and S. D. Pierre (eds.), *Using the arts as an educational model for high-risk individuals*. Denver: University of Denver, School of Art.

Stuhr, P., Petrovich-Mwanki, L., and Wasson, R. 1992. Curriculum guidelines for the multicultural classroom. *Art Education* 45(1): 16-24.

Wilson, B. 1997. *The quiet evolution: Changing the face of arts education*. Los Angeles: Getty Education Institute for the Arts.

BRUCE O. BOSTON

The Arts and Cross-Disciplinary Study

There is now a growing body of evidence that the arts can be utilized successfully in creating cross-disciplinary curricula that also take the arts seriously as disciplines. Many magnet schools use the arts in this way quite fruitfully, as do a number of other experimental programs. But these efforts are not coordinated and their results to date, as is true of cross-disciplinary studies generally, are not conclusive.[1] Arts programs are also rendered even more tenuous by their marginal status in the schools.

Nonetheless, because the arts have been included as a core subject in the National Education Goals and in the Goals 2000: Educate America Act,[2] they can play a more central and productive role in creating cross-disciplinary curricula. This has been reinforced by the development of both content standards *(what students should know)* and performance standards *(what students should be able to do)* for core art forms—dance, music, theatre, and the visual arts. The arts standards have the potential to strengthen the perception of educators, decision makers, and parents concerning the academic rigor inherent in the study of the arts. To the degree that there is lingering concern about cross-disciplinary study, the presence of strong disciplinary standards, in the arts and other areas, can help answer skeptics. Teachers can draw on these standards in designing cross-disciplinary programs.

THE ARTS STANDARDS

The *National Standards for Arts Education* point to five areas of competence:

- Communicate at a basic level in the four arts disciplines;
- Communicate proficiently in at least one art form;
- Develop and present basic analyses of works of art from historical, structural, and cultural perspectives;
- Acquire an informed acquaintance with exemplary works of art in the four arts disciplines from a variety of cultures and historical periods; and

- Relate various types of arts knowledge and skills within and across the arts disciplines.

One frequent criticism of disciplinary standards is the perception that they work against cross-disciplinary studies by reinforcing disciplinary lines. That argument misses the mark because it fails to account for how standards in the arts can be resources in the design and evaluation of cross-disciplinary efforts. Standards are benchmarks against which to measure students' progress. Without standards, assessment of student learning is compromised, and the accountability of a program is undermined. Standards also define what is important for students to know and be able to do. Rigorous standards in the arts identify the fundamental, basic knowledge that is characteristic of the disciplines. With this foundation, curriculum developers can more effectively draw out significant ideas from the arts for use in cross-disciplinary teaching and learning.

ARTS AND CROSS-DISCIPLINARY EDUCATION

Business Raises Some Possibilities.

A further sign that the arts can play a vital integrative role in creating cross-disciplinary curricula is the interest of the business sector in the quality of U.S. education.[3] The educational dimension of the "high-performance workplace," as defined by business, proceeds from a simple premise: better schools are essential to improving the competitiveness of the American workforce and the nation's economic health. The United States Department of Labor, through the Secretary's Commission on Achieving Necessary Skills (SCANS) has concluded that

> Good jobs for American workers increasingly depend on people who can put knowledge to work. Disturbingly our young people leave school without the knowledge or skills required to find and hold a good job. Creating workplace know-how demands two elements: *competencies* and a *foundation of personal qualities*. To establish this foundation and achieve these competencies, the nation needs to reinvent its schools, foster work-based learning, reorganize the workplace, and restructure educational assessment to include the certification of needed skills [4]

Business has an obvious interest in education. The nation's schools produce its customers, employees, and leaders. As Peter Drucker points out in his book, *Post-Capitalist Society,* we live in a time when the basic economic resource is no longer labor or capital, but knowledge itself.

The pursuit of knowledge is increasingly the basic business of American companies and that fact has profound implications for education.[5]

THE SCANS COMMISSION'S EDUCATIONAL FOCUS

The Five Competencies

- Students should be able to identify, plan and allocate resources, such as time, money, materials and facilities, and human resources;
- Students should exhibit the interpersonal skills of being able to work with others, including participating as a team member, teaching others new skills, serving clients/customers, exercising leadership, negotiating, and working with people from diverse backgrounds;
- Students should have information skills, especially the skills of acquiring and evaluating, organizing and maintaining, interpreting and communicating, and using computers;
- Students should be able to understand, monitor, correct, design, and improve the complex interrelationships presented by systems; and
- Students should be able to work with a variety of technologies, including selecting and applying technologies, as well as maintaining and troubleshooting equipment.

The Three-Part Foundation

- Students should have these basic skills: reading, writing, arithmetic and mathematical operations, listening and speaking;
- Students should have these thinking skills: creative thinking, decision making, problem solving, seeing with the mind's eye, knowing how to learn, reasoning;
- Students should have these personal qualities: responsibility, self-esteem, sociability, self-management, integrity/honesty.

Source: *What Work Requires of Schools* (Washington: U.S. Department of Labor, 1991), pp. xvii-xvii.

As the twenty-first century dawns, the definition of an "educated person" is changing profoundly. It can no longer apply to those educated in only the humanities, the sciences, or the arts. Today, the term is more deservedly earned by those who can bridge the gap between liberal learning and applied knowledge, who live as productively skilled members of a global society and economy, who can integrate knowledge and skills across more than one area of academic content, and who can function effectively as members of many organizations and communities.

These changes have implications for the themes of this report and the College Board-Getty Project. For example, both Drucker and Peter Senge, author of the best-selling book on management, *The Fifth Discipline*, express concern about one particularly underdeveloped skill for putting education to work in the real world of defining and solving problems, namely, *the ability to see and think in wholes*. Making a point that has serious ramifications for how the arts and cross-disciplinary learning can reinvigorate education, Senge writes:

> From a very early age, we are taught to break problems apart, to fragment the world. This apparently makes complex tasks and subjects more manageable, but we pay an enormous price. We can no longer see the consequences of our actions; we lose our intrinsic sense of connection to a larger whole. After a while, we give up trying to see the whole altogether.[6]

The perceptual faculties and analytical strategies described by David Perkins, Edmund Burke Feldman, and Harry Broudy all speak to this issue. Perkins argues for the necessity of developing the abilities inherent in what he calls "orchestrating the eye," i.e., training perception to reach out, describe, analyze, reflect, interpret, and make judgments—in other words to look and think more broadly, deeply, clearly, deliberately, adventurously, and holistically.[7] It is a perspective that can also be found in music, dance, and theatre, as well as in other art forms.

For business, better schools are viewed as important means to improving the competitiveness of the American workforce and the nation's economic health. As the basic economic resource of society shifts from labor to knowledge itself, individuals prepared to be part of the high-performance workplace are essential. To help fulfill this aim, schools will need to foster skills associated with creating and utilizing new knowledge in contexts that are increasingly integrated and interrelated. The arts provide unique contexts for exercising those skills and the content for teaching these capacities.

Beyond Instrumentality to Intrinsic Values

Frequently, rationales for the contribution of arts education relate to enhancing students' workforce readiness and the nation's competitiveness in the international marketplace. Increasingly, business leaders are joining arts and cross-disciplinary educators to argue that both arts education and cross-disciplinary studies are highly relevant to the work-place. An education in the arts, as Senge puts it, nourishes "the ability to think in wholes," "the expanded capacity to create," and "new and expansive patterns of thinking." This newfound appreciation of the arts can heighten awareness of their value in bringing curricula together. As a result of this convergence, advocates for both arts education and cross-disciplinary studies have begun to find new allies in the business community.

Other instrumental arguments for the value of the arts for education focus on the contributions they make to acquiring an understanding of diverse civilizations and cultures, the fostering of creativity, the teaching of effective communication, or the teaching of critical assessment of what one sees, reads, and hears.[8]

In the end, however, rationales for arts education—specifically for why the arts and cross-disciplinary studies should be brought together—must rest as much on intrinsic arguments as instrumental ones. Both the arts and cross-disciplinary studies are worth knowing about, understanding, and doing for their own value. The College Board-Getty Project will make the case for both based on the following:

1. *New knowledge is created from the interaction between the known and the questions posed by the "not-yet-known"* Cross-disciplinary studies, by their nature, enable question-asking that breaks open the problem-posing process necessary for new knowledge, in ways unavailable to similar activity that is discipline based.
2. *Knowledge is comprised of both wholes and parts.* Everything we know is related to everything else in some way; further, knowledge of the whole requires knowledge of the interactions of the parts. An intrinsic potential of cross-disciplinary studies, therefore, is this ability to abet and give structure to such processes of combination and recombination in many learning environments.
3. *The relationships of particular realms of knowledge to one another (the disciplines) are, at least potentially, mutually informing and reinforcing.* Their impact is synergistic. Cross-disciplinary study, by its nature, seeks pathways for this process.

Up to this point, we have outlined an intrinsic case for learning in the arts and cross-disciplinary study. Arguments have been offered for the interdependence of arts standards and cross-disciplinary study and for how arts-centered cross-disciplinary curricula might address the needs of business for a high-performance workforce. But these arguments, in themselves, do not make the case for why the arts appear to be well suited to play a unifying role in cross-disciplinary curricula. [The following] will offer reasons for why the arts are particularly well equipped to enable students to pursue the interactive and holistic nature of knowledge. These reasons focus on the inherent characteristics of the arts as ways of knowing, their role as a stimulus to broad and deep thinking, their potential to serve as sources for cross-disciplinary themes, and their connections to multiple forms of intelligence.

THE ARTS AS WAYS OF KNOWING

The arts provide distinctive and unique ways of knowing and understanding that are not offered by other subjects in the general education curriculum. The art forms of dance, music, theatre, and the visual arts represent some of the most significant cultural achievements of humankind. Each has special contributions to make for the broadening and deepening of students' understanding of the world.

To think of the arts as distinctive paths and ways of knowing is a dramatic departure from traditional views which treat the arts as matters of emotion rather than matters of mind, and hence as merely ornamental in education. What does it mean to say that the arts are ways of knowing, and how does this view of the arts relate to cross-disciplinary teaching and learning?

Answers to these questions start with the idea of perception, in particular, how we perceive qualities in the world. As our senses become more acute and refined, they serve as the building blocks for how we think, feel, and imagine.[9] Because the information we acquire through our senses is individual and private, we need a means for sharing it. The arts are a means for making this information public.

The arts are ways of knowing because they provide us with knowledge of human thoughts, feelings, and beliefs. Each art form draws on material from the senses in unique ways and utilizes specialized materials and techniques to communicate these thoughts, feelings, and beliefs. For example, dance is distinctively kinesthetic, draws on the vast capacities of the human body for movement, and organizes these capacities in space and time to communicate. Music is structured sound, using rhythm, melody, harmony, and timbre to communicate thoughts, feelings, and beliefs in an endless variety of musical forms. Theatre communicates them through imitation and representation in characters, narratives, situations, and illusions.[10] The visual arts draw on humans' capacities to see, both literally and metaphorically, and impart information and meaning through looking.[11]

In these ways, the different art forms are unique ways of knowing. But the arts can also be thought of as different paths to "knowing" in general, e.g. posing problems, finding solutions, and creating meanings.

> The arts, when well taught, provide children with opportunities to use their imagination, to create multiple solutions to problems, and to rely on their own judgment to determine when a problem is solved or a project is completed. In the arts, there is no rule to 'prove' the correctness of an answer and no formula to determine when a task is complete. In the arts, children must rely on that most exquisite of human intellectual abilities—judgment.[12]

Learning in the arts disciplines of production/performance, criticism, history, and aesthetics extends the capacity of art forms as ways of knowing in many ways. Production in all the arts and performance in dance, music, and theatre enlist and develop a range of cognitive skills— the creation, interpretation, and organization of expressive forms; planning ahead and re-evaluation of goals; perception of relationships between parts and wholes; and attention to subtleties and nuances. Criticism, especially the interpretation of meanings of works of art, entails a kind of perception not commonly employed. Criticism invites us to explore and probe artworks deeply and can teach us how to look and hear in sustained ways. As a result, cognitive skills of perception, analysis, and interpretation are developed.

Historical inquiry around works of art helps students understand that art does not emerge from or function in a vacuum. Through historical study of works of art, students gain an understanding of relationships between art and culture over time.

> All art is part of a culture. All cultures give direction to art, sometimes by rejecting what artists have made and at other times by rewarding them for it. To understand culture, one needs to understand its manifestations in art, and to understand art, one needs to understand how culture is expressed through its content and form.[13]

Aesthetics, for its part, uses philosophical methods to ask and answer fundamental questions about the nature, status, and value of art works. Philosophical thinking entails an array of cognitive skills of use to students, particularly, the capacity to justify, in clear and defensible language, judgments about qualities and values.

This section on the arts as ways of knowing has made three points:

- the arts are ways of knowing that are distinct from other subjects in the curriculum and provide us with knowledge of human

thoughts feelings, and beliefs that are not duplicated by other
means of learning;
- the arts are different paths to knowing in general, for posing
problems, finding solutions, and creating meanings; and
- learning in the art disciplines enlists and develops a wide range
of cognitive skills.

These points, by stressing art's relationship to the breadth of human
experience and to sophisticated forms of cognition, lay the groundwork
for subsequent arguments for why arts-based cross-disciplinary teaching
and learning can provide curricular coherence.

TOWARD CURRICULAR COHERENCE

Two further arguments can be made for why the arts are particularly well suited to generate cross-disciplinary study: the arts are able to
stimulate and supply the broad and deep thinking required for sophisticated cross-disciplinary study; and the arts, by virtue of their capacity
to create products that embody the diversity, intensity, and complexity
in human experience, are prime sources for meaningful themes that cut
across disciplines. As such, the arts can supply the curricular roots for
coherent cross-disciplinary approaches.

The Arts as a Stimulus to Broader and Deeper Thinking

Elliot Eisner offers guidance about the contribution the arts can make
to both learning and the coherence of a cross-disciplinary curriculum.
He advances two compelling reasons why the arts can be powerful in
improving learning and recasting the curriculum: (1) the arts point powerfully to basic ways we *misunderstand* the ways we know; and (2) the
arts offer alternative, complementary ways of putting reality together.[14]
The arts themselves offer potential for unifying the school curriculum because they provide students with a unique approach and perspective to learning; they stimulate thinking and expand human understanding. But frequently some fundamentally flawed misconceptions
about knowledge constrain or diminish this potential. These beliefs
include:

- Human conceptual thinking requires the use of language.
- Sensory experience is low on the hierarchy of intellectual
functioning.
- Intelligence requires the use of logic.

- Detachment and distance are necessary for true understanding.
- Scientific method is the only legitimate way to generalize about the world.[15]

The arts counter these misconceptions by making the following contributions:

- *An education in the arts helps prepare students for the fact that not all problems have a single, correct answer.* The arts demonstrate that solutions can take a multitude of forms. Unlike one answer endeavors such as spelling and arithmetic, the arts celebrate imagination, creativity, multiple perspectives, and the importance of personal interpretation.
- *In the arts as in life, the form of a thing is part of its content.* The arts teach that form and content go together. A sculptor's form expresses the image in the mind of the sculptor, likewise the actor's delivery of the playwright's lines, the musician's reproduction of the composer's sonata, and the ballerina's steps of the choreographer's ballet.
- *Fixing objectives and following clear-cut methods are not always the most rational ways of leafing with the world.* The arts recognize this by deliberately *not* always assuming that the most effective way to travel between an objective and its realization is a straight line. Solving complex problems requires attention to wholes, not simply to parts. The arts teach purposeful flexibility and experimentation.
- *The arts teach that there is a distinction between expression and discovery.* Some kinds of meaning may require the expressive forms that the arts make possible, as when a work of art seeks to interpret an abstract concept. Through the arts, students discover how to express their individual capacity for imagination.[16]

By revealing misconceptions about knowledge and by making tangible contributions to broad and deep thinking, the arts offer a sound foundation for the achievement of curricular coherence.

The Arts as Sources for Cross-Disciplinary Themes

The second argument for why learning in the arts can lead to curricular coherence lies in their capacity to generate themes that are appropriate and significant for cross-disciplinary study. Learning through themes moves students beyond the confines of a strict content orientation by forging connections between the narrower issues that disciplines focus on and the broader questions posed by the students' social roles, value structure, culture, religion, human identity and psychology, relationships with others, and the physical and biological worlds.

Programs that utilize the arts to integrate across disciplines have a rich and creative variety of theme-based instruction. Among many examples that could be offered, a few are:

- In one California program, studio arts are used as a way for students to express their understanding of course content in humanities classes and to develop a multicultural perspective. In one unit based on Picasso's *Weeping Women*, for example, students learn about Picasso's use of African art and also how contemporary African American artists use African sources.
- In a Florida museum-based program, students use the subject matter of specific works of art (e.g., Joseph Stella's *Brooklyn Bridge)* to reach out to the disciplines of history, geography, literature, engineering, mathematics, design, and even cost-analysis (e.g., students design bridges of their own and consult with local construction companies on costs).
- A program in a small Nebraska town turns the thematic metaphor of "bridges" in another direction—using it not only as an integral part of its internal instructional content, but also as an integrating theme for the entire program, which encompasses the cross-disciplinary study of architecture and design, geography (famous bridges as symbols of cities), intrinsic order in ecosystems, cultural linkages, and other topics.

Perkins and Blythe describe their process for identifying themes as follows: "we look for three features . . . : centrality to the discipline, accessibility to the students, and connectability to diverse topics inside and outside those disciplines."[17] Yet many examples could be cited of themes that lack substance. The following list of questions appear to have relevance for the generation of effective themes in arts-centered cross-disciplinary study:

- What is educationally significant about the theme and will it promote future learning?
- Is it meaningful and appropriate to the students?
- Does it enable students to make generalizations?
- Does it have substance and application in the real world?
- Does it tie in with other units?

- Does it apply to a wide range of subject areas?
- Does it disclose fundamental patterns?
- Does it reveal contrasts and similarities?
- Are relevant materials available?[18]

This section has illustrated how the arts can generate themes for use in cross-disciplinary study. But . . . themes provide only one kind of organizing center. Objects, issues, or ideas can serve this function as well. Other organizing centers for cross-disciplinary work have been suggested, for example, by Gardner and Boix-Manilla:

- Goals related to understanding, i.e., not just *knowing* content but being able to arrive at personal interpretations of essential issues *about* content;
- the demonstration of understanding through performance, e.g., the ability to handle thought-demanding tasks associated with content or the ability to translate disciplinary content into product(s); and
- ongoing assessment of student products to find instances of mature performances of high-quality work and progress from one benchmark to another.[19]

As shown above, the arts can supply the foundation for coherence across the curriculum. First, because the arts offer distinctive ways of learning and understanding, they can form the basis of a coherent curriculum. Secondly, because works of art connect in so many ways to thoughts, feelings, and beliefs, they can generate organizing centers for coherent curricula. These points are augmented in the next section by an additional argument.

CONNECTIONS BETWEEN THE ARTS AND THE INTELLIGENCES

The theory of multiple intelligences, as given currency by Howard Gardner and others, lends further support for the idea that the arts foster the kinds of thinking required for sophisticated cross-disciplinary study. This theory includes seven categories of "intelligences" into which human abilities can be grouped: (1) linguistic intelligence, (2) logical-mathematical intelligence, (3) spatial intelligence, (4) bodily-kinesthetic intelligence, (5) musical intelligence, (6) interpersonal intelligence, and (7) intrapersonal intelligence.[20]

Several points about the theory of multiple intelligences are important to this discussion:

- Each person has capacities in all seven intelligences.
- Most people can develop all seven intelligences to a relatively high level of performance.
- Intelligences tend to work together in complex ways.

The arts appear to offer special opportunities to stimulate ways for intelligences to work together, i.e., the kinds of cognitive capacities required for cross-disciplinary work. For example, in his discussion of musical intelligence, Gardner posits distinct relationships not only between musical and linguistic and mathematical-logical intelligences, but in other relationships as well:

> Young children certainly relate music and body movement naturally, finding it virtually impossible to sing without engaging in some accompanying physical activity; most accounts of the evolution of music tie it closely to primordial dance; many of the most effective methods of teaching music attempt to integrate voice, hand, and body. . . . Ties between music and spatial intelligence are less immediately evident but, quite possibly, no less genuine. The localization of musical capacities in the right hemisphere has suggested that certain musical abilities may be closely tied to spatial capacities . . . [In respect to intrapersonal intelligence] music can serve as a way of capturing feelings, knowledge about feelings, or knowledge about the forms of feeling, communicating from the performer or the creator to the attentive listener.[21]

This latter point lends further evidence to the claim that the arts, in this case music, are unique ways of knowing.

David Perkins offers a different perspective on the relationship between the arts and cognitive processes.[22] Looking at art, he argues, requires thinking, and the practice of looking at art develops a "thinking disposition." Perkins believes that looking at art has an *extrinsic* value—a payoff in the real world—in the form of contributions to four thinking dispositions that also feed directly into cross-disciplinary study. Perkins admonishes those who would develop an intelligent eye to give thinking (looking) the time it needs to yield its benefits; make thinking (looking) broad and adventurous; make thinking (looking) clear and deep; and make thinking (looking) organized. Using these thinking (looking) dispositions enables students to develop their cognitive capabilities in any area of study.

This discussion has offered rationales for why instruction and learning in the arts can be good candidates to serve at the core of cross-disciplinary studies. The *ways of knowing, cognition, curriculum,* and *multiple intelligences* arguments have been examined. It should be remembered that these rationales are not conclusive statements about the value of the arts in the design of cross-disciplinary curricula. They combine the most persuasive thinking about the arts, cognition, and curriculum to suggest why it is reasonable to think that the study of the arts should be at the core of cross-disciplinary teaching and learning. These arguments provide a basis for undertaking a long-term research and development initiative.

Notes

1. See, e.g., Liora Bresler. "Imitative, Complementary, and Expansive: Three Roles of Visual Arts Curricula," *Studies in Art Education* 35, no. 2, 1994, pp. 90-103; Liora Bresler, "The Subservient, Co-Equal, Affective, and Social Integration Styles and Their Implications for the Arts," from "Symposium: The Integration of the Arts into the Curriculum: Part I. The United States," *Arts Education Policy Review* 96, no 5 (May/June 1995), pp. 31-37.

2. In September of 1989, the nation's governors set goals for the nations schools, now eight in number, which the states committed themselves to carrying out and which two successive administrations have endorsed. Among the more significant features of the "Goals 2000" effort, as it has come to be called, has been a renewed focus on the curriculum. Goal 3 specified several areas of "challenging subject matter" in which students would be expected to show competency on leaving grades 4, 8, and 12: English. mathematics, science, history, geography, civics and government, economics, foreign language, and most notably for this report—the arts.

3. See, e.g., the report of the National Commission on the Skills of the American Workforce, *America's Choice: High Skills or Low Wages* (1990), and the two reports of the (Labor) Secretary's Commission on Achieving Necessary Skills (SCANS), *What Work Requires of Schools, and Earning a Living* (1991, 1992); Carol Sterling, "The Evolving Symbiotic Relationship of Arts Education and U.S. Business," Symposium: Control of K-I2 Arts Education: Part 3. Sectors of Influence," *Arts Education Policy Review*. 97, no. 2, November/ December 1995, pp. 27-30.

4. SCANS Commission, *What Work Requires of Schools*, and *Earning a Living* (Washington. DC: U.S. Department of Labor, 1991, 1992). There is a tendency to dismiss much of this discussion as so much special pleading from "inside the Beltway." Some of it is. At the same time, however, the national boards, commissions, and task forces that have generated these and similar studies and reports are heavily weighted with CEOs from American corporations, labor leaders, scientists, researchers, and leading educators from around the nation. They are anything but a clique—or of one mind.

5. Peter Drucker, *Post-Capitalist Society* (NY: Harper Collins, 1993).

6. Peter Senge, *The Fifth Discipline* (NY: Doubleday, 1990), p. 3.

7. See David N. Perkins, *The Intelligent Eye: Learning to Think by Looking at Art*. Occasional Paper No. 4 (Santa Monica, CA: The Getty Center for Education in the Arts, 1994), pp. 70-81. See also E. B. Feldman, *Varieties of Visual Experience:*

Art and Image as Idea, (NY: Harry N. Abrams, n.d.) and H. S. Broudy, *The Role of Imagery in Learning* (Los Angeles, CA: Getty Center for Education in the Arts, 1987).

8. *Toward Civilization: A Report on Arts Education* (Washington, D.C: National Endowment for the Arts, 1988), pp. 13-19.

9. See Elliot Eisner, *Cognition and Curriculum Reconsidered*, 2nd Edition (NY: Teachers College Press, 1994), p. 31.

10. For further discussion of music and theatre as ways of knowing. See Southeast Center for Education in the Arts, *Discipline-Based Arts Education: A Conceptual Framework for Learning and Teaching in the Arts* (Chattanooga, TN: The University of Tennessee at Chattanooga, 1995).

11. Perkins, *The Intelligent Eye.*

12. Elliot Eisner. "Structure and Magic in Discipline-Based Art Education" in *The Role of Discipline-Based Art Education in America's Schools* (Los Angeles, CA: The Getty Center for Education in the Arts, 1988), p. 7.

13. Ibid., p. 20.

14. Elliot W. Eisner, "The Misunderstood Role of the Arts in Human Development," *Kappan* (April 1992), pp. 591-595. The remainder of this section is liberally adapted from this source.

15. Ibid., 592-593.

16. The series is an elaboration of ideas from Eisner, pp. 594-595.

17. David Perkins and Tina Blythe, "Putting Understanding Up Front," *Educational Leadership* (February 1994), pp. 4-7.

18. Susan Kovalik and David Perkins, as quoted in Scott Willis, "Interdisciplinary Learning," *ASCD Curriculum Update* (November 1992), p. 4.

19. Howard Gardner and Veronica Bolt-Mancilla "Teaching for Understanding in the Disciplines—and Beyond," *Teachers College Record* 96, no. 2 (Winter 1994), pp. 203-204; 212-214, emphasis added.

20. See Howard Gardner, *Frames of Mind* (NY: Basic Books, 1983), pp. 122-129, for definition and description of these intelligences.

21. Ibid., p. 123.

22. Perkins, *The Intelligent Eye.*

Reading Suggestions for Part Three

General

Alexander, Kay, and Michael Day, eds. *Discipline-Based Art Education: A Curriculum Sampler.* Los Angeles: Getty Center for Education in the Arts, 1991.

Clark, Gilbert A. *Examining Discipline-Based Art Education as a Curriculum Construct.* ERIC: ART. Bloomington: Social Studies Development Center, Indiana University, 1991.

Delacruz, Elizabeth Manley. *Design for Inquiry: Instructional Theory, Research, and Practice in Art Education.* Reston, VA: National Art Education Association, 1997.

Delacruz, Elizabeth Manley. "Revisiting Curriculum Conceptions: A Thematic Perspective." *Visual Arts Research* 32 (1990): 10-25.

MacGregor, Ronald M. "Curricular Reform: Some Past Practices and Current Implications." In *Issues in Discipline-Based Art Education: Strengthening the Stance, Extending the Horizons.* Los Angeles: Getty Center for Education in the Arts, 1988.

Smith, Ralph A. "Art and Its Place in the Curriculum." *School Administrator* 50, no. 5 (1993): 23-30.

Tollifson, Jerry. "A Balanced Comprehensive Art Curriculum Makes Sense." *Educational Leadership* 45, no. 4 (1988): 18-22

Teaching and Learning

Addiss, Stephen, and Mary Erickson. *Art History and Education.* Urbana: University of Illinois Press, 1993, chaps. 8, 9.

Barrett, Terry, ed. *Lessons for Teaching Art Criticism.* ERIC: ART. Bloomington: Social Studies Development Center, Indiana University, 1994.

Brown, Maurice, and Diana Korzenik. *Art Making and Education.* Urbana: University of Illinois Press, 1993, chaps. 6, 12.

Cromer, Jim. *History, Theory, and Practice of Art Criticism in Art Education.* Reston, Va: National Art Education Association, 1990.

DiBlasio, Margaret, and Raymond DiBlasio. *SmART Curriculum: Sequentially Managed Art Curriculum, Grades 1-6.* 6 vols. St. Paul, Minn.: ARTWORLD Press, 1987.

Erickson, Mary, ed. *Lessons about Art in History and History in Art.* ERIC: ART. Bloomington: Social Studies Development Center. Indiana University, 1992.

Erickson, Mary. In *Art History and Education* by Stephen Addiss and Mary Erickson. Urbana: University of Illinois Press, 1993.

Hobbs, Jack A., and Jean C. Rush. *Teaching Children Art.* Upper Saddle, N.J.: Prentice-Hall, 1997. For the elementary grades.

Hurwitz, Al, and Michael Day. *Children and Their Art: Methods for the Elementary School,* 6th ed. Fort Worth: Harcourt Brace and Co., 1995. For the elementary grades.

Lankford, Louis. *Aesthetics: Issues and Inquiry.* Reston, Va: National Art Education Association, 1992.

Levi, Albert William, and Ralph A. Smith. *Art Education: A Critical Necessity*. Urbana: University of Illinois Press, 1991, chaps. 7, 8.

Katz, Elizabeth L., E. Louis Lankford, and Jan D. Plank. *Themes and Foundations of Art*. St. Paul, Minn.: West Publishing, 1995. For the high school.

Parsons, Michael J., and H. Gene Blocker. "Aesthetics in the Classroom." In *Aesthetics and Education* by Michael J. Parsons and H Gene Blocker. Urbana: University of Illinois Press, 1993, chap. 6.

Smith, Ralph A., and Alan Simpson, eds. *Aesthetics and Arts Education*. Urbana: University of Illinois Press, 1991, Parts 4, 5.

Wolff, Theodore F., and George Geahigan. *Art Criticism and Education*. Urbana: University of Illinois press, 1997), chaps. 4, 12.

Anderson, Tom. "A Structure for Pedagogical Art Criticism." *Studies in Art Education* 30, no. 1 (1988): 28-38.

Battin, Margaret P. "Cases for Kids: Using Puzzles to Teach Aesthetics to Children." *The Journal of Aesthetic Education* 28, no. 3 (1994): 89-104. Also in *Aesthetics for Young People*, ed. Ronald Moore. Urbana: University of Illinois Press, 1994.

Bowler, Susan Ann. "Taming the Beast: The Adventures of J. Paul Getty in the World Wide Web." *Visual Arts Research* 23, no. 2 (1997): 158-71.

Carrier, David. "Teaching the New Art History." In *The History of Art Education: Proceedings from the Second Penn State Conference, 1989*, ed. Patricia M. Amburgy et al. Reston, Va: National Art Education Association, 1992, 28-36.

Geahigan, George. "The Discipline of Art Criticism: Implications for Practice." *Visual Arts Research* 23, no. 2 (1997): 145-157.

Hagaman, Sally. "Philosophical Aesthetics in Art Education: A Further Look Toward Implementation." *Art Education* 43, no. 4 (1990): 33-40.

Hewitt, Gloria J., and Jean C. Rush. "Finding Buried Treasures: Aesthetic Scanning with Children." *Art Education* 40, no. 1 (1987) 40-43.

Kindler, Anna. "Discipline-Based Art Education in Secondary Schools." *Journal of Art and Design Education* 11, no. 3 (1992): 345-55.

Marschalek, Douglas G. "A New Approach to Curriculum Development in Environmental Design." *Art Education* 42, no. 4 (1989): 8-17.

Moore, Ronald. "Aesthetic Case Studies and Discipline-Based Art Education." *The Journal of Aesthetic Education* 27, no. 3 (1993): 51-62.

Olds, Clifton. "Tending Art History in the Eighties: Some Problems and Frustrations." *The Journal of Aesthetic Education* 20, no. 4 (1986): 99-103.

Parsons, Michael J., and H. Gene Blocker. "Aesthetics in the Classroom." In *Aesthetics and Education* by Michael J. Parsons and H. Gene Blocker. Urbana: University of Illinois Press, 1993, chap. 6.

Silvers, Anita. "Vincent's Story: The Importance of Contextualism for Art Education." *The Journal of Aesthetic Education* 28, no. 3 (1994): 47-62. Also in *Aesthetics for Young People*, ed. Ronald Moore. Urbana: University of Illinois press, 1994. Same pagination.

Silvers, Anita. "Multiculturalism and the Aesthetics of Recognition." *The Journal of Aesthetic Education* 33, no. 1 (Spring 1999). Essay review of Chalmers's *Celebrating Cultural Diversity*.

Stelle, Brian D. "Renaissance Art, Education, and History: An Art Historian's Perspective." *Art Education* 46, no. 2 (1993): 41-47.

Wilson, Brent. "Studio-Based Scholarship: Making Art to Know Art." In *Collected Papers, Pennsylvania's Symposium III on the Role of the Studio in Art Education*, ed. Joseph B. DeAngelis. Harrisburg: Pennsylvania Department of Education, 11-20.

Implementation, Evaluation, and Interdisciplinary

Boughton, Doug, Elliot W. Eisner, and Johan Ligtvoet, eds. *Evaluating and Assessing the Visual Arts in Education: International Perspectives*. New York: Teachers College Press, 1996.

Dobbs, Stephen Mark. *Learning in and through the Arts: A Guide to Discipline-Based Art Education*. Los Angeles: Getty Education Institute for the Arts, 1998, 73-81.

Ewens, Thomas, ed. *Discipline in Art Education: An Interdisciplinary Symposium*. Providence: Rhode Island School of Design, 1986.

Wilson, Brent. *The Quiet Evolution: Changing the Face of Arts Education*. Los Angeles: Getty Education Institute for the Arts, 1997.

Admur, David. "Arts in Cultural Context: A Curriculum Integrating Discipline-Based Art Education with other Humanities Subjects at the Secondary Level." *Art Education* 46, no. 3 (1993): 12-19.

Berry, Nancy W. "Making Connections: A Comprehensive Look at Art." *Art Education* 48, no. 6 (1995): 26-31.

Day, Gary and others. "A View from the Field: Discipline-based Art Education for In-service Teachers." *Visual Arts Research* 23, no. 2 (1997).

Day, Michael D. "Evaluating Student Achievement in Discipline-Based Art Programs." *Studies in Art Education* 26, no. 4 (1985): 232-40.

D. Blasio, Margaret Klempay. "Twelve Years and Counting: Tracking a Comprehensive Effort of Instructional and Programmatic Reform through DBAE." *Visual Arts Research* 23, no. 2 (1997); 34-42. Discusses results of impelmenting a DBAE program in a middle-sized upper midwestern school district.

Duke, Leilani Lattin. "The Getty Center for Education in the Arts: A Progress Report." *Phi Delta Kappan* 69, no. 6 (1988): 443-46.

Duke, Leilani Lattin. "The Role of Private Institutions in Art Education." *The Journal of Aesthetic Education* 20, no. 4 (1986): 48-49.

Dunn, Philip C. "Integrating the Arts: Renaissance and Reformation in Arts Education." *Arts Education Policy Review* 96, no. 4 (1995): 32-37.

Erickson, Mary. "Balancing the Art Curriculum: Art Production, Art History, Art Criticism, and Aesthetics." In *Collected Papers, Pennsylvania's Symposium III on the Role of Studio in Art Education*, ed. Joseph B. DeAngelis. Harrisburg: Pennsylvania Department of Education, 1989, 117-23.

Goodson, Carol Ann, and Ed Duling. "Integrating the Four Disciplines." *Music Educators Journal* 83, no. 2 (1996): 33-37.

Greer, W. Dwaine, and Ralph Hoepfner. "Achievement Testing in the Visual Arts." *Design for Arts in Education* 88, no. 1 (1986): 43-47.

Patchen, Jeffery H. "Discipline-based Art Education: A Conceptual Framework for Learning and Teaching in the Arts." *Visual Arts Research* 23, no. 2 (1997): 52-62. Discusses the work of the Southeast Center for Education in the Arts.

Rubin, Blanche M. "Using the Naturalistic Evaluation Process to Assess the Impact of DBAE." *NASSP Bulletin* 73, no. 517 (1989): 36-41.

McMurrin, Lee R. "Principal's Role in Implementing Discipline-Based Art Education." *NASSP Bulletin* 73, no. 517 (1989): 31-34.

Rush, Jean C. "Evaluating Visual Concept Learning according to Within-class Similarities among Students' Art Images." *Art and Learning Research* 5, no. 1 (1987): 14-33.

Thompson, Kathleen. "Maintaining Artistic Integrity in an Interdisciplinary Setting." *Art Education* 48, no. 6 (1995): 39-45.

PART FOUR

Artistic and Aesthetic Development

Introduction

As indicated in the Introduction to this volume, the cognitive revolution in art education has two faces: one face stresses psychological studies of mind and human development and the other the nature of teachable content and knowledge. Although these two faces are fused by certain writers, it is usually clear which is accented, either the psychological or the substantive. What is more, it is evident that psychological studies favor the image of the child as artist and give precedence to creative and manipulative capacities.

The latter emphasis can be found in the developmental studies of Project Zero under the guidance of Howard Gardner. In a 1992 NSSE yearbook devoted to the arts, education, and aesthetic knowing, Jessica Davis and Gardner review the cognitive revolution in human understanding and compare precognitivist and cognitivist perspectives in order to show the influence of cognitive studies on research into child art, aesthetics, and aesthetic education. They further discuss images of learning central to two generations of the cognitive revolution (computer models and symbol systems) and the theory of multiple intelligences (frames of mind) and indicate how they have influenced the work of both Project Zero and Getty policymakers. The former stress the principles of cognitive developmental psychology, while the latter, they believe, feature the concepts and skills of disciplinary learning. The excerpt reprinted here discusses the nature of the cognitivist approach to art education and describes a project, ARTS PROPEL, that highlights the developmental perspective.

Further work in cognitive developmental studies in the arts is reported by David Hargreaves and Maurice J. Galton. In the NSSE yearbook just mentioned, they discuss the special viewpoints of the psychologist, educator, and teacher and indicate ways to bridge the gap between theory and practice, in particular in a project undertaken by the authors. The excerpt reprinted here centers on their psychological perspective and a description of five phases of artistic development.

Research in the cognitive vein that examines the other side of the aesthetic complex, that is, aesthetic response rather than artistic creativeness, is reported in Michael J. Parsons's ten-year study of aesthetic experience. Parsons's work was grounded in the belief that aesthetic meaning is distinctive and requires careful study. From interviews with subjects drawn from different age groups, Parsons formulated five stages

of aesthetic development that follow each other sequentially and produce progressively better understanding of art. Parsons discusses a number of topics and suggests hypotheses for further study. The excerpt reprinted here summarizes the five stages.

Abigail Housen's discussion of stages of aesthetic understanding is
excerpted from a piece on museum education and could have been included in Part Six but is placed here because of her use of research on
aesthetic development. Acknowledging the complexities of addressing
the problems of cultural pluralism and accepting the fact that no single
method will suffice to accomplish the goal of understanding, Housen
states that what is not at issue is the fact that persons do not grasp certain concepts until they attain certain levels of aesthetic development,
and that an understanding of aesthetic development can help educators
perceive the different behaviors of people as they move through different parts of the art world. Accordingly, research in cognitive development
has broad application.

Basic research in the arts has its intrinsic value, but if research is to
affect practice there must be those who not only indicate the possibility
of its relevance but actually translate it into practice. This may be done
in exploratory projects of limited duration or longer-range ventures such
as the Getty's efforts to improve visual arts education through its various institutes in Los Angeles and across the country. Practice can also be
affected through the use of textbooks, such as those by Katz, Lankford,
and Plank and by Hobbs and Rush, which provide useful applications
of research. In the excerpts reprinted here, Jean Rush, who was heavily
involved in implementing the principles of DBAE, discusses the research
that was brought to bear in writing a text, co-authored with Jack Hobbs,
that stresses the DBAE approach. While his remarks do not consist of
reflections on empirical research, Ralph Smith shows how the two faces
of cognition, the procedural and the substantive, can be integrated in an
approach to teaching art that features five phases of aesthetic learning.
He points to areas in the curriculum where attention should concentrate
on creative activities and aesthetic response and on the roles critical and
historical studies play in developing percipience in matters of art and
culture. His account is part of a humanities interpretation of art education
briefly discussed in Part One.

Jessica Davis and Howard Gardner

Symbolic Literacies: The Developmental Portrait Research Has Provided

Development in the visual arts can be described in terms of two aspects of literacy or competency: *perception* and *production*. Perception includes the ability to distinguish the subject matter of a work, the artist's style, and aesthetic aspects like composition and expression. Under perception we also include conceptualization or reflection. This aspect of perception is comprised of an understanding of what is involved in a work of art (such as an individual producing it), as well as an ability to make judgments (as, for example, regarding value). Production is the making of an art (such as the portrayal of a subject) exhibiting stylistic nuances and aesthetic devices. These two dimensions frame the developmental portrait of the acquisition of literacy in the visual arts which synthesizes and further informs our discussion of research.

Perception

The first aspect of a work of art to which the young school child may attend is the subject matter. However, if that element is controlled or the child is asked to sort works according to style, preschoolers as well as six-year-olds have been found to be sensitive to style. With sufficient scaffolding (left on their own, they apparently show little interest in such pursuits), young children can also display sensitivity to the aesthetic aspects of expression, composition, and texture. In terms of conceptualization, however, young children have very limited understandings of art, thinking, for example, that works of art might be made by machines and increase in value according to size. By middle childhood, children seem to have a standard for value: "photographic reality." As adolescents, they may reject those rigid standards and adopt the "relativistic view" that is retained by many adults.[1]

Housen[2] and Parsons[3] have researched aesthetic response as perception and as conceptualization, each uncovering quite similar developmental progressions through five stages. A brief overview of Housen's progression can be articulated in terms of the object of the viewer's attention at each stage: (1) the viewer attends to obvious stimuli like subject; (2) the viewer considers how the painting is made, its value, and how faithfully it replicates the natural world; (3) the viewer considers in which stylistic "school" the painting belongs; (4) the viewer explores the symbolism in the work as it relates to his or her own emotional experience; (5) the viewer conceives of the problems confronted and the solutions negotiated by the artist; the viewer may also actively integrate his or her analytic and emotional responses to the work. At stage five, one sees the merging of production and perception through the perceiver's identification with the producer as well as through his or her own active construction of meaning.

The finding of a five-stage sequence by two researchers offers strong support for a developmental sequence of distinct cognitive stages in aesthetic response. It appears that, with exposure to the domain, individuals become progressively more attentive to the aesthetic properties of individual works of art. They also become progressively more aware of the "others" who create works of art working in a domain that has tradition, context, and values. Finally, they also develop the ability to integrate their own personal aesthetic responses with the contextual knowledge they acquire. One quite reasonable explanation for the observed increase in all aspects of aesthetic perception is the development of skills in language which enable children to *tell* the researcher what they perceive and to have dialogue with the relevant culture in the course of conceptualization about drawing. Whether there are individuals equally sensitive yet less articulate is an important question.

Production

As for production, the developmental portrait depicts the early enjoyment of scribbling as a mere prelude to early representation or the creation of graphic equivalents. Wolf and Perry credit this depiction to an emphasis on realistic portrayal as an endstate in drawing which limits our ability to view early drawing as anything but preparatory stages for this particular goal. Since realistic art is only one option in the aesthetic gambit of representation, they argue, this view seems especially shortsighted. Challenging the dismissal of the drawings of the youngest children (rampant symbolizers in other domains like play) as "purposeless pencillings," they reconceptualize drawing development as the acquisition of a repertoire of visual languages amongst which scribbling will persist as a resource.[4] Their "repertoire" view admits a similar approach to the less flavorful drawings of the literal stage child. Since future artists like Picasso and Klee wholeheartedly enjoyed a literal stage,[5] the literal stage, like scribbling, may be a time of resource acquisition in spite of its dip in aesthetic appeal. Unfortunately, however, scribbling gives way to a next step in drawing; and for the majority, the literal stage heralds its demise.

The portrait we have provided of literate production is shaped like a U:[6] young children and adult artists balanced at the high points, school-aged children hugging the floor with most of them exiting to the right, transforming the U to an L—perhaps "L" for literal as that Project Zero stage and as the condition of most adults—but certainly not "L" for literate as a competent reader and writer of the language of art. This portrait emerges from research intended to inform the new breed of art education which embraced a cognitive approach—an approach that had already found its way into general education.

Effects of Cognitive Revolution on General and Aesthetic Education

The cognitive revolution was introduced to the field of education at a conference in Woods Hole in 1959. Under the leadership of Jerome Bruner, a group of scientists, scholars, and educators responded to the Soviet challenge of Sputnik by gathering to discuss ways to improve science education in America. Cognitive researchers pondered various issues related to the acquisition and employment of knowledge; but the central issue of these discussions was rooted in Piaget. It was that academic disciplines had schema or *structures* that children could learn to ferret out and use—even across disciplines.

Separated by a decade of thought on the subject, two conferences were to art education what Woods Hole had been to science education: the Seminar on Research and Curriculum Development at Pennsylvania State University in 1965 and a conference entitled "The Arts, Cognition, and Basic Skills" in Aspen, Colorado, in 1977. A movement within art education embraced the Brunerian concept of structures within disciplines. Accordingly, scholars in the field wrestled with the challenge of deciding what these structures might comprise in art education, and how they would be implemented and reconciled with curriculum demands. Bruner had forged the gap between cognitive theory and educational practice, and art educators worked to redefine aesthetic education as the education of a process of thought.

As it had with reference to general education, the cognitivist approach introduced new questions to the field of art education, and new theoretical guidelines were needed for appropriate instruction. The notion of aesthetic thinking was paradoxical. Because it was a process of

thought and a way of making meaning through symbols, aesthetic thinking was *like* other cognitive processes; but because the meanings it makes,
like the symbols it uses, are unique, aesthetic thinking was also *different*
from other cognitive processes. In which ways could aesthetic thinking
be taught like other cognitive processes, and in which ways not?

The traditional distinction between a cognitivist and noncognitivist
approach relied on a view of expression in art as a cut-off point between
emotion and cognition. In fact the field of art instruction had been built
in significant measure on a view of the artistic process as a feeling enterprise best accessed through free and untutored expression. However,
the new vision was of something called "artistic knowledge"—a way of
perceiving, thinking, and forming which was basic and therefore essential to education.[7] The cognitivist notion that literacy had to be gained in
the symbolic languages of art resonated in the cry for skills and knowledge to serve art just as vocabulary and syntax served language. The
new perspective left behind the "touchy feely" approach to art and invited (not without trepidation) the inclusion of art education in the "back
to basics" movement. For researchers, the foremost issue was what was
to count as the basics in art education; for practitioners, the question of
who was qualified to teach the basics in art education was equally crucial.

In 1982 the Getty Center for Education in the Arts was formed to
address such issues and to advocate art as a basic to children's education. The results of this effort and the recommendations that were to
rock the boat of art education were presented in 1985 in a volume entitled *Beyond Creating: The Place for Art in America's Schools.*[8] The Getty
Center recommended Discipline-based Art Education (hereafter DBAE)
which attended to four content areas in art instruction. Understanding
in art would result from studying and integrating four kinds of knowledge: (1) art production (knowing how—πραξισ); (2) art history and
culture (knowing about); (3)art criticism (knowing why); and (4)aesthet-
ics (knowing of/within, as through formal aspects).[9] The general consensus among art educators of the early 1980s was that instruction and
measurement of student achievement in the arts had historically focused
on skill development, with not enough attention given to aesthetics, critical judgment, and cultural context. DBAE would right this imbalance.

In 1988, a group of art educators and researchers applauded the good
intention but cited the "ominous flaws" and "potentially dire consequences" of the Getty effort in another volume: *Beyond DBAE: The Case
for Multiple Visions of Art Education.*[10] Between these two bookends, a
collection of publications presented dueling perspectives, most of which

in some way reflected the tenets of the cognitive revolution. Was understanding in art to be skill-based ("knowledge how") or content-based ("knowledge that")? Would it incorporate the integrative nature of information processing, considering aesthetic understanding as a cognitive process of decoding, encoding, and reflecting? In that case, would each part of the process get equal time, or would the field decide which part was most important? Might there even be a way to focus on the interaction, that is, the discipline that grounded the entire process?

The paradox of aesthetic thinking persisted in the attempt to bridge the gap between theory and practice for DBAE. It was feared that DBAE would even be assimilated into a general movement in critical thinking, dissolving the particularities of the special knowledge that is art by focusing on such commonalities with other forms of education as rigor and an interest in excellence.[11] The promise that a cognitive view of art had held, that it might emerge as an essential ingredient in education, appeared as a double-edged sword. Would the recognition that art was as serious a subject as others dilute the differences which were as essential as equal status?

DBAE had introduced a debate that engaged the interest and resources of art educators and researchers. Proponents would explore means of proper implementation; dissenters would devise alternative implementations for a cognitive approach to art education. The spirited crossfire is reflective of the profound effect that the Getty effort has had on those who think about art education and are now looking for ways to expose ordinary students to aspects of artistic knowledge heretofore reserved for advanced students of art. ARTS PROPEL is one result of this energy and direction.

ARTS PROPEL emerged in 1985 as a joint effort involving Harvard's Project Zero, the Educational Testing Service, and the Pittsburgh Public Schools.[12] The acronym is for perception, production, and reflection, with the final L for learning. Initially conceived to devise assessment instruments for measuring artistic learning in middle and high schools, ARTS PROPEL developed with an equal concern for curriculum modules as with their concordant assessment instruments.

Whereas as DBAE thinking and talking about art carry equal weight as the making of art, in PROPEL the emphasis is on process, primarily process as production which necessarily involves the cognitive components of perception and reflection. Two vehicles propel this process approach. The first is the *domain project*, a set of curricular materials which fit into a regular course. The domain project is a central production experience framed by reflection and perceptual activities, with assessment factored therein. The second vehicle is the *processfolio*. As opposed to the traditional portfolio in which artists collect their best final products in hopes of getting work or a show, the processfolio is a resource for students through which they can retain and review works in progress as tracers of their growth in symbolic activities. Consistent with the cognitive approach, the processfolio seeks to capture the phases in the development of a product or the solving of a problem and to encourage the student to reflect upon his or her processes of learning.

Just as the groundbreaking efforts of DBAE embraced the Brunerian concept of structures within disciplines, ARTS PROPEL encompassed many principles of cognitive developmental psychology. Withal, the cognitive revolution had clearly arrived and promised to remain on the permanent scene of aesthetic education.

Notes

1. See Howard Gardner, *Art Education and Human Development* (Los Angeles: Getty Center for Education in the Arts, 1990).

2. Abigail Housen, "Museums in an Age of Pluralism," in *Art Education Here*, ed. Pamela Banks (Boston: Massachusetts College of Art, 1987).

3. Michael Parsons, *How We Understand Art* (Cambridge: Cambridge University Press, 1987). See also chapter 4 in the present volume [i.e. *The Arts, Education, and Aesthetic Knowing*, ed. Reimer and Smith], where Parsons discusses children's understandings of artworks.

4. Dennie Wolf and Martha Perry, "From Endpoints to Repertoires: Some New Conclusions about Drawing Development," *The Journal of Aesthetic Education* 22, no. 1 (1988): 17-34.

5. See David Pariser, "The Juvenile Drawings of Klee, Toulouse-Lautrec, and Picasso," *Visual Arts Research* 13, no. 2 (1987): 53-67.

6. See Howard Gardner and Ellen Winner, "First Intimations of Artistry," in *U-Shaped Behavioral Growth*, ed. Sydney Strauss (New York: Academic Press, 1982).

7. See Rudolf Arnheim, "Perceiving, Thinking, Forming," *Art Education* 36 (March 1983): 9-11. This issue of the journal, edited by Martin Engel, is twice as long as any preceding issue and represents a milestone in the course of the entrance of cognitive science into aesthetic education.

8. Getty Center for Education in the Arts, *Beyond Creating: The Place for Art in American Schools* (Los Angeles: Getty Center for Education in the Arts, 1985).

9. See Elliot Eisner, *The Role of Discipline-Based Art Education in America's Schools* (Los Angeles: Getty Center for Education in the Arts, 1987); Bennett Reimer, *A Philosophy of Music Education*, 2d ed. (Englewood Cliffs, NJ: Prentice-Hall, 1989).

10. Judith Burton, Arlene Lederman, and Peter London. *Beyond DBAE: The Case for Multiple Visions of Arts Education*, sponsored by the University Council on Art Education (North Dartmouth, MA: Peter London, 1988).

11. See Dennie Wolf's remarks in *Issues in Discipline-Based Art Education: Strengthening the Stance, Extending the Horizons* (Report of the invitational seminar sponsored by the Getty Center in Cincinnati, Ohio, May 21-24, 1987).

12. See Howard Gardner, "Zero-Based Art Education: An Introduction to ARTS PROPEL," *Studies in Art Education* 30, no. 2 (1989): 71-83.

DAVID J. HARGREAVES AND MAURICE J. GALTON

Five Phases of Artistic Development

The current state of the research literature has recently been documented in *Children and the Arts*.[1] Our outline of the five phases draws together the main features of this body of research. We have deliberately described *phases* rather than *stages* so as to avoid the connotations of Piagetian stages. We do not seek here to propose functional explanations for the progression across the phases. Rather, we seek to describe the modes of symbolic thought that are typically displayed by children at different ages in their dealings with the arts.

Our descriptive model is summarized in table 1. The five horizontal rows contain brief descriptions of the phases, which we have labeled the *presymbolic, figural, schematic, rule systems*, and *metacognitive* phases. We have assigned approximate age levels to each phase. The first vertical column, "cognitive aesthetic development," refers to research evidence on general symbolic developments. There are six columns describing domain-specific developments. Four of these deal with developments in music and the other two with developments in drawing and writing. This is not intended to imply that musical developments are in any way more significant or important than those in other domains, but probably reflects the relative diversity of musical behavior and of the research that has investigated it.

We have included singing, which has largely been studied by the analysis of recordings of children's spontaneous output; musical representation, in which children are typically asked to make graphic representations of musical stimuli (usually drawings of tapped rhythm patterns); melodic perception, which is largely based on numerous experimental studies of children's ability to recognize similarities and differences between single-note melodies; and musical composition, an area in which very little systematic data have been collected. We have adopted "composition" as a convenient term for musical invention in its broadest sense. The term is intended to cover improvisation and recordings of original performances as well as traditional written compositions.

TABLE 1
FIVE PHASES OF ARTISTIC DEVELOPMENT

PHASE	COGNITIVE AESTHETIC DEVELOPMENT	Domain-Specific Developments					
		DRAWING	WRITING	SINGING	MUSICAL REPRESEN-TATION	MELODIC PERCEPTION	MUSICAL COMPO-SITION
METACOG-NITIVE (15+ years)	independence from cultural styles and context	freedom from artistic styles	self-reflection in relation to social rules				enactive and reflective strategies
RULE SYSTEMS (8-15 years)	development of artistic conventions and style sensitivity	"visual realism," viewer-centered	story grammar analysis of structural complexity	intervals, scales	formal-metric	analytic recognition of intervals, key stability	"idiomatic" conventions
SCHEMATIC (5-8 years)	emphasis on realism and subject matter	baselines, skylines	standard narrative forms	"first draft" songs	figural-metric: more than one dimension	"conservation" of melodic properties	"vernacular" conventions
FIGURAL (2-5 years)	concrete, mechanistic	preschmatic, "intellectual realism"	"frame" or outline stories	"outline" songs: coalescences between spontaneous and cultural songs	figural: single dimension	global features: pitch, contour	
PRE-SYMBOLIC (0-2 years)		scribbling	scribbling, symbolic play	babbling, rhythmic dancing	scribbling: "action equivalents"	recognition of melodic contours	sensory, manipulative

The other two main areas of research have been on children's drawings, on which there is a substantial recent literature,[2] and on children's
writing, which has a smaller but growing literature.[3] There are several
gaps in the table, for which we make no apology; they mostly arise from
the lack of research in particular areas.

The presymbolic phase. Our first phase is described as "presymbolic"
(0-2 years) since representational symbols are not yet fully formed. Most
developments involve physical actions and sensorimotor coordination,
and it is only in the second year of life that abstract symbolism begins to
emerge. Bruner referred to "enactive" representation at this age,[4] and it
takes place in what Piaget described as the "sensorimotor" stage. Thus,
to take our final column first, Swanwick and Tillman's description of
children's early engagement with music emphasizes mastery.[5] Their
spiral model of musical development includes a first "sensory" mode,
in which infants are concerned with the exploration of the qualities of
sounds (especially timbre), and a related "manipulative" mode in which
they gradually master the means of sound production.

Infants' drawings are described as "scribbles," in which the physical action of pencil on paper is most important; scribbles only begin to
take on representational meaning toward the end of this phase.[6] There
is a clear analogy in musical representation; Goodnow used the term
"action equivalents" to describe the marks that preschoolers make when
trying to draw sequences of taps on paper.[7] Although the child's actions
may match the temporal pattern of the taps, what appears on the paper
bears no relation to it.

Early developments in storytelling also take place by means of physical expression. Cowie describes how infants engage in "storying" with
pencil on paper; they imitate the flow of a script, so that a graphic or
scribbled "text" emerges.[8] There is also a great deal of overlap between
early storytelling and symbolic or make-believe play. Smith has suggested that fantasy and sociodramatic play is often the precursor of imaginative writing and that narrative-like and structural features can be
observed in early play.[9]

The link with physical action is also a primary feature of infants'
singing and their response to music. Moog's observations of some 500
children provide a detailed description of the development of physical
responses to music.[10] Babies as young as three to six months were found
to sway or bounce rhythmically in response to music, and the coordination between their dance movements and aspects of the music become
increasingly accurate in the second year of life. Moog also studied early
"babbling songs," which he regarded as a precursor of speech, and

demonstrated that singing became increasingly integrated into imaginative play as infants progressed beyond this phase.

Recent research on melodic perception in infants has revealed that their capacity to recognize musical features may be remarkably advanced. Chang and Trehub, and Trehumb, Bull, and Thorpe, for example, have shown by means of heart rate measurements that babies as young as five months can recognize changes in melodic contour and rhythmic pattern and that these changes are more salient than pitch transpositions.[11] It appears that infants use a kind of "global" processing strategy to recognize melodic contours, which parallels the strategies adults use to recognize unfamiliar or atonal melodies. This finding is an early pointer to the essence of the second phase of artistic development.

The figural phase. The defining characteristic of the "figural" phase (approximately 2-5 years) is the tendency to make "global" or "outline" representations in various artistic media in which the overall shape, or figure, of the representation is clearly discernible, but the details within that shape are imprecise or absent. This has a good deal in common with Bruner's description of "iconic" representation.[13] Extrapolating from the paragraph above, there is good evidence that preschool children perceive or "process" melodies by attending to their overall shapes or "contours."[14]

This is also mirrored in the spontaneous singing of the preschooler. Some of the work of the Harvard Project Zero group[15] suggests the gradual acquisition of sets of song-related expectations, or "song frames," such that "outline songs" are produced. These are shown most clearly in the gradual coalescences between children's own spontaneous songs and those which they learn from the culture that surrounds them, such as nursery rhymes, playground chants, or pop songs.[16]

There are precise parallels in children's storytelling. Cowie describes how preschoolers produce "frame" stories, which "consist mainly of a beginning and an end—about stock characters who experience unbalancing and unresolved adventures."[17] There are also clear parallels in children's drawings at this age, which might be described as "preschematic." One of their central features is "intellectual realism"; children are said to draw "what they know, and not what they see."[18] Examples include "transparencies," such as people's heads being drawn as visible beneath their hats, and "turning over," where two visual perspectives are incongruously combined in the same drawing. Another feature of this stage is the well-known "tadpole figure"[19] in which children universally draw people without bodies. This latter is a good example of the graphic equivalent of "outlines" in other media.

When children represent music by graphic means at this age, they are once again likely to make figural, or outline representations. In fact, the term "figural" was coined in this context by Jeanne Bamberger in her well-known studies of children's drawings of rhythm patterns. [20] In representing the ten-beat pattern of the second and third lines of "One, two, buckle my shoe," for example, preschoolers are more likely to show the overall two-part shape of the sequence than to depict accurately the rhythmic relationships between each beat. Describing some further work on this topic, Davidson and Scripp point out that the children tend to focus on a single dimension of the task, usually the overall rhythmic pulse.

All these developments are clearly domain-specific. Researchers who have looked more generally at what we have termed "cognitive aesthetic developments," such as Gardner, Winner, and Kircher (1975), Parsons (1987), or Wolf (1989), have discovered a tendency for children to be concerned at this age with the concrete feature of art works and with the mechanics of producing them. [22] Gardner, Winner, and Kircher's study also revealed a strong preoccupation with rules, for example, about who is allowed to paint or play an instrument and why; they described these responses as "immature."

The schematic phase. As one might expect, one of the major developments occurring when children's engagements with art works become "schematic" (roughly between the ages of five and eight years) is an increase in the level of organization of "immature" productions, so that they become increasingly congruent with cultural rules and standards. As far as general cognitive aesthetic development is concerned, the researchers mentioned above place a strong emphasis on the subject matter of art works and on the degree of realism of this subject matter. Thus, pictures or drawings are good if they look realistic; *what* they represent is much more important than *how* (that is, in what style) the representation is made. Similarly, in the case of musical composition, Swanwick and Tillman propose a "vernacular" mode of development in which children's output incorporates fairly general musical conventions such as melodic and rhythmic ostinati and sequences and phrasing in 2-, 4-, or 8-bar units. [23]

The acquisition of cultural rules in drawings is clearly evident in children's use of ground lines, or baselines, and skylines. These serve to organize spatially the elements of a drawing which have previously been unsystematically arranged on the paper. [24] Children's stories, similarly, conform increasingly to standard narrative forms with a beginning, a middle, and an end. [25] Their songs at this age have been characterized as "first draft" songs in that they are intermediate between the "outline" songs of the previous part, and the fully accurate songs which occur later in childhood. [26]

One significant and specific development that occurs in the schematic phase parallels Piaget's account of the transition from preoperational to concrete operational thinking. It is embodied in two areas of research on musical development. The first is a direct attempt to create musical analogies of Piagetian conservation tasks. Pflederer carried out a pioneering study of "music conservation" which has stimulated various others to devise and assess similar tasks. She proposed five conservation-type laws for the development of musical concepts. [27] While there is some doubt about the conceptual validity of the Piagetian analogy, the empirical evidence nevertheless lends support to the developmental progression that Piagetian theory would predict. [28] Secondly, studies of musical representation have found that children can typically represent more than one dimension of a rhythmic pattern by graphic means at this age. [29]

The rule systems phase. Although these schematic developments show increasingly fluent use of artistic rule systems, children's output in different domains is still far from completely accurate. Full-scale accuracy in relation to cultural rules only fully emerges between the years of eight and fifteen or so, which we have accordingly labeled the phase of "rule systems." Thus, drawings become "visually realistic," or what Cox has described as "viewer-centered"; objects can be depicted as they might be seen from any angle, or by any viewer, and they are accurate in their use of artistic conventions such as perspective, occlusion, and depth relationships. [30]

The developments that occur in writing have been studied by means of story grammar analysis. Here the emphasis is upon the structural complexity of stories and how this develops with age rather than on the content of those stories. [31] Strictly speaking, this may reflect a development of the *use* of existing rule systems rather than of the acquisition of those systems, since the formal rules of storytelling are less explicit than those in domains such as music.

In singing, musical representation, and melodic perception, the pattern of research findings is fairly similar; children become increasingly accurate at representing and reproducing the precise pitch and rhythmic relationships between notes, so that scales and intervals become stabilized. [32] These "digital" relationships are not only accurate *within* the component phrases of a piece but also in relationship to one another and to the piece as a whole, that is, with respect to its key and time signatures.

In their more general description of the development of children's musical compositions, Swanwick and Tillman propose an idiomatic mode of development at around this age which incorporates the fluent use of conventions such as elaboration, call and response, and contrasting sections, all within an authentic harmonic and instrumental context.[33] This is in line with the general finding from studies of aesthetic perception, shown in the first column of table 1, that children become fully aware of stylistic conventions and interpret works of art in terms of those conventions.[34]

The metacognitive phase. In the "metacognitive" phase, which begins in the teenage years, adolescents not only posses a full and mature understanding of artistic conventions, but they may also begin to see the work of individuals, including themselves, in relation to but independent from those conventions. As Wolf puts it, "They become aware that there are no absolute answers, no certain rules; they realize that different minds will construct different worlds and different ways of evaluating those worlds.[35] Many people may never achieve this mature level of artistic understanding.

In visual art, in music, and in other media, artistic styles can be seen in relation to one another, and the creator can draw on each style to varying degrees in formulating the language of an original statement. Swanwick and Tillman have also proposed a final metacognitive mode of musical composition which involves the capacity to be self-reflective and to relate original musical thought to other areas of experience.[36] Albeit at an earlier age level, Cowie suggested that writing can fulfill a reflective function in relation to the social roles of self and others.[37] By adopting the "spectator role," the writer maintains an independent perspective on the network of social relationships of which he or she is a part.

Musical composition is a notoriously difficult area for empirical study, although the cognitive approach is beginning to make some significant inroads.[38] One finding that emerges from two different cognitive studies deserves mention. In a study in which beginning and advanced music students were given a short composition exercise, Davidson and Welsh found that beginning composition students tended to work "enactively" at the piano: they composed in short units and worked sequentially within one phrase at a time.[39] The more advanced students tended to conceive larger musical units internally before trying them out at the keyboard: they worked at a higher-order symbolic or reflective level.

A parallel finding emerged from a study by Hargreaves, Cork, and Setton in which novice and expert jazz pianists were asked to improvise right-hand solos over prerecorded backing tracks.[40] The novices tended to have no clear advance plan, or to focus on a single musical dimension of the backing track, such as its chords or rhythm; only occasionally was there any evidence of change in their improvisations as a result of feedback. In contrast, the experts approached the task with an explicit yet provisional overall plan, which was frequently changed according to what happened as the solo developed.

These two findings are of particular interest because they seem to represent a recapitulation of the shift from enactive to symbolic modes of thinking which was observed in the early phases of artistic development. Although the student composers and improvisers had achieved a high level of mastery of the component skills of the tasks they were set, a similar developmental progression was apparent. This indicates some degree of coherence in our necessarily very brief account of the five phases of artistic development. Since this is our first attempt to sketch the main features of a growing body of research, it is bound to lack completeness, to have many loose ends, and to need further revision as research proceeds.

Notes

1. David J. Hargreaves, ed., *Children and the Arts* (Milton Keynes: Open University Press, 1989).

2. See Norman H. Freeman and Maureen V. Cox, eds, *Visual Order* (Cambridge: Cambridge University Press, 1985).

3. See Helen Cowie, ed. *The Development of Children's Imaginative Writing* (London: Croom Helm, 1984).

4. Jerome S. Bruner, "The Growth of Representational Processes in Childhood," in Jeremy Anglin, ed., *Beyond the Information Given: Studies in the Psychology of Knowing* (New: W. W. Norton, 1973).

5. Keith Swanwick and June Tillman, "The Sequence of Musical Development: A Study of Children's Composition," *British Journal of Music Education* 3 (1986): 305-339.

6. Glyn V. Thomas and Angèle M. J. Silk, *An Introduction to the Psychology of Children's Drawings* (Hemel Hempstead: Harvester Wheatsheaf, 1990).

7. Jacqueline J. Goodnow, "Auditory-visual Matching: Modality Problem or Translation Problem?" *Child Development* 42 (1971): 1187-2101.

8. Helen Cowie, "Children as Writers," in *Children and the Arts*, ed. David J. Hargreaves (Milton Keynes, Open University Press, 1989).

9. Peter K. Smith, "The Relevance of Fantasy Play for Development in Young Children," in *The Development of Children's Imaginative Writing*, ed. Helen Cowie (London: Croom Helm, 1984).

10. Helmut Moog, *The Musical Experience of the Preschool Child*, trans. Claudia Clarke (London: Schott, 1976).

11. Hsing-Wu Chang and Sandra E. Trehub, "Infants' Perception of Temporal Grouping in Auditory Patterns," *Child Development* 48 (1977): 1666-1670; Sandra E. Trehumb, Dale Bull, and Leigh A. Thorpe, "Infants' Perception of Melodies: The Role of Melodic Contour," *Child Development* 55 (1984): 821-830.

12. W. Jay Dowling, "Melodic Information Processing and Its Development," in *The Psychology of Music*, ed. Diana Deutsch (New York: Academic Press, 1982).

13. Bruner, "The Growth of Representational Processes in Childhood."

14. Dowling, "Melodic Information Processing and Its Development."

15. Lyle Davidson, Patricia McKernon, and Howard Gardner, "The Acquisition of Song: A Developmental Approach," in *Documentary Report of the Ann Arbor Symposium: Applications of Psychology to the Teaching and Learning of Music* (Reston, VA: Music Educators National Conference, 1981).

16. A number of examples of these so-called "pot-pourri" songs can be found in Moog. *The Musical Experience of the Preschool Child* and in Hargreaves, *The Developmental Psychology of Music*.

17. Cowie, "Children as Writers," p. 23.

18. G. H. Lucquet, *Le Dessin Enfantin* (Paris: Alcan, 1927).

19. Norman H. Freeman, "Do Children Draw Men with Arms Coming Out of the Head?" *Nature* 254 (1975): 416-417; idem, *Strategies of Representation in Young Children* (London: Academic Press, 1980).

20. Jeanne Bamberger, "Revisiting Children's Drawing of Simple Rhythms: A Function for Reflection-in-Action," in *U-Shaped Behavioral Growth*, ed. Sydney Strauss (New York: Academic Press, 1982).

21. Lyle Davidson and Lawrence Scripp, "Education and Development in Music from a Cognitive Perspective," in *Children and the Arts*, ed. David Hargreaves.

22. Howard Gardner, Ellen Winner, and Mary Kircher, "Children's Conceptions of the Arts," *The Journal of Aesthetic Education* 9 (1975): 60-77; Parsons, *How We Understand Art*; Dennie P. Wolf, "Artistic Learning as Conversation," in *Children and the Arts*, ed. David Hargreaves.

23. Swanwick and Tillman, "The Sequence of Musical Development."

24. David J. Hargreaves, Philip M. Jones, and Diane Martin, "The Air Gap Phenomenon in Children's Landscape Drawings," *Journal of Experimental Child Psychology* 32 (1981): 11-20.

25. Cowie, "Children as Writers."

26. Davidson, McKernon, and Gardner, "The Acquisition of Song."

27. Marilyn Pflederer, "The Responses of Children to Musical Tasks Embodying Piaget's Principle of Conservation," *Journal of Research in Music Education* 12 (1964): 251-268.

28. See reviews by Mary Louise Serafine, "Piagetian Research in Music," *Bulletin of the Council for Research in Music Education* 62 (1980): 1-21, and by David Hargreaves, *The Developmental Psychology of Music*.

29. Davidson and Scripp, "Education and Development in Music from a Cognitive Perspective."

30. Maureen V. Cox, "Children's Drawings," in *Children and the Arts*, ed. David Hargreaves.

31. B. M. Kroll and C. M. Anson, "Analyzing Structure in Children's Fictional Narratives," in *The Development of Children's Imaginative Writing*, ed. Cowie.

32. Dowling, "Melodic Information Processing and Its Development"; Davidson and Scripp, "Education and Development in Music from a Cognitive Perspective."

33. Swanwick and Tillman, "The Sequence of Musical Development."

34. Howard Gardner, "Style Sensitivity in Children," *Human Development* 15 (1972): 325-338.

35. Wolf, "Artistic Learning as Conversation," p. 33.

36. Swanwick and Tillman, "The Sequence of Musical Development."

37. Cowie, "Children as Writers."

38. See John A. Sloboda, ed., *Generative Processes in Music: The Psychology of Performance, Improvisation, and Composition* (Oxford: Clarendon Press, 1988).

39. Lyle Davidson and Patricia Welsh, "From Collections to Structure: The Developmental Path of Tonal Thinking," in *Generative Processes in Music*, ed. Sloboda.

40. David J. Hargreaves, Conrad A. Cork, and Tina Setton, "Cognitive Strategies in Jazz Improvisation: An Exploratory Study," *Canadian Journal of Research in Music Education* 33 (December 1991): 47-54.

Michael J. Parsons

Stages of Aesthetic Development

We all begin in the same cognitive state. We are born into the world small, speechless, subject to an unorganized plenty of sensory stimuli, possessed of an individual body with pleasures and pains, unaware of our nature of abilities, socially oriented but unable to distinguish our self from whatever happens. We are aware of nothing except as it appears to us. This picture of our original state is common to the cognitive development tradition. From this beginning we construct the ideas with which we understand the world. As we do so, mentally we join the society into which physically we have been born. So the story of our mental development is also the story of our social development, of our membership in society. We learn our society's language, adopt its ideas and values, share its activities; and so both construct our own mind and become a member of our society. Later, if we are so lucky, we are able to think autonomously: to have original ideas, to be creative, perhaps to judge our culture from some independent viewpoint that is independent but still social in constitution.

The basic direction of development is from dependence to autonomy. It is the common theme of developmental theories: the story of the growth of both human freedom and human sociality. It occurs in two great movements. We earn our freedom from the domination of biological impulse by becoming good members of society; and freedom from the domination of society by constructing some viewpoint independent of society. This last movement is no less a growth of sociality than the first. When we are autonomous we are no less members of society, but we are more concerned to improve society than to conform to it. The growth of our social nature underlies the development of aesthetic understanding just as it does other kinds of cognitive development. It is consequently a theme underlying my account here.

Stage one can be thought of as a kind of theoretical zero point in this regard. It is the point at which we are more a biological than a social creature. Though we have immense social potential, we have not yet become a member of society. We are unable to take the perspective of others, and are not really aware of the difference between ourselves and others. We are not clear that others do not see and feel what we see and feel, because we have not distinguished between their point of view and ours. In short, we are aware of only one point of view, the one from which everything appears to us. In a sense this state is a theoretical construction, one which is needed to make sense of the direction of development. It exists, if at all, very early in life, and is largely prelinguistic. In my scheme here I have extended it somewhat, to avoid the unnecessary proliferation of stages. I include in stage one many of the characteristic responses of young children, including at times kindergartners.

Stage One: favoritism
- It's my favorite color!
- I like it because of the dog. We've got a dog and its name is Toby.
- It looks like a big pickle coming down from the sky.
- I don't believe in bad paintings. They're all mostly good.

The primary characteristics of stage one are an intuitive delight in most paintings, a strong attraction to color, and a freewheeling associative response to subject matter. Young children rarely find fault with paintings, no matter what their subject or style. They relish color, the more the better. They are often aware of the subject of a painting, i.e., what it represents; but they allow associations and memories freely to enter their response. The common characteristic is the happy acceptance of whatever comes to mind, not distinguishing between what is and is not relevant.

Psychologically, this is the stage where there is little awareness of the point of view of others. All that is occurs in experience; there is nothing else, and nothing to compare it with.

Aesthetically, paintings are a stimulus to pleasant experience. It does not matter what they represent or whether they are nonrepresentational. Liking a painting is identical with judging it, and it is hard to imagine a bad one. There are no distinctions of relevance nor questions about objectivity.

Stage two: beauty and realism
- It's gross! It's really ugly!
- You expect something beautiful, like a lady in a boat, or two deer in the mountains.

- You can see how carefully he's done it. It's really good!
- It looks just like the real thing.
- It's really just scribbling. My little brother could do that.

The dominant idea of stage two is that of the subject. Stage two is organized around the idea of representation. The basic purpose of painting
is to represent something. It is true that some paintings are nonrepresentational, but they are not really meaningful. A painting is better if the
subject is attractive and if the representation is realistic. Emotion is something to be represented, as in a smile or a gesture; and style is appreciated only as realism. Skill, patience, care are admirable. Beauty, realism,
and skill are objective grounds for judgments.

Psychologically stage two is an advance because it implicitly acknowledges the viewpoint of other people. The notion of representation
requires the distinction between what anyone can see and what one is
merely reminded of. To stick to what is pictured is to understand that
what one associates with the painting is not necessarily what others see.

Aesthetically stage two is an advance because it enables the viewer
to distinguish some aspects of experience as aesthetically relevant (those
having to do with what is pictured) from some that are not (those not
having to do with what is pictured). For example, the Renoir may be
judged good because it pictures a dog, and dogs are nice. But this latter
has become a fact about the dog, and not about the viewer's tastes, as
with stage one. Similarly, the color of the Klee is good; and this is a fact
about the color, not about personal favorites.

Stage three: expressiveness
- That really grabs me!
- You've got to have a gut feeling for it. It doesn't matter what the
  critics say about form and technique.
- You can see the artist felt really sorry for her.
- The distortion really brings the feeling out more strongly than a
  photo would.
- We all have a different experience of it. There's no point in talking
  about good and bad. It's all in the individual.

The organizing insight of stage three has to do with expressiveness.
We look at paintings for the quality of the experience they can produce,
and the more intense and interesting the experience the better the painting. Intensity and interest guarantee that experience is genuine, i.e., really felt. The feeling or thought expressed may be the artist's or the

viewer's, or both. It is always what is inwardly grasped by an individual person.

This insight affects most of one's ideas of art. The purpose of art is to express someone's experience. The beauty of subject matter becomes secondary to what is expressed, and may actually get in the way of expression. Similarly realism of style and skill are not ends in themselves but means to expressing something, and may not be better than their contraries. Creativity, originality, depth of feeling, are newly appreciated. There is a skepticism about the value of talking about painting, and about the possibility of objective judgments, because the important criterion remains the quality of some individually felt experience.

Psychologically, stage three is an advance because it rests on a new awareness of the interiority of the experience of others, and a new ability to grasp their particular thoughts and feelings. There is also a corresponding awareness of one's own experience as something inward and unique.

Aesthetically, stage three is an advance because it enables one to see the irrelevance of the beauty of the subject, the realism of the style, and the skill of the artist. It opens one to a wider range of works and a better grasp of expressive qualities. An example is the difference between finding the Albright ugly and distasteful, and finding it powerfully expressive of empathy with Ida.

Stage four: style and form
- The way the paint is laid on here, and lets the bottom color show through—it sings!
- See the grief in the tension in the lines, the pulling on the handkerchief!
- Look at the way light strikes the tablecloth; the colors are so varied and yet the overall effect is white, and the cloth still lays flat on the table.
- There's a quirky humour in the face. It's basically frontal, but the eyes are done in a Cubist style.
- He's playing with the eyes. They're more like cups or boats, it's a visual metaphor.

The new insight here is that the significance of a painting is a social rather than an individual achievement. It exists within a tradition, which is composed by a number of people looking over time at a number of works and talking about them. As they talk, they find some things more meaningful and others less so. They help each other to see perceptively.

The work exists in a public space; aspects of its medium, form, and style can be pointed to in an intersubjective way; in this way interpretations can be corrected and improved. There are relationships between different works—styles—and a history to their interpretation. All these aspects of a work are public and may have a bearing on its meaning. Its meaning is constituted by what can be discursively said by the group about it, and this is more than what is grasped inwardly by an individual at one time.

The insight affects many ideas about paintings. It places the emphasis on the way the medium itself is handled, on texture, color, form, space, because these are what are publicly there to see; and on style and stylistic relations, because these are how a work relates to the tradition. What is expressed in art is reinterpreted in terms of form and style, and is a public idea rather than a private state of mind.

Psychologically, the advance here is in the ability to take the perspective of the tradition as a whole. This is cognitively more complex than grasping the state of mind of one individual. An example is when one reads several interpretations of a work, and sees how each makes sense in its own terms and yet is a part of the same tradition.

Aesthetically, this is an advance because it finds significance in the medium, form, and style, and distinguishes between the literary appeal of the subject and sentiment and what is achieved in the work itself. It finds significance in the stylistic and historical relationships of paintings, and it expands the kinds of meanings that can be expressed. It enables one to find art criticism useful as a guide to perception and to see aesthetic judgment as reasonable and capable of objectivity.

Stage five: autonomy
- It seems to me that it breaks out of the limitations of the style by emphasizing the flatness of the surface.
- It has a kind of tired feeling to it. I can't be sure if it's because I'm tired of seeing that kind of thing, or if he got tired of painting it.
- In the end the style is too loose, self-indulgent. I don't like that, I want more self-control.
- I go back and forth on this. I used to think it too rhetorical; now I vibrate to it again.

The central insight here is that the individual must judge the concepts and values with which the tradition constructs the meanings of works of art. These values change with history, and must be continually readjusted to fit contemporary circumstances. Judgment is felt as both more personal and more fundamentally social. On the one hand the responsibility for judgment lies inevitably with the self. One's own experience is in the end the only possible testing ground for judgment, and one can affirm or amend accepted views only in light of one's best understanding of one's own response. The result is an alert awareness of the character of one's own experience, a questioning of the influences upon it, a wondering whether one really sees what one thinks one sees. In the same way the values that underlie our judgments are our own responsibility. Though they come from the tradition, they can be affirmed or amended only in light of our own sense of their value. If they fit us, we affirm them; if they do not, we must amend them.

On the other hand, while one is individually responsible, the responsibility is toward others. The reexamination of accepted views is an attempt to fashion a more appropriate judgment in light of the common situation, and it is meant as valid for anyone in that situation. It is important therefore to talk with others about works of art and the common situation. One cannot question one's own experience without dialog, without considering the response of others to the same works. Dialog provides the only leverage one has to question the tendencies of one's own experience and to understand their significance. In sum, while judgment is accepted as an individual responsibility, there is also a clear sense of the need for discussion and intersubjective understanding, and of responsibility to the community for truth.

This insight affects the understanding of other aesthetic concepts. A style, for example, is no longer an established category but a grouping created for some purpose. The value of certain ways of handling the medium or of formal arrangements is no longer taken as a traditional verity, but requires a personal affirmation. What is expressed is no longer the established attitudes of the tradition but the personal choices of an individual made on behalf of others. Art is valued as a way of raising questions rather than as transmitting truths. Judgment is seen as capable of reasonable argument, and at the same time as dependent on personal affirmation.

Psychologically, this is an advance because it requires one to transcend the point of view of the culture. It requires the ability to raise questions about established views and to understand the self as capable of answering them. This implies a perspective on the culture itself.

Aesthetically, it is an advance because it enables one to make subtler responses, and to be aware that traditional expectations may be misleading. One also understands the practice of art, both its creation and appreciation, more adequately as the constant reexamination and

ABIGAIL HOUSEN

Museums in an Age of Pluralism

Of the many changes in art museums over the past century none has been more continuous than the evolving role of education. While the charters of most art museums expressly include education, the substance and boundaries of museum education have been widely interpreted. For some art museums, the preservation of our cultural heritage is educational at the core and a museum's educational mission resides within the charge of conservation. Other museums focus on fostering an understanding of our cultural heritage and center on research and documentation as education. For still others, the educational challenge is to encourage a valuing of objects and knowledge; exhibition and critical evaluation are fundamental to that pursuit. Finally many museums strive to fulfill several educational roles and define their mission as the preservation of objects, ideas, and values through programs in conservation, exhibition, and instruction.

Embedded in a choice of educational mission is a more fundamental decision about what it means to know, to understand, and to value an aesthetic object. America's first museum educators did not shy away from such questions. Charles Wilson Peale, Benjamin Ives Gilman, John Cotton Dana and others sought ways to foster the aesthetic experience. Aesthetic appreciation was a means toward a range of ends such as public education, social improvement, moral instruction, civil responsibility, and community spirit. In pursuing these ends each educator presumed an understanding of his public and concentrated on the most fruitful way to share objects and ideas with that public.

Todays museum educators, facing what the American Association of Museums' Commission report *Museums for a New Century* describes as cultural pluralism do not assume such familiarity with their public.[1] The commission points out that museum educators will face populations with increasingly differing interests and needs. This suggests that museum educators will have to explain works of art to very diverse groups. Developing appropriate and meaningful ways to interpret works of art to such a range of visitors will put educators' understanding of the teaching and learning processes to new tests.

One way to approach a diverse audience is to find some universal way of explaining a work of art to all people of all ages: one tour, one lecture, one slide show, one demonstration that would simultaneously appeal to visitors with varying needs and abilities without shortchanging the art object. Unfortunately, experience and research show that there is no one way for all. What educator has not been struck by the variety of aesthetic assumptions and values in an audience?

Recently much has been written about the cognitive stages of adolescents and adults. This literature suggests that even if cultural pluralism did not confront us, psychological pluralism would. Developmental psychologists have illustrated in fields such as scientific reasoning, moral development, ego development, and epistemological development that people make sense of their worlds in qualitatively different ways. Even persons of the same age and cultural background may bring strikingly different mental sets to the same experience. The work of Piaget, Kohlberg, Loevinger, and others shows that these different frameworks have a significant impact on how people interact with and learn from their environments.[2]

Research in aesthetic understanding confirms these studies of development. A single work of art may evoke distinctly different reactions and interpretations. The understanding of the work of art varies because of differences in conceptual frameworks. Studies indicate that a person grows in the capacity to respond aesthetically and goes through several stages of aesthetic understanding.[3] In a research project, five stages, ranging from naive to sophisticated, were measured in stream-of-consciousness remarks subjects made when viewing a reproduction of a painting.[4] Their statements led to the following generalizations.

At Stage 1, *The Accountive Stage,* viewers lack a framework or responding to works of art and use the tools closest at hand. These naive viewers, relying on perceptual cues, let bold and obvious stimuli in a work of art trigger idiosyncratic associations. With such observations and associations, the viewers create stories about a painting. The following comment refers to a reproduction of the *Bathers* by Picasso: "It puts me in mind of a place called Sasheba. Sometimes it gets very hot. . . . Here, the lady that's standing in the blue. . . I wonder what she's thinking of. . . . If she's thinking of a trip in that sailboat. . . should she bathe or what?"

At *Stage II, the Constructive Stage,* viewers move beyond story telling. They begin to distance themselves from the work of art and show a less subjective way of looking at it by asking how the work of art was made, how long it took to make, how much it cost to buy and how it has been used. Viewers at this stage adopt a conventional perspective reflecting society's values, mores, and standards. The natural world and the conventional world are used as their measuring rods. In reference to the *Bathers*, viewers made the following comments: "And the lighthouse, usually it's supposed to have a big light, but I guess that one doesn't have one." "I don't know if the sea looks like that—a lot of yellow in that." "The cloud formations seem very unrealistic." "I'm surprised not to see a sun, 'cause usually on these kind of pictures, you'll see a sun, you know."

At *Stage III, the Classifying Stage*, viewers use facts, dates, styles, biographies, and histories to place the work of art within its niche, to give the work a fitting label. Analyzing, decoding, identifying, cataloguing new information against old are the viewers' central preoccupations. Referring to the reproduction of the *Bathers*, viewers said, "Well, it's after cubism, almost what synthetic cubism goes on to." "This is not a Picasso I knew, but I immediately flashed on the blues and the pinks of the *Harlequin*." Another viewer said of *Combination Concrete* by Stuart Davis, "The colors are primary and harsh and bold, very expressionistic, very typical of the contemporary offset of the German expressionists."

At *Stage IV, the Interpretative Stage*, viewers seek a more personal experience with the work of art. Each encounter with it becomes a catalyst for a new consciousness. Viewers use intuitions, past experiences, informed emotions and affect-laden memory as guides to interpret the symbolic content expressed in the work of art. One viewer referring to Picasso's *Bathers*, described how the clashing colors "send waves of emotions throughout the canvas." Another mentioned that "there is no light from the lighthouse and there is no sound from her mouth, but you know that the lighthouse is for light and that her mouth is for sound. And you can hear her scream even though it is a painting. And you can see the lighthouse's beam even though it is day It's like the silence of the light coming from the lighthouse of the day."

At *Stage V, The Re-creative Stage*, viewers' perceptions are shaped by a self-aware willingness to encounter the work of art playfully as one would a friend. Viewers try to interpret the work of art by re-creating the problems, choices, and solutions the artist once faced. A long history of viewing makes people at this stage aware of the various ways to analyze a work. Viewers skillfully integrate analytic and emotional responses, as the following comment about the Picasso reproduction suggests: "One can almost say that the combination of the images of the sailboat and the lighthouse draws on our own stock associations with romanticism and serenity and at the same time incorporates some kind of warning. . . . They all—the elements come back to what I felt in my first childlike impression, which is luxuriance and warning, imitation and modification, sensuality and pleasure."

Faced with psychological pluralism as well as cultural pluralism, how can museum educators please everyone? Is it appropriate even to try? There remains the tantalizing possibility that, despite cultural and psychological differences, one good lecture, one good slide show, one good workshop could speak on many levels to a wide range of participants.

Yet research in human development indicates that this is likely to be a false hope. In a classic study on moral reasoning, for instance, James Rest presented subjects of differing moral stages several arguments based on various levels of sophistication in reasoning. When asked to repeat the arguments, Rest found that subjects paraphrased the logic of arguments of stages beyond their own in terms of the logic of their own stages. The subjects could not summarize higher levels of argument without distortion and tended to reject the reasoning of stages below their own.[5] This study strikes a chord in all of us who have unsuccessfully tried to give the same explanation to people of differing ages or experiences. It also explains that "aha" we get when years later we understand a particular piece of wisdom for the first time.

What is clear from empirical studies in aesthetic understanding is that people do not grasp certain aesthetic concepts and issues until they attain particular levels of aesthetic development. The concepts of Stage III viewers are uninteresting and difficult for viewers at Stage I to understand. The style and school of a painting are of no interest to viewers who do not yet understand the concept of intentionality. Similarly concerns of style and school are less interesting and compelling to viewers at Stage IV, who are puzzling over the symbolic messages in works of art. Indeed, research indicates that these differences in aesthetic awareness and understanding are so fundamental that they shed light on other more observable behaviors, such as the way viewers walk through a gallery, talk about works of art, and choose museum programs. Studies show that stages of aesthetic development are evident in the number of pauses viewers make in a gallery, the amount of time they spend there, and the time they take to read the labels and to go through a museum.[6]

These research findings complement intuition. They reaffirm the need for educators to confront psychological pluralism. If educators want to reach a broad audience, they will have to create presentations for each aesthetic level.

Dealing with aesthetic levels need not be overwhelming. The conceptual tools used at each aesthetic stage can serve as guides to the programs educators devise. Developmental psychology which attempts to investigate and describe how individuals understand, offers practitioners and theoretians descriptive pathways. Cognitive psychologists interested in aesthetic behavior have been asking questions about how viewers process information about aesthetic objects. How do viewers solve questions about form and content in a work of art? How do they develop hypotheses and generate knowledge about the nature of aesthetic experience? Researchers have answered these questions by examining the mental steps artists and other viewers take as they assimilate information and solve aesthetic problems.

The museum educator can use these findings in designing presentations, particularly the data collected and catalogued in aesthetic scoring manuals.[7] These indices of aesthetic response show the concepts and interpretations of viewers at each aesthetic level. Scoring manuals can help educators to identify the concepts and issues that are most compelling and provocative for each level. Knowing what the most naturally engaging themes are can help planners program for diverse museum audiences. Without such understanding, planners will find it all too easy to design programs that are conceptually accessible or interesting to only a few. Often programs are limited unwittingly because they are aimed at audiences that already frequent the museums or resemble the educators themselves. With a map of the different mindsets, organized around empirically derived concepts and concerns, educators can develop imaginative programs for each stage.

Notes

1. American Association of Museums' Commission, *Museums for a New Century* (Washington, D.C.: American Association of Museums, 1984).

2. See John Broughton, "The Development of Natural Epistemology in Adolescence and Early Adulthood," unpublished doctoral dissertation, Harvard University, 1975; David Feldman, *Beyond Universals in Cognitive Development* (Norwood, N. J.: Ablex, 1985); Lawrence Kohlberg, "Stage and Sequence: The Cognitive Developmental Approach to Socialization," in *Handbook of Socialization Theory and Research* (Chicago: Rand McNally, 1969); Jane Loevinger, *Ego Development: Conceptions and Theories* (San Francisco: Jossey-Bass, 1976); Jean Piaget, *Judgment and Reasoning in the Child* (New York: Harcourt Brace, 1928); Robert Selman, "Stages of Role-Taking and Moral Development as Guides to Social Intervention," *Learning*, December, 1973.

Abigail Housen

3. Cornelia Brunner, "Aesthetic Judgment: Criteria Used to Evaluate Representational Art at Different Ages," unpublished doctoral dissertation, Columbia University, 1975; Abigail Housen, "The Eye of the Beholder: Measuring Aesthetic Development," unpublished doctoral dissertation, Harvard Graduate School of Education, 1983; and Michael Parsons, Marilyn Johnston, and Robert Durham, "Developmental Stages in Children's Aesthetic Responses," *The Journal of Aesthetic Education*, vol. 12, 1978, pp. 83-104.

4. Housen, op. cit.

5. James Rest, "Hierarchical Nature of Moral Reasoning," *Journal of Personality* vol. 12, 1978, pp. 83-104.

6. Abigail Housen Geer, "A Study of the Role of the Museum as Art Collector or Educator," unpublished manuscript, Harvard Graduate School of Education, 1976; and Abigail Housen Geer, "Levels of Aesthetic Development: A Study of Museum Visitors," unpublished manuscript, Harvard Graduate School of Education, 1977.

7. Housen, "The Eye of the Beholder."

JEAN RUSH

Aesthetic Literacy

Human beings have drawn or painted or modeled images since the Paleolithic era (or Old Stone Age), some twenty thousand years ago. We do not know who or where the first artist was, but we suspect he—we believe it was a man—lived long before the Stone Age. We do know that by the Stone Age, several groups of people inscribed those magic images on cave walls. Moreover, the style of those artists varied from group to group. Cave painters who lived near Altamira and those who lived at Lascaux had different styles, for example. We can only conclude that the older artists in each community taught their younger followers how to paint.

Like our forebears, we can also teach others to understand and use the magic of art. We call that understanding *aesthetic literacy*. It is the hallmark of what developmental psychologist Howard Gardner calls a "genuine (or disciplinary) understanding of art."[1] Only someone who is knowledgeable *about* art can be inventive *in it*.

To illustrate aesthetic literacy, imagine that you want to build a house, but you find yourself unable to measure and saw wood. The boards you nail together are crooked and unstable. You want lights, but electrical circuits and wiring are a mystery. You like hot and cold running water, but you have no concept of plumbing. You would need to understand concepts drawn from many different bodies of knowledge, whose principles have been established by experts, to build your house.

Creating a work of art (as an artist does), or estimating its significance (as an art critic does), or verifying the authenticity of a work made in the past (as an art historian does), or discussing the nature of art (as an aesthetician does) are all inventive activities. Their makers construct something. Each activity uses a different body of knowledge, but each contributes to the house that we call art.

Just as it is difficult to build a house without blueprints drawn by an architect, it is difficult to master inventive activities in the visual arts without "blueprints" that spell out basic principles of construction. Each art object, or piece of art criticism, or documentation of historical

authenticity, or aesthetic argument is a blueprint in the following respect: each conveys certain concepts selected from the body of artistic
knowledge that it represents. The artistic concepts that these objects share
are what we call their aesthetic properties.

Learning to read these aesthetic properties is the process of becoming aesthetically literate. It does not happen by accident. Experience
shows that learning about the arts, particularly those we call the fine
arts, requires a teacher.

What distinguishes arts professionals is the inventiveness of their
acts: making art, analyzing and evaluating it, researching its past, interpreting and debating its meaning. The opportunity for inventive activity through art—not facts about art—is what aesthetic literacy offers all
children. How sturdy a house each of them will build and how innovative it may be depends upon the efforts they make, the knowledge they
accumulate, and whether or not they possess some innate aptitude—
shall we call it talent?—that sets them apart from the rest of society.

Nonuniversal Artistic Development

Since the 1920s, one of the most compelling aims of art teaching has
been to safeguard children's artistic development. Until quite recently,
children's abilities to create graphic images and symbols were thought
to evolve, independently of instruction, in pretty much the same way
all over the world. Many educators have considered child art to be an
observable, dependable developmental activity.

Teaching children knowledge about art intervenes in this developmental process and can produce observable departures from traditional
developmental norms; that is, knowledge can either accelerate or retard
children's performances relative to their levels of maturation. Anyone
who values aesthetic literacy tends to see intervention as positive, and
many teachers today share this view. They reason that children who
have been introduced to the principles of art early will learn them sooner
than they might otherwise, and that this knowledge will increase their
ability to be inventive.

In 1980, developmental psychologist David Henry Feldman introduced a concept of nonuniversal cognitive development that explains
some of the differences in knowledgeability between popular and fine
art, between naive and sophisticated audiences, and between lay people
and professionals.[2] Cognition is the process by which knowledge is acquired. Feldman observed that although all children's thought processes
develop in similar ways up to a certain age, their ways of thinking diverge
as they become increasingly influenced by their surroundings.

Further, the acquisition of advanced knowledge is not automatic; it depends on each individual's level of experience (that is, education) in any particular area. In other words, something more than native ability accounts for the differences between "blue collar" and "white collar" jobs in any society. Something more than native ability accounts for the differences of taste among art appreciators and differences of skill among arts practitioners.

Although in real life these distinctions may not always be clear-cut— many people are difficult to classify—Feldman's ideas are particularly useful for explaining the function of formal education. Although young children throughout the world demonstrate similar thought processes, as adults some of them will achieve more advanced levels of knowledge and skill than others. During education, an individual undertakes a long, slow climb toward knowledgeability, beginning at the universal level.

Feldman distinguishes the following regions within the developmental continuum as individuals master any discipline: *universal, cultural, discipline-based, idiosyncratic,* and *unique.* In the visual arts, there are specific kinds of art objects, art practitioners, art institutions, and art audiences whose levels of competence correlate with each of Feldman's developmental regions. Competence increases from the universal level to the unique.

Feldman theorizes that certain kinds of environmental conditions account for the advances of some individuals over others, perhaps in combination with a natural predisposition for art, sometimes called talent (or, these days, artistic intelligence). One of these environmental conditions is formal education. If Feldman is correct, individuals must make a decision to become aesthetically literate—it requires choice.

Levels of Competence and Education

We all recognize the term *old master.* We are accustomed to judging art, particularly from times past, according to the degree of mastery with which it is made. We know that some artists (and art critics, art historians, and aestheticians) are more capable than others. In fact, we characterize every aspect of the domain of art—not only the objects and the art professionals, but the art institutions and even the art audiences themselves—according to an ever-increasing degree of competence.

Objects (such as works of art) or documents (such as reviews of exhibitions, historical attributions, and aesthetic theories) are an important, if not the most important, component of the art domain. Art professionals who make, authenticate, catalog, interpret the meaning of, evaluate, exhibit, sell, publicize, and teach art form a second component.

TABLE 1. Characteristics of Discipline Competence in Art

	Domain of Art			
Levels of Competence	Objects Criticism History Theory	Artist Art Critic Art Historian Aesthetician	Institutions Parents Tradition Teachers	Audiences Amateurs Collectors Appreciators
I. Universal: Early childhood arts	Earliest nonrepre- sentational graphic expressions Acultural	Common Worldwide Young children Spontaneous Inevitable, invarient Widely acknowl- edged	Parents No instruc- tion Preschool	Family Friends
II.A. Cultural: Folk arts	Discipline- related Culture- specific Applied Handcrafted Skillful	Common Amateur Indigenous Nonspon- taneous Popular	Tradition Informal Instruction Unschooled Cottage Industry	Many people Discipline- expert to discipline- unaware Wealthy to poor
II.B. Cultural: Popular and applied arts	Discipline- related Culture- specific Applied Electronic media, film Hobbies Kitsch	Common Professional and amateur Adult to early childhood Nonspon- taneous Popular	Mass media Mass marketing Popular literature Formal instruction General education Elementary school High school College	Most people Discipline- aware (basic lit- eracy) to discipline- unaware Wealthy to poor

Terms denoting levels of competence (universal, cultural, discipline-based, idiosyncratic, and unique) are taken from figure 1.2, Developmental Regions from Universal to Unique, in *Beyond Universals in Cognitive Development*, by D. H. Feldman (Norwood, N.J.: Ablex, 1980), 9. Table from Hobbs/Rush, *Teaching Children Art*, 1997. Adapted by permission of Prentice-Hall, Upper Saddle River, N.J.

The social institutions that display art and educate the public about it constitute a third component consisting of art museums, schools, publications, and even families. A fourth component consists of audiences—the consumers who appreciate art, buy it, enjoy it, and often make it themselves on recreational bases.

Although we recognize that members of each component have attributes in common, we also find that their internal characteristics are quite diverse. Take art objects as an example. When we say art, what objects do we have in mind? The *Mona Lisa*, hanging in the Louvre? A contemporary film? A 1953 yellow Cadillac convertible? A drawing by a two-year-old child? Each of these is a work of art in someone's mind.

Applying Feldman's developmental regions can help us to sort out these artworks and other objects, professionals, institutions, and audiences in terms of their levels of competence. In table 1, I attempt to show how one might assign various components of the domain of art to Feldman's regions. If your expertise is in an art form other than the visual arts, the table may allow you to translate the following arguments into your own discipline. As you read the table, remember that many art educators now believe the visual arts to contain four components or disciplines: the practice of making art, art criticism, art history, and aesthetics.

To illustrate the relationship of Feldman's levels of competence to education, let us examine the path to competence taken by the visual artist. Using the artist as an example allows you, if you wish, to compare Feldman's nonuniversal continuum to the better-known universal continuum of children's graphic development, and also to the less well-known pattern of aesthetic development proposed by Parsons and others.[4] It goes without saying that if space permitted, we could also expand upon patterns of inventive activity for critics, historians, and aestheticians. They too begin at the universal level and extend to the unique.

Universal Level

We can observe universal behaviors in art when children are quite young by examining what they draw. Children remain in the universal stage of graphic achievement only until the time they begin to modify their earliest drawings in response to suggestions from adults; this means that the universal level lasts only until the age of three or thereabouts, on average. These earliest artistic behaviors occur in every human being, are spontaneous, and are widely reported throughout diverse cultures around the world.

Cultural Level: Folk Arts, Popular and Applied Arts

Quite soon after beginning to make spontaneous images, children respond to and learn from their environments. In early childhood, their education is usually informal rather than in a classroom. They make images that purposely represent specific objects and ideas. As soon as youngsters begin to adapt their artwork in response to other people or to other influences in their environment, we can consider them to be at Feldman's cultural level.

Within each culture, there are certain kinds of knowledge that all members of the culture inevitably acquire: no one is surprised when a child in France begins to speak French, rather than Swahili or English at about the age of two. In the visual arts, for example, a school child in Japan is likely to draw calligraphic characters with a brush. A child in the United States may create comic books that include the spatial conventions of the television screen. A child of the Muslim faith may draw designs without using the human figure.

The acquisition of these and more advanced culture-specific forms of nonverbal communication are widespread throughout every society. Child art reflects children's experiences with visual images prevalent in their cultures. Two kinds of images found at the cultural level are those called folk arts and the popular (and applied) arts.

Folk arts. Think of folk arts as those arts representing traditional skills in any geographic area or ethnic group. They are culture specific and their practice is passed on by means of informal schooling. Many folk artists produce highly skillful aesthetic objects, like the carved wooden masks from West Africa or the wool Bayeux tapestry from eleventh-century France. Folk arts are made by hand and generally serve some practical or symbolic purpose in the lives of their makers.

Popular and applied arts. The popular arts today require a high level of competence, some degree of which may be learned informally, but much of which is learned formally in schools. All cultures expect their children to understand and practice things like reading, writing, computing, history, and the rules of their government; these expectations define a basic level of verbal and numerical literacy. Think of understanding and making popular and applied art as a basic level of artistic literacy.

Basic artistic literacy shares many concepts and skills with the fine arts, just as, for example, computing does with mathematics. Advertising art, commercially released films, the high-volume production of hand-crafted ceramic dinnerware, and computer-imaged logos generated for television stations are created by highly competent artists.

Artistic activity at Feldman's popular level, however, is not necessarily practice of the art disciplines, any more than being able to add, subtract, multiply, and divide makes someone a mathematician. In Feldman's matrix, popular and applied art might be called discipline related. Popular and applied art are discipline related when they are done extremely well and their production demonstrates high levels of skill.

Discipline-based Level

An excellent sign painter does not necessarily paint pictures that would be welcomed in art galleries. The differences between the sign painter, operating at Feldman's cultural level, and the fine artist, considered to be discipline based, have to do with the level of cognitive abstraction at which each works. In many cases, the philosophical distinction between today's highly skillful applied artists and fine artists is exceedingly narrow, if not erased altogether.

Discipline-based careers are called professions, and fewer people practice them than the number who perform jobs at the cultural level. There are fewer doctors than nurses, for example, fewer engineers than mechanics, fewer architects than contractors, and fewer fine artists than applied designers. Professional people take longer to prepare themselves because they prepare in more depth before society considers them ready to enter the workplace.

Professional people internalize the ideas and practices of their disciplines; they set the standards; they define the disciplines. In art, discipline-based professionals are most closely associated with the fine arts. The fine arts are often defined as works of art that have aesthetic meaning rather than a practical function. Works of art in all societies become metaphors for important cultural values and ideas, and in the fine arts, we find the most complex visual messages that exist in our civilization.

Idiosyncratic Level

Only a relatively few artists can be placed at Feldman's idiosyncratic level of competence. If literacy in the discipline is uncommon, proficiency at the idiosyncratic or highly personal level may be said to be unusual. Artists at this level are the experts, the boundary breakers, the conspicuous ones. They are the "household names" (at least to other artists), the ones whose art brings "megabucks" in the New York or Los Angeles or Houston galleries. Andy Warhol was such an artist in his day; Christo is one now. They belong to the avant-garde; they innovate; they are the artists à la mode, the trend setters. Contemporary critics give them their approval. Their ultimate reputation must wait for the perspective of history; it will depend on whether or not tomorrow's audiences will still find them significant.

Unique Level

On Feldman's highest level of competence, we find the artists of whom it may be said there is, and always will be, only one for all time. One Rembrandt van Rijn. One Kathe Kollwitz. One Katsushika Hokusai. One Diego Velasquez. These are the kinds of artists who, as we look at their works, have the power to transform our understanding of the world from that point on. No one will ever take these artists' places.

Such unique individuals are rare in any discipline. They are the visionaries, the people who unequivocally deserve to be called creative because each changed forever the shape of art. The works of these artists are known and loved the world over. They transcend national boundaries. Exhibitions of their art attract thousands of visitors. Over time, the innovations of artists who are unique have proved to be so enduring that they and their creators eventually become part of the popular culture.

Notes

1. Howard Gardner, *The Unschooled Mind: How Children Think and How Schools Should Teach* (New York: Basic Books, 1991), p. 9.
2. David Henry Feldman, *Beyond Universals in Cognitive Development* (Norwood, N.J.: Ablex, 1980).

Ralph A. Smith

Phases of Aesthetic Learning (K-12)

At their best, works of art require years of study and half a lifetime of experience and growing familiarity may be necessary for their full appreciation. So opined Harold Osborne in *The Art of Appreciation*.[1] Aesthetic learning in the schools is likewise a long journey. It begins early and gradually extends into the middle and secondary years and its overall purpose is the cultivation of percipience, which in this context implies the possession of a well-developed sense of art that may be attained through a number of learning phases that culminate in a learner's rich apperceptive mass. Such learning should recognize the demands of the current society, the subject of art, and the requirements of the learner. These latter requirements have been articulated in cognitive studies which assume that learning occurs most efficaciously when new information is related to a young person's conceptual framework. Concepts organized in a hierarchy undergo change as new information is assimilated. This view of learning means that teachers must have a good grasp of the conceptual character of art and an understanding of how to relate new information to learners' existing schemes of knowledge.[2]

Learning may thus be said to proceed from simple exposure and familiarization with things as well as making and rudimentary perceiving in the elementary grades to more demanding historical, appreciative, and critical studies during the secondary years. As particular objectives change, so will teaching and learning methods. Assessment will center on the progress that learners make in expanding their conceptual frameworks. The entire scheme is built on the assumption that phases of aesthetic learning are instrumental to the goal of greater percipience and the special satisfaction and benefits it affords.

Phase One: Perceiving Aesthetic Qualities (K-3)

Although very young children are hardly prepared to engage works of art in all their formal complexity and dramatic intensity, to say nothing about their thematic and symbolic import, they are sensitive to the simple sensory and expressive qualities of things, and the years from

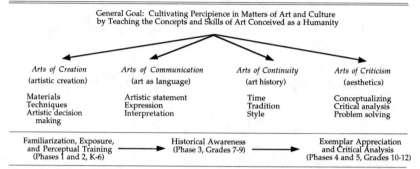

General Goal: Cultivating Percipience in Matters of Art and Culture
by Teaching the Concepts and Skills of Art Conceived as a Humanity

Arts of Creation	*Arts of Communication*	*Arts of Continuity*	*Arts of Criticism*
(artistic creation)	(art as language)	(art history)	(aesthetics)
Materials	Artistic statement	Time	Conceptualizing
Techniques	Expression	Tradition	Critical analysis
Artistic decision	Interpretation	Style	Problem solving
making			

Familiarization, Exposure, and Perceptual Training (Phases 1 and 2, K-6)	Historical Awareness (Phase 3, Grades 7-9)	Exemplar Appreciation and Critical Analysis (Phases 4 and 5, Grades 10-12)

Teaching and learning proceed along a continuum from exposure, familiarization, and perceptual training to historical awareness, exemplar appreciation, and critical analysis, stressing discovery and reception learning, didactic coaching, and dialogic teaching methods. Evaluation of aesthetic learning concentrates on the development of aesthetic conceptual maps and the conditions conducive for doing so. Reprinted with permission from A. W. Levi and R. A. Smith, *Art Education: A Critical Necessity* (Urbana: University of Illinois Press, 1991). Slightly edited.

kindergarten through third grade are the time to exploit and expand this capacity. This can be done through exposure to the aesthetic qualities of all sorts of things, whether in nature or in ordinary objects or in works of the children's own making. During this phase it might be said that the general goal is an appreciation of the qualitative immediacy of life. The young learn to enjoy things for their freshness and vividness; they cultivate a delight in the looks, sounds, tastes, and smells of things around them. But since visual, auditory, and verbal works of art are the principal loci of such qualities, it is important that young students' attention also be directed toward artworks. Learners in the early grades should be encouraged not only to note their aesthetic qualities but also to understand that artworks are special objects found in special places that society maintains at considerable effort and expense. Thus do young learners begin to develop an elementary sense of art and the art world. At the same time they intuitively acquire a sense of object directedness, a fundamental feature of aesthetic experience.

In short, formal aesthetic learning begins during phase one. The understanding the young bring to school undergoes modification and expansion. The job of building dispositions gets underway. An initiation occurs into the mysteries of art and into a cultural institution known as an art world. In making their own works of art, young learners also gain insight into the nature of the artistic creative process. They come to realize that a work of art is a product of an artist's having composed the special qualities of materials into an aesthetic object that features medium, form, and content. They learn, in other words, the ways of aesthetic communication. In terms of a humanities interpretation of DBAE, this is, in effect, to bring the skills of artistic creation and aesthetic perception to bear on the study of art. Learning during phase one should not be inordinately formal, and a child's propensities should constantly be kept in mind. And although all phases of aesthetic learning are instrumental to the achievement of a certain level of percipience, there will be numerous moments of intrinsic satisfaction when ulterior objectives tend to recede from awareness.

Much of what now goes on in the early years of school can suffice for achieving the objectives of phase one. However, if teachers plan these activities and lessons with the long-term goal of aesthetic percipience in mind, they might go about their teaching in slightly different ways. The important consideration is that all learning should have point and lead in a certain direction, the direction in phase one being toward greater perceptual finesse in phase two of aesthetic learning.

Phase Two: Developing Perceptual Finesse (Grades 4-6)

A precise dividing line between learning phases cannot, of course, be drawn, but by the upper elementary years the young are capable of concentrating their energies and powers. They can perceive greater complexity in works of art, their own as well as those of more mature artists. Gradually, however, attention shifts more and more to the latter, for it is only by perceiving works of some complexity that perceptual skills can be honed and developed.

In addition to the immediate qualities of artworks, their complex webs of relations and meanings are now also brought more fully and clearly into view. It is time for looking at artworks more closely while simultaneously learning about the art world in which works of art find a home and guardians. Still not inordinately formal, phase-two learning is more structured than that of phase one. In addition to making, seeing, and listening, students during this period also begin to acquire a vocabulary or language for talking about art and its various components.

Although it is possible to teach even the very young a methodical way to do something, it is especially during phase two that some system can be introduced. Harry S. Broudy recommends paying close attention to a work's sensory, formal, expressive, and technical aspects. Scanning such aspects is a way to make initial contact with artworks, and it can be effective provided excessive claims are not made for it and the method is not oversimplified.[4] To guard against the latter outcome, it might be helpful to see scanning within a larger pattern of response. Kenneth Clark, the distinguished art historian, once described his own perceptual habits this way. First, there is the initial impact a work of art makes. That is followed by a period of close scrutiny and examination during which one attempts to find what is actually in a work to be perceived and enjoyed. The phase of scrutiny is followed by one of recollection. Relevant kinds of information, for example, biographical and historical, are summoned in order to help render a work intelligible. Additional periods of scrutiny and recollection then renew and revitalize aesthetic responses. The point is that aesthetic experience is difficult to sustain for very long and the senses need time to regroup. What is more, although one's initial impressions of a work are fresh and spontaneous, they are often not a reliable key to a work's real character or import.[5]

At the end of phase two, far more than at the end of phase one, students should be able not only to convey to others the character of their first impressions (impact), but also to engage in formal analysis (scrutiny) and apply what knowledge they have acquired (recollection) in sustaining their interest in a work (renewal). When they practice the skills of aesthetic perception during what may be called the complete act of informed aesthetic response, learners experience, though not necessarily self-consciously, those additional features of aesthetic experience that Beardsley termed felt freedom, detached affect, and active discovery, that is, feelings of freely taking up a special point of view toward something for the sake of what can be discovered in doing so. During phases one and two it is, of course, appropriate to show and discuss works created by members of different groups and from other cultures and civilizations. A humanities curriculum, in other words, should have a multicultural dimension. However, I understand multiculturalism not as an ideological attack on the values of Western civilization but simply as a recognition that the study of alternatives is a revered humanistic objective, a way to avoid a narrow ethnocentrism.[6] Indeed, a well-developed sense of art implies an awareness of a broad range of artworks.

Phase Three: Developing A Sense Of Art History (Grades 7-9)

Having learned how to perceive the qualitative immediacy, relational properties, and meanings of works of art, students are now ready to examine works under the aspects of time, tradition, and style. In what should be a well-designed survey course, students discover how artists have both celebrated and criticized a society's beliefs and values. Learning still serves the same general goal of a percipience curriculum, but now the development of historical awareness deepens the learners' cognitive stock and helps them to expand their sense of art. Not only that; discovering something new about what is important and valuable and interesting to perception is intrinsically satisfying.

Phase three also contributes to an appreciation of the ways works of art reflect the growth of civilization. They do so by providing records of extraordinary efforts to impose form and style on raw, unshaped material.[7] This is to say that works of art are preeminent symbols of efforts to free human existence from a life of necessity in order to enjoy one of freedom and leisure in which human powers can be cultivated for their own sakes. The study of such works further serves to emphasize that just as works of art have survived their severance from religion, magic, and myth,[8] so also, we may say, do they have the capacity to transcend gender, class, and race. Finally, the study of art history leads to an appreciation of the idea of a tradition.

In contrast to the pedagogy of the first two phases of aesthetic learning, phase three by necessity is more formal and requires systematic instruction. Although there won't be time in a survey course to linger long over any particular work, students will develop important insights into the processes of historical continuity and change and will come to realize that continuity is by far the greater part of the story.

An appreciation of tradition and of continuity and change can, of course, be attained through the study of practically any culture or civilization. But it is only natural that American youth should be initiated first into the major cultural heritage of their own society. Even Richard Rorty, a philosophical revisionist, acknowledges this as common wisdom.[9] The "war against Eurocentrism" currently being waged by certain advocates of multiculturalism is thus ill-advised and counterproductive. It generates cultural particularism instead of promoting the nobler goal of cultural pluralism.[10] . . .

Phase Four: Exemplar Appreciation (Grades 10-11)

The purpose of phase four is neither skill training nor historical study so much as appreciation in the best sense of the term. This is the time to study works of art in some depth without which any talk about excellence in arts education is mere rhetoric. During phase four, students pause simply to admire some of the greatest achievements of humankind—works of art resplendent in their beauty, form, significance, and mystery as nothing else is. It matters not, moreover, the ethnic origin or gender of the artist; we are talking about human excellence.

As I conceive of it, exemplar study also provides an opportunity to understand the role of contextual factors in appreciating art. One can, of course, appreciate a work of art on its own terms without much regard for the historical factors that helped to shape it, but we fail to give the arts their due as humanities unless we pause to understand the ways they reflect and integrate the different cultural elements of a society or even of a whole epoch. We may call this the figure-ground relationship of exemplar appreciation, with the artworks being the figure. But this relationship should not be reversed; contextual information is primarily an aid to appreciation. Above all, a work of art should not be simply dissolved into its context.[11]

Given the aim of cultivating an appreciation of artistic excellence during the fourth phase of aesthetic learning, it follows that examples of artistic excellence from different cultures are also candidates for appreciation. Although one would expect masterworks from the Western cultural heritage to be featured, efforts should also be made to appreciate artistic exemplars of non-Western cultures.

Phase Five: Critical Analysis (Grade 12)

Beyond exemplar appreciation the percipience curriculum offers critical reflection on the role of art in human life and society and on the innumerable conundrums such relations generate.[12] But the principal purpose of the last phase of aesthetic learning is to provide opportunities for young adults to fashion something of their own philosophies of art, to formulate beliefs and to stake out positions, at least tentatively, on such questions as the relations of art and morality, art and the mass media, art and the environment, art and politics, and so forth. Certainly not least among the questions that should be considered are those about artistic value and worth. When students address these questions the rich apperceptive mass they have built up through previous phases of learning will now be put to good uses. Given the public controversy that has attended a number of recent artistic events, there should be no difficulty stimulating the interest of twelfth-graders. In truth, older students are curious about artistic controversies and their teachers' views on them. In senior seminars a start can be made in asking the right questions and sorting out the relevant issues.

Toward Needed Reform

A humanities justification of arts education is grounded in a redefinition of the traditional humanities in procedural and substantive terms. Under this redefinition the teaching of the arts involves bringing to bear in appropriate ways and at relevant times the arts of creation, communication, continuity, and criticism. The mastery of these arts at levels suitable for the ages of learners eventually yields percipience in matters of art and culture, the ultimate goal of arts education. Aesthetically percipient, the well-educated nonspecialist can be expected to traverse the art world with intelligence, tact, and a measure of autonomy. A student achieves this level of percipience through a series of learning phases: exposure and familiarization, perceptual training, historical study, exemplar appreciation, and critical analysis.

Obviously, before a percipience curriculum could be implemented in the schools, major progress would have to be made in the reform of teacher education.[13] Prospective teachers of art would need considerably more work in the humanities. And there would have to be a greater commitment on the part of society to the importance of providing aesthetic studies so that the young can realize as fully as possible significant aesthetic capacities. Such capacities can be understood in connection with the constitutive and revelatory powers of art, powers that can shape the human personality in positive ways and provide humanistic understanding. Such benefits have both personal and social value. What is more, a society is more likely to enjoy greater cultural health when inhabited by persons with aesthetic intelligence and sensitivity. In this sense then, arts education is a critical necessity.

Notes

1. Harold Osborne, *The Art of Appreciation* (New York: Oxford University Press, 1970), p. 36.

2. For a discussion of such principles, I have found the writings of Joseph D. Novak quite helpful. See his *A Theory of Education* (Ithaca: Cornell University Press, 1986), and David P. Ausubel, Joseph D. Novak, and Helen Hanesian, *Educational Psychology: A Cognitive View*, 2d ed. (New York: Holt, Rinehart and Winston, 1978).

3. The following discussion is a condensed version of the accounts given in Ralph A. Smith, *The Sense of Art: A Study in Aesthetic Education* (New York: Routledge, 1989), chap. 6, and in Levi and Smith, *Art Education: A Critical Necessity*, chap. 8.

4. Harry S. Broudy, *The Role of Imagery in Learning* (Los Angeles: Getty Center for Education in the Arts, 1987), pp. 52-53.

5. Kenneth Clark, *Looking at Pictures* (New York: Holt, Rinehart and Winston, 1960), pp. 16-17.

6. For example, in his *The Future of the Humanities* (New York: Thomas Y. Crowell, 1977), Walter Kaufmann writes that the objectives of the humanities are four: the conservation and cultivation of the greatest works of humanity, the teaching of vision, the fostering of a critical spirit, and thoughtful reflection on alternatives (pp. xvii-xxi).

7. This is the theme of Kenneth Clark's *Civilisation* (New York: Harper and Row, 1969) and a government report, *Toward Civilization: A Report on Arts Education* (Washington, D.C.: National Endowment for the Arts, 1988).

8. Hannah Arendt, *The Human Condition* (Chicago: University of Chicago Press, 1958), p. 167.

9. Richard Rorty, "The Dangers of Over-Philosophication—Reply to Arcilla and Nicholson," *Educational Theory* 40, no. 1 (Winter 1990): 41-44.

10. Diane Ravitch, "Multiculturalism: E Pluribus Plures," *The American Scholar* 59, no. 3 (Summer 1990): 337-354. See also, idem, "Multiculturalism: An Exchange," *The American Scholar* 60, no. 2 (Spring 1991): 272-276 for the author's response to a critique of "Multiculturalism: E Pluribus Plures" by Molefi Keti Asante that also appeared in the Spring 1991 issue of *The American Scholar*. See also my "Forms of Multicultural Education in the Arts," *Journal of Multicultural and Cross-cultural Research in Art Education* 1, no. 1 (Fall 1983): 23-32; and Rachel Mason, *Art Education and Multiculturalism* (London: Croom Helm, 1988), esp. pp. 1-2, "Four Types of Multiculturalism."

11. What one must avoid is what Hilton Kramer (*The New Criterion* 9, no. 4 [December 1990]) calls the postmodernist mode of analysis termed Deconstruction, whose aim is "to deconstruct every 'text'—which is to say, every art object—into an inventory of its context and thus remove the object from the realm of aesthetic experience and make it instead a coefficient of its sources and social environment" (p.7).

12. For a number of such conundrums, see Margaret P. Battin, John Fisher, Ronald Moore, and Anita Silvers, *Puzzles about Art: An Aesthetics Casebook* (New York: St. Martin's, 1989).

13. I have discussed some initiatives toward such reform in my *Excellence in Art Education: Ideas and Initiatives*, updated version (Reston, Va., National Art Education Association, 1987), chap. 5.

Reading Suggestions for Part Four

Arnheim, Rudolf. *Thoughts on Art Education*. Occasional Paper 2. Los Angeles: Getty Center for Education in the Arts, 1989.

Gardner, Howard, and David Perkins, eds. *Art, Mind, and Education: Research from Project Zero*. Urbana: University of Illinois Press, 1989. First published as a special issue of *The Journal of Aesthetic Education* 22, no. 1 (1988).

Gardner, Howard. *Art Education and Human Development*. Occasional Paper 3. Los Angeles: Getty Center for Education in the Arts, 1990. Extensive references.

Golumb, Claire. *The Child's Creation of a Pictorial World*. Berkeley; University of California Press, 1992. Also the symposium on the volume in *The Journal of Aesthetic Education* 28, no. 2 (1994): 51-70.

Moody, William J., ed. *Artistic Intelligences: Implications for Educators.* New York: Teachers College Press, 1993.

Burkett, Mary Frances. "Developmental Stages of Children's Concepts of Art and Educational Implications." In *Collected Papers: Pennsylvania's Symposium on Art Education, Aesthetics, and Art Criticism,* 1986, ed. Evan J. Kern. Harrisburg: Pennsylvania Department of Education, n.d.

Csikszentmihalyi, Mihaly, and Ulrich Schiefele. "Art Education, Human Development, and the Quality of Experience." In *The Arts, Education, and Aesthetic Knowing.* Ninety-first Yearbook of the National Society for the Study of Education, Part II, ed. Bennett Reimer and Ralph A. Smith. Chicago: University of Chicago Press, 1992, 169-91.

Feldman, David Henry. "Developmental Psychology and Art Education: Two Fields at the Crossroads." *The Journal of Aesthetic Education* 21, no. 2 (1987): 243-59. Also in Ralph A. Smith, ed. *Discipline-Based Art Education: Origins, Meaning, Development.* Urbana: University of Illinois Press, 1989, same pagination.

Koroscik, Judith. "The Function of Domain-Specific Knowledge in Understanding Works of Art." In *Inheriting the Theory: New Voices and Multiple Perspectives.* Los Angeles: Getty Center for Education in the Arts, 1990, 10-11. Seminar summary of remarks.

Parsons, Michael J. "Can Children Do Aesthetics: A Developmental Account," *The Journal of Aesthetic Education* 28, no. 3 (1994): 33-45.

Rush, Jean. "Bridging the Gap Between Developmental Psychology and Art Education: The View from an Artist's Perspective." *Visual Arts Research*, 10, no. 2 (1984): 9-14.

Wolf, Dennie Palmer. "The Growth of Three Aesthetic Stances: What Developmental Psychology Suggests about Discipline-Based Art Education." In *Issues in Discipline-Based Art Education. Strengthening the Stance, Extending the Horizons.* Los Angeles: Getty Center for Education in the Arts, 1988, 85-100.

PART FIVE

Professional Development

Introduction

A Getty seminar on preservice and inservice education produced a number of informative addresses and responses on the topic. In a major address, Frances Schoonmaker, after construing the interrelationships between preservice and inservice education as a continuum concerned with the construction and reconstruction of meaning in light of new experience, discusses how such a continuum can be maintained by emphasizing three strands. These strands accommodate the acquisition of knowledge, analysis and reflection, the problems of reconstruction and application, and experimentation and critique, all of which presuppose supervision. Because of its character she cautions against likening DBAE to other subjects and believes the goals of DBAE will not be realized without reforming mainstream education.

Michael Day, in introducing a collection of essays that were first presented at a Getty-sponsored symposium on teacher preparation in art education, refers to national efforts to reform education and underlines the need of the field of art education to recruit, prepare, and retain excellent teachers of art if it is to further the reform effort. To assist in this task he discusses twelve components of any viable teacher-preparation program and suggests ways in which these components can be strengthened. Not believing that every program needs to be reformed, he alludes to several existing ones that can serve as models.

It is one thing to talk reform and quite another to undertake it, as the Greer and the Wilson and Rubin essays in Part Three demonstrate. Katherine A. Schwartz provides a case study of such efforts in her account of experiences with the Alaska Center for Excellence in Education in implementing DBAE. In the excerpt reprinted here, she describes a study that illustrates the numerous factors involved in reforming the way art is taught and provides data for changes that were actually made and that indicate the possibility of significant reform.

I've mentioned that several of the writings in this collection could be subsumed under more than one topic. E. Louis Lankford's discussion of the weight given to aesthetics in Wilson's *The Quiet Evolution*, for example, could be placed under both curriculum issues and professional development. I've chosen the latter because it concerns the role of aesthetics in the preparation of art teachers. After remarking the strengths of Wilson's report, not least Wilson's extensive knowledge of the schools and art programs, suggestions for implementation that stress overlapping forms of inquiry directed toward works of art expressing significant individual and social themes, and his critique of an approach to art education that confuses means and ends, Lankford questions Wilson's skepticism about the usefulness of aesthetics in preparing teachers of DBAE. The excerpt reprinted here concentrates on this question.

Frances Schoonmaker

The Interrelationship between Preservice and Inservice Education for Art Teachers and Specialists

I have one basic premise: teacher growth and development occur along a continuum of experience in the life of the teacher. I will argue that if there is to be an interrelationship between preservice and inservice art education, then it must account for this continuum. Because I am not an art educator, I take comfort in Gilbert Clark, Michael Day, and W. Dwaine Greer's recent comment that "Art is viewed as a subject with content that can be taught and learned in ways that resemble how other subjects are taught in schools" (1987, 131). My remarks will relate to pre- and inservice education of teachers and I will leave it to the educators of art teachers and specialists to draw the connecting threads.

The Continuum in Teacher Education

Webster's Unabridged Dictionary defines the word continuum as:

That which is absolutely continuous and selfsame; that of which no distinction of content can be affirmed except by reference to something else (as duration and extension, which are capable of support distinctions only by reference to numbers or to such relations as those of now to then, here to there, before to after); secondarily, that of which the only assessable variation is variation in time or space.

John Dewey argued that, "The thing needful is improvement of education, not simply by turning out teachers who can do better the things that are now necessary to do, but rather by changing the conception of what constitutes education" ([1902] 1974, 338). If we were to reconceptualize teacher education as a continuum—an activity that is altogether in keeping with Dewey's idea, I believe—we would include at least three key strands in both pre- and inservice education. We would begin by focusing on what is continuous in the experience of the individual who is being educated to teach—that is autobiography. Next we would equip our students to be good observers of the complex, dynamic contexts in which they work. Finally, we would develop in our students a mind-set about teaching as a profession requiring continuous scholarship.

Preservice Teacher Education

1. *Focusing on autobiography.* That which is absolutely continuous and selfsame in the life of the individuals who present themselves to us in preservice programs is personal biography. When an individual makes the decision to teach and to begin a program of formal preparation, it is with reference to countless experiences with teachers. Some of these will have been positive and others negative. In any case, the individual who chooses to become a teacher has had at least twelve to sixteen years of direct, laboratory experience in schools where impressions have been formed about who teachers are and what they do, or ought to be doing. These impressions are so powerful that they are likely to furnish the basic approach an individual takes in teaching and, more often than not, provide the model of teaching that is utilized once a teacher education program is completed. Sociologists such as Dan Lortie (1975) tell us that beginning teachers tend to set aside what they learn at colleges and universities in favor of generalized impressions and past experience that soon become entrenched ways of doing in the classroom. Dewey ([1902] 1974) referred to this phenomenon, describing it as the development of habits of work sanctioned by empirical rather than scientific evidence. Classroom practice is adjusted, not to principles of teaching, but to what succeeds or fails from moment to moment.

If this is the case, then what we do as preservice teacher educators is, more than likely, beside the point. It makes perfect sense for art educators to debate issues such as whether there should be more or less studio experience in preservice education. But unless art educators pay attention to sociological and psychological dynamics that influence the practice of teaching, these debates are academic.

A preservice program, however we might conceive it, must provide opportunity for the student to identify what is likely to be an unarticulated theory of education that guides interpretation of experience. Autobiography, classroom experiences remembered, remembrances that emerge as a result of fieldwork may help the student identify this theory.

Peter Berger (1963, 56-57) noted that as individuals we interpret and reinterpret our own experiences, reconstructing our past in accordance with present ideas of importance.

This means that in any situation, with its near-infinite number of things that could be noticed, we notice only those things that are important for our immediate purposes. The rest we ignore. But in the present these things that we have ignored may be thrust upon our consciousness by someone who points them out to us.

It is the preservice teacher educator's responsibility to thrust upon the consciousness of students his or her own philosophy of education and guiding theory. Admitting to a theory of education, searching for its sources, and exposing it to critique will enable the student to continuously reconstruct experience instead of being a slave to experience. Then teacher education is not a new box full of experience stacked on top of a pile of boxes, but a repacking of all the boxes of the student's experience. It is not added on, but part of that experience.

Writing an autobiography and philosophy of education is a way to incorporate this strand into the preservice program, but there are countless other opportunities to draw on the student's lived experience. Dewey (1902, 323) pointed out that isolation of the preservice program from this experience is both unnecessary and harmful.

> It is unnecessary, tending to futility, because it throws away or makes light of the greatest asset in the student's possession—the greatest, moreover, that ever will be in his possession—his own direct and personal experience. . . . But it is more than a serious mistake (violating the principle of proceeding from the known to the unknown) to fail to take account of this body of practical experience.

By beginning with the student's autobiography and drawing on it to illustrate principles of teaching and learning, we are already facilitating the construction of personal meaning from the experience of teaching. Arthur Jersild (1955, 4) notes that:

> The search for meaning is not a search for an abstract body of knowledge, or even for a concrete body of knowledge. It is a distinctly personal search. The one who makes it raises intimate personal questions: What really counts, for me? What values am I seeking? What in my existence as a person, in my relations with others, in my work as a teacher, is of real concern to me, perhaps of ultimate concern to me?

2. *Studying the complex, dynamic context of schools.* Students need to learn from the beginning of their programs that teacher education is applicable to the extent that they can figure out how to apply it. Then we need to give them the tools for doing so. Perhaps the most important tool we can give them is an ethnographic approach to their work. At its core, ethnography is concerned with the meaning of actions and events

to those we seek to understand (Spradley 1979). Prospective teachers will need to learn to be good observers, learning how to study the school and classroom that are familiar as if they were strange. They must learn to ask themselves what the people who are actors in the school setting can teach them through overt behavior and language and implicit meanings that will enable them to be more effective.

Seymour Sarason ([1971] 1982) has reminded us that schools have their own culture where social relationships, rules, and standards have been developed over time. Despite their commonalities, each school has unique differences. Each has a profound influence on the teachers who enter the school for the first time and on those students who are in the school trying to make sense of it. Willard Waller (1932), in his classic *Sociology of Teaching*, pointed out that the school is a unity of interacting personalities, a despotic organization that is always in a state of perilous equilibrium. While schools are organized on the principle of authority, their authority is always being challenged by those who have a vested interest in their work. For the public, school outcomes are often more important than the details of education, and these outcomes are most often assessed in gross utilitarian terms (Stanley 1981). This has served to hide issues that ought to be held up to careful scrutiny—issues related to the quality of life that goes on inside the school, to the development of dreams and imagination in students and teachers, to the fostering of personal meaning. Focus on utilitarian outcomes has served to hide the complexity of entering a particular school and being able to apply one's knowledge and skill in some kind of standard way. Neither children, schools, nor communities are standard, and they can confound those who attempt to institute widespread curriculum changes without regard to each school's uniqueness.

An ethnographic approach is crucial if we want our students to bring about change in the schools. It will enable them to take into account the strong beliefs that other people may have about the curriculum and make wise choices about how to proceed when there is conflict.

3. *Developing an experimental attitude.* In the final analysis, the way we enable our students to think about their work will probably have more impact on their future as teachers than any specific methods that we may teach. Perhaps this is why Dewey believed the laboratory experience to be superior to the apprenticeship in teacher education. Dewey argues that while specific methodology may render a more capable teacher for the first year or so, it will not render a more thoughtful teacher. Dewey's assumption is that teachers should promote learning in the broadest sense. A laboratory experience challenges the student to develop

an experimental approach to teaching so that practice will be intelligent, rather than accidental and routine.

Activities such as less planning are ways of thinking about teaching. Evaluation is a way of thinking about the value students place on their experiences and the value that a community places on particular traditions and ideas. Disciplines of knowledge are ways of organizing thinking about the world or content to be taught. Skills are ways of gaining access to knowing and new ways of doing. Every method and practice that we teach should be, to use Dewey's words, developed under "the inspiration and constant criticism of intelligence" (1902, 320).

It is crucial that the teacher learn how to study context and draw from experience in order to make wise decisions about what to teach, because the real work of becoming a teacher is a difficult, complex, and lonely task. Teachers are not initiated into a world of meanings or a teacher craft and culture that they interpret with the help of mentors. And while there has been recent attention to development of mentoring and master teacher programs, most new teachers are on their own— expected to be skilled, knowledgeable, and understanding. The principal and board of education do not anticipate assisting them, over time, in acquiring the skill, knowledge, and understanding that are necessary to becoming a master teacher (Lortie 1975). Nor do parents want new teachers "learning" on their children. Admission of ignorance or uncertainty places the new teacher in a vulnerable position.

Teacher educators tend to want to look at the problem of induction into teaching as a transfer-of-learning problem. We imagine that if we gave teachers better pedagogical tools, they would be better prepared to make the transition from pre- to inservice teaching. Sevigny (1987, 121), for example, suggests that the state of knowledge in discipline-based art education is such that "The foremost question for the immediate future is no longer *what* to teach, but rather *how* to teach." Undoubtedly art educators know a great deal more than ever before about what ought to be taught in the schools, but knowledge and context are dynamic. Even if we were able to identify the specific content that teachers need to know, hold it in a stable, suspended state, and discover *the* pedagogy that teachers most need and get them to perfect it in student teaching—even then, we could not be sure that this perfected practice would transfer into classroom practice during the first years of teaching. The process of learning to teach is too complex. Transfer of learning from the preservice program to practice requires experience, support, and time. The fact is, there are no generic schools or generic classrooms. Should our beginning teacher have the good fortune to complete an internship in the school where he or she begins to teach, the uniqueness of the various individuals who make up each classroom, the dynamic nature of the arts, and the complexities of teaching would make a direct transfer impossible—impossible, that is, unless we are willing to concede that teaching is telling and learning is receiving, without reference to context, a concession I am unwilling to make.

Teaching, like learning, is experiential in nature. Once our teacher educators, entering students of teaching, and school people have a mindset that sees preservice as a launching rather than a docking, a departure rather than an arrival, then we all can be more realistic in our approach to classroom improvement and continuing inservice education. Developing a continuum in teacher education requires more than some minor shifts in vocabulary. It requires the development of true laboratory settings at the college and university and it requires conscious attention to inservice teacher education.

Inservice Teacher Education

Unfortunately, the interrelationship between pre- and inservice teacher education as a whole is more problematic than positive. It is most often one of mutual suspicion and blame. We preservice educators recognize severe constraints on our time and resources. We are often angered by the difficulty we have finding appropriate field placements and lack of cooperation from the schools in preparing teachers. Sometimes we are angered by what we see happening to our graduates as they seem to be swallowed up into the schools and we are appalled at the bad habits they develop. We in inservice education are appalled at how little beginning teachers know and are frustrated over having to show them how to do every little thing—like how to keep an attendance register! We are angered over the college's insistence that it call the shots in student teaching and see cooperation with the local university as having to buy into the university's research agenda, which is usually far removed from our concerns and needs.

I do not believe that this situation would exist if we were to reconceptualize teacher education in terms of the continuum. At the inservice level, the continuum would build on the same three strands that were begun in preservice: (1) autobiography, (2) study of context, and (3) continuous scholarship.

1. *Focusing on autobiography.* Maxine Greene (1973, 270) points out that teachers are often treated as if they were disembodied, not persons, but a role to be played. She writes:

The numerous realities in which. . . [the teacher] exists as a living person are overlooked. His personal biography is overlooked; so are the many ways in which he expresses his private self in language, the horizons he perceives the perspectives through which he looks on the world.

Strategies utilized in implementation of discipline-based art education must not deny teachers—whether these are art specialists or "ordinary classroom teachers" being asked to add DBAE to the curriculum—their own expertise and their vital role as curriculum decision makers. A great deal of what I read about curriculum reform in the arts sounds like what I read about curriculum reform in the 1960s and 1970s in other disciplines. It would be a serious mistake if art educators ignored the lessons learned from failed curriculum reform efforts of this period. It is apparent from studies of these curriculum implementation efforts that teachers will not follow through on implementation of a curriculum unless they have an investment in it (Bolin 1987). The investment has to be more than bringing them all into a workshop where they are told what they should do, how to do it, and what materials to utilize.

Here I find that I am in strong disagreement with those who advocate a teacher-proof DBAE where the objectives and strategies have all been settled. Michael Apple (1987) has referred to this as the "separation of conception from execution." As teachers are handed material to implement, without thought to their own expertise either in the discipline or in pedagogy or in human growth and development, their skill in these areas begins to atrophy. As Apple points out, "lack of use leads to loss."

Increasingly, teaching methods, texts, tests, and outcomes are being taken out of the hands of the people who must put them into practice. Instead, they are being legislated by state departments of education or in state legislatures, and are being either supported or stimulated by many of the national reports . . . which are often simplistic assessments of and responses to problems in education . . . and which demonstrate the increasing power of conservative ideologies in our public policy discourse.

Clark, Day, and Greer (1987, 167) argue that a written curriculum is necessary in DBAE to ensure articulation and avoid repetition across grades, to utilize educational objectives that provide sequences of learning and encourage effective program evaluation, and to incorporate art curriculum into the mainstream: "If art is to be taught regularly in every classroom throughout an entire district, some means are required to ensure implementation. In art as in other subjects, such means include a written curriculum with plans that follow a scope and sequence for teachers in all grades." The concern expressed here is that we will expect too much of the ordinary classroom teacher if we ask that he or she become expert in art history, criticism, production, and aesthetics. My concern is that we will ask too little. As Apple points out (1987, 70), when curriculum becomes too centralized, focusing on competencies measured by standardized tests, the consequences are most often exactly the opposite of what has been intended. "Instead of professional teachers who care greatly about what they do and why they do it, we may have alienated executors of someone else's plans."

I have argued elsewhere that it is at the level of curriculum in use that curriculum thinkers have most often been frustrated over the past two decades (Bolin 1987, 96-97).

> The link between intention and actuality in curriculum development is often a weak connection at best, and curriculum change is a tedious process. If one sees the curriculum as a document that outlines a set of objectives, implementation is not necessarily a curriculum problem but an instructional problem.

The teacher must be an active participant in curriculum development and implementation. Participation by the teacher begins when the teacher is intellectually engaged with subject itself. This is where the art specialist has a vital role to play with classroom teachers who do not have needed knowledge and skills in art, assisting them in making appropriate curriculum choices. The teacher examines a curriculum document, analyzing its substance (assisted by the art specialist if it is the classroom teacher who is working with a DBAE program), modifying and supplementing it in light of the realities of that teacher's own classroom and school situation. The teacher must be seen as one who utilizes a given curriculum as a basis for decision making—real decisions, not shallow choices about whether to use *suggested activity A* or *suggested activity B*.

2. *Studying the complex, dynamic context of schools.* Inservice teachers are often unaware of the complexities of their own setting and how these shape practice. Often the constraints of the workplace are accepted as personal failure—for example, the teacher may believe that if she tried harder or had better skills students would be more responsive, when in reality, the school has failed to provide her with a reasonable class load, appropriate materials, or adequate supervisory support. The teacher who has learned to study the school context is less likely to confuse institutional constraint with personal failure.

Understanding the complexity and dynamic nature of schools is a key concept if one is interested in involving teachers in curriculum change. At the outset I noted that I take comfort in Clark, Day, and Greer's comment (1987, 131) that in programs of discipline-based art education, "Art is viewed as a subject with content that can be taught and learned in ways that resemble how other subjects can be taught in schools." I also find discomfort in that statement. There is a lot to concern us about how other subjects are taught in schools today. Mainstream thought on schooling is far less concerned about education for personal meaning, education of imagination and feeling—in short, education of the whole person—than it is concerned with development of those human capacities that are most easily verified by observation or measured by objective criteria. Though most educators may recognize the need for both analytical and imaginative thinking, and I know few teachers who are indifferent to personal meaning, they are under enormous pressure to teach a narrowly conceived, test-driven curriculum. If we attempt to place art education into the present school milieu as another subject to be taught in ways similar to other subjects, we are in grave danger of allowing the arts to be treated as objective knowledge in the narrowest sense of that term. In the current political context of schooling, programs in creative and critical thinking, art, music, dance, and aesthetics—if they are present at all—are asked to follow rules of cognition for political purposes related to objective measurement as a means of accountability. The tragedy is not just a distortion of subject. The tragedy is that through the arts and their symbolic language many students have found a retreat from an oppressive, technical approach to learning that has been disinterested in their personal concerns. Too much that goes on in our schools has the consequence of rendering knowledge useless or meaningless to the student. Art education, or the disciplines of art education in their most rigorous sense, cannot be allowed to be one more set of subjects. Art educators can ill afford to accept schools as they are or feel that an advance has been made for art in education with acceptance of the arts in terms of mainstream education.

Teacher educators who are interested in implementing DBAE have often expressed concern over art teachers who favor studio art, supposing that this is the case because there is more studio art in preservice programs. While this is undoubtedly true for many art teachers, it is too simplistic an answer to teacher resistance to DBAE. Art teachers may tenaciously cling to studio classes because they recognize how little opportunity students have for symbolic expression in the schools. To limit the studio in order to include history or aesthetics, if these are to be taught by mainstream rules, would be to sell students short. Many art teachers will need to be reassured that there will be alternatives to the narrow approaches to teaching and learning that they observe around them.

Inservice teachers who are convinced of the value of DBAE must learn how to carefully study the school context in order to develop thoughtful strategies for instruction. These teachers will be far more capable of dealing with the realities of mainstream education than will outside experts who do not understand the particular school milieu.

3. *Developing an experimental attitude.* The inservice teacher in a continuum should be thought of as a scholar teacher, one who is a continuing student of subject, pedagogy, and human growth. Research, inquiry, and writing are not the exclusive property of university scholars. Teachers, too, should be challenged to see themselves as scholars. Dewey (1929, 32) argued that it is not research that will be most helpful to teachers, but the research as it is critically examined and tested in light of their own understanding, experience, and particular circumstances: "The final reality of educational science is not found in books, nor in experimental laboratories, nor in the classrooms where it is taught, but in the minds of those engaged in directing educational activities."

Teacher scholarship needs to be supported, however. Becoming a teacher is a lifelong process. The very least that a teacher ought to be able to expect of the profession is that appropriate supervision be provided. Supervision is the right of teachers, though they are unlikely to ask for supervision as many presently experience it. Elliot Eisner (1981, 62) likened the supervisor to the critic in the arts: "The critic's function—and I would argue one of the major functions of the supervisor— is to help others appreciate what has transpired." Supervision should be directed toward enabling the teacher to be more thoughtful and reflective about practice. This perspective is not served by the supervisor who observes the teacher's performance in a few isolated instances, noting details such as writing the objective on the board, presence or absence of anticipatory set, increasing motivation through altering level of concern, or whether the teacher looks professional. As Dewey pointed out, "Such methods of criticism may be adapted to giving a training-teacher command of some of the knacks and tools of the trade, but are not calculated to develop a thoughtful and independent teacher" (1902, 335). When it is not possible to provide the specialist with a supervisor who is an experienced art teacher, the supervisor must at least be guided by an art educator. Although it is true that there are many generic skills in teaching, there is always need for specific, subject-centered feedback.

In a continuum, supervision is the right of the teacher. Here we benefit again, by borrowing images from the arts. Think of the skilled pianist who continues to study with a teacher, moving beyond the teacher in skill and achievement, but returning for the discipline, practice, and critique. Teachers of art need to continue to study their craft—including subject matter, human learning, pedagogy, and studio work. Teacher scholarship may exist without supervisory support, but for it to flourish in the schools, we must not leave it to chance. Every teacher should be a scholar teacher.

Toward a Continuum in Teacher Education

I have argued that the interrelationship between preservice and inservice art education should be that of a continuum. I have suggested three strands that characterize a continuum in teacher education. The form that DBAE will actually take has not been addressed. There are many specific questions to be answered in any attempt to implement a wide-sweeping curriculum reform such as DBAE. Undoubtedly, the appropriate relationship between pre- and inservice education in discipline-based art will require certain agreements about who should do what and when. These are legitimate, pressing concerns that I have ignored. Art educators are far more equipped to work out specific details than I am.

I have presented some prior considerations that must be taken into account if DBAE is to find its way into the schools and stay. If preservice teacher education makes little difference in teacher practice, then content of preservice teacher education is irrelevant. If inservice education does not contribute to improvement of the schools and lasting curriculum reform, then talk about content of inservice programs is idle talk. Questions of content and organization become important only as we are able to offer programs that are likely to make a difference in the way teachers do their work. I believe that the continuum does and will make a difference.

A continuum presupposes that education is concerned with construction of meaning through continuous reconstruction of experience in light of new information and experience. To be consistent with a continuum, all preservice and inservice instruction should give attention to autobiography of those who participate, study of the context of schooling, and continuous scholarship or developing an experimental attitude about teaching. These should be placed within a framework that will provide for (1) acquisition of knowledge, (2) analysis and reflection, (3) reconstruction and application, and (4) experimentation and critique.

Acquisition of knowledge is critical when new areas are being introduced. This may be presented in a variety of ways—lecture, briefing session, teacher (or student) study group, assigned readings. Too many preservice courses and staff development programs stop with direct input, however. *Analysis and reflection* time should be built in to any program that seeks to provide new information. In a staff-development context, it often makes sense to present information to a large group. When this is the case, resource people should follow up with small group discussions, providing participants with the opportunity to question and consider the material. Allowing time for a few questions at the end of a lecture does not serve this purpose. Sometimes analysis and reflection can be promoted through writing reflective or dialogue journals that are read by appropriate supervisory personnel.

Once opportunity for analysis and reflection have been provided, *reconstruction and application* should be expected. When there is a specific innovation, such as DBAE, with concepts and organizing principles related to a strong philosophical base, there is always concern that contamination of the model will occur. The fact is, contamination occurs in every top-down model—contamination, resistance, and subversion. In a continuum, reconstruction of knowledge is not looked on as a necessary concession, but the best possible representation of the innovative idea—it is represented, transformed by the one who will receive it. If there are invariant guiding principles in DBAE, then these will survive the teacher's intellectual activity as they will survive the student's. As teachers are involved in thinking through and applying information in terms of their knowledge, expertise, and understanding of the school context, they will begin to apply it.

There is a place for carefully sequenced curriculum guides that are prepared with teachers, but the key to their use is the word *guide* and the words *prepared with* teachers. Activity and sequence must always be subject to expert teacher judgment. It is far more likely that an innovation such as DBAE will become a part of the schools and recognizable ten years from now if this plan is followed.

Reconstruction and application are followed by *experimentation and critique*. Teachers need to modify, redesign, try out, experiment with ways to teach specific content to students. Their understanding of content needs to be assessed. They need supervisory support as they do this. The supervisor focuses on curriculum intentions—intentions outlined in the curriculum materials, teacher intentions, student intentions—and engages the teacher in dialogue about those intentions. In this way, the teacher will know when more information is necessary or that better application of principles of learning could be made, not because the supervisor has said so, but because the teacher's own critical skills are enlarged.

The strands of a continuum and framework for its development that I have outlined will provide broad guidelines for going beyond, exploring, and discovering how to better educate teachers in DBAE programs. A continuum will always be unfinished—there is always an overlapping horizon of what could yet be (to use Berger's words) when we are more likely to want some certain answers. In the past, teacher educators have been too ready to give answers to, rather than find answer with, teachers. Answers, in a continuum, will always hinge on the uncertainty and unpredictability of pre- and inservice students with whom we work. The continuum is their continuum.

John Westerhoff (1987, 193) has remarked:

> It is easy to forget that nothing—no media, film, field trip, teaching method, or educational resource—can replace a person. After everything has been said about methods, skills, knowledge, technique, or program, what finally surfaces as most important is the person who teaches.

I suspect that if art educators bear this in mind, discussions and plans about discipline-based art education will not have to end up in the tradition of past curriculum reform movements that never got very far beyond the minds of the reformers.

References

Apple, Michael. 1987. The de-skilling of teaching. In *Teacher renewal: Professional issues, personal choices*, ed. F. S. Bolin and J. Falk. New York: Teachers College Press.

Berger, P. L. 1963. *Invitation to sociology: A humanistic perspective*. Garden City, N.Y.: Anchor Books, Doubleday.

Bolin, F. S. 1987. The teacher as curriculum decision maker. In *Teacher renewal: Professional issues, personal choices*, ed. F. S. Bolin and J. Falk. New York: Teachers College Press.

Clark, G. A., M. D. Day, and W. D. Greer. 1987. Discipline-based art education: Becoming students of art. *The Journal of Aesthetic Education* 21(2):129-96.

Dewey, John. [1902] 1974. The relation of theory to practice in education. In *John Dewey on education*, ed. R. D. Archambault.

Dewey, John. 1929. *The sources of a science of education*. New York: Horace Liveright.

Eisner, E. W. 1982. An artistic approach to supervision. In *Supervision of teaching*, ed. T. J. Sergiovanno. Alexandria, Va.: Association for Supervision and Curriculum Development.

Greene, Maxine. 1973. *Teacher as stranger*. Belmont, Calif.: Wadsworth.

Huebner, Dwayne. 1987. The vocation of teaching. In *Teacher renewal: Professional issues, personal choices*, ed. F. S. Bolin and J. Falk. New York: Teachers College Press.

Jersild, Arthur T. 1955. *When teachers face themselves*. New York: Teachers College Press.

Lortie, Dan C. 1972. *Schoolteacher: A sociological study*. Chicago: University of Chicago Press.

Sarason, Seymour. 1971. *The culture of the school and the problem of change*. 2nd ed. Boston: Allyn & Bacon.

Sevigny, Maurice J. 1987. Discipline-based art education and teacher education. *The Journal of Aesthetic Education* 21(2):95-126.

Spradley, J. P. 1979. *The ethnographic interview*. New York: Holt, Rinehart, and Winston.

Stanley, M. 1980. Education and public policy discourse. *Teachers College Record*, p. 81.

Waller, W. 1923. *The sociology of teaching*. New York: John Wiley and Sons.

Westerhoff, John. 1987. Teacher as pilgrim. In *Teacher renewal: Professional issues, personal choices*, ed. F. S. Bolin and J. Falk. New York: Teachers College Press.

MICHAEL D. DAY

Preparing Teachers for Excellence

The task of improving art teacher preparation programs in the United States and developing the corps of art teachers is of central importance for the field of art education. Regardless of its difficulty, it is one that can and must be addressed by professional art educators at all levels, especially by those in higher education. The assignment for higher education is to strengthen and improve current art teacher preparation programs, to assure that all programs are at least adequate and preferably better than adequate, and to encourage programs with no intention of meeting high standards to withdraw.

Art education is surely one of the most dynamic fields in education in the sense that so much change has taken place within a relatively brief time period. For many years, art was on the periphery of general education, a "nice" subject that everyone liked but surely not "necessary" within the core of basic subjects (Broudy 1987). Art was a subject that served education at the whim of the local board or superintendent but remained the easy target for budget cuts.

Both the direction of art education and its place in the school have changed significantly in recent years. It is this broad change of approach—or "paradigm shift," as some have claimed—that has major implications for contemporary art education. Changes that can be traced back to the Penn State Seminar of 1965 (Mattil 1966) have drastically altered today's art education expectations and practices, including the conduct of art teacher preparation programs. A major change for university undergraduates, for example, is the expectation that they will study art history, art criticism, and aesthetics as well as becoming proficient in the domain of art production (Clark, Day, and Greer 1987). As well, they are expected to incorporate concepts from these disciplines within the curriculum they prepare for public school children and young people.

. . .

Profiles For Art Teacher Preparation

There is no accepted model for the "best" undergraduate art education program. Virtually every college or university art teacher preparation program differs from others in significant ways. Nevertheless, all programs deal with many of the same factors: admission to the program; curriculum content in art; education and pedagogy coursework; physical, and educational resources; uses of technology; field experiences and practice teaching; relationships with public and private schools; assessment and endorsement; and placement, to name a few. Program emphases and curricula vary from school to school, as do requirements for practicum or student teaching experiences. Some programs collaborate closely with school districts, while others do not. Control of program content might reside within the art education program, the art department, or the college of education, or it might be prescribed to some degree by state departments of education through licensure requirements.

A program profile that relates to these common factors can be constructed for each art teacher preparation program. This profile is defined by the unique way in which each common factor is resolved. For example, the proportion of coursework in art versus coursework. in education varies from program to program. The content of study in art, art history, art criticism, and aesthetics varies as well. Like the profile of a person's figure, all the parts are similar to those of other people yet have their own distinguishing characteristics. The various combinations of similar parts result in individual profiles, and these profiles have much in common.

The twelve items listed below appear to be pervasive components among many art education programs. Although they are numbered for convenience, no hierarchy is intended. These and other items of significance might be described and analyzed individually, then combined to form a profile of the particular art education program. This descriptive profile might then serve to illuminate strengths and weakness of the program and suggest targets for improvement. Following insights derived from this process, program leaders could develop a plan of action for improving specific components in their respective programs.

TWELVE PROGRAM COMPONENTS: DESCRIPTION AND ANALYSIS

1. *Discipline Content: Art Studio/Design, Art Criticism, Aesthetics, Art History*

How many studio art credits are required for the art education program? How much breadth and depth do students achieve with these credits? What level of preparation do art education students receive in the disciplines of art history, aesthetics, and art criticism? In what departments are these courses taught? Do students gain insights regarding the teaching of content from the art disciplines as they attend these courses? Are students prepared sufficiently in the art disciplines to implement the requirements of the National Visual Arts Standards? Are they prepared to meet recommendations implicit within NBPTS? [National Board for Professional Teaching Standards]

Suggestion: Prospective art teachers have an intensive course of study in their major. They take courses in the studio areas of drawing, painting, printmaking, ceramics, and sculpture. They study color, composition, and design. They are expected to develop advanced capability in at least one studio or design area. By the time they go out to look for a job, art education majors are expected to have a strong portfolio of studio work.

In order to meet the requirements of the discipline-based approach to art education and to implement the National Standards for the Visual Arts, prospective art teachers need to take coursework in art history, aesthetics, and art criticism. Along with study of the Western traditions of art, they need to learn about the art of other cultures in the world, including Asian, African, and Native American art. It is also important that they gain knowledge about the art of their own time: contemporary art.

The range of study for art education majors includes the applied arts. At least at a basic level, they need to know about and understand the arts of architecture, graphics, illustration, interior design, and industrial design. As teachers they will need to be aware of the roles art plays in society and culture (Chalmers 1996).

2. *Education Requirements*

What are the relationships between the art education program and the college of education? What is the source for certification requirements? Is the art education program administered within the college of education, the department of art, or some other department? How does location of the program affect its emphasis and character? What are the education requirements for art education programs in professional schools of art and design? What proportion of the art education student's program is dedicated to professional education requirements?

3. *Clinical Experiences*

At what point in the art education program do clinical experiences begin—classroom visits, visits to other educational institutions, student teaching, internships, and so on? How are visitation sites selected? How are students encouraged to learn from clinical experiences? Do students participate in critiques of videotaped teaching episodes? How are cooperating teachers selected? How are cooperating teachers rewarded for their participation? How are local schools associated with the college or university teacher preparation program? What means are employed for evaluation of student teaching performance and other clinical activities?

Suggestion: Socialization is an essential part of the preservice program at the college or university. Art education students should be engaged in a student chapter of their professional organization and should have opportunities to function as part of a social and professional group.

4. *Teaching Methods*

How are prospective art teachers introduced to various teaching methods? How is teaching modeled in art education classrooms? Do students analyze the teaching methods of their university professors? How many specific teaching methods are introduced? How many are practiced? How many are mastered? Are students introduced to the concept of having a repertoire of teaching methods? What teaching methods are unique to teaching the visual arts? Do students observe master teachers applying methods in response to different learning situations?

Suggestion: Art teachers are expected to be able to teach using a repertoire of teaching methods: slide and lecture, demonstration of art techniques, discussions, group study, supervision, interviews, and others. Students should learn about inquiry-based approaches to teaching. They will need to use these methods fluently, responding to the interests of students within the unpredictable and unique environments of each individual art classroom.

5. *Technology*

In what ways are contemporary computer technologies relevant to art education? Is utilization of computer technology antithetical to traditional art values? Or are computer skills necessary for the development of professional art teachers? If so, what computer skills do prospective art teachers need to gain? How are computers instrumental for creating art? For developing curriculum? For conducting research? For making materials for teaching? What other technologies are applied in art teacher preparation programs?

Suggestion: As college students, prospective teachers are prepared to use computers for their teaching. They learn to use the Internet within the art curriculum, to gain competency with basic computer graphics programs, to use computers for creating curriculum and for developing worksheets and learning aids for students. There is no limit to the level of computer proficiency to which art education students might profitably aspire.

6. *Curriculum*

What are the different definitions of the term curriculum as it is used in education? Which senses of the word carry most meaning for art education? What are the implications for curriculum presented by the Visual Arts Standards and NBPTS? What skills for curriculum development are needed by prospective art teachers? Do students analyze and critique commercially prepared art curricula and teaching materials? Are students prepared to evaluate and select commercial curricula? To adapt commercial curricula to local requirements? To develop art curricula for local use? Are students prepared to consider integration of the art curriculum with other school subjects?

Suggestion: Art education students are expected to write an art curriculum. They need to be able to write comprehensive lessons with all the essential components, including objectives, learning activities, and assessment of student progress. They are expected to write units of instruction with scope, sequence, content, and methods of inquiry derived from the four art disciplines. These units are organized around works of fine and applied art from a range of the world's eras and cultures. Prospective art teachers are prepared to relate, integrate, cooperate, and collaborate across the curriculum. They are taught to work with other teachers to further their school's mission and curriculum.

7. *Assessment*

How are prospective art teachers prepared to assess student learning and progress? What range of assessment/evaluation methods are emphasized? What do students learn about portfolio assessment, its history in art education, and its contemporary applications? Are students prepared to evaluate their own art programs and their own teaching? How is assessment connected with curriculum and with instruction? What is the role of assessment in relation to other components such as teaching methods, diverse student populations, and discipline knowledge? How much of a teacher's time and effort should be dedicated to assessment/evaluation? How does assessment relate to and interact with grading, reporting progress, and communicating art program goals? How does assessment relate to communication with school officials, parents, and students? What are the implications of the NAEP assessment of art learning?

8. *Classroom Management*

What skills are required to manage a contemporary art classroom? Do prospective art teachers learn about ordering, storing, distributing, and accounting for materials? About maintaining tools, equipment, and supplies for art production activities? How do prospective art teachers learn about classroom organization, exhibition of student artwork, and classroom environment? How are teaching materials such as art prints, slides, videotapes, CD-ROMs, and books stored, used, and accounted for? How is a discipline-based classroom different from a traditional studio classroom? What skills and strategies for maintaining a positive learning environment are studied and practiced by prospective art teachers? How are they taught to deal with student behavior problems? What do they learn about the way public and private schools typically deal with behavior problems? What do they learn about school law?

Suggestion: Prospective art teachers must develop skills of classroom management, including management of potentially hazardous tools and materials. Art teachers must know and apply safety cautions and standards. Contemporary art education assumes use of electronic media such as slides, television, videos, CD-ROMs, computers, and the Internet in the classroom.

By the time, they enter the art room as teachers, college students need to be able to maintain a positive learning environment for their students. This means that they need to acquire the knowledge and skills necessary to maintain discipline, deal with potential behavior problems, and understand school policies and procedures with respect to student department.

9. *Diverse Student Populations*

Do prospective art teachers have opportunities to work with diverse student populations? What training do they receive to prepare them as teachers of students with various handicaps? Different first languages? Various ability levels? Diverse learning styles? Various ethnic and cultural backgrounds? How do the National Visual Arts Standards and the NBPTS recommendations address diverse student populations? How are prospective art teachers prepared to work with parents, school, and community, as well as with students in their classrooms?

Suggestion: Teachers need to know a great deal about learners; they should study the psychology of children and adolescents. Art teachers need to be very well informed about children's artistic development. Prospective art teachers must be cognizant of different learning styles among their students and be able to adapt instruction to meet the needs of all learners. They should be aware of new information from the field of cognitive psychology, including fundamentals of higher-level thinking and the benefits of a thinking curriculum.

As they enter the mainstreamed classroom, art education students ought to be able to relate positively to children and young people from all cultures and backgrounds, including those who speak English as a second language; to children of nearly all mental and physical capabilities; and to children with a range of disabilities. Art teachers need to be sensitive and responsive to the values of the local communities in which their students reside.

10. *Professional Art Education*

Are prospective art teachers prepared for the roles they will be expected to perform as professional educators in their schools and communities? Does the art education program sponsor a college student chapter of the NAEA? Do college students receive and read professional publications? Do they participate in local, state, and/or national professional meetings? Are they prepared to promote and advocate the arts and art education as an essential part of general education? Are students familiar with the range of national, state, and local education and art education organizations and their functions? Are prospective art educators prepared to assume the roles of professional leadership?

Suggestion: Prospective art educators need to understand the profession they are entering: how school districts are run; the role of the board of education; the role of parent groups; the role of superintendents; the role of central office staff, and especially the role of the principal, the most influential person in a school building. They need to know basics of school law and their responsibilities and liabilities as teachers.

Art teachers should participate in their professional organizations at the local, state, and national levels; subscribe to professional journals; stay abreast of developments in the field; and become leaders in their communities. Very likely they will need to become effective advocates for the arts in education.

11. *Certification/Licensure*

What certification or licensure system applies to graduates of this art education program? How is the program directed or influenced by certification requirements? Is certification reciprocal with other states? How do certification/licensure requirements or lack of requirements affect the content of this art education program?

12. *Museum/Community Resources*

How are students prepared to integrate art museum resources, art galleries, public art, community artists, art critics, and other art professionals for the purposes of art education? Have the benefits of viewing original artwork, as compared with art reproductions, been emphasized? Do students have experiences with the local community as a resource for art education? Are students aware of art teaching resources available from many museums? Do they know how to access and use such materials? Are they cognizant of ways teachers prepare their students for visits to museums, galleries, and other community resources? Are they able to evaluate such educational experiences?

Suggestion: When they enter the teaching force, new art teachers should be familiar with art museums and galleries and how to utilize the various art resources of the community. They should have extensive experience in viewing, studying, and responding to original art objects and should recognize the potential educational values to be gained by students through their experiences with original art. Prospective art teachers need to understand how the resources of museums can be used for inquiry-based learning, art history, art criticism, and investigations in aesthetics.

These twelve items or components address a few significant questions and issues that pervade the enterprise of art teacher preparation. This list is not exhaustive and could be elaborated extensively; it is intended only as a beginning point for discussion. Although some significant topics are not included on it, this list does suggest the complexity and range of issues, knowledge, and skills that every art teacher education program must address.

. . .

CONCLUSION

During the millennium of the 2000s, American schools will continue to need well-prepared, well-qualified teachers, including teachers of art. Art education programs in many colleges and universities are currently meeting this demand and will continue to provide competent and caring art teachers for the schools. These sound programs will need to remain active and engaged with the professional field of art education in order to maintain high standards.

Other programs do not meet minimum standards for art teacher preparation. Students are graduated and certified in art education, yet are not well prepared to teach art according to the best recommendations of the professional field. Unless they are willing to make the necessary investments to improve, these inadequate art teacher preparation programs should stop accepting students, close their operations, and place their resources elsewhere.

The National Standards for the Visual Arts, the National Board for Professional Teaching Standards, the National Assessment of Educational Progress in Art, and numerous other publications, organizations, and resources provide art educators with an abundance of guidance for strengthening art teacher preparation programs. Although each is unique, all art education programs are engaged in similar activities, issues, and practices. Professors of art education can assess and improve their programs through a process of description of various components to create a program profile, followed by analysis of strengths and weaknesses. With the profile in mind, professors can then develop action plans to prioritize and guide the direction and pace of program improvement. This process can be ongoing and responsive to new challenges and demands for art education in the schools.

This discussion has reinforced the well-accepted notion that making positive changes in education is neither simple nor easy. This is an accurate but incomplete observation, because there are also several very positive realities that need no change: well-prepared art teachers who devote decades of their lives to teaching receptive youngsters, enjoying every day of their careers; schools with admirable art programs valued as central within the school curriculum; strong art teacher preparation programs that recruit enthusiastic students, prepare them well, and place them in satisfying positions. These are our models for professional development, and they are worth all our efforts in the pursuit of excellence.

References

Broudy, H. S. 1987. *The role of imagery in learning.* Los Angeles: J. Paul Getty Trust.

Chalmers, F. G. 1996. *Celebrating pluralism: Art, education, and cultural diversity.* Los Angeles: J. Paul Getty Trust.

Clark, G., M. Day, and D. Greer. 1987. Disciplined-based art education: Becoming students of art. *The Journal of Aesthetic Education,* 21(2): 129-93.

Mattil, E. L., ed. 1966. *A seminar in art education for research and curriculum development.* University Park: Pennsylvania State University.

KATHERINE A. SCHWARTZ

DBAE and Staff Development

The Alaska Center for Excellence in Art Education (ACEAE) promotes visual art education that helps students to understand and create art. Discipline-based art education (DBAE) is used as a guide for designing staff development and university courses, because in addition to performance and production skills, students are taught how art relates to every subject in the curriculum. As presented by Greer (1984), DBAE programs demonstrate that when students study art images and have opportunities to create them; (1) they learn to express their own ideas and feelings in visual form, (Art Production); (2) they acquire knowledge about the contributions artists and art make to culture and society (Art History); (3) they respond to and make judgments about art (Art Criticism); and (4) they learn to recognize the expressive character of particular works of art (Aesthetics). In addition, the art content in DBAE is consistent with the goals of the National Art Education Association (1986) and the National Standards for Arts Education (1994).

The theoretical foundation that defines this approach to teaching art has been debated among art educators for more than thirty years. The content, curriculum characteristics, and contexts for DBAE instruction were defined by Greer (1984), and expanded upon by Clark, Day, and Greer, (1987). Research priorities for DBAE were identified by Rush (1986) and the role of DBAE in America's schools was proposed by Eisner (1987). The dimensions of DBAE were compiled for staff development by Schwartz (1987), and an excellence curriculum for art education was provided by Smith in 1986, updated in 1995. For more than a decade, The Getty Education Institute for the Arts, an operating program of the J. Paul Getty Trust, has consistently promoted DBAE through extensive publications, conferences, and regional art education institutes.

The education components of ACEAE include staff development and a graduate course. Staff development is provided on request throughout the year, and is tailored to address the unique needs of school districts. Presentations are provided in several geographic locations to encourage individuals from remote villages to participate. Local committees provide leadership, funding, and in-kind contributions. Staff development programs focus first on the role of art in education and secondly, on appropriate curriculum and teaching methods.

A graduate course, *Improving Visual Art Education,* is available to teachers and administrators following each staff development presentation. After an introduction to the role of imagery in learning as discussed by Broudy (1987), the course demonstrates how DBAE contributes to other subjects and reinforces general education objectives. Course activities model successful strategies for teaching and evaluating art instruction. Participants learn about art by working directly with artists, educators, original art, and cultural artifacts.

Purpose of the Study

This study examines the effectiveness of DBAE staff development, and of a graduate course provided by the Alaska Center for Excellence in Arts Education (ACEAE) from 1991-1996. The study also summarizes progress made by 90 educators to improve art education in their communities. The study addresses the following questions:

(1) How are Alaskan educators in this study connecting DBAE theory and practice to improve teaching?
(2) Why are educators using DBAE theory and practice to improve teaching?
(3) What difference does DBAE-influenced art education make in the education of Alaskan students?
(4) What are the long range benefits of the *Improving Visual Art Education* course?

Methods

This study employed two research methods: narrative progress reports from nine partners in the effort to improve art education, and survey responses from 90 teachers and administrators who completed the graduate course *Improving Visual Art Education.* The combination of the narrative progress reports and survey data shows how and why individual teachers and administrators are changing their approach to teaching or administrating art education programs.

Narrative Progress Reports

The narrative progress reports are limited to nine organizations and school districts which hosted DBAE staff development and the *Improving Visual Art Education* graduate course in their communities. The narratives describe their art education programs, recent progress made to provide comprehensive art education programs, strengths of the programs, and benefits to students. The narratives provide individual interpretations of what works for improving art education in Alaska in diverse communities.

The partners included in the study are: Alaska Department of Education, Arts in Education Program of the Alaska State Council on the Arts, Anchorage Museum of History and Art, Anchorage School District, Fairbanks North Star Borough School District, Juneau School District, Kenai Peninsula Borough School District, Matanuska Susitna Borough Schools, and Petersburg City Schools.

Survey

The survey was created through the joint efforts of an advisory committee representing participating school districts. The components of Discipline-based Art Education (DBAE) presented by Clark et al. (1987) were used to design the survey. Following the completion of the *Improving Visual Art Education* graduate course, participants completed the survey and identified how they might change their approach to art teaching or administration. Their responses were filed in a data base.

To determine long-range benefits, one year after completing the course, participants responded to a second survey in which they were asked to identify how they were changing the content, curriculum, and instruction used for teaching or administrating art education. Questions were added to the second survey to identify the assistance participants were receiving from district administration; recommendations for follow-up activities; content needed for staff development; art education curriculum currently used, resources used, generation of new lessons, and students' benefits from art education.

Population

The population for the study was limited to 210 certified teachers and administrators who completed the graduate course and who returned the second survey. A total of 102 surveys were returned, representing a 48% return rate. Twelve surveys were eliminated because they were not completed. Comparisons were made between the first and second survey responses.

The population represented 7 school districts and 75 schools which provide education to about 47% of Alaska's total (K-12) student population. The participants averaged 16.44 years of teaching experience, and they comprised five groups: 38 elementary teachers, 9 middle school teachers, 7 high school teachers, 15 administrators, and 21 certified art specialists. The elementary teachers in this study were responsible for teaching the district art curriculum to their students. Only 9 of the elementary teachers received assistance from art specialists. The middle school teachers and high school teachers in this study did not teach art classes. The administrators in this study included elementary principals, librarians, museum educators, and art supervisors.

Discussion of Results

How are Alaskan educators in this study connecting DBAE theory and practice to improve teaching?

The results of the survey responses with supporting information from the narrative reports identify how educators are changing art content, curriculum, and instruction to improve teaching.

Content. Percentages of changes made in art education content by elementary teachers, middle school teachers, high school teachers, administrators, and certified art specialists are seen in Table 1.

Table 1. Art Education Content Changes.

Content	Total	Elem	Middle	High	Adm	Art Sp
Aesthetics	71.1%	71.1%	66.7%	42.9%	86.7%	71.4%
Art history	61.1%	55.3%	44.4%	28.6%	73.3%	81.0%
Art criticism	70.0%	60.5%	55.6%	57.1%	100%	76.2%
Art production	67.8%	86.8%	66.7%	00.0%	66.7%	57.1%

Art specialists are making the greatest number of content changes in art history (81%), art criticism (76%), and aesthetics (71%), which suggests they are broadening their traditional art production teaching focus. Elementary teachers are changing art production content, moving away from seasonal activities towards comprehensive instruction.

Curriculum. The changes made in art curriculum by elementary teachers, middle school teachers, high school teachers, administrators, and certified art specialists are seen in Table 2.

Art specialists (81%) are making the greatest number of changes in the use of written and sequential art lessons. The administrator group (93%) is making most changes in the use of art images. Administrators traditionally have more money for resources, which may account for the higher rate of change.

Table 2. Art Education Curriculum Changes

Curriculum	Total	Elem	Middle	High	Adm	Art Sp
Written lessons	58.8%	44.7%	55.6%	57.1%	60.0%	81.0%
Sequential	63.3%	57.9%	55.6%	42.9%	53.3%	90.5%
Art images	76.7%	78.9%	66.7%	28.6%	93.3%	81.0%

Most of the participants (80%) report generating new lessons or teaching resources. Art specialists, administrators, and elementary teachers have generated the most (95%, 86%, and 80% respectively). The middle school and high school teachers in this study do not teach art classes, yet more than half of them are generating new art lessons or resources to use in the classes they teach.

Instruction. Art instruction is scheduled at least once a week by 48% of those responding. Most of the participants (71%) use teacher-generated lessons, and half of them are using the school district curriculum. Participants (45%) are using more local artists as resources for instruction and a number (38%) are coordinating the Artist in the Schools Program with the school art curriculum.

The middle school and high school teachers are integrating art with other subject areas. Participants recorded 65 examples of generating new art lessons or teaching resources. Several teachers said they have completely revised their art programs. Most art teachers indicated that they are coordinating elementary and secondary art programs to provide sequential and systematic instruction.

Curriculum areas mentioned for integration included: social studies, literature, science, language arts, math, poetry, music, writing, reading, and health. Elementary teachers (67%) are integrating art into grade level themes. Several elementary teachers commented that their entire curriculum is taught within themes (thematic units), and art is now included in every theme. Two selected teacher comments reinforce this finding:

1. I completely changed my focus for teaching after hearing the lecture. For 18 years, I was the teacher he [W. Dwaine Greer] was talking about — the one who taught art on Friday afternoon, after all the academic work was completed. Now I start every week with a focus on an art theme. I include art into every subject I teach. My students love it.
2. I am now able to create a whole series of art lessons integrated with class themes.

Why are educators using DBAE theory and practice to improve teaching? The survey responses suggest several reasons why educators are using DBAE theory and practice to improve teaching. In addition to completing the DBAE course, assistance has been provided to participants in the form of advocacy, help from art education consultants, and new teaching resources. One teacher reported,

> First, the course helped me to understand the role of art in education. Then I led staff development on that topic to teachers in my school. Next, the interest and support from the teachers led to the creation of an art specialist K-6 position in my school.

A review of the narrative reports indicates the art educators in the participating school districts are experienced, active in national issues, and have a very good understanding of DBAE. Many of the art educators helped to schedule the DBAE staff development and the *Improving Visual Art Education* course provided in their communities, and most of them assisted with teaching the course. The reports also indicate that districts are making video tapes of DBAE staff development for teachers who are not able to attend. In addition, certified art educators are incorporating art history, aesthetics, and art criticism into art studio courses offered in schools and museums. The art educators who participated in this study are creating DBAE art resources and lessons that encourage teachers to learn right along with their students. They generate excitement and enthusiasm in classroom teachers by providing demonstration lessons. In every participating school district, the art educators are readily available and willing to assist with staff development.

Many of the classroom teachers perceive a need to teach an "art" program and not just a "craft" program. They demonstrate a commitment to art education by taking additional classes and attending seminars. Teachers are deliberately working to incorporate art into the daily curriculum, because the study of art provides a thematic focus for classroom instruction.

Administrators are supporting efforts to improve art education by allocating money for art curriculum, instruction, and assessments. Even more important, school districts are allocating time for teaching art and on-going opportunities for certified art teachers and art curriculum committees to revise or write district art curriculum.

What difference does DBAE-influenced art education make in the education of Alaskan students? Most (80%) of the participants indicated they see students benefiting from art education through problem solving, discovering patterns, comparing and contrasting, decision making, choosing appropriate tools, and creating a product. Elementary teachers, middle school teachers, and high school teachers indicated decision making and choosing appropriate tools were equal in importance in creating a product. One of the most important benefits identified is improved quality of instruction.

Art specialists (95%) identified creating a product as the most important benefit to students, followed by decision making, choosing appropriate tools, and problem solving. Art specialists recognize that creating a product requires thinking and problem solving. One art educator stated, "When students create products they have many opportunities for problem solving, discovering patterns, comparing and contrasting, decision making, and choosing appropriate tools."

The narrative progress reports indicate that Alaskan students who participate in comprehensive art education programs are learning how art contributes to understanding themselves, society, and civilizations. Students are learning how art is reflected in their personal lives as they experience art at many different levels, with increasing competence and sophistication. Along with learning art production skills, students are developing an appreciation for aesthetics, art criticism, and art history.

The narrative reports also indicate that art education helps students to see the connections between the visual world and the analytical world, to stretch their vocabularies and perceptions and create links between the humanities and sciences. The knowledge students gain in art class helps them in other classes. Art education teaches children to understand concepts and it exposes them to great art. In addition, when students graduate from school districts with comprehensive art programs, many go on to make art their life's work, in fields such as commercial design and illustration, computer graphics, and architecture.

References

Alaska Department of Education. (1988). *A status report: Curriculum, instruction, and assessment in Alaska school districts 1987-88.* (Available from Alaska Department of Education, 801 W. 10th St. Suite 200, Juneau, AK 99801.)

Alaska Department of Education. (1995). *Alaska student content standards in the arts.* (Available from Alaska Department of Education, 801 W. 10th St. Suite 200, Juneau, AK 99801.)

Broudy, H. S. (1987). *The role of imagery in learning.* (Occasional Paper 1). Los Angeles, CA: The Getty Education Institute for the Arts.

Broudy, H. S. (Speaker) (1988). *The role of art in general education.* (Videotape). The J. Paul Getty Trust, Getty Trust Publications, 401 Wilshire Boulevard, Suite 850 Santa Monica, CA 90401-1455.

Broudy, H. S. (1989). Art as general education. *The Alaska Journal of Art*, 1 (1989): 4-9.

Clark, G. A., Day, M. D., & Greer, D. W. (1987). Discipline-based art education: Becoming students of art. *The Journal of Aesthetic Education*, 21 (2), 129-193.

Eisner, E. W. (1987). *The role of discipline based art education in America's schools.* Los Angeles, CA: The Getty Education Institute for the Arts.

Fullan, M. G. & Miles, M. B. (1992). Getting reform right: What works and what doesn't. *Phi Delta Kappan*, 73 (10), 745-752.

Greer, W. D. (1984). Discipline-based art education: Approaching art as a subject of study. *Studies in Art Education*. 25(4), 212-218.

National Art Education Association. (1986). *Quality art education goals for schools: An interpretation*. Reston, VA: Author.

Music Educators Conference. (1994). *National standards for arts education.* Reston, VA: Author.

Rush, J. C. (1986). DBAE: pragmatic priorities for realistic research. *Journal of the Australian Institute of Art Education*, 10(1), 23-35.

Schwartz, K. A. (1987). *Educators' perceptions of an instructional supervision system for discipline-based art education* (Doctoral dissertation, University of Arizona, 1987).

Schwartz, K. A. (1989). Improving art education in Alaska through discipline-based art education. *The Alaska Journal of Art*, 1 (1989): 16-21.

Schwartz, K. A. (1996). *Improving Visual Art Education in Alaska, 1991-1996.* (Available from Alaska Center for Excellence in Arts Education, Kenai Peninsula College, 34820 College Drive, Soldotna, AK 99669-9789.)

Smith, R. A. (1986). *Excellence in art education: Ideas and initiatives.* Reston, VA: National Art Education Association.

Smith, R. A. (1995). *Excellence II: The continuing quest in art education.* Reston, VA: National Art Education Association.

Welter, C. H. (1989). To go where no publication has gone before. *The Alaska Journal of Art*, 1 (1989): 2-3.

E. Louis Lankford

Aesthetics in Teacher Preparation

Throughout his report [*The Quiet Evolution*], Brent Wilson lauds the selection and curricular application of themes that offer insights into profound human concerns, such as freedom, justice, and ecological crises. The trick, however, is that the theme must be *derived from* the key work of art (p. 103). "The most important learning takes place when several school subjects are taught simultaneously within the context of the large themes that illuminate conceptions of human purpose and well-being. Works of art provide these themes" (p. 211). Yet, how does one select a pithy thematic work of art unless one already has a pithy theme in mind? Aimlessly browsing museum galleries and art history books waiting for a work of art to reach out and slap you in the face with its theme doesn't seem like a very effective, goal-oriented educational process. Clearly, the concept must guide the search and selection of the work of art, yet the interpreted work of art does ultimately further shape and refine the concept. Although Wilson warns against the popular curriculum webbing model which places the thematic concept at the center (he claims that artworks are too often used as mere illustrations of the theme (p. 106), in practice even his model requires that the theme precede and overlay the key work of art.

A second problem is more substantive and strikes at the intent of the model. By focusing on key works of art, teachers must be willing to set aside abstract topics and issues except as they are epitomized through the works of art. This has implications not just for the scope of the curriculum but for the manner in which professional development in comprehensive art education occurs.

In Chapter Two, Wilson describes with delight the "passage" of teachers into and through the "Art World" via Getty-sponsored inservice programs. Familiarity with the roles and functions of art museums, galleries, artists studios, and the like provide teachers with valuable information and insights into the richness and complexity of the visual arts. "After attending a summer DBAE institute program, participants are probably unable ever again to think of art objects devoid of contexts" (p. 79).

Ironically, by basing curriculum exclusively on key works of art, Wilson relegates topics and issues central to those contexts to the role of being explanatory fodder for understanding and appreciating a necessarily limited number of art works. Overarching issues, no matter how vital, that fail to serve that function might never come to light in instructional contexts. For example, suppose a teacher selected Richard Serra's celebrated and notorious *Tilted Arc* as the key work of art for a unlit of instruction. Surely one reason why *Tilted Arc* would be selected in the first place is because of the historic struggle in the 1980s between those who wished for it to remain at Federal Plaza in New York City and those who wished to have it removed. Central to the debate were concepts of censorship, freedom of expression, taxpayer support for the arts, and the relationship between the art world and the rest of society. In support of Wilson's model one could claim that *Tilted Arc* is in fact an ideal choice as a key work of art, as it epitomizes multiple crucial concerns of the Art World. But how close to home must one stick in exploration of these concerns? Censorship alone is a vast, multidimensional and important subject crossing history and cultures and intersecting the arts in America through Constitutional interpretations of freedom of speech. Even though Wilson's model encourages examination of "related visual works" and "related historical, critical, and philosophical writings" (p. 103), to do so in comprehensive ways would require veering far from the originating key work of art. If the key art work is supposed to be the crux of the unit, then such investigations would be a frank betrayal of the unit's focus.

The fact is, the Art World is imbued with overarching topics and issues. Among the DBAE disciplines, aesthetics in particular concentrates a large measure of its energies on such stuff. Questions of value, ethics, objecthood, the veracity of interpretations, the social dynamics of the world of art are grist for philosophical contemplation. Aestheticians often put the concept or issue, as opposed to any particular work of art, at the center of inquiry. Ironically, (again), Wilson's own definition of art (p. 86) is the result of such inquiry; it would have been impossible to derive it from a work of art.

Despite the fact that such inquiries are characteristic of the contexts of art, Wilson wants all teachers to understand and be conversant with, he discourages this form of inquiry in classrooms. In Chapter Five he graphically describes the reason why art works must always be centralized: "Children who are lost when classroom conversation turns the least bit abstract begin to respond, because when works of art are discussed, their features are pointed to continually" (p. 141). Are teachers, then, always to shy away from sticky and complicated abstract topics? Such an attitude would constitute a major setback to gains achieved in raising the status of art education as an academic subject. There are other ways to keep children with diverse learning styles in the loop; instructional strategies abound in the literature.

The solution is simple enough: admit *ideas*, *issues*, and *themes* as central to curriculum units. Works of art needn't be treated as illustrations, but rather as exemplars, archetypes and paradigms of concepts. Such a model would not replace Wilson's key-work model, but stand as a viable alternative to it. A full year's curriculum could incorporate both.

Of course, to effectively centralize ideas, issues, and themes, teachers would have to be knowledgeable about the pertinent concepts and familiar with forms of inquiry appropriate to them. Determined to keep key works of art at the core of theory-to-practice in art education, Wilson discourages the sort of concentrated study needed to gain such knowledge and familiarity. He repeatedly finds fault with efforts to provide discipline-specific inservice education, citing aesthetics as a particularly troublesome case. Questions central to aesthetics "are often asked without reference to specific works of art," and discussions are focused "almost entirely on understanding the discipline of aesthetics through consideration of the issues addressed by aestheticians, not on discussing issues such as whether Andy Warhol's Brillo boxes should be considered art" (p. 86). This is another chicken-or-egg proposition: How can one intelligently discuss the Brillo box case without delving into larger aesthetic issues? The notion of trying to understand aesthetics *without* consideration of the issues addressed by aestheticians is extraordinarily puzzling, especially given Wilson's sincere wish that teachers engage in "historical and philosophical study" in order to expand their "understanding of cultural contexts in which works of art are created" (p. 79).

At issue is the development of expertise on the part of teachers. As a six-year veteran of The Ohio Partnership for the Visual Arts—one of the inservice projects evaluated in Wilson's report—I can't tell you how many times I was confronted by teams of teachers "wanting to have aesthetics explained to us." For these participants, and their inservice instructors and facilitators, the evolution referred to in Wilson's title was anything but quiet. This was new material, and difficult. Although I might have waxed eloquent about Warhol's Brillo boxes or Serra's *Tilted Arc*, that was not what they felt they needed. They needed the big picture. What, fundamentally, *is* aesthetics, what do aestheticians do, why do they do it, and how? Such information is not easily transferred through holistic multidisciplinary lessons centered on individual works of art. More importantly, teachers cannot be expected to incorporate information and processes of inquiry from the discipline of aesthetics into their curriculum, holistically or otherwise, unless they possess a substantial understanding of aesthetics. To apply Wilson's own metaphor, how can he expect teachers to help students view works of art clearly if the lenses are fuzzy and out of focus, or they can't find the glasses, or worst of all, they didn't know they needed glasses until they bumped into a wall? I shudder to think of all the art educators out there who may be throwing an "Is this art?" into their Wilsonesque key-work curricula believing they've got aesthetics covered. Do they understand the implications of the question? Are they familiar with a variety of historical and contemporary responses to the question? Are they able to theoretically analyze, compare, contrast, evaluate, and reformulate those responses and others offered by students? Can they cite a variety of exemplars, including "borderline cases" that might not qualify as "key" works of art but which nevertheless serve to illuminate the nuances of concepts? Are they able to demonstrate the close relationship of the question to other issues in the philosophy of art?

Wilson is absolutely right in his assertion that teachers be able to seamlessly integrate the disciplines in curriculum and instruction. He is right to assert that works of art as they are created and understood are "the principal content of art education" (p. 85). But his insistence on placing key works of art at the center of instructional unit design may be too constraining to do full justice to the richness and complexity of the Art World. And his assertion that the education of art teachers be accomplished without discipline-specific instruction is an invitation to shallow curriculum, or at least it makes such an outcome more likely. The philosophy and methods that Wilson propound are good, sound, and meaningful. But there is more than one route to the top of a mountain. Perhaps in this case, paths should merge.

Reading Suggestions for Part Five

Day, Michael D., ed. *Preparing Teachers of Art*. Reston, Va.: National Art Education Association, 1997.

Getty Center for Education in the Arts. *The Preservice Challenge: Discipline-Based Art Education and Recent Reports on Higher Education*. Seminar Proceedings. Los Angeles: Getty Center for Education in the Arts, 1988.

Getty Center for Education in the Arts. *From Snowbird I to Snowbird II: Final Report of the Getty Center's Preservice Education Project*. Los Angeles: Getty Center for Education in the Arts, 1990.

Schwartz, Katherine A. *Alaska Center for Excellence in Art Education: Improving Visual Art Education in Alaska, 1991-1996*. Soldotha Alaska Center for Education in the Arts. Kenai Penninsula College, 1996.

Wilson, Brent. *The Quiet Evolution: Changing the Face of Arts Education*. Getty Education Institute for the Arts, 1997.

Feinstein, Hermine. "Redesigning Preservice Programs to Implement DBAE: Institutional Realities." *Art Education* 42, no. 2 (1989): 6-9.

Greer, W. Dwaine, and Jean C. Rush. "A Grand Experiment: The Getty Institute for Educators on the Visual Arts." *Art Education* 37, no. 1 (1985): 24, 33-35.

Lovano-Kerr, Jessie. "Implications of DBAE for University Education of Teachers." *Studies in Art Education* 26, no. 4 (1985): 216-23.

Martin, Anna C. "Effects of Feedback on Preservice Teachers' Questioning Strategies." *Arts and Learning Research* 7, no. 1 (1989): 95-106.

Redfern, H. B. "Philosophical Aesthetics and the Education of Teachers." *The Journal of Aesthetic Education* 22, no. 2 (1988): 35-46.

Sandell, Renee, and Cherry-Schroeder. "Talking about Art from Past to Present, Here to There: Preservice Art Teachers Collaborate with a Museum." *Art Education* 47, no. 4 (1994): 18-24.

Sevigny, Maurice J. "Discipline-Based Art Education and Teacher Education." *The Journal of Aesthetic Education* 21, no. 2 (1987): 95-126. Also in Ralph A. Smith, ed. *Discipline-Based Art Education: Origins, Meaning, Development*. Urbana: University of Illinois Press, 1989, same pagination.

Silverman, Ron. "Testing the In-service Hypothesis: The Getty's Los Angeles DBAE Institute." *Visual Arts Research* 23, no. 2 (1997): 4-11.

Stastny, Kimm. "Ideal Instructional Competencies for High School Art Teachers." *Design for Arts in Education* 90, no. 1 (1988): 40-43.

Troeger, Betty Jo. "Delineating a Model of a Knowledge Base for Art Teacher Education: A Response to NCATE." *Visual Arts Research* 16, no. 2 (1990): 31-35.

PART SIX

Issues

Introduction

In certain respects the problems of DBAE are not unique; any interpretation of art education must contend with problems of aims and policy, curriculum design, teaching and learning, implementation and evaluation, professional development, research, and so forth. The major difference with DBAE is that such problems take on a certain coloring and twist. In the literature of DBAE, for example, there is the problem of understanding the nature of definitions generally and the roles traditional and modern definitions of art and art education should play in a theory of DBAE. Likewise with definitions of teaching and curriculum. Should emphasis be placed on teaching art as a distinct subject with special aims and outcomes? Or should the principles of DBAE also inform the teaching of other subjects and try to reform schooling generally? What kinds of problems emerge, moreover, when advocates say interdisciplinary studies should prevail over domain-specific learning? DBAE has, of course, unsettled many in the field of art education by insisting that art making should be complemented by historical and critical studies. Yet the curriculum question remains: What relative weight should be given to creative, historical, and critical studies?

Such considerations raise further questions about the potential benefits realizable through the study of art. Should art be studied primarily for its intrinsic or extrinsic values, that is, noninstrumentally or instrumentally? Is the quality of personal experience afforded by art sufficient? Or is the study of art expected to achieve a range of nonaesthetic objectives? Assuming that all schooling and learning are inevitably instrumental, what can a study of art reasonably bring about? In short, the resolution of issues like these is central to the justification of aesthetic studies.

Inasmuch as the teaching of art in this country occurs in a democratic society, another question is whether it is elitist in the condemnatory sense of the term to have students study and appreciate masterworks even at that stage of their development when they are capable of experiencing them with some understanding. Or, as some theorists hold, should the teaching of art include the whole gamut of art from traditional and modern masterworks to folk art and popular entertainment? By what criteria, in other words, should works be selected for study: cultural representativeness, personal relevance, artistic excellence, social and historical significance, or some other? Such questions become important in the consideration of a range of options, for example, multiculturalism, modernism, postmodernism, and feminism, all general terms that require working definitions.

In a discussion of an issue that characterizes contemporary debate in art education, Michael D. Day examines the relevance for contemporary art education of the artist-teacher as a professional role model. He stresses the limitations of the model for preparing secondary school teachers by exposing a number of considerations that restrict a teacher's professional development. For example, the model perpetuates an over-concentration on art production that is at odds with the tendency in contemporary theory of art education, including that of DBAE, to expand the scope of aesthetic learning.

In *Excellence II: The Continuing Quest in Art Education* (1995), in effect the second edition of *Excellence in Art Education: Ideas and Initiatives* (1986, 1987) written in response to the excellence-in-education movement of the eighties at the behest of the National Art Education Association, Smith recalls the origin of the first edition and discusses subsequent developments in education and the field. The second edition expands the discussions on excellence, aesthetic experience, and elitism found in the first edition and adds new chapters that address the topics of multiculturalism and postmodernism and provide an interpretation of art education from a humanities point of view. The excerpt reprinted here attempts to reconcile elitism and populism in an analysis that distinguishes between open and closed elites and argues for the right of all in a democratic society to have access to excellence.

Inasmuch as DBAE emphasizes the grounding of the teaching of art in a number of traditional disciplines and insofar as such disciplines are often regarded as inherently patriarchal, it is not surprising that DBAE has been subjected to criticism by feminists. The approach taken by Georgia Collins and Renee Sandell points out what they consider imbalances in the treatment of the role of the child, subject, and society in theories of DBAE. Questioning DBAE's preference for a subject-oriented curriculum, Collins and Sandell ask for a "feminine" responsiveness to the needs of the child and society that would stress the cultivation not so much of cultural literacy as of visual literacy. Such an orientation would avert not only the defeminization but the dehumanization of art teaching that the writers fear.

The issues and the questions options like these generate are often the subject of partisan and acrimonious debate, which makes them difficult to resolve rationally. In *Aesthetics and Education*, a volume in the Disciplines in Art Education series, Michael J Parsons and H. Gene

Blocker address such topics in a calm and reasonable voice. In addition to discussing the nature of art and aesthetic objects, the relations of art and audiences, the nature of representation, artists' conception of art, contexts of art, and classroom applications of aesthetics, they also suggest ways to form opinions about modernist and postmodernist thinking and multiculturalism. The excerpt reprinted here, written by Blocker, compares and contrasts modernism and postmodernism and emphasizes that neither is a single theory but rather a loose collection of different views and movements.

Michael D. Day

Artist-Teacher: A Problematic Model for Art Education

The power of imagery is well established within the literature of aesthetic education, especially in the writing of H. S. Broudy.[1] Images can convey ideas, represent ideals, and even shape thought and feeling. The model of artist-teacher is an example of a pervasive and powerful image that has shaped educational practice in art education for decades,[2] and the term remains in the everyday vocabularies of many in the field. This essay suggests that the substance of the artist-teacher image is questionable in the context of contemporary art education.

The notion of an artist who is also a teacher is historically, geographically, and culturally common. Artists have regularly learned about art making from other artists. The most pervasive contemporary manifestation of the teaching artist is found in college and university departments of art where men and women selected for their artistic accomplishments are paid to teach art to students enrolled in the institution that employs them. It is perhaps at the college level that the hyphenated appellation is most appropriately applied,[3] for art department faculty are formally recognized and paid for their teaching services on a regular basis, while the clear expectation is maintained that they continue to produce art.

At the public school level, however, the artist-teacher model becomes problematic. The image of the artist-teacher conveys a complex of ideas within the field of art education: it means that the teacher is one who can also do, or perform artistically; that teaching emphasis is on art production rather than on art history, criticism, or other approaches to learning about art; and it implies that courses in studio art should dominate the college preparation of art specialists who are certified to teach in the public schools.[4] In light of current professional recommendations for best educational practice in art education that emphasize a broader approach to understanding art, these assumptions are questionable.[5]

Arguments in favor of the artist-teacher model are found in the expressive-creative approach to art education. For example, when the educational goal is the development of creativity, self-expression, and personality integration,[6] art activities are viewed as the best, most engaging way to foster growth in pupils. "The goal of the artist is to express one's self aesthetically at the highest human level," writes J. Michael,[7] and this lofty goal is considered important for pupils as well. The teacher is unable to raise pupils to the "highest human level" unless the teacher is also an artist.

A sensitivity to the platitude that "those who can't do, teach" underlies the artist-teacher image. C. H. Anderson rejects the notion that art educators are a group that couldn't make it as artists and insists that "the art teacher must be competent . . . in technical skills required to create art." She suggests that nonproducing art teachers are liable to "creative, intellectual, personal, and professional stagnation."[8]

On the other hand, because of the demands of teaching, in her case at the college level, B. Hammer writes that "I no longer think it is necessary to create personal work while teaching full time. In fact, I suggest the opposite. When teaching, teach; when making art, don't teach."[9]

Issues of time or place for art creation are difficult questions for the artist-teacher, but it is the image of the artist as an independent creator that is the source of most conflict within the artist-teacher image. The basic problem with the artist-teacher model in secondary schools, in addition to the exclusive focus on art production, centers on incompatibilities between the artist's agenda and the teacher's responsibilities to pupils. R. Smith points out that the aims and purposes, contexts and modes of working, and ultimate commitments are different for artists and teachers. "The conceptual frameworks which inform the work of the professional artist and the professional teacher of art are made up of different items."[10]

Art teachers usually receive their preparation from college departments of art, and typical programs of coursework are heavily loaded with studio courses taught by college artist-teachers. Perhaps more influential on prospective teachers than the actual curriculum is the effect of the studio mystique and the charismatic aura that has developed around the role of the artist, especially the fine artist. The following profile of values, implicitly conveyed to art students in the college setting, is probably not typical of any one art department, but some combination of these beliefs and attitudes will likely typify many of them.

A value that one might expert to find in an art studio is a *strong commitment to art*. Researchers report that college art students hold strong aesthetic values, and this commitment is attended by a correspondingly lesser concern for economic and social values.[11]

In some art departments a belief in the *predominant value of art* places the pursuit of artistic excellence above other commitments. In this environment the college student is taught that an overwhelming dedication to art is required and that sacrifice of lesser values is necessary for success in art. The artist has a special "calling," almost a religious commitment and must pursue it at all costs. For example, H. Rosenberg wrote of the Abstract Expressionists: "Based on the phenomenon of conversion the new movement is, with the majority of the painters, essentially a religious movement."[12]

Very often a high premium is placed on *strong individualism*, which is associated with creativity and personal expression. According to this value, personal uniqueness is prerequisite to innovative artistic expression" "If we truly do our 'own thing,' it will be original and unique just as the person, himself, is unique."[13] The painter Hans Hofmann advised, "everyone should be as different as possible. There is nothing that is common to all of us [artists] except our creative urge."[14]

The artist who follows this approach relies on his or her individuality and cannot afford to be conventional. Thus, *nonconformity* is often a strong value promulgated in college art studios that adhere to this view of the artist. In some instances this means rejection of commonly accepted standards for speech, dress, and social behavior in order to convey an "artistic" image to the world.

The environment in this setting is sometimes uninviting to artistic neophytes or dilettantes, such as non-art major students who wish to take a class or two in art production. Only those art majors who are willing to make the aforementioned commitment are considered worthy of serious attention. In some cases art education students, prospective public school art teachers, are considered almost the same as non-art majors, causing some to disguise their major when entering studio classes in order to receive respectful consideration.[15] For future secondary art teachers in this situation the message is clear that art values supersede considerations about educational issues. An additional comment with respect to the relative status of the roles of artist and teacher is made by college studio instructors and professors who repudiate their roles as art educators, perhaps because the overt admission that they gain their livelihood from the teaching function in an accredited, often bureaucratic institution detracts from the image of nonconformist individualist.

Many art teachers in the public schools are able to sort out their priorities as educators and avoid conflicts inherent in the artist-teacher image. However, the art teacher who holds some of the values described above will have philosophical grounds for resisting current recommendations with respect to educational issues such as goals for art education, content for teaching organization of the curriculum, conception of the learner, the role of the teacher, and evaluation of educational progress. The image of individualist nonconformist is not compatible with the performance of many teaching responsibilities that require placing the welfare of students first.

Focus on the role of artist might mean that students are not made aware of the real world of art that they will encounter during their adult lives, the world of art galleries and museums; art from many cultures, times, and places; the contemporary world of fine and applied art.[16] The following comments of a secondary art teacher from a recent study exemplify this isolationist tendency:

> The artist is what art is. It's not galleries; I mean, galleries have nothing to do with it, it's the artist. Artists are visual, exciting, flamboyant people and without that tremendous energy you don't have artists. Ninety-nine percent of what I teach is the extending of energy and if you have enough energy to work, art will follow.
>
> I always consider that I'm the artist, I'm their model, and kids get to respect me as their art model and they'll learn more from me. There's nothing that they don't see in demonstrations; and I don't bring in films of somebody throwing pots. I throw pots for them, I paint for them, I draw for them, so everything is live and in color.[17]

Following are some of the questions and issues that attend the artist-teacher image today:

1. Does the term, which places the artist before the teacher, place teaching in a position of secondary importance?
2. Does the term imply that a person must first be an artist in order to qualify as a teacher? This implication is contracted by common place instances of good artists who are poor teachers and excellent art teachers who do not engage in art production.[18]
3. Do the physical, emotional, and time demands of teaching detract from the artist-teacher's art production? Does the distraction of teaching responsibilities tend to be resented by the artist-teacher?
4. Is the inward focus of the artist on personal creative expression incompatible with the outward focus on the welfare of students required of the teacher?
5. Does the artist-teacher receive primary personal and professional satisfactions from the production of art or from the educational

growth of pupils? If the artist role provides primary satisfaction, isn't this a conflict of interest in light of the source of
remuneration?

6. Why is art the only field or subject in education that employs a
hyphenated image for the teacher? Parallel terms such as math-
ematician-teacher, athlete-teacher, or scientist-teacher are rarely
seen in practice or in the literature. Doesn't the artist-teacher label place importance on the teacher rather than on the student or
on the subject to be taught and learned?

7. Isn't the basic assumption of the artist-teacher model, that art education means only art production, an obsolete assumption? Current recommendations suggest that students have opportunities
to learn about art from the perspectives of art criticism, art history, and aesthetics as well as from art production.[19]

The artist-teacher model, once the dominant image for secondary
art teachers, conveys an image that is rife with problems in relation to
contemporary art education. Its narrow emphasis on production limits
the scope of art learning; its aggrandizement of the artist's role relegates
educational considerations to a secondary position; and its focus on the
artist limits the development of the teacher as a professional educator.

Notes

1. Harry Broudy, *Enlightened Cherishing* (Urban: University of Illinois Press, 1972).

2. Laura Chapman, *Instant Art, Instant Culture* (New York: Teachers College Press, 1982), p. 89.

3. Harlan Hoffa, "The Roots of Art Education in the United States." *Art Education* 37, no. 1 (January, 1984): 24-26.

4. Fred Schwartz, "Graduate Education in the Fine Arts for the Artist-Teacher," *Peabody Journal of Education* (April 1975): 205-12.

5. National Art Education Association, *Quality Art Education* (Reston, VA.: NAEA, 1985). This brochure states that quality programs include sequentially organized study of art production, art criticism, art history, and aesthetics; California State Department of Education, *Visual and Performing Arts Framework* (Sacramento: California State Department of Education, 1982); The College Board, *Academic Preparation in the Arts* (New York: College Entrance Examination Board, 1985).

6. Viktor Lowenfeld, *Creative and Mental Growth* (New York: Macmillan, 1947).

7. John Michael, "Studio Art Experience: The Heart of Art Education," *Art Education* 33, no. 2 (1980): 16.

8. Constance H. Anderson, "The Identity Crisis of the Art Educator: Artist? Teacher? Both?" *Art Education* 34, no. 4 (July 1981): 46, 45.

9. Barbara Hammer, "The Artist as Teacher: Problems and Experiments," *Boston University Journal of Education* 166, no. 2 (1984): 186.

10. Ralph A. Smith, "The Deschooling of Art Education: How It's Happening and What to Do About It," *Art Education* 33, no. 3 (March, 1980): 10.

11. J. W. Getzels and M. Csikszentmihalyi, "The Value-Orientations of Art Students as Determinants of Artistic Specialization and Creative Performance," *Studies in Art Education* 10, no. 1 (1968).

12. Harold Rosenberg, "The American Action Painters," *Art News*, December 1982, pp. 22-23.

13. Michael, "Studio and Experience."

14. Hans Hofmann, in *Theories of Modern Art*, ed. B. Chip (Berkeley: University of California Press, 1968), p. 564, from transcribed session with abstract artists in New York, 1951.

15. Chapman, *Instant Art*, p. 91.

16. Michael Day, "Child Art, School Art, and the Real World of Art," in *Art Education and Back to the Basics*, ed. S. Dobbs (Reston, Va: NAEA, 1980).

17. Michael Day, "The District That Could," in *Art History, Art Criticism, and Art Production* (Los Angeles: Rand, 1985), p. 35.

18. Lee S. Shulman, *Research on Teaching in the Arts: Review, Analysis, Critique* (East Lansing, Mich.: The Institute for Research on Teaching, May 1979). Shulman questions the artist-teacher model in favor of direct instruction, see pages 8-10.

19. W. Dwaine Greer, "Discipline-Based Art Education: Approaching Art as a Subject of Study," *Studies in Art Education* 25, no. 4 (1984); Getty Center for Education in the Arts, *Beyond Creating: The Place for Art in America's Schools* (Los Angeles: J. Paul Getty Trust, 1985).

RALPH A. SMITH

Eliltism

> Art can thrive only insofar as the practitioner or appreciator looks be-
> yond himself and assumes some standard for the thing made .... It is
> "popularized" art, art as a mere commodity, that in its lack of standards
> and its glorification of easy and stereotyped availability, is the enemy
> of distinction. And of *distinctions*.
>
> Robert Penn Warren[1]

Is it elitist in a maleficent sense to stress excellence in art and art education? Is it acceptable to the democratic egalitarian ethos to speak of things
eminently superior and good of their kind? Is it consistent with democratic values to recognize and reward excellent performance? I argue
that the pursuit of excellence is not elitist in any condemnatory sense
and that commitment to and praise of excellence are traditional democratic
virtues.

That it is still necessary to raise such questions attests to the perva-
siveness and intensity of the conviction that excellence and democratic
values are somehow incompatible. It is not, to be sure, a belief that is
consistently held. In many areas of life the ideal of excellence and the
recognition of excellent performance are taken for granted: artists and
writers earn awards for outstanding artistic, scholarly, and journalistic
accomplishment, exemplary athletes achieve well-deserved fame, and
talented entertainers receive the accolades of their peers and publics.
Yet when it comes to matters of education and schooling, and particularly arts education, derision often greets those who recommend that
the best that has been said, written, and created should be of central importance. It is strange, then, that many who are willing to accept the fact
of excellence and its recognition in many other areas of endeavor balk at
emphasizing excellence when it comes to the teaching of art. Misgivings suddenly surface about making value judgments and the appropriateness of admiring exceptional performance. To shore up their
doubts, skeptics resurrect old nostrums and marshall them against the
argument for high standards. Despite the debates over matters of taste

that are in fact going on everywhere, skeptics maintain that there can be no disputing of tastes. Oblivious to the truism that masterpieces from past ages often transcend their origins and speak to subsequent eras, anti-elitists declare that traditional art is irrelevant and has nothing to say to persons living today, especially to members of the working class and ethnic groups. There seems to be some apprehension that behind the promotion of excellence lurks a sinister intention to superimpose the values of one group on those of another, a fear that, to repeat, appears to be more pronounced among art teachers than among teachers of other subjects in the curriculum. It has even been suggested that emphasizing excellence in education is nothing more than a vile strategy to oppress minorities and eradicate student creativity. The following remarks lay to rest such unfounded fears.

Consider first some of the points anti-elitists make. Even if, they might say, discussion of artistic exemplars has something of the effect claimed for it, is it really necessary? Should not students have at least one opportunity in the school day to express themselves freely and make decisions on the basis of their individual interests, and should not this opportunity be provided by the art class?. . . .Is there not something to the notion that tastes cannot be disputed? Is it not true that experts disagree among themselves and often look foolish when works certified as originals are later found to be forgeries? Is the relevance of the past really a foregone conclusion? Should not student interests and the values and backgrounds of various groups figure somewhere in planning curricula and teaching? Such questions deserve to be considered carefully, but first some preliminary considerations are in order.

Although the notion of elitism is often opposed to that of populism, as in the phrase "elitism versus populism," I think it is more useful to seek an accord between them. . . .Consider elitism. Elitists are not necessarily hidebound traditionalists who instinctively turn away from popular, minority, and vanguard art. Nor do self-styled populists necessarily rule out the study of traditional masterpieces; their intention may be simply to include today's popular art in the range of works young people study in school. Neither do the differences between the elitist and the populist invariably turn on the importance each assigns to standards; populists may favor the development of critical standards but, again, in connection with the study of works they assume are of more immediate interest to students.[2] Certainly the distinction between elitism and populism cannot be based on what is popular. One has only to consider the interest the public increasingly shows in "the old masters." A more promising approach to the matter is to recognize what is valuable in both elitism and populism. In order to do this, it is necessary to make some distinctions.

To begin with, we are justified in condemning *closed elites* that permit membership solely on the basis of a person's wealth, class, or social standing. But not all elites are like this. There are *open elites* of demonstrated merit that control admission by insisting on adherence to professional standards. No advanced society can exist without such elites, and even less developed societies depend on them. The professions of medicine, law, and engineering are examples of open elites. No matter that professionals make mistakes from time to time, it is still for sound reasons that we prefer certified engineers to design the bridges we cross and licensed physicians to write our prescriptions. Nor do we want to dilute professional standards. Professional elites come under scrutiny only when they set arbitrary admission criteria, insist on unearned benefits, or tend toward unwarranted exclusiveness. If trust in the professions is somewhat guarded today it is because they too, like so many other sectors of society, are in need of remoralization, that is, a recentering of their efforts on social responsibility and human values.

If we think of elitism in terms of open elites and acknowledge their indispensability, then the term elitism loses many of its negative connotations. Having acknowledged the need for beneficent elites, we may proceed to a discussion of cultural elitism. Stuart Hampshire has stated that an elitist is a person who believes four propositions. The first is

> that there is a tradition of great, and of very good and interesting work, in each of the liberal arts, and that there is good reason to expect (with some qualifications) that these traditions are being prolonged into the future. Second, that at any time a minority of otherwise intelligent persons, including artists, are deeply interested in one, or more, of the arts, and have devoted a considerable part of their lives to their involvement with them, and to thinking about them. The judgments of artistic merit by such persons, who are not difficult to recognize, are the best guides to artistic merit that we have; and in fact they usually tend towards some consensus, with a periphery of expected disagreement. Third, that enjoyment of one or more of the arts is one of the most intense and most consoling enjoyments open to men, and also is the principal source of continued glory and of pride and of sense of unity for any city, nation, or empire. Fourth, very often, though not always, a good artist does not create his own public within his lifetime and needs support, if he is to work as well as he might.[3]

Little comment is needed on the first proposition: good work has been and is being done and so we pass to the second one. It points out that not only connoisseurs, art historians, and art critics constitute the elites that make distinctions of value among works of art, but artists also participate in the formation of critical opinion. The historical record abounds with their judgments of past and contemporary work; indeed, evaluations made by artists are often the harshest of all.[4] What is more, with some notable exceptions, the judgments of critical elites have been remarkably stable; they tend to withstand the test of time. There is now a core of classics and masterpieces that is largely accepted by those whose primary concern is with matters of culture; controversy is less about the core than about its periphery. And movement between periphery and core does not occur haphazardly; it is attended by intensive critical debate. Witness, for example, the controversy generated by the so-called canon wars.

It is difficult to disagree with Hampshire's third proposition: the experience of art at its best is one of the most vivid and often most consoling forms of human gratification. It is precisely this kind of gratification that the writer Rebecca West had in mind when she spoke of the intense emotion, deep and serene, that she felt when in the presence of artistic greatness. Such emotion, she wrote, "overflows the confines of the mind and becomes an important physical event," yet it "does not call to any action other than complete experience of it." Likewise, Kenneth Clark describes such satisfaction in terms of heightened perception, possession, self-discovery, and incandescence.[5]

Further, it is obvious that works of art not only dramatically illustrate cultural continuity, but are also symbols of civilization and expressions of national and civic pride. Nations and cities build and maintain museums and performing arts centers for more than purely aesthetic reasons. Next to its record of humanitarianism and compassion nothing reflects more positively and tellingly on an era than its cultural achievements and the attitude taken toward them. The identities of New York, Chicago, Los Angeles, and Washington, D.C. are as dependent on their cities' museums, works of public art, symphony orchestras, and ballet companies as they are on their financial districts and sports facilities.

It is a popular misconception, moreover, that elitists yearn only for the art of past golden eras and turn their backs on contemporary art. As their writings attest, cultural elitists of the sort Hampshire talks about easily traverse cultural spaces and periods. "Style and Medium in the Motion Pictures" by Erwin Panofsky, a distinguished art historian, is one of the most anthologized essays on film. William Arrowsmith, a classical scholar, discovers value in both Homer's *Iliad* and Alain Resnais's film *Hiroshima, mon Armour*, believing the latter to be an unconscious imitation of the ancient work. Meyer Schapiro finds something important to remark in both Romanesque sculpture and modern painting. Leo Steinberg is fascinated with the perplexities not only of Michelangelo's but also Jasper Johns's work. Charles Jencks, the British architect, theorist, and critic, defines postmodernism as the intermingling of modernism with traditional ideas of Western humanism. And if, like Hampshire and Robert Penn Warren, we include artists among the elitists, we discover numerous instances of painters and sculptors who looked for inspiration and artistic challenges to the masters of the past: Cézanne who wanted to redo Poussin in the presence of nature; Picasso who was intrigued by the relations of reality and illusion in the art of Velázquez; Frank Stella who became preoccupied with the spatial volumes of Correggio, and so forth.[6] In short, the elitist's supposed domination by the dead hand of the past is a myth. Artists and others undertake journeys into the past not only for the purpose of enjoying the intrinsic values of the travels themselves but also for receiving help with understanding contemporary problems. Consequently we should not regard scholarship and artistic inquiry of this kind with suspicion but should instead discover ways to impart its insights to the young.

Elitists therefore are correct in setting store by critical judgment and believing that it is proper for tastes not only to be disputed but to be cultivated as well. That tastes differ and are contested is obvious; at issue is the proposition that assertions made in behalf of one's taste should be subject to rational scrutiny.[7] The proposition is, I think, defensible; persons often welcome help in thinking about their preferences and upon reflection may well decide to alter their opinions, and subsequently their tastes. Hampshire even goes so far as to say that to treat people as if they already know what they want or ought to learn is in effect to treat them as less than human. Thus, our reticence about disclosing what we believe valuable is a disservice to the young, and will not help them overcome their indecisiveness. Learning to appreciate the excellence of art is, after all, part of learning to become self-sufficient in the cultural domain. That domain, we should remember, consists of a cultural heritage that, being both and conservative and revolutionary, contains not only the fruits of systems of thought and creativity, but also the critical tools for appraising these fruits. Young people armed with the standards of judgment and the perspectives available in the cultural heritage may well be less susceptible to the stereotypes of pseudo-art and better able to demand better art. Certainly there can be no doubt that the standard of taste prevailing in a society is important for cultural progress for, by determining what people will tend to appreciate, it will also affect what artists create. William Faulkner once remarked that a low level of the writing produced in a society may not be entirely the fault of writers and that literature may not improve until readers do. He therefore urges us to be concerned about the health of that sector of the cultural environment that is composed of the general ability and skill of readers.[8] Does not the same kind of thinking apply to the quality of visual art produced?

The elitist says that the enjoyment of excellent art is one of the higher forms of human enjoyment, not necessarily *the* highest, but one that nonetheless ranks importantly among the features of the good life. The elitist is also correct in this belief. If the pursuit of happiness is a democratic right, then providing the young with opportunities to appreciate art for its capacity to induce worthwhile experience is hardly undemocratic. Failing to acquaint the young with some of humankind's finest achievements would be irresponsible.

In summary, nothing in Hampshire's four propositions suggests that elitism is necessarily maleficent. Nothing implies that elitists hold themselves socially superior or are insensitive to minority or ethnic art, contemptuous of popular culture or contemporary art, or antidemocratic. Certainly there is no indication that access to excellence and the cultural heritage should be restricted to certain groups or that a taste for the best cannot be acquired by people from all walks of life. Much of the criticism leveled at elitism therefore does not apply to it. While it is possible to speak of harmful, undemocratic elitism, it is *beneficent* elitism that Hampshire characterizes—an elitism that prizes knowledge of the cultural tradition, the value of cultural continuity, acts of critical judgment, and excellence. It would be an exceedingly crimped view of human nature that asserted such values are beyond the ken of the large majority of persons.

Notes

1. Robert Penn Warren, *Democracy and Poetry* (Cambridge: Harvard University Press, 1975), 85-86.

2. I believe this is the position of Vincent Lanier. See his "Aesthetic Literacy as the Product of Art Education," in *The Product of a Process*. Selection of papers presented at the 24th INSEA World Congress (Amsterdam: "De Trommel," 1981), pp. 115-21.

3. Stuart Hampshire, "Private Pleasures and the Public Purse," a review of Janet Minahan's *The Nationalization of Culture* (New York: New York University Press, 1977), *Times Literary Supplement*, 13 May 1977, 579.

4. In *Other Criteria* (New York: Oxford University Press, 1972), Leo Steinberg writes: "No critic, no outraged bouregois, matches an artist's passion in repudiation" (p. 4).

5. Rebecca West, *The Strange Necessity* (London: Johnathan Cape, 1928), 57, and Kenneth Clark, *Moments of Vision* (London: John Murray, 1981), 7. Both West's and Clark's views are discussed in Albert William Levi and R. A. Smith, *Art Education: A Critical Necessity* (Urbana: University of Illinois Press, 1991), pp. 23-25.

6. See, e.g., Erwin Panofsky, "Style and Medium in the Motion Pictures," in *Film Theory and Criticism*, 2d ed., Gerald Mast and Marshall Cohen (New York: Oxford University Press, 1979); William Arrowsmith, "Film as Educator," in *Aesthetics and Problems of Education*, ed. R. A. Smith (Chicago: Rand McNally, 1966); Meyer Schapiro, *Romanesque Art: Selected Papers* (New York: George Braziller, 1977) and *Modern Art: 19th and 20th Centuries* (New York: George Braziller, 1978); Leo Steinberg, *Jasper Johns* (New York: George Wittenborn, 1963), and *Michelangelo's Last Paintings* (New York: Oxford University Press, 1975); Charles Jencks, *Post-Modernism: The New Classicism in Art and Architecture* (New York: Rizzoli, 1987); Meyer Schapiro, *Cézanne* (New York: Harry N. Abrams, 1952); Susan Galassi, "The Arnheim Connection: *Guernica* and *Las Meninas*," *The Journal of Aesthetic Education* 27, no. 4 (Winter 1993): 45-56 (a special issue on Arnheim's work); Frank Stella, *Working Space* (Cambridge: Harvard University Press, 1986), to mention but a few examples of the point at issue.

7. An instructive discussion on this point is Monroe C. Beardsley's "Tastes Can Be Disputed," in *Classic Philosophical Questions*, 3d ed., ed. James A. Gould (Columbus: Charles E. Merrill, 1979).

8. Faulkner's remarks are referred to by Philip K. Jason in "The University as Patron of Literature: The Balch Program of Virginia," *Journal of General Education* 34, no. 3 (1983): 178.

GEORGIA COLLINS AND RENEE SANDELL

Informing the Promise of DBAE: Remember the Women, Children, and Other Folk

To anticipate the costs of DBAE's conditional promise from a feminist point of view, it is helpful to begin with a graphic comparison of the triangular paradigm often used to describe three areas of legitimate educational concern: the child, society, and subject. In the equilateral triangle of Figure 1: "Paradigm for Identifying Balanced Educational Emphasis," art education is surrounded by its balanced educational considerations: child-centered, society-centered, and subject-centered concerns. If we compare the shape of art education in Figure 1 to the shape of art education as envisioned by the proponents of DBAE in Figure 2:

Figure 1. Paradigm for Identifying Balanced Educational Emphasis (adapted from Elliot W. Eisner, *Educating Artistic Vision*, New York: The MacMillan Company, 1972, p. 58).

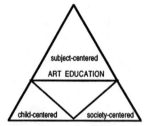

Figure 2. An Interpretation of DBAE's Approach to Educational Emphasis in Art Education.

"An Interpretation of DBAE's Approach to Educational Emphasis in Art Education," we can see a dramatic flattening of art education, produced by overemphasis of subject-centered concerns. As a simple illustration of the major condition of the DBAE promise, this comparison should call our attention to a diminished concern for child and society and an exaggerated concern for subject in DBAE's proposals for increasing the curricular status of art education. If DBAE is trying to correct for an overemphasis on feminine-identified concern for the child in current art educational practice, the proposed correction does not call for a balance between the three basic educational concerns, nor does it call for their pluralistic enlargement (Collins & Sandell, 1984, p. 1973). It would in effect replace one distorting educational emphasis with another. The reduction of child- and society-centered concerns decreases their equalized connection with the subject, implying a defeminization and even a potential dehumanization of art education, which is what happens when the needs of the individual and society are not attended to.

It is important to note that many American schools have tried to maintain a semblance of balance between educational concerns by asking art education to attend to the nurturance of the child and the needs of the school community (if not the larger society), to provide a counterweight within the general curriculum to that heavy subject-centeredness found in the higher-status subjects that DBAE would emulate. Indeed, the one thing that has redeemed art in its marginal curricular status has been the opportunity it has provided to disciplinary concerns. One anticipated side effect of extending a subject-matter emphasis to art education might well be that the educational needs of child and society will have to go begging.

DBAE's emphasis on subject-centered concerns finds is precedent in the structure of the disciplines movement of 20 years ago (Clark, Day, & Greer, 1987; Mason, 1972). Analyses of the conditions that tended to undermine the educational effectiveness of this earlier effort at discipline-based education in other subjects include as negative factors a neglect of child- and society-centered concerns (Clark, Day, & Greer, 1987, pp. 131-132). There is reason, then, to anticipate that even in its own terms, the educational effectiveness of DBAE might be ironically diminished because of its preoccupation with the less frivolous or more serious study of the concepts and intellectual structures of art as a discipline (Efland, 1988).

Although individual educators and even school districts will tend to emphasize one or the other of the three basic orientations to educational values (that is, the child, the society, or the subject), the uniform distortion of the paradigm proposed by DBAE for all art teaching in America's public schools short-circuits the safety mechanism built into the equilateral tripartite of educational concerns. The equality of educational value assigned to each of these areas in the traditional paradigm allows for the monitoring and modification over time of one set of concerns by the other two. If, for example, art education's subject-centered concerns were at some point confined to only those that could find precedent in an elitist art tradition, competing educational concerns related to the child and/or the society would provide the art teacher with a ready and educationally relevant basis for a critique and revision of these narrowly prescribed subject-centered concerns. DBAE's overweening focus on subject-centered education should serve as a warning that, as proposed, this approach to art education is neither likely to recognize nor correct for any social or psychological injustices or irregularities within those art professions and disciplines that they assume comprise the subject of art.

Forgotten Identity

If the conditions of DBAE's promise do not provide for the enlargement of all three bases of educational concern, they do involve a broadening of the definition of the subject upon which art educational concern is to be centered. In addition to art production as exemplified by the professional artist, DBAE will require the teaching of responses to art as exemplified by professional art historians, art critics, and aestheticians. Not surprisingly, the art world has reacted positively to the DBAE proposal, as reflected in recent art media coverage about developments in art education (Brown, 1988; Esterow, 1987). Potentially, the DBAE shift away from child- to discipline-centered concerns could produce a larger, better-informed art audience ready to support museums, buy art, and respect the work of professional artists, art historians, art critics, and aestheticians. If DBAE proponents argue that the by-products of informed audienceship will enhance the quality of life for individuals and society, the concerns of the art world are more parochial. The quality of life as influenced by nonmainstream art production and nonprofessional levels of art appreciation has not been a major concern of mainstream art professions and institutions. These aspects of life, on the other hand, have been a defining concern of that art profession pointedly omitted by DAE as a legitimizing source for the content of art education, that is to say, the profession of art education itself. Unidentified as a source of art content by the DBAE model, the traditional concerns of art educators for child and society as well as for art are therefore twice banished from the DBAE approach to art education.

By excluding art education from its list of exemplary art professions, DBAE reinforces the second-class status of this already highly feminine-identified art profession (Collins & Sandell, 1984, pp. 31-33), even while promising to increase the status of the subject they are to teach. Rather than ratifying the independence and expertise of the art educator, under the DBAE plan art teachers are slated to play out the more negative aspects of the feminine role by becoming more dependent on experts form other art disciplines for the prescribed ideology and content of the art curriculum. There is a painfully familiar irony in the DBAE effort to defeminize art education by divesting the art teacher of all but the most debilitating aspects of the feminine role. One result we might anticipate from DBAE's circumscription of the art teacher's professional concerns and competence is a less-than-whole-hearted compliance on the part of independently minded art teachers who "know their kids." Once again, these professionals may find their only compensation in pursuing low-profile, idiosyncratic approaches to teaching art behind the closed classroom door (Grumet, 1988).

Forgotten Content

In current practice, the content of art education has typically been selected by the teacher in response to the perceived life interests, abilities, and expressive needs of the child and the teacher's understanding of art and its role in the school, larger society, and human cultures. DBAE proposes to defeminize both the content of art education and the intuitive methods by which that content has been determined. To increase the curricular status of art, DBAE declares that the selection, if not the teaching, of art content must be placed in the hands of curriculum designers or district-wide committees who will base this content on concepts, values, and skills exemplified and legitimized by adult professionals in studio art, art criticism, art history, and aesthetics. The proponents of DBAE have failed to acknowledge, however, the degree to which these mainstream art professions have been and continue to be biased with regard to gender, class, racial, and ethnic art activities and values. The discipline of art history, for example, must be recognized as "A component of cultural hegemony maintaining and reproducing diminutive social relations through what it studies and teaches and what it omits or marginalizes, and through how it defines what history is, what art is, and who and what the artist is" (Pollock, 1983, p. 40). Although extensive critiques of these biases have been mounted by socially concerned professionals practicing within these and other disciplines, DBAE's global descriptions of content drawn from the exemplary practice of these professions have not included a keen awareness of these critiques nor provided for corrections of bias. As Hamblen (1987) pointed out in her article, "An Examination of Discipline-Based Art Education Issues," "In technique, focus, interpretation, and final history, Linda Nochlin is an art historian prototype vastly different from H. W. Janson." Furthermore, an "accomplished folk artist could be as worthy a prototype as an artist whose work is discussed in *Art News*" (p. 71). Even if only by default, the narrow, socially and psychologically unresponsive delimitation of art's content by DBAE ignores the progressive separation of art from life in western culture and fails to address the need for greater human relevance and social responsibility in mainstream art and its related professions. In its concern to elevate the content of art by basing it on mainstream models, DBAE does not recognize how even art's mainstream might be revitalized by attending to the cultural roots and life experiences of our students and the particular society in which they live or would like to live.

Like a strong current, the promise of DBAE has propelled the field of art education into motion and has already altered its sense of direction. To better navigate our course (before we sail off into the promising sunset), we have attempted to raise consciousness with regard to forgotten equity concerns that address considerations, identity, and content of the field of art education. Informing the promise of DBAE involves mindfully addressing these neglected areas as well as the notion that discipline itself may not be a sufficient base for art education or any other subject taught in the public schools. A realistic and positive self-concept of the field of art education, that is, trying to be better at what we are instead of what we are not, strengthens our identity. This occurs when we remember and respect our roots as we attempt to expand our domain. Further, our field is enhanced by its collaboration with other arts disciplines in efforts to promote equity in art and society. Rather than applying a few corrective revisions to the DBAE promise for improved curricular status, we are asking for a balanced-concern model for art education. The latter includes acceptance of what we have been and would allow for continuous modifications of art education—indeed of art itself—by a "feminine" responsiveness to the needs of child and society (ranging from micro to macro) for greater artistic relevance. Without this, the current trend toward defeminized, nonstudio approaches to art learning could transform the efforts of the field to resemble humanities education for cultural literacy rather than art education for visual literacy (Sandell, 1988). In embracing the DBAE or any other enticing promise, the field of art education must strive to sail beyond its boundaries without going off its navigational course and disappearing out of sight.

Notes

Beyond creating: The place for art in America's schools. (1985). Los Angeles: The J. Paul Getty Trust.

Brown, J. C. (1988, January). Art education flunks out. *Artnews, 87,* 190.

Clark, G. A., Day, M. D., & Greer, D. W. (1987). Discipline-based art education: Becoming students of art. *Journal of Aesthetic Education, 21 (2).*

Collins, G. (1979). Women and art: The problem of status. *Studies in Art Education, 21(1),* 57-64.

Collins, G., & Sandell, R. (1984). *Women, art, and education.* Reston, VA: National Art Education Association.

Efland, A. (1988). How art became a discipline: Looking at our recent history. *Studies in Art Education, 29(3),* 262-274.

Eisner, E. W. (1972). *Educating artistic vision.* New York: MacMillan.

Eisner, E. W. (1987). *The role of discipline-based art education in America's schools.* Los Angeles: The Getty Center for Education in the Arts.

Esterow, M. (1987, April). Changing the look of art education. *Artnews, 86,* 112-113.

Ewens, T. (1988, March/April). In art education, more DBAE equals less art. A reprint from *Design for Arts in Education.*

Garrard, M. (1976). Of men, women, and art. *Art Journal, 35 (4),* 324-329.

Grumet, M. R. (1988). *Bitter milk: Women and teaching.* Amherst: University of Massachusetts Press.

Hamblen, K. (1987). An examination of discipline-based art education issues. *Studies in Art Education,28 (2)* 68-78.

Huber, B. W. (1987). What does feminism have to offer DBAE? *Art Education,* 40 (3), 36-41.

Mason, R. E. (1972). *Contemporary educational theory.* New York: David McKay.

Pollock, G. (1983). Women, art, and ideology: Questions for feminist art historians. *Women's Art Journal,* 39-40.

Sandell, R. (1988, June). *DBAE: From a teacher's point of view.* Paper presented at seminar on DBAE at University of Maryland, College Park, Maryland, 1988.

Wayne, J. (1974). The male artist as stereotypical female. *Arts in Society, 2* (1), 107-113.

H. Gene Blocker

Art Education and Postmodernism

For most of us, postmodernisms are both attractive and disturbing. On the one hand, many of the teachers we talk with agree that contemporary art is eclectic, pluralistic, and not moving in a single direction. They welcome the opening of the art world and of art education to disenfranchised traditions and groups and the richness they bring. And they approve an emphasis on what makes art most meaningful to each student in our classes. Art traditions have often been too elitist, too exclusive, and too remote from students' experience. Art educators have often paid little attention to their students' interpretations and to the connections the students make between the artworks they study and the concrete realities of their lives.

On the other hand, however, most of us want to retain the idea of art traditions that shape the meanings of works and are important for students to understand. It seems hard to deny that there are established conventions and expectations of art that help one make sense of many individual works and that therefore students should know them. And most of us think that art tells us something about ourselves individually and collectively and want our students to learn something of its insights. In short, we want *both* for our students to approach art individually and to love it freely *and* also to understand art and to learn what is valuable in it. The problem for most of us, therefore, is not whether to accept modernism or postmodernism, but how to strike the right balance between those approaches and to take from them what is most valuable to us.

When new movements challenge established positions, it often happens that initially the genuine differences are exaggerated. There is a tendency for those who embrace new positions to be more concerned with dissociating themselves from the old views than with explaining the new. This contributes to a sense of an unbridgeable gulf between the two. Each side feels that its views are simplified and caricatured by the other and genuine debate becomes difficult. Certainly, there has been plenty of confrontational writing in the postmodernist debates, writing oriented more to attacking and defending than to achieving clearer understandings. But when we look at the situation rather generally, it appears that many of the differences between modernism and postmodernism are in fact not unbridgeable. When we look at the work of actual modernists we see many anticipations of postmodernism and it seems that the more sophisticated modernists have been evolving for years in that direction. And when we look at the actual analyses of artworks by postmodernists we see that they retain some very traditional elements of modernist analysis.

An important example has to do with the postmodernist denial that there is a real (i.e., absolute) difference between facts and interpretations. This is often presented by postmodernists as a black and white issue. But we can happily accept this denial without abandoning the *relative* use of the distinction as a heuristic device. That is in fact what most of us do in our ordinary affairs. We speak in one context about "facts" that are given various "interpretations" and yet understand that in another context those same facts might be treated as interpretations. For example, it may be a "fact" that Jones committed suicide by jumping out of a fifteen-story window, and we look for interpretations of the fact; why did he do it? Only if the fact is later called into question by new evidence will we treat it as an interpretation. Perhaps new evidence suggests he may have been murdered. Then the fact is that he fell from a fifteen-story window, and the interpretive question is whether he was murdered or committed suicide. In this relative use of the distinction, a fact is simply what is not disputed by a group of people at a particular time and an interpretation is what is disputed. Understood in this way, it is still a very useful distinction, though not an absolute one, because it enables us to discuss issues in a reasonable way. We can discuss the adequacy of particular interpretations just because we can, at least temporarily, treat other features of the case as facts. When we interpret an artwork, it is usually possible to establish some facts about it. That is to say, at any given time there are usually some reasonably established conventions and expectations that help us reach a range of agreements about the work and these agreements help us to identify and discuss the issues on which we don't agree. If there were no "facts" at all to begin with, it is hard to see how we could discuss anything at all.

The same sort of point can be made about the claim that we have no direct knowledge of reality and that all knowledge involves a subjective and linguistically mediated point of view. This also is often presented as an all-or-nothing issue. But in fact we can regard the distinction between reality and appearance as useful and even as necessary, even though it is not ultimate. We call things real when we are relatively sure we know what they are; we call them appearances when we are unsure. Suppose we disagree who that person is standing over there on the corner. I say it is Mary; you say it is Taiwo. We approach more closely and see that it is Taiwo. I was "wrong," you were right. Relative to the situation, we can distinguish reality from appearance and truth from falsity, although the distinction is not absolute if that means that it removes all possibility of error. Later it may turn out that it was Taiwo's twin sister, or a holograph of Taiwo, or an artwork by Duane Hanson. But if we do find out that one of these latter possibilities is the case, it will be because we have new evidence, and then in the context of that evidence we will again be able to distinguish the reality from appearance, though again not without possibility of error. The point is that, so long as we do not call the same thing both true and false *in the same context*, it is useful to distinguish truth from falsity and reality from appearance. We can talk with each other about the same work, or tradition, or culture. This is so, even if at the same time we know that interpretations of the work, tradition, or culture, have varied over the centuries and that we have no knowledge of it except through these interpretations. In short, the distinction between reality and appearance is useful, though not ultimate, because it enables us to compare interpretations and to learn from their variety. Modernists and some postmodernists can agree on this.

And finally, the same sort of point seems to apply to the question of objectivity. It is true that no knowledge is completely free of subjective bias and all knowledge must be interpreted through particular conceptual frameworks that embody particular interests. But it is still useful to distinguish between objectivity and bias, between history and propaganda. We can today recognize biases in the history of art that only recently were unchallenged: the Eurocentric bias, for example, or the male bias. It is because of arguments that we can recognize these biases. Multiculturalism and feminism are not merely advertising campaigns but have objective arguments to make; and we have not merely changed our minds but have come to see that we really did have a bias. These arguments are based on the assumption that we can distinguish between bias and objectivity and they have been successful because we can recognize the distinction. But again this does not mean that we assume that we now are operating in a *fully* objective fashion and have no more biases that we are yet unaware of. We assume only that we are more objective, relatively, now that we have recognized some of our biases. In this way, we can make good sense of the relative, though not ultimate, use of the distinction between objectivity and bias.

The conclusion is that we should learn from postmodernisms a measure of modesty about our claims and a sense of the historical character of our understanding. They can help us be more aware of power and political relations than we were. At the same time we should be skeptical of the more extreme claims about the failure of basic distinctions and should continue to do what makes sense to us, not absolutely in all times and places but in our own time and place. Art traditions and conventions have elements of continuity as well as of change, and it is the former that allows us to make sense of the latter. Teaching has always been the attempt to pass on our best understanding of the present so that our students will make sense of the future. Postmodernism shows us how important and difficult that task has become.

Reading Suggestions for Part Six

Blandy, Doug, and Kristin G. Congdon, eds. *Art in a Democracy*. New York: Teachers College Press, 1987.

Burton, Judith, Arlene Bederman, and Peter London, eds. *Beyond DBAE: The Case for Multiple Visions of DBAE*. North Dartmouth: Art Education Department, Southeastern Massachusetts University, 1988.

Getty Center for Education in the Arts. *Issues in Discipline-Based Art Education: Strengthening the Stance, Extending the Horizons*. Los Angeles: Getty Center for Education in the Arts, 1987. Seminar proceedings.

Getty Center for Education in the Arts. *Inheriting the Theory: New Voices and Multiple Perspectives*. Los Angeles: Getty Center for Education in the Arts, 1990. Seminar proceedings.

Getty Center for Education in the Arts. *Discipline-Based Art Education and Cultural Diversity*. Santa Monica: Getty Center for Education in the Arts, 1993. Seminar proceedings.

Anderson, Albert A. "Issues in Art Education: Discipline-Based Art Education." *American Craft* 52, no. 2 (1992): 68-69.

Arnstine, Donald. "Art, Aesthetics, and the Pitfalls of Discipline-Based Art Education." *Educational Theory* 40, no. 4 (1990): 415-22.

Broudy, Harry S. "DBAE: Complaints, Reminiscences, and Response." *Educational Theory* 40, no. 4 (1990): 431-35.

Burton, Judith M. "The Arts in School Reform: Other Conversations." *Teachers College Record* 95, no. 4 (1994): 477-93.

Chalmers, F. Graeme. "Beyond Current Conceptions of Discipline-Based Art Education." *Art Education* 40, no. 5 (1987): 58-61.

Clark, Gilbert. "Critics, Criticism, and the Evolution of DBAE." *Visual Arts Research*, 23, no. 2 (1997): 12-18.

Ecker, David. "The Disciplines of Multicultural Art Education." In *Discipline in Art Education: An Interdisciplinary Symposium*, ed. Thomas Ewens. Providence: Rhode Island School of Design, 1986, 81-88.

Eisner, Elliot W. "Discipline-Based Art Education: Conceptions and Misconceptions." *Educational Theory* 40, no. 4 (1990): 423-30.

Garber, Elizabeth. "Implications of Feminist Art Criticism for Art Education." *Studies in Art Education* 32, no. 1 (1990): 17-26.

Hagaman, Sally. "Feminist Inquiry in Art History, Art Criticism, and Aesthetics: An Overview for Art Education." *Studies in Art Education* 32, no. 1 (1990): 27-35.

Hamblen, Karen. "An Examination of Discipline-Based Art Education Issues." *Studies in Art Education* 28, no. 2 (1987): 68-78.

Hamblen, Karen. "Approaches to Aesthetics in Art Education: A Critical Theory Perspective." *Studies in Art Education* 29, no. 2 (1988): 81-90.

Hart, Lynn M. "Aesthetic Pluralism and Multicultural Art Education." *Studies in Art Education* 32, no. 3 (1991): 145-59.

Hicks, Laurie E. "A Feminist Analysis of Empowerment and Community in Art Education." *Studies in Art Education* 32, no. 1 (1990): 36-46.

Holt, David K. "Post-Modernism vs. High Modernism: The Relationships of DBAE and Its Critics." *Art Education* 43, no. 2 (1990): 42-46.

Johnson, Nancy R. "DBAE and Cultural Relationships." *Journal of Multicultural and Cross-cultural Research in Art Education* 6, no. 1 (1988): 15-25.

Lanier, Vincent. "Discipline-Based Art Education: Three Issues." *Studies in Art Education* 26, no. 4 (1985): 253-56.

Lovano-Kerr, Jessie. "Cultural Pluralism and DBAE: An Issue (Fall 1988) Revisited." *Journal of Multicultural and Cross-cultural Research in Art Education* 8, no. 1 (1990): 61-71.

MacGregor, Ronald N. "Post-Modernism, Art Educators, and Art Education." ERIC: ART. Bloomington: Social Studies Development Center, Indiana University, 1992.

Maquet, Jacques. "Cross-cultural Understanding of Visual Objects: Three Approaches." In *Inheriting the Theory: New Voices and Multiple Perspectives*. Los Angeles: Getty Center for Education in the Arts, 1990, 23-24. Seminar Summary of remarks.

McFee, June. "Art and Society." In *Issues in Discipline-Based Art Education: Strengthening the Stance, Extending the Horizons*. Los Angeles: Getty Center for Education in the Arts, 1988, 104-112.

Ravitch, Diane. "Multiculturalism: E Pluribus Plures." *The American Scholar* 59 (Summer 1990): 337-54.

Schlesinger, Arthur J. *The Disuniting of America*. New York: Norton, 1992.

Silverman, Ronald. "The Egalitarianism of Discipline-Based Art Education." *Art Education* 41, no. 2 (1988): 13-18.

PART SEVEN

Museums and Museum Education

Introduction

The Getty Trust's commitment to art museums and education is well known. Indeed, the Trust now maintains two art museums: one devoted to ancient art and another that is part of the new Getty Center. It is not surprising then that the support of art museum education and the uses of art museums by schools have been priorities of the Getty's educational efforts. The first two selections reprinted here, by Harold Osborne and Albert William Levi, are from a Getty-subsidized special issue of *The Journal of Aesthetic Education* (Summer 1985). Both discuss the functions of art museums and the various ways collections can be arranged and exhibitions displayed. Concentrating on the aesthetic functions of museums, Osborne mentions those of patronage, which is a precondition for continual artistic production and, through it, the direction of public taste. But the chief aesthetic function of museums, he believes, is to provide occasions for aesthetic experiences, which he characterizes as exercises of a particular skill in the sphere of percipience that extends perceptive powers and yields aesthetic enjoyment. Although acknowledging the importance of knowledge about art, he cautions against the tendency of museums to provide excessive information that could negatively affect the cultivation of percipience. Levi likewise addresses the art museum as an instrument in the task of aesthetic education. The museum in this regard may be seen as a place for the contemplation of masterpieces, an agency of cultural history through featuring period rooms, an adjunct to the history of art through exhibits arranged by period and style, and a promoter of art's humanizing potential within the framework of humanistic or liberal education, that is, an education that understands art in terms of communication (art as a language), continuity (art history), and criticism (philosophy of art).

    Drawing on a study supported by the Getty to discover the dynamics of aesthetic experiences in museum settings, Mihaly Csikszentmihalyi defines aesthetic experience in terms of Monroe C. Beardsley's symptoms of the aesthetic (object directedness, felt freedom, detached affect, active discovery, and wholeness) and construes aesthetic experience as a species of "flow experience," instances of which he describes. Both types of experience, he believes, come about through the meshing of specific challenges and skills. But while he finds similarities between the aesthetic experiences of museum professionals and those extracted from visitor reports in a Getty summary of museum focus groups, he mentions a list of obstacles that impede the aesthetic experiences of museum visitors. He further cautions that without a theory of aesthetic experience, research will prove less useful in systematic experimentation, correction, and improvement.

Museum studies cover a wide range of topics that cannot be surveyed here but that may be followed in the suggestions for reading. Certainly the impact of DBAE on museum education is evident in these studies, several of which took their lead from the assessment of museum-educational policies and practices conducted for the Getty Center by Elliot W. Eisner and Stephen Mark Dobbs, for example, Betty Lou Williams's follow-up study of changes in museum-school partnerships. Issues and difficulties involved in evaluating the effectiveness of museum educational programs are discussed by Elizabeth Vallance. She refers not merely to explicitly articulated programs but also to the indirect effects of the forms and contexts of installations. Difficulties of assessment range from identifying measures of success, understanding audiences, and delayed effects of museum experiences to uncertainty about museum education jobs, the tendency of researchers to inflate claims of success, and the inappropriateness of instruments to measure different kinds of effects.

HAROLD OSBORNE

Museums and their Functions

Corresponding to the different categories of collection are different attitudes of interest in the public whom the museums serve—and this must be a major consideration in all museum planning. By and large, the concern of the public who visit the historical and ethnological museums is *knowledge*: knowledge of the history and multiplicity of mankind's cultural tradition. The interest of those who use the aesthetic category of museums is *appreciation*, a difficult concept to define but one for which knowledge is at the most incidental, knowledge for its own sake inapposite. The aesthetic appreciation of works of art is not limited by time, place, or nationality. It embraces the present and the past, from Palaeolithic cave drawings to conceptual art, productions of all peoples and cultures. Of course these two attitudes of interest overlap as the collections in museums overlap. Ethnological collections, historical collections, collections of fine craftsmanship, contain objects which invite and reward aesthetic attention. And collections selected by aesthetic standards may reward students of the history of ideas, the sociology of culture or—that young and dangerous discipline—the history of art.

In the rest of this essay I shall concentrate on the museums organized on aesthetic principles and on two major functions of these.

Certainly it is a major function of museums to preserve the artistic heritage of mankind and to make it widely available. This is done both by building up permanent collections and by arranging temporary loan exhibitions devoted to the work of one artist, one period, or one school. Such assemblages provide a context within which individual works can be appreciated more fully. Learned catalogues and art historical information generally can be helpful or can defeat the purpose which they should serve. If properly used, information *about* works of art can enrich their contemplation; but there is a danger lest it encourage the very general tendency to substitute the acquisition of information for the art of appreciation. For aesthetic awareness, which is appreciation, is not a matter of just opening the eyes and seeing the object upon which attention is directed as one sees the gallery appurtenances and the clothes of other visitors. It is a skill which needs to be cultivated and developed, as does any other skill . . . . And this is the more difficult because it runs counter to our normal way of perceiving the world around us. In ordinary life we look at the world in order to know, to discriminate our visual impressions into things and their relations to each other. In the contemplation of fine art we look for the sake of looking. In the words of Monroe C. Beardsley, we direct attention on the "formal unity and/or the regional qualities of a complex whole." This way of looking, when directed upon a suitable object such as a work of art, induces an intensification and enrichment of the activity of perception itself, and it is in that that aesthetic enjoyment resides. A certain amount of learning properly used (e.g., information about different modes of perspective in different ages and styles) can help to direct and deepen this mode of seeing. But when information takes the place of aesthetic observation it encourages the very natural tendency to look at works of art in the same manner that we look at the environment in daily life. It is surely a function of museum directors to help and encourage their public to develop the skill of aesthetic vision, to see holistically and intensify their perceptiveness of expressive qualities in the artworks to which they are exposed, to contemplate art objects as denizens of a new world of their own creating rather than things existing on the same footing as others in the practical world of everyday life. It is a job which museums do indifferently well. The natural addiction of museums and their directors to the recent science of art history encourages a contrary tendency and falls in line with the natural tendency of the untrained public to bring with them into the gallery their spontaneous habits of analytical and discriminative seeing as in practical life. It is an occupational hazard of art historians that they may know all there is to know about a work of art, all that anyone else has ever said about it, and yet be unable to contemplate it aesthetically as a work of art. Fortunately not all art historians fall into this trap. But too often one can see innocent members of the public traversing the rooms of a gallery with machines glued to their ears pouring art historical information about works which they ought rather to be seeing.

Today we should be able to look to the museums—where else?—not only to combat the insidious substitution of learning *about* for cultivated aesthetic awareness *of*, but also to neutralize the pernicious influence of reproduction. Reproductions can be useful instruments for the furtherance of learning about visual art and in some cases can aid in reviving the memory of what has been seen. In the past, when steel engravings "after" this or that work were the only form of reproduction available, there was little temptation to use them improperly. But the very excellence of modern reproductive techniques blinds people to their shortcomings and makes many people insensitive to the impoverishment and distortion they inevitably produce when used as objects of aesthetic contemplation in their own right. Sculpture in the round must not only be seen from every point of view; it must be seen as *solid*, not merely a collection of contours, in a way which photographs are unable to achieve. Even when matched with the help of the finest computers, colors formed from the mixing of a limited number of printer's dyes inevitably in most cases distort the qualities of oil or gouache colors. Even the reduction of a reproduction to the size of a book page can change what in the original is a harmonious interplay of light and shaded color into garishness and blatancy, or in the attempt to avoid that must underemphasize the vividness and precision of interaction. Yet many people nowadays obtain their introduction to the visual arts through book illustrations, decorate their homes with reproductions, and become so habituated to reproductions that they are unaware of the meager and miserable substitute they afford. Not a few people are even better able to look at the reproduction than the real thing. I remember that I once gave dinner to a cultivated and intelligent gentleman whose professional occupation was not unconnected with the furtherance of interest in the arts in America. He had spent the afternoon at the National Gallery in London, had been disappointed with the Vermeers he saw there (not so striking as he had obviously expected), but had bought reproductions of them at the museum shop as he went out. Museum men are not entirely free from reproach in this matter—they have indeed a bent toward art historical learning as well as showmanship—and the lavishly illustrated catalogues produced by them are, to speak most kindly, often ambiguous as to the purposes they are designed to serve. The proper use of reproductions is one of the most delicate and tricky problems today, and we look in vain to the museum men for guidance.

The second major function of museums today should be patronage and, as has been said above, patronage is linked to the direction of taste. Changed social conditions have eliminated or enormously reduced the sources of patronage which were active in the past. But without enlightened patronage, art production must ossify or cease. When every town has its own flourishing art school, we are producing far more would-be artists than society can possibly absorb. Without enlightened and farsighted direction of taste, the few who are capable of great things must sink into oblivion with the rest. The meager opportunities offered by industry and so forth cannot select the potentially great. The enormous sums which are spent at art auctions, the exaggerated prices at which acknowledged masterpieces change hands, are motivated by profit considerations. Even workers' pension funds invest in art objects, because it is hoped that with continually rising prices this will prove most profitable. But this does not help those artists whose name is yet to be made. It is parasitic upon fluctuations of taste which are otherwise determined. Into this vacuum the public galleries should step, though as presently organized they are patently incompetent for the direction of taste. Private endowments and private collections can to some extent undertake a similar function, without indeed the impediment of bureaucratic domination. But in their case it would be a gratuitous service to mankind, a supererogatory contribution arising from public spirit and concern rather than social duty.

Public taste today is in a turmoil. In the struggle to attract notice to themselves artists strive for novelty as a virtue and confuse originality with difference. And the commercial galleries foster this tendency. Oddity and eccentricity are at a premium, and few people—not all artists even—can distinguish what is nonsense from what is new, the spurious from the true. If the museums took on the burden of patronage, they would also of necessity have to assume a responsibility for discriminating taste. In the 1930s some museum men did regard it as part of their job to judge and pronounce. And they made many mistakes. I remember there were some who said that their young children could do it better than Picasso and thought that Henry Moore would have done better to go down the mine. Now, whether from consciousness of past mistakes or from the realization that directors of museums are not chosen for flair or aesthetic foresight, there is a general assumption that it is their job to follow, not lead, public taste. No artist today stands an outside chance of seeing his work in a public museum unless his name has been already made, and one who has made his name, by whatever means and however undeservedly, is unlikely not to be taken up by the public galleries. It can happen that if a private exhibition is successful, the gallery will select from what is left over on the last day. France is still in advance of other countries in the ability to obtain the best from the production of contemporary artists for her public collections.

With the failure of the museums to step in, public taste today flounders without guidance. Perhaps the strongest influence in suggesting a direction is that of the critics and the newspaper reviewers, whose job does not necessarily fit them for the task. What are needed are men of vision and foresight and a flair for quality. To be effective, such men should be invested with the power not only to voice their judgment, but to confirm it by the control of patronage. It is not easy to find such men in a profession which is heavily biased in the direction of art history and attribution on the one side, the theoretical understanding of technique, restoration, and showmanship on the other. Perhaps it is precisely here that the great private endowments such as the Getty Trust could discover a sphere of particular usefulness where the public museums have floundered and miscarried.

The following may help to clarify the foregoing remarks on the functions of museums in so far as these include the furtherance of appreciation and the provision of material for appreciative commerce with the fine arts.

We are doing very different things, are very differently occupied, when we admire the architectural beauties of Toledo cathedral with rapt astonishment, lose or almost lose the awareness of self in listening to Emil Gilels playing a Beethoven concerto, contemplate a sculpture by Brancusi, or attend a performance of *King Lear*. Indeed so different are works of art from one another, and so diverse are the aspects whose interplay and interpenetration in a single work may demand as many characteristic attitudes of apprehension, that some people have concluded it is impossible to define what is meant by the expression "work of art" in terms of sufficient and necessary conditions applicable to all, declaring that ultimately any artifact is properly a work of art which people (or some select set of people) choose to call a work of art. This is mistaken thinking. Linguistic meanings are indeed conventional. But linguistic conventions are deeply engrained and cannot be changed by arbitrary fiat or whim. Over the last two centuries or so "work of art" has come to acquire an implicit meaning in relation to aesthetic experience or appreciation, which are cognate terms. When used in the context of the fine arts and our commerce with them, the word "appreciation" means, not assessment, though assessment may *result* from acts of appreciation, but the deliberate aesthetic experience of a thing; and aesthetic experiencing is the exercise of a particular skill in the sphere of percipience. It is a mode of perception which is differentiated by the fact that it is practiced for its own sake and not for the practical purposes of everyday life or for theoretical categorization or for scientific and analytical discrimination.

As elementary examples of perception for its own sake we may mention the smell of newly cut grass after summer rain or the scent of fresh basil, the deep pale blue of sky and water during the half hour before darkness in Venice, the ripple and susurration of lapping water as one basks in a canoe on a hot summer's day. But such experiences, though memorable, are ephemeral. They cannot occupy and activate the full waking mind for long but attention drifts, thoughts and imaginings intrude, or we lapse into happy coma. They exemplify the *kind* of direct percipience which underlies aesthetic experience, but they are not yet fully aesthetic. We speak of aesthetic experience when a complex object, such as a work of art, can hold attention in this mode of percipience and extend our perceptive powers to ever greater tension, fullness, and vivacity. A work of art may conveniently be defined as an artifact which has the complexity and the unity to do this. Unity of a particular kind, which may be called "perceptual unity," is necessary in order to accomplish this, for unless there is perceptual cohesion, we perceive the object in parts and relate the parts theoretically in understanding instead of perceiving the object as a whole. Complexity too is essential, though it must be understood that theoretical and perceptual complexity are not the same. The shapes of Jean Arp are simple but are as empty of perceptual significance as are the turds upon which he himself once confessed they were modelled. In the richly fraught simplicity of a Brancusi sculpture, by contrast, every millimeter of every contour contributes essentially to the unified complexity of the whole. Many people again may find the complexity of a Tinguely fountain too "intellectual" for direct visual apprehension.

As perception, aesthetic experience is cognition. But there are two kinds of knowledge. There is the familiar, everyday knowledge which enables us to sort our impressions into signs and indications of things, to sort the things into categories, and so to string verbal propositions together into systems of theoretical understanding and the manipulative rules upon which the techniques of practical living are built. From the unmanageable mass of impressions which impinge upon our senses at every waking moment, only a meager fraction come fully to conscious awareness, selected by discriminatory attention guided by practical interests for the formation of a body of abstract relations, similarities and differences. It is this category knowledge which enables us to say, "This house like most houses has two doors and a roof" and to repudiate "A circle has five sides." Not only does it pervade daily life, but it is this type of knowledge which is expanded almost beyond recognition by modern science. Astronomy tells us that we inhabit a small and undistinguished planet, one of the 200 billion stars in the galaxy, that in the known cosmos there are several hundred billion other galaxies beside the Milky Way. Our minds boggle but assimilate the information; imagination falters and fails. Modern physics speaks in terms of quarks and other elementary particles, molecular biology is a science of chromosomes and DNA, all of which are in principle outside the realm of possible experience. In ordinary life too category knowledge tends more and more to squeeze out knowledge by direct percipience which is its base. We know more than was ever known before *about* people and things, but the vital knowledge of direct contact shrivels and shrinks. We are becoming strangers in a foreign world and live only in a ghost world of our own creating, the world of categories and minds, of abstractions and rules. This is the meaning of alienation, the soul-searing cancer of the contemporary world. And the verbal interchange of hypertrophied conceptualization becomes ever more vapid as its nourishment of direct perceptual contact with reality diminishes. Only occasionally, very occasionally, as in the examples instanced above, is reality allowed to impinge. Aesthetic experience is the opposite to all this. And perhaps it might prove an antidote to the tendency we deplore. But the reality of it is becoming so rare that people are already doubtful what the very term means.

I have discussed the contrast between aesthetic appreciation as percipience and the practical knowledge of daily life more fully in chapter 2 of my book *The Art of Appreciation* (1970) and in an article entitled "The Cultivation of Sensibility in Art Education" contributed to the *Journal of Philosophy of Education* (Vol 18, No. 1, 1984). In the former I wrote that

> it is perhaps not too far-fetched to suggest that the recent massive expansion of interest among people who are neither patrons nor professionals of the arts may stem in part from an unrecognised impulse to find some compensation for an imbalance in contemporary life and education whose tendency is to cramp and confine the faculties of perception. Be that as it may, there is certainly prevalent a belief that through the visual even more than the literary arts can be found occasion and inducement to exercise faculties of perceptiveness which otherwise are in danger of becoming blunted through neglect.

I would add here to avoid possible misapprehension that theoretical knowledge and learning such as are contributed by art history, iconography, and so forth, have a positive function in relation to our appreciation. But it is important to remember that their use and justification are as a propaedeutic and ancillary to more complete and unified apprehension. At its most elementary, for example, where the meanings of words and expressions have changed in the course of time it may be necessary to learn the former meanings in order to apprehend a poem from a previous century. References and allusions which are woven into the texture of a work may require external information for their understanding. And iconography may play a similar role to enhance our apprehension of the visual arts—apprehension which is an essential part of full perception. But the value of discursive and analytical knowledge *about* any work of art lies only in its capacity to facilitate our perception of the work. And this is no easy thing. Percipience for its own sake, that is percipience which mediates aesthetic experience, the percipience which we call appreciation, is a skill that is very unevenly distributed among people and which always needs to be cultivated and developed. It is the more difficult to acquire because it invokes a mode of perception which runs counter to the perceptual habits we practice in practical life. It is easier to absorb a body of elementary facts about the works displayed in a museum than to master the ability of intense and prolonged perception necessary for seeing them complete and unabridged as the unified wholes they should be. Hence there is a temptation to substitute catalogue learning for seeing. And there is a temptation for museum curators to fill catalogues and guidance pamphlets with extraneous information which pleases their public and themselves but which distracts from instead of aiding perception. Yet it is still and always a major function of museums to foster and encourage the skills of appreciation by every possible means.

ALBERT WILLIAM LEVI

The Art Museum as an Agency of Culture

In what has gone before I have tried to explore the historical process by which the modern art museum has come into being and the various transformations by which it has finally established itself as an instrument of culture and a primary agency in the task of aesthetic education. And to this end I have used the paradoxical attack which Dewey makes upon the entire museum idea in the first few pages of *Art as Experience*. But anyone with some degree of philosophic sophistication will recognize that something infinitely more is taking place here than a mere institutional critique and that underneath this attack lies an unexpressed philosophical premise. It is the virulent opposition between the atomistic independence, the stark isolationism, the unregenerate individualism of John Stuart Mill and the pervasive organism, contextualism, and institutionalism of Hegel. Dewey's attack merely gives this opposition a local habitation and a name. It espouses the Hegelian alternative and applies it aesthetically by demanding for the aesthetic object a living institutional embodiment which should resist the isolating, bracketing, insulating influence of museum residence. And indeed the occasional strategy of individualistic, timeless presentation in the museum, as opposed to the much more usual historical contextualizing practice through the use of such classifications as "Renaissance," "Baroque," "Rococo," "Impressionist," and the like, does show that even the philosophical quarrel between Mill and Hegel has implications for museum policy and practice. Earlier we dealt with the art museum in terms of institutional role. Here we will be more concerned with philosophic approach, inner significance, and ideological commitment.

It is certainly true that the presentation of the individual work of art by itself alone is a relatively rare practice by the contemporary art museum and generally used only to call attention to perhaps the latest notable acquisition which the museum has made, as in the case of the New York Metropolitan which displayed Rembrandt's *Aristotle before the Bust of Homer* in a room by itself. But the public that flocked to see it was probably drawn more by rumor of the fabulous price that had been paid for its acquisition than by thirst for any genuine aesthetic experience. On the other hand, another Rembrandt—the great *Company of Captain Frans Banning Cocq*, better known as *The Night Watch*, completely cleaned, revarnished, and repaired, has been placed freestanding and alone in an enormous room of the Ryksmuseum in Amsterdam, huge in its dimensions, breathtakingly beautiful in its coloration, volcanic in its sheer dramatic impact; a permanent invitation to aesthetic contemplation, one of the great aesthetic adventures of the Western world.

Strangely enough, it may even be that what on the surface appears as Hegelian contextualism is in reality invitation to purely individual contemplation. This I think is the case for one of the most genial, exquisite, and deeply satisfying museums that I know, the sumptuous palace at 70th Street and Fifth Avenue in New York, which Henry Clay Frick had constructed in 1913-14 and planned primarily as a setting for his paintings.

The entire case of Frick is instructive. A fabulously wealthy industrialist, he retired at fifty and began to collect pictures. His early taste was "popular" and of questionable merit: he bought Bouguereau, Rosa Bonheur, Daubigny, and Mauve, which, as his taste matured, he subsequently disposed of. He began to study painting assiduously, slowly acquiring the capacity of real taste and discrimination, finally becoming a true "connoisseur" in the Berenson sense. In 1899 he purchased his first Rembrandt; in 1919 his last painting was Vermeer's *Lady Reading a Letter*. In between was the superb Bellini, the Holbeins, the Ruisdaels, El Grecos, Velázquezes, Dürers, and at least fifteen Rembrandts more. To the end he continued to improve his collection by exchanging earlier purchases for works of higher quality.

The results are breathtaking. When one first walks through the Frick museum and notes the fabulous collection of paintings spread out within their sumptuous background of early Italian furniture, French eighteenth-century pieces, and enormous and infinitely beautiful Isfahan rugs, one has the sense of Hegelian contextualism at its most sensitive; but further reflection convinces one that this is far from being the case. There is embodied here no *unified* sense of time, space, or culture. Instead one walks from a Rembrandt *Self Portrait* to Vermeer's *Lady Reading a Letter* to Holbein's *Sir Thomas More* to Giovanni Bellini's *St. Francis in the Desert*. And from there to Velázquez's *Philip the Fourth*, a second Holbein, *Sir Thomas Cromwell*, and from there to a wonderful but *limited* quantity of works by Ruisdael, Vermeer, Titian, Van Dyck, and Veronese, each individually inviting the spectator to stop, attend, regard; each soliciting its own measure of rapt contemplation, formal appreciation, and sustained admiration. And one begins to sense here not a synthesized organic whole, but a loose and almost random aggregate of Millian singulars, each making its individualistic aesthetic claim.

Then, finally, when one begins to be aware of the small-scale bronzes on the Renaissance tables, the names here are those of Benvenuto Cellini, Giovanni da Bologna, Verrocchio, and Michelangelo. And when one begins to notice the Black Hawthorn vases of the K'ang and Hsi period placed almost at random, it is apparent that they are among the choicest in existence! Only then it begins to dawn on one what the Frick museum really is: a presentation of works of art in their naked individuality, a temple of pure aesthetic experience, a virtual embodiment of the idea of *the art museum as an exclusive assembly of nothing but masterpieces*. (Reflection on the essence of the Frick museum suggests that this too is not without its suggestiveness for what the Getty museum has in it to become: the consequence of a private trust, with infinite financial resources of acquisition, and guided by the most enlightened artistic knowledge, and with directive powers with both creative imagination and the appetite for perfection.)

The concept of the art museum as an exclusive assemblage of nothing but masterpieces invites an interpretation of pure aesthetic contemplation, of a consideration of the work of art for its own sake alone. And this reinforcement of the "purity" of the aesthetic experience, like the purity of the apprehension of logical and mathematical universals, places the entire transaction outside of space and time. There is no effort within the Frick collection to call specific attention to date, original function, or place of origin of any of the masterpieces it contains. In this sense the entire enterprise is profoundly antihistorical.

But there is another conception of what an art museum ought to be which is directly antithetical to this—one, in fact, which views it as a lesson in, and an illumination of, cultural history. Here the Hegelian notion of "context" is central, and the entire enterprise is guided by what I should like to call "the doctrine of essential temporality." The shift here is drastic, and it has profound epistemological consequences as well. A contemplative act in the pure present is very different from an act of historical comprehension whose goal is somehow "to recapture" the past, an act of "recovery" or "restoration" of materials only incompletely and inferentially known. To use the art museum as a demonstration of how the various arts and crafts are *associated as a way of life* constituting a particular historical period like "the Middle Ages" or "the Italian Renaissance" or "the Dutch seventeenth century" or "Georgian England" means the use of techniques of assemblage and presentation which stimulate a particular and very elusive attitude—one which a very important philosopher of historical method of the last century, Wilhelm Dilthey (1833-1911), used two words to describe *Verstehen* (or sympathetic intuitive *understanding*) and *Nacherleben* (or profoundly imaginative *re-experiencing*). Here contextualizing, the placement in space and time of art objects in their interconnectedness, is what makes *Verstehen* and *Nacherleben* possible, and the aesthetic and the historical sense may even unite cooperatively in two very different but mutually supportive acts.

One further thing must be presupposed in conceiving the art museum as primarily an institution for instruction in cultural history: some prior agreement upon the conventions of historical classification; one must know in advance what it means to be a historical epoch. Once again, our origins here go back to the eighteenth-century Enlightenment and chiefly to Voltaire's short but revolutionary treatise, the *Siecle de Louis XIV*, published in 1751. Here, probably for the first time, the concept of a *Zeitgeist* is taken seriously, and a historical epoch is defined less in terms of politics, power, and dynastic conquest than in terms of the advance of literature and the arts. Only from this time onward is it possible to write books with titles like Karl Vossler's *Mediaeval Culture* or the Oxford *Legacy of the Middle Ages* or Walter Pater's *The Renaissance* or Burckhardt's *The Civilization of the Renaissance in Italy* or the two notable Oxford collections, *The Age of Shakespeare* and *The Age of Johnson*, respectively. Any one of these titles might also be the title of an exhibit arranged by any art museum devoting itself to the illumination of cultural history.

In fact, there are at least three ways in which this illumination can be carried out. The first is by total dedication. The Musée de Cluny, situated in the heart of Paris, a stone's throw away from the Sorbonne and the College de France, houses perhaps the finest collection of mediaeval arts and crafts in the world, all superbly exhibited in a mansion of the Middle Ages—one of only two surviving examples of mediaeval domestic architecture in the city of Paris. Its riches are incalculable. It contains sumptuous tapestries like *La Dame à la Licorne*, *La Vie Seigneuriale*, and *Saint Etienne*, chalices and reliquaries of chased gold and silver, illuminated manuscripts with brilliantly painted miniatures, limoges enamels on religious subjects of the twelfth century, fragments of stained glass and cathedral sculpture, psalter covers in carved ivory, carved wooden chests and cupboards of the twelfth, thirteenth, and fourteenth centuries, embroidered taffeta robes, richly carved choir stalls, limoges caskets and plaques of cloisonne, massive stone fireplaces of the period with their cooking utensils, chairs, tables, and other pieces of domestic furniture, and, in fact, innumerable exemplars of the decorative and industrial

arts, both for ecclesiastical and domestic purposes, all arranged to promote maximum intelligibility, all calculated to stimulate just that
Verstehen and *Nacherleben* of which Dilthey spoke.... After one has carefully and attentively worked one's way through the Musée de Cluny,
one does not feel that one has "walked around" the Middle Ages, but
that one has "entered into" them!

A lesser way is the single room or series of "period" rooms. Almost
any art museum of size or distinction has to some degree the interest to
exhibit its aesthetic treasures in historical context, as icons of the aristo-
cratic way of life in a notable period of Western culture. If it is lucky
enough to have transported the fireplace and wood paneling from some
stately townhouse of Georgian England, it hangs a Joshua Reynolds
portrait over the mantel, a Gainsborough landscape over the mahogany
Sheraton sideboard, which already holds a massive Georgian coffee-and-
tea service, and its finest Spode or Wedgewood or Chelsea china on the
polished Hepplewhite dining room table surrounded by its Hepplewhite
chairs which already occupies the center of the stage. And in the same
spirit it can equip other "period" rooms as well its "Louis XV Boudoir,"
its Austrian "Biedermeier," and its American "Federal" parlors. The
possibilities are endless, and their variety and quality are dependent only
upon the state and quality of the collections the art museum possesses.
(Occasionally, such assemblages are actually authentic. In the Museum
der Stadt Wien, for example, I have seen both the Biedermeier drawing
room of the great Austrian dramatist Franz Grillparzer (1791-1872) and
the interesting and bizarre self-designed study of Adolf Loos (1870-1933),
the real European founder of architectural modernism, both taken bodily
from their respective original apartments and reassembled whole.)

A third and least way is simply to promote suggestiveness by the
loose association of such cognate works of fine art or craft as the museum possesses and sees as historically related. I saw just such a display
at the rather modest art museum of the city of Detroit. In at least one of
its very long and rather narrow galleries, at intervals of perhaps fifty
feet, it had hung pictures done by the better-known of American Colonial portrait painters—Copley, Stuart, Hoppner, and a few others—and
standing against the walls between these pictures were splendid examples of the furniture made by the finest American Colonial cabinet-
makers of Boston, Baltimore, and Philadelphia: exquisite and imposing
Chippendale highboys in mahogany made in Philadelphia, lowboys and
tables of Virginia walnut made in Baltimore, block-front desks from
Newport, Rhode Island, and a multitude of Hepplewhite and Sheraton

chairs made in all four cities. And on some of the flat surfaces of the lowboys and tables were placed elegant silver tea services and pitchers and porringers of the period and style of Paul Revere. The overall impression was both casual and stately and led the mind inevitably to a sense of the elegance, dignity, and culture of patrician Colonial America—a total civilization, if you will, but constructed out of an array of disparate particulars.

Hitherto I have taken up the ideologies of the art museum (1) as the temple of pure aesthetic experience, as ideally a collection of masterpieces, and (2) as an agency for the presentation of cultural history, as illumination of the major cultural "epochs" in the history of the West. Now I want to turn to (3) the art museum as the special protege of the academic field of art history and (4) the use of the art museum to present the fine arts as "liberal arts," that is to say, the exploration of "art" as a "humanity." In the case of (3) there is less original material to explore, since in some sense that is the way that most art museums currently function. Most of those responsible for the direction of art museum aesthetic policy have been trained as art historians, and it is therefore natural that they should be subconsciously aware of the doctrines they have absorbed by the influential theorists of their field: Berenson's emphasis upon "tactile values," Fry's emphasis on "significant form," Wölfflin's distinction between the "painterly" and the "linear" styles, Panofsky's obsession with "iconographic meanings," Gombrich's investigations of "the a priori of the spectator's anticipations." These distinctions have probably often subconsciously influenced the placement of the individual artwork in the museum space.

But there are other art historical conventions which are even more powerful classificatory designations like "Mannerist," "Baroque," "Rococo," "Impressionist," and the like, and these may even guide the sophisticated visitor to the museum as to where to go and what to look for. It is therefore much more traditional to present the painterly materials by historical placement than, say, by genres. So one might have a Dutch seventeenth-century room combining landscapists like Hobbema, Ruisdael, and Van Goyen with the interior wizards like De Hoogh, Ter Borch, and Vermeer, or a French nineteenth-century room in which Renoir's portraits, Monet's country landscapes, and Pissarro's and Sisley's paintings of the Grand Boulevards of Paris are all projected into one giant "Impressionist" space. But imagine the educational potential if a revolution occurred (and, if one can appeal to a musical analogy, the "serial" was supplanted by the "variation" form) and *genre* took priority over the principle of mere temporal succession. Then Titian and Joshua

Reynolds, Copley and Franz Hals, Ingres and Modigliani, Rembrandt and Holbein, Goya and Van Dyck, Raphael and Memling, Manet and Dürer, El Greco and Velázquez might hang together in fascinating opposition, leaving the spectator in bemused but active consideration of valences of attitude, style, characterization, technique, and ultimate value. Then portraiture might take its rightful place in the spectrum of human concern, and painting might be transformed before our very eyes from a "fine art" into a "humanity."

This, of course, leads directly into our final topic (4) the art museum devoted exclusively to *the presentation of art as a humanity*. Here again I wish to concentrate my attention primarily upon painting. The humanities, I have long maintained, are identical with the liberal arts, and the liberal arts consist primarily of the languages and literatures, history, and philosophy. Thus the humanities may alternatively be defined as the arts of *communication*, the arts of *continuity*, and the arts of *criticism*. Any move, therefore, to turn the fine art of painting into a humanity involves its being interpreted simultaneously as an act of communication, of historical significance, and of moral, social, or political criticism.

First the matter of communication. Painting is, of course, nonlinguistic; its magic is created neither with speech nor with words, but with paint and canvas in the form of shapes and images. Yet it is highly suggestive to consider paintings metaphorically as acts of writing or of speech, with each individual painter having his own unique "vocabulary" of line, color, calligraphy, and overall mood. Consider the obvious matter of chromatic preference. Van Gogh loved yellow, Rembrandt brown, El Greco alizerin crimson. Chardin paints in the darker "shades," Bonnard in the lighter "tints," Fra Angelico in "tones" of purest blue, red, and purple. Monet, like Bonnard, works in tints, especially lavender, turquois, and powder blue, whereas Mondrian with his black lines will have only the unmixed primaries red, yellow, blue, and green.

Or, consider the vocabulary of line ; the clarity of Raphael, Holbein, and Ingres compared with the cloudiness of Rembrandt and the Impressionists. Or, in our own time, the hard edges of Albers and Noland compared with the smudginess of DeKooning or the careless drips and blots of Jackson Pollock. Or the actual calligraphy of the brush strokes: the rough ones of Franz Hals or Van Gogh compared with the smooth ones of Manet and Van Dyck, or the obsessive fussy dots of the Impressionists and Seurat. How did Cézanne get from the gutteral speech of his early thick impastos to the whispers of those thin washes (almost like watercolors) of the very last paintings? Isn't some brushwork bold or nervous, careless or deliberate, slashing or exact? Or consider the matter of characteristic mood: the violent gesturing of Michelangelo and Van Gogh, the good humor of Franz Hals; the angry and violent Soutine, the gloomy Munch, the sullen Vlaminck; the serenity and sweetness of Raphael and Cima da Conigliano, the quiet peacefulness of Vermeer and De Hoogh.

Finally as to content. What does the painter talk about? What are the subjects of his conversation? Mostly religion and God as with Giotto, Fra Angelico, and Giovanni Bellini. Or important people as with Clouet, Holbein, and Van Dyck. Or fine clothes and interior decoration and beautiful domestic objects as with Ter Borch, Vermeer, and De Hoogh. Or the East Anglian countryside by Constable, or the countryside around Aix-en-Provence by Cézanne, around Arles by Van Gogh, or around Delft, Leyden, and The Hague by Ruisdael, Hobbema, and Van Goyen. Or perhaps they speak about beautiful nude women, as with Boucher, Ingres, and Titian as he grew old. Or about old men, rabbis, solid citizens, and himself, as did Rembrandt throughout his life.

The last two categories need hardly detain us further: they are almost too obvious to require elaboration. For painting as ingredient in history, as an "art of continuity," it is only necessary that the museum display and discuss it as finding its place in a determinate *tradition:* say, that of portraiture from Titian to Modigliani, or that of still life from Claez to Braque, or that of landscape from Bellini to Cézanne. And for painting as philosophy, as social criticism, for example, it might be highly instructive to display examples of painters like Gentile Bellini and Carpaccio, whose pageants and processions glorify and revere the city of whose life they are a part, close to, but in opposition with, the spirit of that other persuasion—of those like Goya and Hogarth and Daumier, or like Ben Shahn or Jacob Lawrence in our own century, whose works are living critiques of courtly corruption or of civic poverty, squalor, and vice.

To conclude. In the first half of my consideration of the art museum as an agency of culture, I have tried to examine its institutional role (1) as warehouse, (2) as showcase and custodian of the aesthetic valuables of the community, and finally (3) as indispensable instrument in the great task of aesthetic education. Analogously, in the second half I have tried to present four conceptually different strategies through which the art museum's efforts of aesthetic education might be directed (1) by the idea of the art museum as a collection of supreme masterpieces presented for pure aesthetic contemplation, or (2) by the idea of the art museum as an agency of cultural history, or (3) by the idea of the art museum as primarily an adjunct of the discipline of art history, or finally (4) by the idea of the art museum as the presentation of fine art as a humanity.

I have not meant that these last four alternatives should of necessity be mutually exclusive. It is only necessary, I think, that they should be unambiguously clear in the minds of those who are currently responsible for the direction of art museum policy.

MIHALY CSIKSZENTMIHALYI

Notes on Art Museum Experiences

The Role of Museums in Society

In answering this question, it will be useful to make a distinction between *latent* and *manifest* functions. By manifest functions I mean the stated goals that institutions are expected to accomplish, while the latent ones are those discreetly ignored goals that no one talks about in polite company, either because they are too obvious or because they are slightly embarrassing. Nevertheless, without taking care of their latent functions, most institutions would soon cease to exist.

Like other cultural institutions, such as universities, churches, libraries, baseball clubs, or symphony orchestras, art museums must exercise financial acumen so as to raise funds for an increasingly expensive staff and physical plant; they must be worldly and fashionable so as to bestow status on trustees and donors; they must have good enough public relations to be seen as sources of civic pride in the community and, if possible, attract tourists to it. To accomplish all this a certain amount of mystification might be required. Museum professionals, like the "priests" of other cultural entities, sometimes must exaggerate the importance of their mission, or veil it in momentous mystery, so as to convince lay people of the importance of their offerings. Although these latent functions have to be met if art museums are to survive, one hopes they are not the only reasons they exist.

What, then, are the manifest goals of an art museum, the ones that make it a unique institution and justify its existence? Two main functions seem to be preeminent. The first concerns the *preservation and restoration of the best examples of human craft* (or *art*, as the Romans called it). The second aim is *to use art as a medium for communicating aesthetic experiences to visitors*. It is probably safe to say that, historically, the first goal has been viewed as the sole or predominant task of art museums, whereas the second goal has gained in importance only over the past few decades. Correspondingly, a certain tension is built into the staff structure of museums. Curators naturally see the acquisition, restoration, critical appraisal, and proper storage or exhibition of works as the museum's main priority; whereas the educational staff often feels that art objects are primarily a means of communication, and what counts is not necessarily their aesthetic or monetary value, but what the visitors get out of encountering them.

What follows will deal exclusively with the second manifest function of art museums, namely, their task of providing visitors with unique and presumably valuable experiences. This focus is appropriate for two reasons: first, because the properly curatorial functions are relatively better understood and unproblematical; second, because the two surveys under consideration deal almost exclusively with what happens to viewers when they encounter works of art.

Dimensions of the Aesthetic Experience

Both the museum professionals we interviewed, and the audience focus groups agree on a limited number of reasons why encounters with works of art can be meaningful and desirable. Although most professionals are probably well acquainted with these reasons, it might be useful to summarize them once again. The first column of Table 1 includes the four categories we used in our report to the Getty Museum; the second column lists the main categories that emerged in the study of the focus groups. Although the terms are sometimes different, the content of the categories seems to translate rather easily from one study to the other. Apparently the kind of experiences expert museum professionals and visitors report when they encounter works of art share many commonalities.

Both groups speak of the aesthetic experience as having four major components. One is a cognitive dimension through which the art object appeals to prior knowledge and extends its boundaries. Another appeals to emotions that are difficult to express in rational terms, yet appear to enrich our lives. The third dimension concerns the purely visual impact the object makes and the perceptual refinements it causes in the viewer. And the last category includes the ways in which works of art help us understand ourselves and other people by making us reflect on what transpired in the encounter with the work of art.

Professionals and visitors naturally differ in their respective emphasis on these dimensions of experience. Museum curators, especially those with a Ph.D. and those who specialize in classical art, respond to art primarily along the cognitive dimension. They are fascinated with issues of provenance, attribution, and precise location in the artist's oeuvre. The artwork is above all else a glorious intellectual puzzle waiting for a creative solution. Understandably, this dimension of the encounter is much less salient, if not entirely absent, among visitors. Yet the responses from lay audiences suggest that they too would relate to this aspect of the aesthetic experience if they had the necessary knowledge.

Table 1.   Dimensions of Aesthetic Experience Reported in the Two Studies

From *The Art of Seeing* (Interviews with museum professionals)	From the *Museum Focus Groups Summary Report*, pp. 21-30 (Visitors' museum experiences)
Knowledge	Understanding of history and of various cultures
Emotion	Emotional experience—curiosity, fantasy, exhilaration
Perceptual impact	Beauty of objects; stylistic and technical comparisons
Communication	Self-discovery, introspection; personal connectedness with objects; universal concerns across cultures and times

In general, however, visitors do not expect intellectual thrills from attending a museum. They are, rather, hoping for surprise and excitement as they escape temporarily the predictable confines of existence in an environment where the constraints of everyday life appear to be suspended. The more sophisticated viewers may hope, in addition, to learn something important about their own joys and sorrows as these are reflected in the expressive strivings of fellow human beings. Although the term *magic* rarely appears in the sober responses of these two surveys, it seems clear that what the audience expects from an art museum is, above all, a magical transformation of experience.

Cognitive challenges, emotions, visual impact, and empathy leading to self-communication are the "stuff" out of which the aesthetic experience emerges in consciousness, but by themselves these components do not add up to what we mean when we say we had a genuine encounter with a work of art. An aesthetic experience is more than the sum of its parts; in fact, it begins precisely when the various dimensions of consciousness meld together and we are no longer aware of "thinking," "feeling," "seeing," or "communicating" as separate processes. Total immersion in the work of art is the magic experts and laypersons alike hope for when they visit a museum, but rarely attain.

From this perspective, the aesthetic experience is a species of the genus *optimal experience*, which in my studies I have also called *flow experience*. This is a state of consciousness characterized by intense concentration bordering on oblivion, yet requiring complex mental or physical activity. Various art forms, games, sports, meditation, religious rituals, and mathematical and scientific investigations are among the activities that usually provide flow experiences. Despite the enormous differences in the content of such activities, these experiences are remarkably similar. Both men and women from a great variety of cultures, social classes, levels of education, and ages report these experiences in the same terms.

As an example, I will quote Charles Lindbergh, who uses the analogy of the aesthetic experience of a theatergoer to describe how it felt to fly the *Spirit of Saint Louis* across the Atlantic. But his words are very similar to how Navajo braves describe hunting a deer with bow and arrow, Thai women describe weaving rugs, or Japanese teens describe racing motorcycles:

> It's been like a theater where the play carries you along in time and place until you forget you're only a spectator. You grow unaware of the walls around you, of the program clasped in your hand, even of your body, its breath, pulse and being. You live with the actors and the setting, in a different age and place. It's not until the curtain drops that consciousness and body reunite.

It is my contention that Lindbergh describes not only what it feels like to see a good play, or to fly solo across the ocean in 1927, but also a great variety of other flow experiences, of which encountering a work of art is one. It is this flow that "carries you along in time and place" that constitutes the magic we seek in art, and it is to its closer analysis that I shall now turn.

The Structure of the Aesthetic Experience

To see how the dimensions of knowledge, emotion, perception, and empathy are structurally united in the wholeness of the aesthetic experience I would like to compare an aesthetician's description of the criteria defining aesthetic experiences and my description of the criteria defining flow experiences reported by rock climbers, chess masters, ballet dancers, surgeons, and other such folks. This comparison, presented in Table 2, reveals remarkable similarities.

In both cases, the experience is made possible by the active exercise of powers (e.g., cognitive, emotional, perceptual, and communicative skills in the case of aesthetic encounters) in meeting environmental challenges (e.g., the visual, emotional, conceptual, symbolic residues left by the artist in the artwork). The engagement of skills with challenges requires concentrated attention. This in turn leads to further concentration on the limited stimulus field of the artwork—or the cockpit of the plane, or the baseball diamond—resulting in a focusing on the present moment, on the flow of consciousness, to the exclusion of past and future concerns, or of any mental content extraneous to the tiny, yet fully satisfying, world created by the interaction.

Table 2.	Comparison of Criteria Defining the Aesthetic Experience and the Flow Experience	
	Criteria for the Aesthetic Experience* (From Beardsley, 1982, pp. 288-89)	Criteria for the Flow Experience** (From Csikszentmihalyi, 1975, pp. 38-48)
	1. Object focus "Attention fixed on the intentional field."	1. Merging of action and awareness "Attention centered on activity."
	2. Felt freedom "Release of concerns for past and future."	2. Immersion in the present "No awareness of past and future."
	3. Detached affect "Objects of interest are set at a distance emotionally."	3. Loss of ego "Loss of self-consciousness and transcendence of ego boundaries."
	4. Active discovery "Active exercise of powers to meet environmental challenges."	4. Control of actions "Skills adequate to overcome challenges."
	5. Wholeness "A sense of personal integration and self-expansion."	5. Transcendence of ego boundaries; experience is autotelic, or satisfying in itself.
		6. Clear goals, immediate feedback

* From Beardsley, M.C. (1982). *The aesthetic point of view: Selected essays*. Ithaca, NY: Cornell University Press.

** From Csikszentmihalyi, M. (1975). *Beyond boredom and anxiety*. San Francisco: Jossey-Bass.

This immersion in the ongoing moment frees the actor from the ego-related concerns and defenses that take up so much of our attention in everyday life. Immersion in flow produces "detached affect" because there is no attention left over to worry about what will happen to our precious selves. Yet, paradoxically, as we return to normal life after experiencing this temporary loss of self-consciousness, we tend to emerge with a greater sense of wholeness and integration—a stronger sense of self.

These are some of the similarities between the aesthetic and the flow experience, the broader class of subjective states that people find enjoyable and rewarding for their own sake. But assuming it is true that looking at a painting and, let us say, skiing down a mountain slope provide experiences that are in some important respects similar, we must still answer the question, in what way are the two experiences *dissimilar?* Or, to put it another way, what is the specific difference that distinguishes the act of looking at a painting from skiing?

Activities that provide flow differ from each other in terms of the challenges they present, and thus in terms of the skills needed to become involved in them. The challenges of rock climbing, for instance, derive from the existence of vertical slabs of stone that, given the laws of gravity, make it possible for a person to experiment with actions and related states of being that defy ordinary reality. The *sui generis* challenges of art are very different in kind. They consist in visual representations of a person's unique ideas and feelings, expressed in the symbolic vocabulary of a particular human community embedded in a specific historical period. The skills necessary to engage these challenges involve the ability to decode and recreate—through historical knowledge, emotional responsiveness, visual sophistication, and communicative empathy—some aspects of the process by which the work of art was created. It is through this meshing of challenges and skills that the aesthetic flow experience comes about, and the potential magic of art becomes actualized.

A person who has a high level of skills for decoding the content of artworks needs no help from the museum to achieve this experience. All he or she needs is for the work to be accessible to viewing, and the less fuss about it the better. A friend of mine well-schooled in music prefers to get his Bach directly by reading the written score of a composition rather than by listening to its performance, because he claims he can get a more perfect musical experience without the distractions of a concert hall and of actual sounds. In a similar vein, the ideal visitor would be one so well prepared that he or she would not even need to look at a painting. Given a label and a blank wall, such a visitor could recreate in his mind the work in all its details and partake of the aesthetic experience. Most of us, however, fall far short of such ideal expertise. The average museum visitor needs help to become involved with the artwork.

Historically art museums have evolved as the institutions of a relatively homogeneous elite sharing a common education, similar tastes, and largely interchangeable backgrounds. Museums could take for granted a common symbolic matrix uniting works and visitors. The time for such homogeneity is long past. The ethnic mix of our metropolitan areas is becoming ever more varied, and the kind of education that would prepare a person to interpret a traditional artwork is becoming ever more rare. Even more important than these demographic changes is the change in the museums' attitudes toward their mission. Instead of being content to cater to the elite, museums are now attempting to appeal to a much larger constituency—seemingly coterminous with the entire population of their community. Democracy rather than demography is responsible for the current mismatch of what works of art can potentially offer and what visitors can obtain from them.

If art museums wish to achieve the goal of becoming mediators of aesthetic experiences for the community, they must find ways to facilitate the interaction between the challenges contained in artworks and the aesthetic skills visitors bring to the museum encounter. We might now turn back to the conclusions of the *Focus Groups Summary Report* for some ideas as to how this could be accomplished. None of these ideas will be entirely new to museum professionals, but it may be helpful to summarize them again in this context.

Obstacles to a Meaningful Aesthetic Experience

The *Focus Groups Summary Report* lists a variety of reasons why visitors claim they did not get as much out of their museum visits as they had hoped. The major obstacles listed include lack of orientation to the contents of the museum, insufficient information (e.g., about the artist's life and about the particular work's iconography, art history, cultural context, and technique), confusing layout and organization of exhibits, daunting physical surroundings, intimidating employees, and failure of the museum to communicate the benefits to be expected from the visit.

These items at first may seem like a hodgepodge of unrelated reasons, a laundry list of fatuous complaints. However, if we use the flow model to interpret what these results might mean, it becomes clear that the obstacles fall into reasonable categories having to do with various ways in which the aesthetic experience can be inhibited.

For example, it is difficult to become involved in an activity that will provide a flow experience unless the participant has a clear idea what he or she can do. Clear goals are a prerequisite. Yet most potential museum visitors just do not know what they are supposed to do in front of a work of art. This ignorance not only makes them feel self-conscious and embarrassed but it also effectively prevents all but the most superficial encounter, which remains on the mundane level of everyday life experience. Hence, the visitors list "communication of benefits" and "orientation" as things they miss, and with good reason. What can museums do to help set goals for a meaningful visit? I do not pretend to have the answers, but as Einstein and many others before him have said, having the right question is already half the solution.

Clear goals are useless without skills; to enter the flow state one must use some personal resources to engage the external challenges. Visitors are very aware that they sorely lack the background for getting the full benefit of what they are exposed to. Museum professionals agree that the main preparation necessary for enjoying a work of art is simply having looked at a great deal of art. The more one looks, the more one is able to discriminate and to immerse oneself in what one sees. Past experience settles in memory as knowledge and enriches future encounters. But most museum visitors have not looked long and well enough in the past to see what there is to see. Therefore they list the lack of information as perhaps the crucial obstacle to a meaningful museum experience. They feel that if they know more about the artist, the symbols he or she used, the cultural background and technique, it would be easier to become immersed in the interaction with the work. While the problem is clear, the solution is again not obvious. Museums have tried for a long time now to provide increasing amounts of information to visitors, often to the chagrin of the already informed, who feel that their own experiences are disrupted by the intrusiveness of lengthy labels, voluble guides, and audiovisual aids. An understanding of what makes the aesthetic experience possible, however, should help provide guidelines for how to optimize the conflicting needs of the audience.

Many of the obstacles listed under the headings of "layout and organization" and "physical surroundings" cause problems because they disrupt the concentration necessary for achieving the aesthetic experience. Too many people, too much noise, unclear boundaries between areas, confusing signs and labels are only some of the intrusions that bring the viewer back from the magic interaction to the hassles of everyday reality. Similarly, guards and other employees sometimes disrupt the immersion in the experience by being too conspicuous or rude.

Just because these obstacles exist, however, it does not mean that museums must concern themselves with removing them. There is no necessary step from *is* to *ought;* facts by themselves do not implicate action. Whether one wishes to make museums accessible to an ever wider segment of the population is a matter of choice based on goals derived from values and principles, not from facts alone.

If the goals of the museum do include facilitating the aesthetic experience, then the answers gleaned from the focus groups, as interpreted within the framework of a theory of aesthetic response, provide useful directions for change and implementation. In conclusion, I should like to stress the advantages of a theoretical approach. A good theory helps explain facts, and above all else it allows generalizations from single instances to entire classes of future events that it helps anticipate. For example, visitors occasionally complain of rude guards. Without a theory, one might be tempted to conclude that the cure for this problem was to train guards to be solicitous. But theory helps us see that it is not rudeness per se that is the problem, but the intrusion rudeness provides; hence, one would conclude that solicitous guards could be equally intrusive, and hence problematic.

Perhaps the greatest advantage of a theory of aesthetic response is that it allows for systematic experimentation, for correction as a result of disconfirming evidence, and, therefore, for gradual, incremental improvement. Without a theory, facts generated by surveys tend to have an ad hoc, temporary significance. They might help solve local problems, occasionally they could even lead to generalizations, but facts alone lack the power to explain and predict. Of course, a theory that is not exposed to factual checks is quite useless. Hence, as in all other domains of knowledge, it is through a dialectical interchange between facts and theory that we shall understand better what happens inside museums.

Elizabeth Vallance

Issues in Evaluating Museum Education Programs

The challenges to evaluating museum education programs . . . include the difficulty in identifying meaningful measures of success, the fact that our audience is transient and hard to pin down, the fact that our students' comfort and familiarity with art vary enormously, the likelihood that some of the strongest effects of our programs may be so long term and ephemeral that we might never be aware of them, and the related difficulty of knowing whether our "graduates" ever become art consumers generally.

In short, we work in a very open system with few controls on our student population or on what they learn from our programs. These challenges to effective program development and evaluation in turn pose special problems for evaluating museum education programs. These problems include the following:

1. We only rarely have a clear sense of what our goals are for any specific program. Most museums offer a variety of programs in various formats to attract varied age groups, and the overall goal of these programs is to "reach" the broadest possible audience with appropriate programs. But I know of no instances where the educators set specific goals in advance aside from the usual ones of "good turnout" and "nice (read: varied) crowd." Museum educators' general goals of providing accessible art information to a broad audience are passionately felt and argued for in many forums.

But program to program, I believe we settle too often for numerical success and a feeling by the instructor of having covered the content appropriately. We have not been in the business of developing goals. As a result, our evaluation efforts have lagged behind those in schools.

2. The spontaneous responses to programs tend to be *mostly positive.* The fact that our audience has, by its very (and completely voluntary) presence, made a commitment to learn something and to be open to new ideas predisposes visitors to enjoy the program and to tell us so.

A program has to be pretty poor, or somehow offensive to someone, before we will hear a complaint. It is easy to overestimate the instructional effectiveness of our programs by attending to explicit audience reaction. (Anecdotal evidence of public response to the art itself tends to be skewed more to the negative. It is curious how many people will approach a guard, or an Information Desk volunteer, to comment on how much they dislike a particular work of art—the Serra sculpture, for instance—or to wonder aloud how anyone can really consider that circle of stones on the floor—Richard Long's *Mississippi Circle*—to be art. In a day I spent in a guard's uniform overhearing comments in the contemporary art galleries, most indicated puzzlement or rejection. Rarely do visitors convey their love of any particular piece to our staff.)

3. We estimate program success to some extent by the size and return rate of our audiences, and yet this practice also tends to *overemphasize the positive*. We notice when participants return and become "regulars in our programs" (we recognize them in crowds and see their names recurring on registration lists), but without specifically tracking the nonreturns, we have only a very vague sense of how many people do not come back for more. Nonreturning participants simply do not come back; it is difficult to notice the absence from a program of a person who had attended a related program earlier.

4. It is extremely *difficult to follow up* on our programs to gauge the impact they might have had on people's subsequent relationship to art. Aside from new regulars that we can identify in our own programs, we do not know whether a program has made any difference at all to most participants' future interactions with art. Are we educating better art consumers? How would we know?

5. Even the most carefully designed program with the most appropriate publicity will depend for its success on the underlying *hidden curriculum* of the art museum: the messages conveyed by the solemnity or openness of the setting, by the comforts available to tired visitors, by the sparseness or usefulness of the object labels and other interpretive text, and by the ease or difficulty of finding one's way around the building. An excellent program in an unwelcoming museum will surely have a different reception than the same program in a museum that is open and accessible to all.

A great educational program of exhibitions and other programs can be lost on the public if the PR department does not promote it. Parents finding nothing in the museum shop but scholarly books may decide not to bring their children back for a second visit. Overzealous or unfriendly guards may make a family feel unwelcome near valuable paintings and discourage subsequent visits until the children are older. No museum education program can fairly be divorced front its context, and the contextual factors are even more difficult to assess than the straight programmatic ones.

6. It is more tempting, because it is easier, to assess the *prior public appeal* of a program than to assess its eventual instructional effectiveness. Our tendency to emphasize head count and other quantitative measures skews our attention to the size of a program's "draw"—the crowd that appears at the start of the program—and away from concerns with its real quality once it is completed. Family Days at our museum are usually enormous: Thousands of people come for a Sunday afternoon of activities focused on a special exhibition, and it is plain in watching them and overhearing their conversations that they are enjoying themselves. As an effort to portray the museum as a friendly, accessible public place, the event clearly succeeds.

Are people really learning about the paintings featured in the exhibition? Probably. But we are less sure about the instructional effectiveness than we are about appeal. In some cases we assume that the "delayed effects" of a few strong memories and the sheer enjoyment of being there will suffice as educational goals for the day. Does this assumption ever violate our real purposes?

7. Many of the most appropriate instruments for assessing the effectiveness of museum education programs would *violate the informal nature of the learning* that we seek to foster. Pre- and posttests of art historical knowledge, intensive visitor interviews, pop quizzes, and even careful ethnographic observational data could intrude on the comfortable visits we hope our visitors will have, and we can engage in these activities only occasionally for special purposes. Portfolio assessment is available as an evaluation tool for studio art classes, but on the whole our visitors come too erratically for us to be able to track them easily.

8. Do we know *what constitutes a fruitful dialogue* about the Serra sculpture? Serious art educators know what they mean by effective discussion of aesthetics, or by criticism. But what of the many visitors who do not stop long enough to really discuss the piece, and merely pass by it with a nice comment? Are we overestimating the power of this provocative piece when we assume it is serving an educational function if it provokes a comment? Is any conversation about art better than none at all? How do we know?

I suspect that museum educators take a lot for granted about how well our programs work. We are, I think, fairly well in tune with the public, and we do have a good sense of what the "average visitor" can handle in terms of content level and intensity program. Over time, we learn what seems to attract both first-timers and repeat visitors to our programs; any three museum educators describing the qualities of an effective public talk would agree remarkably well. We live daily with the uncertainties and frustrations posed by the four "challenges" I've discussed here and have adapted well to the need to create programs that stand alone and are appropriate to wide ranges of participants.

We know, as any teacher does at the end of the day, whether the program has been "good" or disappointing, using qualitative measures and sheer professional judgment. And we do not believe all of our programs are equally good: we make distinctions routinely and can assure any potential funder about which sorts of programs are most likely to be worth an investment. We think we know what we are doing.

But the problems in evaluating museum education programs are many, and they reflect basic questions yet to be answered about the purposes of our programs. Museums lag behind formal educational settings in being able to assess their educational programs reliably using standards shared by similar institutions. As public or quasi-public institutions with no captive audience, art museums revel in "capturing" what they can of their publics, and their evaluation methods reflect this first-level need. But as museums mature in their roles as educational institutions and learn to balance their interpretive functions more equitably with their responsibilities to display art well, they will discover the need to better document their considerable successes in the important business of complementing school learning with informal and lifelong learning in the arts.

Regular and reliable evaluation of programs, when it comes, will attest to the coming of age of art museums as educators.

Reading Suggestions for Part Seven

American Association of Museums. *Museums for a New Century.* Washington, D.C.: American Association of Museums, 1984.

American Association of Museums. *Excellence and Equity: Education and the Public Dimension of Museums.* Washington, D.C.: American Association of Museums, 1992.

Csikszentmihalyi, Mihaly, and Rick E. Robinson. *The Art of Seeing: An Interpretation of the Aesthetic Encounter.* Santa Monica, Calif.: Getty Center for Education in the Arts, 1996.

Eisner, Elliot W., and Stephen M. Dobbs. *The Uncertain Profession: Observations on the State of Museum Education in Twenty American Museums.* Los Angeles Getty Center for Education in the Arts, 1986.

Getty Center for Education in the Arts. *Insights: Museums, Visitors, Attitudes, Expectations: A Focus Group Experiment.* Los Angeles: Getty Center for Education in the Arts, 1991.

The Journal of Aesthetic Education 19, no. 2 (1985). Special Issue: Art Museums and Education.

Brigham, Diane. "Museum Teaching as Learning Laboratory." In *Collected Papers: Pennsylvania's Symposium on Art Education, Aesthetics, and Art Criticism,* ed. Evan J. Kern. Harrisburg: Pennsylvania Department of Education, n.d., 195-206.

Dobbs, Stephen M., and Elliot W. Eisner. "The Uncertain Profession: Educators in American Art Museums." *The Journal of Aesthetic Education* 21, no. 4 (1987): 77-86.

Feagin, Susan L., and Craig Allen Subler. "Show Pictures: Aesthetics at the Art Galley." *The Journal of Aesthetic Education* 27, no. 3 (1993): 63-72.

Funch, Bjarne Sode. "Educating the Eye: Strategies for Museum Education." *The Journal of Aesthetic Education* 27, no. 1 (1993): 83-98.

Housen, Abigail. "Three Methods of Understanding Museum Audiences." *Museum Studies Journal* 2, no. 4 (1987): 41-49.

Newman, Alan. "Report: What Did the Focus Groups Reveal?" In *Insights: Museums, Visitors, Attitudes, Expectations: A Focus Group Experiment.* Los Angeles: Getty Center for Education in the Arts, 1991, 112-22.

Ott, Robert William. "Art Education in Museums: Art Teachers as Pioneers in Museum Education." In *The History of Art Education: Proceedings from the Penn State Conference,* ed. Brent Wilson and Harlan Hoffa. Reston, Va.: National Art Education Association, 1985, 286-94.

Pitman, Bonnie. "Taking a Closer Look: Evaluation in Art Museums." In *Evaluating and Assessing the Visual Arts in Education,* ed. Doug Boughton, Elliot W. Eisner, and Johan Ligtvoet. New York: Teachers College Press, 1996, 249-66.

Rice, Danielle. "Museums and Visual Literacy." *The Journal of Aesthetic Education* 25, no. 4 (1991): 127-36.

Soren, Barbara. "The Museum as Curricular Site." *The Journal of Aesthetic Education* 26, no. 3 (1992): 91-101.

Vallance, Elizabeth. "Art Criticism as Subject Matter in Schools and Art Museums." *The Journal of Aesthetic Education* 22, no. 4 (1988): 69-81.

Walsh-Piper, Kathleen. "Museum Education and the Aesthetic Experience." *The Journal of Aesthetic Education* 28, no. 3 (1994): 105-13. Also in *Aesthetics for Young People*, ed. Ronald Moore. Reston, Va.: National Art Education Association, 1995. Same pagination.

Williams, Betty Lou. "Recent Changes in Museum Education with Regard to Museum-School Partnerships and Discipline-Based Art Education." *Visual Arts Research* 23, no. 2 (1997): 83-88.

Williams, Patterson B. "Educational Excellence in Art Museums: An Agenda for Reform." *The Journal of Aesthetic Education* 19, no. 2 (1985): 105-23. Shorter version in *Museum Studies Journal* 2, no. 4 (1987): 20-28.

Afterthoughts

As one who has helped advance the idea of discipline-based art education since its inception in the early eighties under Getty auspices, I am hardly a disinterested compiler of its extensive literature. Consequently, while I think the writings reprinted are representative I've no doubt that it would be possible to assemble a collection with a somewhat different character. To understand my support of DBAE and its emphasis on grounding the teaching of art in the art-related disciplines of art making, art history, art criticism, and aesthetics, or, more simply, creative, historical, and critical studies, it may be helpful to say a few more words about my background and interests.

My early years were spent growing up during the Great Depression and my adolescence extended through a period that experienced World War II and the beginning of the Cold War. Young adulthood consisted of undergraduate and graduate studies, with a span of military service in between, which culminated in a teaching position in higher education at a time when the civil rights movement was relatively quiet and the din of the counterculture was less numbing. Like everyone, I'm a product of stages along life's way. For example, reared in a working-class industrial environment in which the children of immigrants had far less opportunity to attend college than they now do, I was upon entering Columbia College in the early fifties a serious student eager to taste the fruits of higher learning. Fortunately, Columbia at that time was a haven of liberal learning and the city a dramatic contrast to the drab life of an industrial valley. With its celebrated core courses in the humanities and contemporary civilization and a distinguished faculty, Columbia could hardly disappoint. It was in Columbia's humanities sequence, the courses in the arts, music, and literature, that I discovered the great ideas and works of the cultural heritage, largely of course the riches of Western civilization inasmuch as cultural revisionism had not attained the influence it was later to have on academia. Ultimately, these courses and my sojourns into the art world of New York were to have a decisive influence on my choice of career.

As I've noted elsewhere,[1] the fifties in New York was a decade when contemporary American art blossomed and Manhatten became the center of the international art world. Everywhere culture was expanding and enjoying a new popularity, especially as the decade wore on. Confining myself to academic matters, at Columbia Meyer Schapiro was stimulating graduate students with lectures and writings on both Romanesque and Modern Art, while to equally appreciative undergraduates Howard Davis was revealing the excellences of Northern and Italian Renaissance painting. Dustin Rice and George Collins paved the way for an understanding of modern art and architecture, while William Dinsmore, the distinguished classical scholar, was likewise opening eyes with descriptions of Greek sites and temples he had himself helped to excavate. In perhaps the most popular course with undergraduates, Mark Van Dorn was revealing to students the pleasures and powers of poetry. Lionel Trilling was performing a similar task with English literature as well as writing about the liberal imagination and how the values of literature constitute important antidotes to the abstractions and distortions of ideology.

Across the way at Teachers College, Lawrence A. Cremin, not yet the eminent historian of American education he was to become nor, for that matter, president of Teachers College, was anticipating his later interpretation of the genius of American education in terms used by Matther Arnold, as a grand experiment to humanize knowledge by bringing the best that's been thought and said to bear on matters that most concern us. Those who tried to do so, Arnold believed, were the true friends of equality. However, in his study of anti-intellectualism in American life the historian Richard Hofstadter reminded that such a task will never be an easy one in an egalitarian society given to invoking the commonplace over the superior and where judgments of value often encounter resistance. Indeed, in his analysis of intellect Jacques Barzun went so far as to say that we must now contend not just with the anti-intellectualism of those commonly associated with hostility toward the life of mind but also with the anti-intellectualism of intellectuals, those who have been the beneficiaries of the very best education. My experiences at Columbia Teachers College, moreover, were not those normally the subject of so much criticism of this institution. Again, my timing was good. I had the benefit of excellent instruction in the history and philosophy of education which sparked my interest in the philosophy of art and the humanities, and what I would eventually call aesthetic education.

The fifties are often characterized as a conservative decade, as the "Eisenhower Years." Yet for one with an energetic curiosity the big city provided more than enough excitement. Indeed, when compared to the decade that followed the fifties now seem not just a quieter decade but in intellectual and cultural respects a saner one as well. Consequently, I could not view with equanimity the sixties' radical bent that consisted of, among other things, assaults on sensibility and authority and the decline of decency and manners. The radicalism of the sixties reinforced my belief in the traditional ideal of humanistic learning and the realization that the only ideal for a democratic society is one that prizes excellence and the pursuit of the best possible self. Such an ideal, far from being elitist in any maleficent sense, is one that wants for the large majority what has heretofore been the prerogative of the minority and for the attainment of which substantive universal schooling is an enabling means.

It was also during the sixties that I began to think seriously about the justification question in aesthetic education. This involved making a case for the completed work of art as an important locus of value so as to counteract what I and several others believed was excessive emphasis on self-expressive activities in the teaching of art. Understandably, interest in the art object reflected my studies in art history and experiences in the art world. Taking leads from writings in philosophy of education and aesthetics (principally philosophy of art), I was persuaded that a useful way to draw attention to the object of art was to understand it as a humanly fashioned artifact that has a capacity to induce a high degree of aesthetic experience, at least a work of some complexity and significance, and that contrary to conventional thinking the locus of creativity was to be found not in the creative act so much as in the work of art as it lives in the experience of a beholder. In short, I favored an instrumental theory of aesthetic value. Aesthetic education could then be characterized as instruction in the concepts and skills of aesthetic perception and all that informs it so far as understanding and appreciating art are concerned, and other things from an aesthetic point of view. At this point I found the writings of Harold Osborne and Monroe C. Beardsley, at the time the deans of British and American aesthetics, respectively, useful in returning interest to the object of art. I came to realize, however, that it is less important to agree on a single theory of aesthetic experience than to acknowledge the relevance of a range of such theories in the never-ending task of probing the mysteries of art and our response to it. Contextualist theories, for example, confirm what I had always taken for granted, that external knowledge is obviously relevant in matters of understanding and appreciation. Such knowledge fuels and animates perception, or what a percipient thinks and feels with.

Armed with a theory of aesthetic education that featured aesthetic value as a capacity of an artwork to induce aesthetic experience, in the eighties I synthesized my interests in a number of publications and gave increasing attention to the nature of public policymaking for arts education.[2] But by the eighties multiculturalism, cultural studies, postmodernist theory, feminism, and social reconstructionism were on the rise. Theorists of art education began to stress social interpretations of art education that relied heavily on the methods and insights of the social sciences, notably sociology and anthropology. Granted that art education should encompass a broad range of artworks, non-Western and indigenous, and include the study of works by women (all acknowledged incidentally in the early Clark, Day, and Greer monograph-length definition of DBAE, but overlooked by many critics), the tendency to redefine art education in social science terms, to "anthropologize" it, as one writer has put it, would, I think, make it difficult to justify aesthetic education as a serious field of study deserving separate curriculum time.[3] School principals, for example, could simply say let social studies take care of the arts. Sacrificed would be the understanding of art as a distinctive way of knowing with a history of accomplishment and source of aesthetic delight.

If I have tended to draw on philosophical aesthetics to help clarify the problems of aesthetic education, it has not been, as I've said, for lack of interest in the other disciplines of DBAE. Both my early and later publications make this clear, certainly not least my general editorship of a series of five volumes devoted to indicating the relevance of DBAE's disciplines to teaching art (excerpts from which are included this collection). Appeal to scholarship, moreover, is consistent with Arnoldianism, that is, the obligation to humanize knowledge for purposes of illuminating matters of pedagogical importance. Such a concern also animated my founding of the *Journal of Aesthetic Education* in the sixties and subsequent editing of it for over thirty years. Accordingly, when Getty policymakers adopted an approach to art education grounded in relevant disciplines, I had no difficulty embracing it; my thinking had been proceeding along similar lines for quite some time. Getty policymakers, it should be mentioned, wisely eschewed originality of conception in favor of adopting ideas in the substantive literature of art education.

But, once more, the Getty educational venture arrived on the scene at a time when the cultural and educational atmosphere was becoming politically charged. Moreover, the literature produced in this atmosphere often proved dense, difficult, and intimidating. Consequently, many teachers were ill-prepared to digest the complexity of the ideas or to react to harsh accusations of racism, sexism, and elitism. It wasn't always clear, moreover, that critics fully understood the arguments they advanced or anticipated undesirable consequences for the field of art education if they were adopted, some of which are discussed in the issues section of this collection. Without going into detail , I have said elsewhere[4] that an unchecked multiculturalism is in danger of evolving into a cultural particularism that would split a democratic pluralism held together by shared common beliefs and values; that interpretations of scholarship and art education in terms of race, class, and gender risk reductionism and devaluing of what is most special and valuable about the arts and aesthetic education; that a rejection of elitism when the term is associated with excellence invites cultural decline and mediocrity and flies in the face of democratic values that feature aspiration and self-improvement; and that interpretation of human relations, including those between teacher and student, in terms of adverse hegemonic relations fails to appreciate the liberating and empowering character of such relations. In short, the revisionist critique of art education in my view fails to appreciate (or chooses to ignore) the power of works of art to transcend particular interests. Totalitarian regimes should also have taught us by now that the cost of politicizing art is the stifling of imagination and the creation of bad art. Not only that. The politicizing of teaching and learning and its insistence on political correctness diminishes academic freedom.

In other words, I am partial to nonpolitical interpretations of DBAE, by which I mean interpretations that keep the abstractions and distortions of ideology at bay and are sensitive to an appreciation of what Trilling in his sympathetic critique of the liberal imagination called variousness, difficulty, complexity, and possibility. It should not be surprising therefore that I also favor teacher-preparation programs grounded in solid undergraduate liberal studies that include course work in the arts and humanities and professional studies that, in addition to foundational courses in the problem areas of art education, incorporate relevant concepts, methods, and values from the art-related disciplines of art making, art history, art criticism, and aesthetics, the four disciplines of DBAE.[5]

Regarding pedagogy, by virtue of background and temperament I likewise endorse a more intellectual conception of art education, one, however, that need not be dry and insensitive to the interests of learners. For example, like other contributors to this collection I appreciate the value of inquiry learning but not at the expense of good didactic teaching that can perform an important role in any worthwhile education. Moreover, respect for learners and their inclinations is obviously a desideratum. Harry Broudy has characterized teaching in terms of a triad consisting of didactics, heuristics, and philetics,[6] that is, the imparting of knowledge, discovery learning, and caring. Ideally teachers should be proficient in all three, but given their idiosyncracies and dispositions a synthesis is rarely achieved. To be kept in mind, especially in the arts and humanities where the subject is more obviously human and personal, is that didactics and heuristics without philetics limit the possibility of maximum learning while inordinate philetics without didactics and heuristics deprives the young of the substance, discipline, and skills they need.

Originally, I had intended to include in this collection a part on the future of DBAE, but both space limitations and scarcity of writing on the topic advised against it. Doubtless, the future of DBAE—or as it has also been called, comprehensive art education—will be evident in reformulations of art education that place a greater emphasis on intellectual development and appreciation of the important roles the disciplines of the art world play in understanding and teaching art. This tendency is already evident in writings not just in the field of art education but also in dance, music, and theater education.[7]

But if I were to conjecture about the future of DBAE, by whatever name it might be called, it would include a recommitment to the study of excellence in art, that is, the initiation of the young into the artistic riches of past and present for the sake of their redeeming values. I do not consider such values to be the specific political objectives of special interest groups so much as what the study of excellence can reasonably be said to instill, an awareness of human creativeness. At a time when the pressures of the world weigh so heavily on human lives and civilizations and there is a pervasive lowering of standards in the culture, a "defining down," the study of serious and worthwhile works of art can revive memories of human accomplishment. While I do not believe art education can solve or even seriously ameliorate major social problems, it can, I think, instill confidence and engender a sense of possibility. The distinguished art historian Kenneth Clark expressed this prospect eloquently in his little essay *What Is a Masterpiece?* "Just when we are beginning to despair of the human race, "he writes, "we remember Vézelay or Chartres, Raphael's *School of Athens* or Titan's *Sacred and Profane Love*, and once more we are proud of our equivocal humanity."[8] And to these works we can add many others in the history of the arts. Such historical memory is an antidote to cultural amnesia and recalls the ideal of excellence and the cherishing of quality. Commitment to high standards, moreover, was central to William Penn Warren's Jefferson lecture, *Democracy and Poetry*, and by poetry he implied all art not just literature. This country's first Poet Laurate, Warren emphasized that both practitioners and appreciators of art must assume some standard for things made, and that commonplace art, that is, art as a mere commodity with its easy acceptance and glorification of stereotypes, is the enemy not only of distinction, but of distinctions.[9] A study and appreciation of excellence, moreover, can be responsive to those insisting that art education have greater social and personal relevance. Inasmuch as the great works of tradition and modernity address a range of human concerns, they can hardly be called irrelevant.

The turn of a century is a propitious time to look back as well as forward, a time to review and recall commitments as well to envision new prospects. At its inception Getty policymakers placed discussions of DBAE in the context of the excellence-in-education movement of the eighties. I can think of no more fitting commitment for its future than a rededication to excellence and all that this indispensable term subsumes.

Notes

1. "Building a Sense of Art in Today's World," *Studies in Art Education* 33, no. 2 (Winter 1992):71-85.

2. See, e.g., *The Sense of Art: A Study in Aesthetic Education* (New York: Routledge, 1989), and *Public Policy and the Aesthetic Interest: Critical Essays on Defining Cultural and Educational Relations*, co-edited with Ronald Berman (Urbana: University of Illinois Press, 1992).

3. For some insightful observations on aesthetics and the social sciences, see Anita Silvers "Multiculturalism and the Aesthetics of Recognition: Reflections on *Celebrating Pluralism*," *The Journal of Aesthetic Education* 33, no. 1 (Spring 1999): 95-103.

4. See *Excellence II: The Continuing Quest in Art Education* (Reston, Va.: National Art Education Association, 1995), esp chaps. 6, 7, 8.

5. See "Arts Education as Liberal Education," *The Journal of Education* 175, no. 3 (1993): 1-14.

6. Harry S. Broudy, "Didactics, Heuristics, and Philetics," *Educational Theory* 22 (1972): 251-61.

7. See, e.g., Southeast Center for Education in the Arts, *Discipline-based Music Education: A Conceptual Framework for the Teaching of Music* (Chattanooga: Southeast Center for Education in the Arts, 1944); Jeffery Patchen, "Overview of Discipline-Based Music Education," *Music Educators Journal* 83, no. 2 (1996):19-26, 44; Elsa Posey, "Discipline-Based Art Education: Developing a Dance Curriculum," *Journal of Physical Education, Recreation, and Dance* 59, no. 9 (1988): 61-63. Bennett Reimer, "Would Discipline-Based Music Education Make Sense?" *Music Educators Journal* 77, no. 9 (1991): 21-28.

8. Kenneth Clark, *What Is a Masterpiece?* (New York: Thames and Hudson, 1979), 5.

9. Robert Penn Warren, *Democracy and Poetry* (Cambridge: Harvard University Press, 1975), 85-86.

Contributors

RALPH A. SMITH is Professor Emeritus of Cultural and Educational Policy at the University of Illinois at Urbana-Champaign where since the mid-sixties he has taught courses in aesthetic education, advised graduate students, and edited *The Journal of Aesthetic Education*, which he founded in 1966. He has been a consultant to numerous educational and cultural organizations and served for several years as Executive Secretary of the Council for Policy Studies in Art Education. Among his recent publications are *The Sense of Art: A Study in Aesthetic Education, General Knowledge and Arts Education,* and *Excellence II.* He has also co-edited *Aesthetics and Arts Education, Public Policy and the Aesthetic Interest,* and the NSSE Yearbook *The Arts, Education, and Aesthetic Knowing,* and is general editor of the Getty-sponsored series of five volumes titled Disciplines in Art Education: Contexts of Understanding, to which as co-author he contributed the first volume titled *Art Education: A Critical Necessity.*

H. GENE BLOCKER at the time of his retirement was Professor of Philosophy at Ohio University where he taught and wrote widely on Western and non-Western aesthetics, interests which resulted in his spending time studying and lecturing in Hong Kong, China, West Africa, and Scotland. He has authored *Philosophy of Art* and *The Aesthetics of Primitive Art,* co-authored *Aesthetics and Education,* which is excerpted in this volume, and co-edited *Contemporary Philosophy of Art* and *Contextualizing Aesthetics: From Plato to Lyotard.*

BRUCE O. BOSTON is president of Wordsmith, Inc., a writing and editorial consultancy serving primarily clients in the Washington, D. C. area. He served as a team or principal writer for a number of reports, including *A Nation at Risk, What Work Requires of Schools,* and the *National Standards for Arts Education,* and has contributed to such publications as *Business Week, School Psychology, Teaching Music,* and *Executive Speechwriter.*

HARRY S. BROUDY (1905-1998) spent most of his career as a philosopher of education in the College of Education at the University of Illinois at Urbana-Champaign. Over a long, distinguished career he addressed a range of educational topics, notably the nature of general education, the professional training of teachers, aesthetic education, and the uses of knowledge. His interest in aesthetic education provided philosophical guidance in the initial efforts of the Getty to implement DBAE in the Los Angeles School District. Among his publications are *Building a Philosophy of Education, Democracy and Excellence in American Secondary Education* (with B. Othanel Smith, and Joe R. Burnett), *Enlightened Cherishing: An Essay on Aesthetic Education, Truth and Credibility: The Citizen's Dilemma, The Use of Schooling,* and *The Role of Imagery in Learning.*

MAURICE BROWN studied painting at the University of Tennessee and The Ohio State University where he received his doctorate in painting and philosophy. He taught at Bradley University and the University of Wisconsin at Oshkosh before accepting a position at the State University of New York at New Paltz, from which he retired. He has received a number of awards and fellowships and his works are represented in major collections throughout the country.

F. GRAEME CHALMERS is Professor of Art Education at the University of British Columbia, Vancouver. He has published extensively on various aspects of art, culture, and education and has been recognized for his service to both national and international organizations in which he has played leadership roles. In addition to authoring the Getty-sponsored study *Celebrating Pluralism* excerpted in this volume, he has published in such journals as *Art Education, Studies in Art Education, The Journal of Aesthetics and Art Criticism,* and *The Journal of Aesthetic Education.*

GILBERT A. CLARK is Professor Emeritus of Art Education and Gifted Talented Education at Indiana University. Active in state, national, and international art education associations, he has contributed numerous articles on curriculum and the gifted and talented to such journals as *Art Education, Studies in Art Education, Visual Arts Research,* and *The Journal of Aesthetic Education.* In addition to the excerpt reprinted in this volume, he has authored *Art/Design: Communicating Visually, Understanding Art Testing,* and *Examining Discipline-Based Art Education as a Curriculum Construct* and co-authored *Educating Artistically Talented Students, Resources for Teaching Art from a Multicultural Point of View,* and *Issues and Practices Related to Identification of Students Gifted and Talented in the Visual Arts.*

GEORGIA C. COLLINS at the time of her retirement was Professor of Art Education at the University of Kentucky. Her research interests include women's concerns, contemporary issues, and theory of art education. She has published in such journals as *Art Education, Studies in Art Education, The Journal of Aesthetic Education,* the *Journal of Multicultural and Cross-*

cultural *Research in Art Education,* and the *Journal of Social Theory in Art Education.* She has also co-authored *Women, Art, and Education,* co-edited *Gender Issues in Art Education,* and contributed chapters to a number of volumes addressing women's concerns and art education research. For her contributions and leadership she has received a number of awards from educational organizations.

MIHALY CSIKSZENTMIHALYI is Professor of Psychology and Education at the University of Chicago. His principal interest lies in the study of the more positive aspects of human experience about which he has authored and co-authored numerous articles and books, including *Beyond Boredom and Anxiety, Flow: The Psychology of Optimal Experience, Creativity: The Work and Lives of 91 Eminent People,* and *Creativity: Flow and the Psychology of Discovery and Invention.* The results of his study for the Getty Center for Education on the nation of aesthetic experience were published in *The Art of Seeing*

JESSICA DAVIS has worked as a practicing artist, teacher of the arts in school and community programs, and visiting artist and administrator. She is currently director of the Harvard Graduate College of Education's Arts in Education Program, which she originated. The results of her research as a cognitive development psychologist are reflected in such publications as *Safe Havens, The Co-Arts Assessment Handbook, The Wheel in Motion, The Music Book,* and *The Art and Science of Portraiture.*

MICHAEL D. DAY is Professor of Art at Brigham Young University where he has served as head of both the art department and the art education program. He has held major offices in a number of state and national organizations and is a principal advocate of DBAE. His influence has been felt primarily in the areas of curriculum implementation and assessment and professional development. Among his writings are case studies contributed to *Art History, Art Criticism, and Art Production: An Examination of Art Education in Selected School Districts* and numerous articles in such journals as *Art Education, Studies in Art Education,* and *The Journal of Aesthetic Education.* He is the co-author of *Children and Their Art* and co-editor of the Getty-sponsored *Discipline-Based Art Education: A Curriculum Sampler.*

STEPHEN MARK DOBBS is an independent consultant who has been a professor of Arts and Humanities at San Francisco State University, a program analyst with the JDR 3rd Fund, and a senior program officer of the Getty Center for Education in the Arts. Upon leaving the Getty he held the position of CEO and executive director of the Koret Foundation and president and CEO of the Marin Community Foundation. He has authored *Perceptions of Discipline-Based Art Education and the Getty Center for Education in the Arts,* co-authored *The Uncertain Profession: Observations on the State of Museum Education in Twenty American Museums,* and edited *Research Readings for Discipline-Based Art Education.*

LEILANI LATTIN DUKE directed Getty educational activities for seventeen years (1981-1998) during which she exemplified unparalled leadership in the reform of art education. Her efforts included the support of research and development in implementing and evaluating the Getty's approach to teaching art known as discipline-based art education. The effects of her leadership were realized when the basic premises of comprehensive art education were incorporated into statements of aims by local, state, and national organizations, including the National Standards for Art Education and the National Assessment in the Arts. Her periodic reports about the nature of the Getty's educational programs appeared in a number of publications, notably *Beyond Creating: The Place for Art in America's Schools* and in such journals as *Art Education, Phi Delta Kappan, Design for Arts in Education,* and *The Journal of Aesthetic Education.*

MARCIA MUELDER EATON is Professor of Philosophy at the University of Minnesota where she has served as head of the department. Among her publications are *Art and Nonart: Reflection's on an Orange Crate and Moose Call, Basic Issues in Aesthetics,* and *Aesthetics and the Good Life.* She has also contributed an essay to *Aesthetics for Young People* and a chapter to the NSSE Yearbook *The Arts, Education, and Aesthetic Knowing.* A past president of the American Society for Aesthetics, she lectures extensively in this country and abroad. Her current work addresses the relations of aesthetic and ethical values.

DAVID EBITZ, director of the John and Mable Ringling Museum of Art in Sarasota, Florida, has taught art history at the University of Maine and was Head of Education and Academic Affairs at the J. Paul Getty Museum before accepting his current position. In these capacities he has curated exhibitions, lectured extensively, published articles and reviews on medieval art, connoisseurship, and art education, and presented workshops on museums, education, and visitor experience.

ELLIOT W. EISNER is Professor of Education and Art at Stanford University and one of the principal interpreters of DBAE. For his contributions to art education and curriculum theory he has received recognition in the form of awards and elected offices in a number of national and international associations. In his writings he has addressed such topics as qualitative thinking, cognition in artistic expression, and the art of teaching, administration, and educational criticism. Among his publications are *Educating Artistic Vision, The Educational Imagination: On the Design and Evaluation of Educational Programs, The Enlightened Eye: Qualitative Inquiry and the Enhancement of Educational Practice,* and *Cognition and Curriculum.*

MARY ERICKSON is Professor of Art Education at Arizona State University, Tempe. She has taught in the public school and community college systems of Illinois and Indiana and was a faculty member of the Department of Art Education at Kutztown University before accepting her current position. In addition to her publications in such journals as *Art Education, Studies in Art Education,* and *The Journal of Aesthetic Education,* she has developed a number of learning resources and pedagogical games for the teaching of art, as well as curriculum materials for the Getty online service ArtsEdNet. In addition to co-authoring *Art History and Education,* she has contributed discussions of curriculum and the disciplines of DBAE to a number of conference proceedings and edited *Lessons about Art in History and History in Art.*

MAURICE GALTON, a former Dean of Education at Leicester University, United Kingdom, is now a member of the faculty of Homerton College, University of Cambridge. Long interested in the nature of teaching and learning in primary schools, his research has been reported in a number of studies, for example the ORACLE and DELTA projects, and is based on direct observation of classroom practice. His ORACLE study first published in the seventies has been replicated and published as *Inside the Classroom: 20 Years On.*

HOWARD GARDNER is the John H. and Elizabeth Hobbs Professor in Cognition and Education at the Harvard Graduate College of Education. He also holds a position as Adjunct Professor of Neurology at the Boston University School of Medicine and is Co-director of Harvard Project Zero. He is widely known as a theorist and interpreter of the cognitive revolution in modern philosophy and psychology and for his theory of multiple intelligences set out in *Frames of Mind*. He has further written about the nature of thinking, creativity, and understanding in such publications as *Creating Minds, Leading Minds,* and *Extraordinary Minds*. Two works devoted to the problems of schooling are the *Unschooled Mind: How Children Think and How Schools Should Teach* and *The Disciplined Mind: What All Students Should Understand*. For his accomplishments he has been the recipient of numerous awards and honorary degrees.

GEORGE GEAHIGAN is Professor of Art and Design at Purdue University where he coordinates the doctoral program in art education and teaches courses that integrate the disciplines of DBAE. In addition to co-authoring *Art Criticism and Education*, he has published articles on criticism and its role in art education in such journals as *Art Education, Studies in Art Education, Visual Arts Research,* and *The Journal of Aesthetic Education*. He has also contributed discussions of criticism to a number of national and international conference proceedings and contributed the introductory chapter to the NSSE Yearbook *The Arts, Education, and Aesthetic Knowing*.

W. DWAINE GREER is Professor of Art of the University of Arizona. He has been active in state, regional, and national curriculum activities in which he has held office and was formerly director of the Southwestern Regional Laboratory (SWRL) aesthetic education program located in Los Angeles. He has also served as director of the Getty Institute for Educators on the Visual Arts and contributed to its national diffusion project. He has authored *Improving Visual Arts Education* and *Art as a Basic: The Reformation in Art Education*, which consists of reflections of his tenure with the Getty Center for Education in the Arts and the future of art education. He has published in such journals as *Art Education, Studies in Art Education,* and *The Journal of Aesthetic Education* and is currently engaged in the development of curriculum materials for teaching art.

DAVID HARGREAVES is Professor of Education at the University of Durham and Visiting Professor of Research in Music Education at the University of Gothenburg, Sweden. His research is well known internationally and has been translated into several languages. He is also a jazz pianist and composer and has appeared on BBC television and radio. Among his publications are *The Developmental Psychology of Music, Children and the Arts* and *The Social Psychology of Music*.

ABIGAIL HOUSEN is a co-director and principal researcher in *VUE: Visual Understanding in Education,* a nonprofit, developmentally based educational research group. Her theory of aesthetic development is the basis for a growing number of museum programs and school curricula through the country. From 1979 through 1994 she was a professor on the faculty of the Massachusetts College of Art where her duties included directing the graduate program in art education and teaching courses in the psychology of viewing, museum education, and interactive video.

RICHARD LACHAPELLE is a Professor of Art Education at Concordia University, Montreal. He is principally interested in the nature of aesthetic learning, museum and community-based education, the use of new technologies in research and teaching, and qualitative inquiry. In addition to the article excerpted in this volume, he has published in the *Canadian Review of Art Education* and *Studies in Art Education* and contributed essays to *Le Musée, un lieu éducatif, Actes du colloque sur la recherche en enseignement des arts visuels,* and *L'education et les musées: visiter, explorer et apprendre.*

E. LOUIS LANKFORD is E. Desmond Lee Foundation Endowed Professor in Art Education at the University of Missouri-St. Louis where his chief responsibilities include developing and implementing teacher preparation and inservice programs and collaborating with the staff of the St. Louis Art Museum in developing educational materials associated with special exhibitions. Prior to his move to St. Louis he served for fifteen years on the art education faculty of The Ohio State University. He has contributed numerous articles and chapters to professional publications, including *Art Education, Studies in Art Education,* and *The Journal of Aesthetic Education.* His book *Aesthetics: Issues and Inquiry* published by the National Art Education Association has been well received in the field, and his co-authored high school text *Themes and Foundations of Art* is noteworthy for its cross-cultural, thematic, and inquiry-based approach to teaching art.

ALBERT WILLIAM LEVI (1911-1988) devoted much of his career to addressing the nature of the humanities and culture and was at the time of his death David May Distinguished University Professor Emeritus in the Humanities at Washington University. He was also a member of the faculty of the experimental Black Mountain College and served for a period as its Rector. Among his major publications are *Philosophy and the*

Modern World, Philosophy and the Imagination, Humanism and Politics, The Humanities Today, and *Philosophy as Social Expression* . He was also the co-author of *Art Education: A Critical Necessity,* an interpretation of DBAE from a humanities point of view.

HAROLD OSBORNE (1905-1987) exerted a major influence in British aesthetics through his editing of the *British Journal of Aesthetics* and participation in the British Society for Aesthetics. Among his major publications are *Aesthetics and Criticism, Aesthetics and Art Theory: An Historical Introduction, The Art of Appreciation,* and *Abstraction and Artifice in Twentieth-Century Art.* He further edited *The Oxford Companion to Art,* and *The Oxford Companion to the Decorative Arts.*

MICHAEL J. PARSONS is Professor of Art Education at The Ohio State University where he has served as chairman of the department. He has contributed significantly to thinking about aesthetic development with the research published in his *How We Understand Art: A Cognitive Developmental Account of Aesthetic Experience* and through his participation in the Getty Regional Institute that was responsible for implementing and assessing a discipline-based approach to teaching art. His articles have appeared in such journals as *The Journal of Aesthetics and Art Criticism, Educational Theory,* and *The Journal of Aesthetic Education,* and he contributed chapters to the NSSE Yearbook *The Arts, Education, and Aesthetic Knowing* and *Aesthetics for Young People.*

DAVID N. PERKINS is Co-director of Project Zero where he studies the nature of cognitive development and skills in both the arts and sciences with a view to improving the teaching of understanding, creativity, problem-solving, and reasoning. In addition to *The Intelligent Eye* excerpted in this volume, he has authored *The Mind's Best Work, Knowledge as Design, Smart Schools: From Training Memories to Educating Minds,* co-authored *The Teaching of Thinking,* and co-edited *Art, Mind, and Education.*

STUART RICHMOND is concurrently Dean of the School of Creative Arts, Sciences, and Technology at the Hong Kong Institute of Education and Professor of Art Education at Simon Fraser University, British Columbia. In addition to the article excerpted in this volume, he has recently published articles on the philosophy of art education and the nature of aesthetic perception in such journals as the *Journal of the Ontario Society for Education through Art* and the *Proceedings of the XIIIth International Congress of Aesthetics.* He has further served as editor of the *Canadian Review of Art Education* and is a practicing photographer.

BLANCHE M. RUBIN is an independent consultant in art education and educational evaluation. She was co-evaluator of both the Getty Los Angeles Institute for Educators in the Visual Arts (1984-1990) and its Regional Institute Grants Programs (1993-1995), assuming the leadership of the national evaluation team in 1996 and 1997. Before consulting for the Getty Center she served as evaluator for numerous art and museum education programs in Indiana, Illinois, and California. Her writings have appeared in a number of publications including *Visual Arts Research* and *The NASSP Bulletin.*

JEAN RUSH is Professor Emerita of both the University of Arizona and Illinois State University where prior to her retirement she held the position of Professor and Chair of the Department. A principal interpreter and implementor of DBAE, she has authored numerous articles on the nature of aesthetic learning and perception in such journals as *Art Education, Studies in Art Education, Arts Educational Policy Review* and *The Journal of Aesthetic Education.* She is also the co-author of a text for the elementary years titled *Teaching Children Art* that incorporates the principles of DBAE and is dedicated to Harry S. Broudy for his contributions to aesthetic education.

RENEE SANDELL is Professor of Art Education at The Maryland Institute, College of Art in Baltimore. Her research and teaching interests include gender concerns, multicultural and current issues in art education, studio pedagogy, and the professional development of teachers. She has co-authored *Women, Art, and Education,* co-edited *Gender Issues in Art Education: Content, Contents, and Strategies* and contributed chapters to books on such topics as research methods and methodologies, preservice education, and sex equity. Her writings have also appeared in such journals as *Art Education, Woman's Art Journal,* and *Studies in Art Education.*

FRANCES SCHOONMAKER is Professor of Education in the Department of Curriculum and Instruction at Teachers College, Columbia University. Her principal interests lie in the theory and practice of teaching, teacher preparation, caring and values education, and religious education. She has authored numerous articles and books and collaborated on several others, including *Growing Up Caring: Exploring Value and De-cision-Making, Teacher Renewal: Professional Issues, Personal Choices,* and *Thinking about Teacher Empowerment.*

KATHERINE A. SCHWARTZ is the director of the Alaska Center for Excellence in Arts Education at Kenai Peninsula College where she teaches courses in art methods, aesthetics, and philosophy of education and serves as a specialist for the Kenai Peninsula Borough School District. She also directs the Kennedy Center's Alaska Alliance for Arts Education and is the coordinator of the Arts Education Summer Institute: Integrate the Arts with Integrity: Dance, Drama, Literary Arts, Music, Visual Arts. She has developed and evaluated comprehensive arts education programs in Alaska which has involved developing arts standards and assessment instruments and providing art education staff development in remote communities through distance education.

ANITA SILVERS is Professor of Philosophy of San Francisco State University. She has published in such journals as *The Journal of Aesthetics and Art Criticism,* the *Journal of Philosophy and Medicine,* the *Journal of Social Philosophy,* and *The Journal of Aesthetic Education.* In addition to her observations about DBAE reprinted in this volume, she has contributed essays to *Aesthetics for Young People* and *Aesthetics: A Critical Anthology.*

MARILYN STEWART is Professor of Art Education at Kutztown University in Pennsylvania where she teaches undergraduate and graduate courses in art criticism and aesthetics. She has been a Visiting Scholar at the Getty Education Institute for the Arts and currently serves as general editor of a Davis Publications series titled Art Education in Practice. In addition to her contributions to *Aesthetics for Young People,* she has written *Thinking Through Aesthetics* and contributed to numerous journals, including *Art Education, Studies in Art Education,* and *The Journal of Aesthetic Education.*

ELIZABETH VALLANCE is Director of Education at the St. Louis Art Museum and a specialist in curriculum theory. She has served as Vice-President for the AERA division in Curriculum Studies and co-edited *Conflicting Conceptions of Curriculum.* Her research and museum articles have been published in such journals as *Educational Researcher* and *The Journal of Aesthetic Education.* She is also a practicing photographer.

BRENT WILSON is Professor and Head of the Department of Art Education at Penn State University. His interests encompass a broad range of art-related disciplines and research topics in art education. In addition to *The Quiet Evolution*, the extensive Getty evaluation report of its regional institutes, he researched and wrote the first draft of the Arts Endowment report on arts education titled *Toward Civilization*. He has also published in such journals as *Art Education, Studies in Art Education, Arts Education Policy Review*, and *The Journal of Aesthetic Education*.

THEODORE F. WOLFF, an independent painter, writer, and art critic, served for several years as art critic for the *Christian Science Monitor*. The recipient of several awards for art criticism, he has authored *The Many Masks of Modern Art, Morris Graves Flower Paintings, Enrico Donati: Surrealism and Beyond*, and a monograph on the American painter Joyce Treiman.